BRIDGES OF THE BODYMIND

BRIDGES OF THE BODYMIND

BEHAVIORAL APPROACHES TO HEALTH CARE

Jeanne Achterberg
G. Frank Lawlis

With Foreword by Lawrence LeShan

INSTITUTE FOR PERSONALITY AND ABILITY TESTING, INC.
CHAMPAIGN, ILLINOIS

Library of Congress Cataloging in Publication Data

Achterberg, Jeanne, 1942-
    Bridges of the Bodymind.

    Bibliography: p.
    Includes index.
    1.   Medicine and psychology.   2.   Mind and body.
3.   Imagery (Psychology)   I.   Lawlis, G. Frank, 1940-
joint author.   II.   Title. [DNLM: 1.   Psychophysiologic
disorders.   2.   Neoplasms--Psychology.   3.   Diabetes
mellitus--Psychology.   4.   Backache--Psychology.
5.   Arthritis, Rheumatoid--Psychology.   6.   Alcoholism--
Psychology.   WM90 A179b]
R726.5.A23   616'.001'9   80-16596
ISBN 0-918296-14-5
ISBN 0-918296-19-6

Institute for Personality and Ability Testing, Inc.
P. O. Box 188, Champaign, Illinois 61820

Printed in the United States of America.

CONTENTS

Table

FOREWORD

This book brings a unique synthesis of approaches and skills to bear on the concepts of health, disease, and treatment. Combine a thorough knowledge of ancient and modern usages of these concepts with trained ability in experimental design and scientific method, an extensive clinical experience and a warm appreciation for the patterns and meanings, joys, and pains of their patients' lives and one has a very rare synthesis indeed.

Such a synthesis is exactly what Achterberg and Lawlis have achieved in their work. This volume takes up where their earlier *Imagery of Cancer* left off, and we can now begin to see the long-range philosophical implications, not only of their own work, but also of the work of such other students in the field as Engel, Baltrusch, Greene, and Simonton.

It is very difficult to address the basic problems of psychophysiology and their implications for clinical treatment without becoming either a pedant or a dilettante; without either using a great deal of technical language that can only be understood by a specialist or else taking a completely superficial approach to the matter. The authors walk this fine line well. One does not need to be a physiologist to understand the book, but I have rarely met a physiologist who could not profit a great deal from it.

Certain themes repeatedly come through in this book. One is the fact that disease and health are processes, not static situations. There is no single "condition" called "health," nor is there one called "disease." Rather, an individual is in fluid motion throughout a lifetime, experiencing certain paths as more health oriented and certain as more disease oriented; some paths increase the individual's total ability to enjoy life and function effectively in the environment, while others detract from these abilities. Another basic theme stresses that the terms "health" and "disease" only make sense when one considers the total organism, not just the symptom or organ. A third theme emphasizes the positive value to the individual at any level of integration—psychological or physiological—of taking as much control of personal destiny as possible. (This last, as the authors repeatedly point out, is a factor that must be taken into account when evaluating therapeutic approaches, including their own! The very fact that the patients come to the program may mean that a skewed treatment population group already exists.)

There should be a wide audience for this book. It can be read with benefit by both healthy laymen and those with a wide variety of dysfunctions. Individuals can gain from it a sense of how to orient their total life patterns toward healthier paths. For professionals in the health field, I heartily recommend it. It not only expresses the philosophy, but also teaches the "nuts and bolts" of what we will someday mean by "holistic medicine."

Lawrence LeShan, Ph.D.

PREFACE

The physician of the future will give no medicine, but will interest patients in the care of the human frame, in nutrition, and in [the] causes and prevention of illness.

Thomas Edison

Last year, following what we believed to be one of our rather nonsensational, factually based presentations on stress and disease, one of the members of the mixed-professional audience approached us excitedly and said, "I feel like we are finally all coming out of the closet!" Perhaps we are. The movement in health care predicted by Edison (quoted above) appears to be emerging from the fog and discontent spawned by an ultra-specialized health-care system. The pressure to change comes from health consumers seeking respect for their human needs, from researchers bombarding the current treatment models with hard data supporting the role of the individual in health, and from dissatisfied practitioners successfully trying nontraditional approaches to the treatment of disease.

We appear to be in that most uncomfortable stage of scientific revolution provoked by this pressure and described by Kuhn (1962) as the transition period where there is "a large, but never complete overlap between the problems that can be solved by the old and by the new paradigm." As the transition in thinking comes to conclusion, the profession as a whole will have altered its methods and goals and assumed the new paradigm (or set of laws, theories, applications, and instrumentation). As yet, however, we in medicine remain temporally distant from that kind of drastic alteration because our tremendous investment in years of tradition permits change only in small, measured increments.

Nevertheless, new directions are evolving under many names, such as behavioral medicine, humanistic medicine, holistic health, and health psychology. The evolution embraces a myriad of different techniques. Some of them are as old as recorded history. Others required space age technology in order to develop. All, however, focus on adding to health care new dimensions beyond those which typically view the patient as a system of organs or tissues or bones—dimensions which stretch, instead, to totality of function and well-being.

xi

The work and writings of the great 19th-century experimental scientist and physician, Dr. Claude Bernard, grant us perspective on the current state of events. Bernard, throughout his illustrious career, expressed the Gestaltist principle that the whole is greater than the sum of its parts, especially in understanding human physiology. Pasteur, his contemporary, attempted to conquer the microbes which caused the great infections that plagued humanity, and thus embarked on a controversy with Bernard that spanned decades. Bernard maintained that illnesses hover constantly about us, but do not take root in the "terrain" unless it is ready to receive them. To Bernard, the condition of the terrain—the milieu interior of the body—and the maintenance of a homeostatic balance within, were the appropriate concerns in understanding health and disease. Pasteur eventually conceded this position on his deathbed, reportedly exclaiming "Bernard was right, the microbe nothing, the terrain everything" (McQuade & Aikman, 1974).

Our research was devoted to understanding the differences in this internal milieu—particularly from a psychological point of view—that in one person allow the development of disease and in another promote immunity. We sought, further, to clarify the circumstances that permitted one person to overcome illness, while another with an identical diagnosis became crippled or died. Our clinical practice evolved by putting into operation our findings and promising techniques that seemed appropriate to our patients' needs. We cannot claim patent rights on any procedures. Some of the work that we describe was practiced in ancient Greece, in American Indian cultures, and by mystical sects such as Rosicrucians. If we fail to give credit to deserving sources, it is merely because there are so many such just desserts or because original sources have been lost in antiquity.

Because we have been trained in the tradition of scientific psychology, and because we continue to ascribe to the procedures required to establish a data base, we have anchored our statements as soundly as possible with statistical conclusions. However, a treatise based solely on research findings would be barren, indeed, and particularly inappropriate in behavioral or psychological approaches to medicine, a field containing a wealth of individual expression. Those individual expressions we will try to share, acknowledging our most gracious appreciation to our patients. Each has been our teacher; and collectively they constitute the most intriguing group imaginable. We believe everyone who lives with a physical disease has a unique observation about that condition that deserves to be voiced and heard. Our patients were certainly no exceptions. Often, though, we had to create, with them, new means of communicating their own intuitions, so that they could become part of our mutual reality. In doing so, we developed intense relationships which frequently taxed our imaginations and sapped our energies. Our forte in this work, however, was that there were two of us committed to a mutual task. We could substitute for each other, encourage, and give support when the obstacles appeared onerous and insurmountable.

The patients discussed in this book were referred to us by several sources. Many sought us out, having read something of our research in the paper or heard some other tidbit of information about our procedures. Others were sent to us from physicians via hospital networks, and they were often quite surprised to find themselves in our care. (After all, nothing was wrong with their heads, it was their bodies that were in distress.) None of them had problems amenable to standard medical procedures, though virtually all had been sick long enough to be classified as "chronic." Often they had been passed through innumerable sets of diagnostic and treatment procedures.

Thus, we were doing what was, in effect, last-resort or tertiary medical care. This sub-basement of the medical world is not altogether a negative place to be, since any medical improvement is better than what has previously transpired on the patient's downhill course. Our success in achieving our goals for patients has varied as much as any practitioner's. It is contingent upon the type of clientele, our own motivations, and our previous experience with the issues involved. Since there were, and are, no blueprints or protocols for what we were doing, we often made up the rules as we went along.

The unification of all of our work resides in the imagery process, and this has served as a framework upon which to build and embellish. The reader will soon become aware that, for us, "imagery" conveys a very broad meaning related to cognitive function, while the current popular connotations of the word typically relegate it to visualization experience. We cannot think of a more descriptive word, however, unless it is "cognitive representations," but one's tongue trips over that. Thus, we retain "imagery," with all of its surplus meaning, because we feel it best describes the bridges between body and mind.

Imagery is the construct that represents the underlying assumption in psychophysiological approaches to disease; i.e., that psyche and soma are indeed inextricably linked. We use the term "bodymind"[1] to denote this unity of being. It is a

---

[1]We thank Ken Dychtwald (1977) for our introduction to the usage of *Bodymind* as a reference to the physical and psychological aspects of an individual, as well as for his astute observations which both guided and supported our own.

reactionary term, intended to move conceptually beyond the restrictions of the traditional physiologic and psychologic approaches.

In addition to using the umbrella of imagery, for our presentation we have divided many of the chapters into taxonomies of disease, because that is the way the medical world within which we work functions.

During the past few years, a variety of affiliations and agencies permitted and supported the gathering of data and clinical insights. Information for the cancer chapter is derived from the experience of both authors: as co-directors of the evaluation team for the Cancer Rehabilitation Demonstration Project (NCI #N01-CN-45133) conducted in the Department of Physical Medicine, Southwestern Medical School, Dallas, Texas; from Dr. Lawlis's work as psychological and statistical consultant on the Comprehensive Rehabilitation of the Laryngectomee Study (NCI #R18-CA-18629), conducted at the Department of Otolaryngology, University of Texas Health Science Center, San Antonio, Texas; and from Dr. Achterberg's tenure as Research Director, Cancer Counseling and Research Center, Fort Worth, Texas. Complete results from the NCI-funded projects are available as final reports from the agency. The findings from several substudies within these projects have been published and are cited in the bibliography. Clinical insights are derived from over eight combined years of working with cancer patients in both private practice and in a county hospital setting.

The results of the approach described for low back pain are to be found in technical reports from Caruth Hospital, Dallas, Texas, a private rehabilitation facility where Dr. Lawlis served as staff psychologist. Additional information on low back pain specific to an indigent population was obtained from his experience with a back pain "school" conducted at Southwestern Medical School, at which patients were educated in methods of appropriate care.

The arthritis studies were conducted with the assistance of a grant from NIH awarded to Dr. Achterberg. Patients were studied from a variety of sources, including clinics in the teaching hospital affiliated with Southwestern Medical School, and with the aid of the local chapter of the Arthritis Foundation. Additionally, a segment of the work represents a dissertation conducted by Dr. Phillip McGraw under our auspices, in partial fulfillment of the Ph.D. requirement at North Texas State University. Also, imagery information from acutely ill patients was collected by Pat Heidt, a Ph.D. candidate in nursing at New York University, in conjunction with her dissertation requirements.

The diabetes chapter was written as an outgrowth of a dissertation conducted at East Texas State University by Dr.

Carol Kershaw which brought her and us, as collaborators, in contact with many diabetics in the course of the study. A very rich source of information for the diabetes chapter, as well as the others, were the individuals who came to us as private patients for counseling, biofeedback, or bioenergetics. Being unconstrained by experimental design, we were able to explore new avenues of observation and therapy with them.

The miscellaneous notes obtained from intensive and programmed strategies in specific disease groups grew from our combined experiences in four medical school settings and two private clinics.

Comments on the training and role of a somatic psychologist were derived from Dr. Lawlis's experience as Director, Behavioral Medicine Program, North Texas State University, and from the involvement of both authors in supervising graduate students in medical settings.

Miscellaneous notes on the role of psychologists in medicine were obtained from our combined experiences in four medical school settings and two private clinics, from Dr. Lawlis's experiences as Director of the Behavioral Medicine Program at North Texas State University, and from the involvement of both authors in supervising graduate students in research and practice.

This book deals with many issues and with no particular claims to the reader, except our hope that by expressing our learning experiences as sensitively as possible, and with as much referencing and data backup as we can, we may assist in advancing the art and science of psychological care for those diagnosed as having physical disease.

CHAPTER I

INTRODUCTION
The Basic Perspective

Disease
as a
Lifestyle
Health is one value of universal concern. Its presence or absence affects every aspect of life: spiritual, vocational, and social. A healthy, functioning body seems to be a prerequisite for the pursuit of all the values held dear to the "American Way of Life." We borrow money for ventures and recreation upon the assumption of expected health. We consider our bodies to be the churches which harbor our spiritual energies. For the most part, the structure of our bones, skin, and muscles affects personal relationships and self-concepts.

In the spirit of unifying all levels of well-being, we refer to "bodymind" as a term intended to convey each component of a person's functioning. The emphasis is on the individual as a whole organism reacting to the environment as it is perceived and construed. These reactions are based on perceptions both internal and external to the individual.

Throughout an individual's development, all body responses are recorded at both conscious and unconscious levels. Each cell in the human body possesses memory. If one continues to shock a living cell one hundred times, that cell will reorganize itself chemically so as to deal with the irritation. Perhaps it will build thicker walls, or it may change its size or substance. In some ways the noxious stimulation will create a specific reaction in the cell. In this sense the cell is developing a memory of counteraction.

As collections of living cells interrelate, more sophisticated responses become possible. The bone structures realign themselves in response to new pressures. Muscles become stronger as heavy demands are made of them. Skin grows calluses to protect itself against friction. The body is made up of a concert of small but significant intelligences, only a small fraction of which are within the realm of conscious awareness. The process of stimulus awareness and integrated intercellular response is carried out each moment.

In essence, the bodymind is a total collection of receptive and reactive units capable of responding to the environment. If its responses are repeated at frequent intervals, over a period of time they will become part of a lifestyle. When the

1

responses are adaptive, the bodymind is called "healthy." If, however, these total responses are inappropriate or overwhelming, they will, in due time, be diagnosed as some disease.

An examination of disease process in the 20th century makes it apparent that a new perspective on health care is needed. Hospitals are full, but people by and large are no longer "catching" anything but influenza, colds, and infections that are usually controllable with antibiotics. We submit that the major cripplers are diseases that people consciously or unconsciously produce themselves and which are, in fact, diseases of lifestyle. We must then consider the possibility that we as individuals can take personal responsibility, if not for preventing, then at least for delaying the onset of the diseases.[1]

Common Causes of Death: Examples of Bodymind Disintegration

The role of the bodymind concept in disease process can be well illustrated by considering the ten most common causes of death in the United States. The number one cause of death this year in males age 35-44 was heart disease; number two was cancer; three, accidents; four, cirrhosis of the liver; five, stroke; six, suicide; seven, homicide; eight, pneumonia and influenza; nine, diabetes; and ten, emphysema. Among females in that age group, the cause and order are approximately the same, with the exception that the tenth cause of death in females is nephritis.

Most of these are lifestyle diseases, the result of things that we do to ourselves or things that we expose ourselves to without proper defense. Some of the exposure, of course, is unavoidable. Other exposures *are* avoidable. The advice usually given for maintaining oneself after diagnosis of the leading killers is as follows:

1. Heart disease—The advice typically given to patients who are coronary prone is to eat properly, exercise moderately, avoid smoking altogether, and do not expose oneself to any psychological or physiological stress beyond individual tolerance.

2. Cancer—Believe it or not, the advice for forestalling or alleviating this disease is approximately the same as for heart disease: eat properly, avoid carcinogens in the atmosphere and in food whenever possible, avoid certain types of food,

---

[1]It is important at this point to mention that in no sense do we deny any genetic predisposition for diseases. The leading position today is that one does not inherit disease, but that there are certain weaknesses, predispositions, and genetic preprograms for various dysfunctions.

exercise, keep the body in healthy shape, and avoid significant stressors. The basic idea here is to preserve the integrity of the immunological system, as well as to avoid known cancer-producing agents.

3. Accidents—As far as accidents are concerned, it is well documented that individuals are more accident prone when they are undergoing a profound psychological trauma or stress, or when they are involved in a series of life changes. Inattention, reaction-time deficiencies, and depression are all stress concomitants and can all contribute to accident proneness. Obviously, then, stress levels should be monitored and some means of immunizing against excessive stress adopted.

4. Cirrhosis of the liver—This condition is almost exclusively related to physical abuse to the body by excessive intake of alcohol. If one wished to avoid the fourth leading cause of death, one could drink moderately or not at all.

5. Stroke—The advice to individuals who have suffered a stroke is generally akin to that offered to victims of heart disease.

6. Suicide—This is obviously a self-inflicted ordeal. In most cases, it seems to be a final response to some situation and is indicative of a general inability to cope with life stresses. Suicide is thus the end point of a diseased lifestyle.

7. Homicide—Once again, the cause is a clear reflection of stress beyond the tolerance of individuals. Most people are killed by someone close, usually a friend or relative, in an unfortunate attempt to resolve a problem.[2]

8. Pneumonia and influenza—These are two infectious diseases which still maintain their status as major killers. Interestingly, exposure to the germs which cause pneumonia and flu does not typically induce those diseases. The germs need a receptive terrain, and that terrain only becomes receptive when bodies are abused by poor diet, poor health habits, a general lack of physical maintenance, and a certain exposure to stresses—all of which deteriorate the protective cushioning mechanisms of the terrain.

9. Diabetes—The advice typically given to control this disease or to alleviate it altogether is not much different from what we have already discussed. Control the diet, exercise to burn off excess sugar in the blood, and avoid excessive stress, because stress raises blood sugar levels (even in non-diabetics).

_____

[2]Both suicide and homicide fit only peripherally within the scope of our current treatises, since they are not physical diseases in the taxonomical sense. However, we can presume that the same general laws for prevention hold true; that is, if a person is well nourished, physically fit, and has developed some means for interacting in a healthy fashion with environmental pressures, then these particular diseases of lifestyle could be avoided.

10. Emphysema—Need we elaborate? One does not "catch" emphysema. It is normally self-inflicted through excessive tobacco usage. There are other causes of and reasons for emphysema as well, such as living in highly polluted areas. It is, then, a disease of society. Therefore, it remains our responsibility to control its expression.

Disease as Reaction to Energy Deficiency   Many researchers, in looking at physical disease in our society, have concluded that humans are endowed with only a finite quantity of energy. It may vary from individual to individual and from day to day, but once depleted, it is gone. Coffee and other stimulants do not provide us with any more energy; rather, they only help us to use more rapidly that which is already available. We use energy when we adapt to life change and when we involve ourselves in situations that produce a great deal of anger and/or anxiety. When energy is used in this manner, less is available for keeping the body healthy, for repairing damaged tissues, damaged joints, and for renewing the cells that are used in the fight against disease.

In fact, research by Thomas Holmes (1967) and his associates has shown that every time we involve ourselves in a life change, whether it be positive change, such as a joyful marriage, or negative change, such as illness or a jail sentence, we apparently use up a quantity of this energy. They have devised a scale which lends insight into how much energy is being worn away in any one period of time as a result of the stresses that we are facing in our lives. According to their research, virtually every disease can be predicted or precipitated by an uncommonly large number of life changes. Accidents, too, can be similarly predicted or precipitated. This kind of research has necessitated revisions in the previous notions of psychosomatic disease. Thus, all disease is viewed as having psychological components. Every thought affects the body in some way, and every physical movement or change is accompanied by some mental alteration.

Disease as an Evolutionary Determinant. When adopting new prescriptions for health, we also need to consider that we have evolved from a species with very particular kinds of adaptiveness. For example, we have the ability to gear up our bodies to flee, fight, or do whatever else is necessary to survive when under pressure or when facing a threatening situation. Now, of course, when we experience feelings of anger, hostility, or fear, we generally do not fight physically due to society's prohibitions. However, the same physiological response that accompanied these emotions millenia ago still occurs. Adrenal flow is increased and the sympathetic nervous system is activated, although now there is often no opportunity for discharge. Unless we exercise vigorously, the anger must be turned inward. Continuously turning inward the anger and the physiological response to anger results in tissue damage.

Society has played a trick on us. It evolved certain mannerisms before our bodies learned how to handle them adaptively. It is interesting to speculate what would happen, for example, if one were allowed to act out feelings of fear, anger, or hostility. In our pilot research with the criminally insane, who indeed do act out these feelings, we found very little if any cancer. This is quite surprising in view of the fact that most of them smoke and otherwise abuse their bodies. Perhaps these people are, in a sense, protecting their bodies from physical disease by turning their anger outward.

Research on voodoo death, too, indicates the profound physiological response that people have when they are extremely afraid. People do die with no known cause of pathology when they fear that they have been cursed or hexed in some way. We have often wondered if diagnoses of diseases that are accompanied with a great deal of fear, such as cancer and heart disease, do not have a component of voodoo death about them. People may feel that they have been hexed or cursed and a death sentence placed upon them, so they die in compliance.

Bodymind and Other Theories of Disease Intervention

Because of our emphasis on bodymind, we are often accused of not believing in the germ theory. For many diseases, among them cancer, rheumatoid arthritis, and diabetes, the cause of the disease is around us all the time. Most of us have malignant cells. Many of us have the rheumatoid factor. But only a few of us are unfortunate enough to be diagnosed with a disease. It is apparent that our bodies are designed to protect us from invasion, and, regardless of what kind of seeds or germs we carry around with us, the normal course of events is toward health. As Hans Selye once indicated, the microbe is in and around us all of the time; it causes no disease until we are exposed to stress. What, then, is the cause of our illness—the microbe or the stress?

"Aren't you really talking about psychosomatic medicine?" is a question frequently asked of us. The question is appropriate in the context of the existing topology in medicine, but it is extremely limited in bodymind formulation. Psychosomatic medicine has as its base the Freudian notion that there are specific disease manifestations of neurotic repressions. Under the classic hysterical rubric, the individual places a somatic symptom in the way of doing a deed that he or she is afraid to do.

For example, a bride may develop paralysis rather than marry, or a reticent individual may develop hiccups every time a large group must be addressed. These physical symptoms allow escape from otherwise unbearable situations. If the person can admit or reach some insight through psychotherapy, the symptom may or may not persist. Although the rational ego can consciously expose the anxiety, the unconscious or habit formation may have to be overcome. A next step is to change the significant others, the ego objects, into supporting a less neurotic behavior.

It is not our intention to undermine the concept of hysteria in disease formation. We affirm it as a diagnostic reality occurring with great frequency. Behavioral or somatically oriented approaches to disease intervention account for these hysterical features of personality, but also extend beyond hysteria to the link between mental and physical health.

Dimensions of Bodymind Intervention

Techniques for intervention in physical disease are growing at an exponential rate, although only a few have been researched with any degree of rigor. As shown in Figure 1.1, we have divided the most well-recognized interventions into two general categories, Active and Passive, which describe the extent of patient participation and investment of energy in the actual treatment. Passive treatment is traditional and does account for a wide range of positive outcomes, especially with regard to acute distress. Active treatment, which is less traditional, requires patient participation, and is probably more appropriate after the acute care needs are met.

Under the active category, there are three subdivisions indicating the mode of treatment: cognitive, physical, and behavioral. The cognitive styles include relaxation therapies, biofeedback, etc., all of which involve stress adaptation through cognitive change. These may or may not include insight into a psychodynamic or an habitual response to a stimulus.

The physical dimension includes therapeutic modes that focus primarily upon a structured set of patterned activities designed to bring about a beneficial change in health. Besides physical exercise and yogic breathing training, we include deep massage, as practiced by Rolf and by Bioenergetics, and sedative massage. These techniques are included in this category because the individuals' responses are anticipated and shaped according to known healthy patterns. For example, such exercises often utilize the perception of pain as

Figure 1.1

**INTERVENTION TECHNIQUES
IN PHYSICAL DISEASE**

Active Techniques

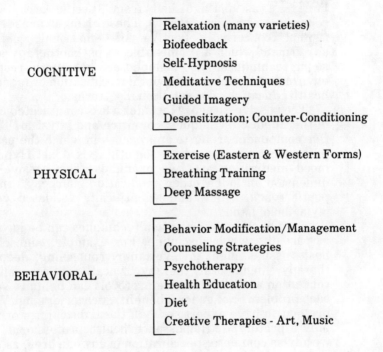

COGNITIVE
- Relaxation (many varieties)
- Biofeedback
- Self-Hypnosis
- Meditative Techniques
- Guided Imagery
- Desensitization; Counter-Conditioning

PHYSICAL
- Exercise (Eastern & Western Forms)
- Breathing Training
- Deep Massage

BEHAVIORAL
- Behavior Modification/Management
- Counseling Strategies
- Psychotherapy
- Health Education
- Diet
- Creative Therapies - Art, Music

Passive Techniques

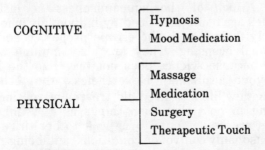

COGNITIVE
- Hypnosis
- Mood Medication

PHYSICAL
- Massage
- Medication
- Surgery
- Therapeutic Touch

both a diagnostic and intervention feature. The responses to these sensations can be used to modify stress reactions in very specific ways. It is also impossible to remain aloof and non-involved in these therapies because of the often painful physical sensation.

Although all of these general dimensions overlap to some degree, we have included as behavioral techniques those interventions that emphasize behavioral changes in general lifestyles, as distinguished from specific areas of either cognitive or physical activity. These changes include the attitudinal concerns reflective of emotional conflict and adjustment which are amenable to psychotherapy and counseling techniques. Also included are behavioral responses to environment, such as behavioral modification or management, health education, and nutritional patterns.

The passive category includes a less complicated clustering of therapeutic techniques: cognitive and physical. The cognitive components refer to approaches in which the patient is a passive recipient to whom something is done. Hypnosis and mood medication are two examples. The passive physical dimension includes other medication, surgery, and therapeutic touch, a new and scientifically validated version of laying on of hands.

Each of these intervention techniques can be incorporated as part of a whole discipline. For example, counseling with health issues might involve family counseling, deep psychotherapy, behavioral therapy, vocational counseling, and relaxation as well. Exercise protocols can be quite specific to each problem or of general benefit, such as jogging. We do not pretend to have expertise in all these disciplines or to exemplify a prototype "Renaissance health professional." Nor do we advise complete specialization in any one area, as that only perpetuates the existing model of medical specialization.

Many of the therapies which are categorized under our various headings cause the medical world to emit a collective shudder. Much of the squeamishness is justified. The techniques are being practiced by individuals who frequently are poorly trained and who escape proper credentialing and professional licensing. They are also immune to scientific scrutiny because science does not travel to the hinterlands (i.e., beyond academia). Nevertheless, the techniques are breathing new life into tired old treatment routines, and it is refreshing to note that such things as T'ai Chi meditative exercises are being found beneficial to health (when tested under reasonably controlled conditions) and being reported on in prestigious medical journals (Bell, 1979).[3]

---

[3] Dictionary-type treatments of the newer therapies can be found in *Mind Style, Life Style* and *Healing: The Coming Revolution in Holistic Medicine,* by Jack LaPatra (1978).

Role of the
Patient's
Agendas Interacting with patients day after day, walking through the wards of a county hospital, and observing a nation of individuals—the majority of whom flaunt habits of poor hygiene and behaviors detrimental to health—has led us to the conclusion that illness serves many functions. Some of the functions are so complex that we do not pretend to understand the conditions that provoke and sustain the disease. Nevertheless, in keeping with our thesis, we believe that disease does not strike in a mystic, random fashion. It strikes, as Claude Bernard believed, only when the "terrain," i.e., the body, is receptive. One's reactions to disease, including behaviors more or less likely to promote health, are certainly amenable to conscious control, particularly when patients are educated regarding some options for controlling or overcoming disease.

We are not assuming that behavioral or psychological intervention, in combination with medical treatment, has a set of answers, or that "if only the patients would listen, they would enjoy better health." Quite the contrary, many of the patients we encounter are, in fact, being treated with experimental medication and surgery, all of the usual protocols having been exhausted. Obviously, this will continue in our profession for some time, until eventually psychology is elevated to a place of consultation nearer to the acute care stage of illness. Furthermore, we as psychologists will continue to see patients for whom most medical treatment has been unsuccessful, and for whom, therefore, the disease is either incurable or is supposed to exist somewhere in that amorphous region between their ears.

These two groups, i.e., the last resorters and the presumed psychogenic cases, pose special sets of problems which are addressed in various places throughout the text. At the same time, a profile of the malingering patient, or the patient who will not readily respond to treatment, would be highly desirable. Unfortunately, none exists.

Other people of concern, though, are the diabetics who defy dietary controls and neglect insulin injection; the hypertensives who fail to take medication; the coronary patients who continue to smoke; and the patients referred for biofeedback and relaxation training with admitted stress-related disorders who would like to learn to relax, but just cannot find the time. And yes, they all do "know" it's important for their health. For these patients, health behaviors have a lower priority than the behaviors that make them sick. There is great therapeutic value in assisting the patient to identify his or her life priorities, examine them closely, and then openly reach some conclusion together regarding their wishes for health.

It has been our experience that patients will not readily admit they want to be ill, much less that they want to die, unless, of course, they are in severe pain or hopelessly disabled. In the latter case, many plead for a swift demise. It becomes a delicate issue, then, to challenge their verbalizations of desire for health and to directly confront those behaviors which are antagonistic to that health.

Such challenge and confrontation, of course, take time and courage. Try, for example, suggesting to a blue collar factory worker that low back pain could be relieved if it were not so enjoyable to stay at home watching TV while collecting Workman's Compensation payments. That kind of confrontation is ridiculous; most patients are not psychologically aware enough to intellectualize any kind of mind-body relationship without assuming that they are being accused of craziness or crass dishonesty. The control that can be exerted over behavior must be gradually taught, not confronted with shock tactics and accusations.

Various standardized diagnostics have been used to determine treatment responsiveness, but these are only partially successful. We have reported in the cancer chapter on studies associated with rehabilitation or treatment response in various categories, including rehabilitation after ostomy surgery, laryngectomees' learning of esophageal speech, physical recovery following mastectomy, and response following diagnosis of incurable cancer. In using these diagnostic criteria, we cannot assume that those individuals who scored low on scales associated with successful recovery did not wish to return to health. They may have experienced too much tissue damage to be counteracted by the usual mechanisms that establish a homeostatic bodily condition, or by any known treatment.

For every disease there appears to be a point of no return, which also varies considerably from individual to individual: the diabetic, for example, with numerous severe neuropathies; the cancer patient with significant vital organ damage; the rheumatoid arthritic with Stage IV disease; or the spinal cord injured quad or paraplegic. To accuse these patients of not wanting to get well is inappropriate at the advanced stage of disease or trauma. The effort required may be beyond their capacity to respond.

Patients Who
Want to Be Sick The wish to remain ill may be totally unconscious. Once we identify these patients, we normally continue them in treatment for at least a short period of time, because they do sometimes require psychological services, and we do want to leave the option for change open.

Their decision to remain ill, however, is antithetical to our own philosophical bent. That is, a purposeful decision to remain in the sick role signals preplanned failure in the treatment and communication models which we have devised and within which we work most comfortably. We commend these patients to therapists or researchers in the more supportive models, both in rehabilitation psychology and in disciplinary groups, who are expert in administering to the emotional needs of the dying patient.

Our own path is predicated on an optimistic future vista of a society of enlightened individuals who not only attend to the needs of their bodies and have awareness of the tremendous amount of inner healing and self-regulation that is possible, but who also see other ways of resolving needs than through physical decompensation. A future society is envisioned where it is possible to call into work "well" instead of "ill" and take a day off to relieve pressure or celebrate wellness; where "stress breaks" would be the usual happenstance in the workday instead of "coffee breaks," which nutritionally and emotionally may adversely affect the human condition. Good health would be rewarded by a rebate system of health insurance premiums to the well subscribers, or by companies' offering bonuses for staying well.

In view of the fact that many, many powerful reinforcers exist for poor health, it should surprise no one that many patients consciously or unconsciously cling to disease.

Passive Suicide Patients. We treat the group of patients within this category, "passive suicide," with a great deal of consideration. Many have led very productive lives, have never been sick a day, and have decided in some secret way that it is time to end a good life with as little trauma as possible.

We first became aware of this pattern while surveying the psychological aspects of breast cancer literature. The older patients were very different psychologically from the younger patients. They generally felt better about their roles in life, such as their motherhood and womanliness in general. A disease diagnosed as terminal represented to them not so much a culmination of intolerable stresses, but rather a natural ending. This was not so with the younger patients. This latter group clearly expressed numerous maladjustments. For them, cancer often could be viewed as a result of the depression of an immunological system by psychological factors.

How unfortunate that we generally believe we must be sick in order to end life: that death cannot be a decision rather than a feared specter! Many of the patients we see in the county hospital are "passive suicides." God has called them home and He signals His desires with a diagnosis of physical deterioration. Few can argue with this beckoning.

While we could cite numerous case histories of patients who might be included in this category, we choose to give a family example which demonstrates the dynamics involved in "passive suicide."

J's grandmother was an extraordinary woman, born and reared in Montana. She was lovely and eloquent, and, despite obvious social pressures to marry young, she married late by her generation's calendar and to a man with a charismatic reputation that outlived him by two decades. She was never ill a day in her life, bore each of her five children at home (the last when she was well into her 40s), courageously withstood her husband's idiosyncrasies, and lived until the age of 73 with no maladies except "rheumatism," which was significantly relieved by aspirin.

After the death of her husband, however, she began a methodical journey, traveling and visiting each of her children for a period of time. Then, returning to Montana, she leased a small apartment in a town close to her sister. Having acknowledged the wellbeing, yet separate lives of her children and the vacuum of her own existence, she became ill and was diagnosed with cancer of the pancreas. This type of diagnosis signals an immediate physical deterioration, even though there are contrary instances. It is one of the most rapid and deliberate courses toward death. She felt no pain during the few months that she lived after the diagnosis and died quietly in her sleep at precisely the time her physician predicted.

To presume any disease intervention, medical or otherwise, for patients in this situation doesn't make much sense. What does seem to have substance, however, is to encourage or allow the body to shut down in as natural a way as possible, without remorse or recriminations. In treating such patients, especially if we have been seeing them for some time, we continue the relationship even though their decision made it fairly clear that the needs of dying, not living, were the counseling focus.

The Disease-Dependent Patient. Two types of patient may be characterized under this classification. The distinction is quite important for designing intervention techniques. On the one hand, some individuals seem to fit into this category because disease is the only thing holding their lives together. We refer to such people who seem to need to be ill in order to fill the void of an otherwise empty life as illustrative of the "My Disease Is My World" syndrome. Others are, in a sense, favored with a fuller life and have a multitude of interests or resources which could be redirected. These "Prisoner of Disease" patients may recognize their dilemma, but cannot bring themselves to initiate the changes necessary to achieve improved health. They have become prisoners, so to speak, of their condition and are so used to their confined existence that the "outside" world is now more threatening than the status quo of continued suffering.

Both types of individuals in this category generally have been ill for a very long period of time or may have been acutely ill for a short period. Nevertheless, all the activities in their lives have had to be shifted to accommodate the demands of disease. They may have had tremendous hospital costs and purchased special equipment (beds, inhalators, prostheses) at great expense. Moves to healthier climates may have been necessary. Family members may have had to shift roles and responsibilities. Vacations and recreation may have been adjusted to the ups and downs of the disease. The patient may have had to quit work, and, as often happens, the spouse may also have stopped working in order to provide continuous nursing care. All of these events point to *disease-dependent* life activities. In some cases, virtually *all* aspects of lifestyle are disease related.

An example of the "Prisoner of Disease" patient is a 50-year-old woman diagnosed with bronchial asthma. Her attacks were provoked by many things (weather, pollen, dust), but were always exacerbated during periods of emotional stress. Our initial goals for therapy were to teach relaxation and bio-feedback in an attempt to short-circuit the emotional component of the disease and also to provide her with images to counteract the spontaneous visualizations which she had of bronchia closing or shrinking. These fearful images, which occurred whenever an attack was imminent, only made the physical situation worse.

Her treatment could be termed successful from two standpoints. She *was* able to deal effectively with stress-induced attacks, although those related to weather changes and other environmental conditions continued. In addition, the attacks she had were of shorter duration. That was as far as we got. She was considerably overweight and a heavy smoker, which obviously interfered with her health. We made several futile attempts to design a behavior modification program, but it was quite clear that both eating and smoking were high priority behaviors and would continue.

Somewhat in frustration, we requested a session with her, her husband, and extended family (five children and their spouses who kept nearly daily contact with their parents). During the session, which was a classic of family disease dynamics, it became apparent that her children felt Mother's asthma had ruled their lives. They resented the intrusion but admitted, on the other hand, that considerable adjustment would have to be made if she ever returned to health and that it would be difficult at best. One daughter, for example, had assumed the mothering role and would have to abandon it. The parents, too, had desires of extricating themselves from the children's demands for extended vacations when Mother felt well.

The family constellation was thus threatened with change. More than that, however, the family fully recognized that *they* themselves would have to change in order for Mother to get well. In the past, when she had tried to quit smoking, smokers in the family continued to smoke in her presence. Eating was also a major family social function, and no one was willing to stop the festive rounds of the cities' finer restaurants so that she could diet. Not one of the children would agree to discontinue the big birthday celebrations, even though they were a major source of stress. They also fought and argued in her presence, using her as a sounding board, a behavior which they all felt affected her health. Yet they were obviously caring, loving children who truly desired that their mother should become well, as did she. The cost, in terms of life adjustments, was simply too great.

She terminated her treatment sessions after three months, and we did not disagree with the decision. An impasse in progress had been reached from our point of view, and she had obviously achieved the original goal of treatment, i.e., to circumvent the stress-related attacks.

Therapeutic interaction with this type of patient is predetermined by (1) the amount and nature of lifestyle changes required to escape the sick "prisoner" role, and (2) the priorities set by the patient and family on behaviors that sustain the illness or that would disappear should good health be discovered. If (1) is "few" and (2) is "low," therapy will be successful. Unfortunately, many sessions may be required to determine that (1) is many and (2) is high, in which case you've wasted the patient's (and your) time. Given the least glimmer of hope, however, we tend to maintain the counseling relationship. These patients generally have numerous resources and supports; when the illness goes away, the interactions and activities will change accordingly. Potentially, they can be removed from disease dictatorship, even if familial stress is encountered initially.

Our second example indicative of "My Disease Is My World" syndrome presents a different set of issues and treatment (or lack of treatment) implications. This patient has a basically empty life except for the disease. She is a 65-year-old lady diagnosed with rheumatoid arthritis which was not crippling, but quite uncomfortable. We allowed her to participate in two adjunctive treatments which were available: biofeedback and physical therapy. For 12 weeks she passively accepted the treatment from the physical therapist and the biofeedback technician. There was no objective evidence that she ever heeded the instructions to relax or that she learned even a modicum of physical control. Unlike most R.A. patients, she didn't express variance in pain or discomfort or disease flare-ups, but rather always was "bad." Nothing seemed to make her feel better, though her medical doctor asked her point blank why she kept coming to the clinic if she didn't benefit from medication and didn't want to take it. She was taking Prednizone and complaining of destructive reactions. She had been on every known treatment for R.A. and had been taken off each drug because of reported side effects. She was moderately well educated about her disease, however, and offered us coherent and vivid images of her body's improper functioning. She exhibited no anger about her condition, nor toward those who treated her, and was placid and overtly pleasant throughout the sessions. Apparently she continued coming for treatment because dealing with her disease was not only her major focus, it seemed to be the *only* focus in her life.

In examining her lifestyle, it seemed to us that her disease was the glue holding her life together. Without it, she would have nothing left, no place to go, nothing to do. She lived alone, had few, if any, church or social activities, and seldom saw any family even though they lived nearby. Her only activities were coming to the clinic and reading Gothic novels (when she didn't feel well enough to move about, which was apparently often).

Unlike the first patient we described, whose activities would shift if health replaced disease, this second patient and others like her would have a vacuum in their lives without the disease. If she didn't hurt, what in the world would she get up and do? What would she talk about? Who would care for her (perhaps the most important issue)?

We may have unknowingly contributed to her behavior by providing $5.00 per session to defray transportation expenses. A grant allowed that provision to needy patients and, if they had their own cars (as she did), the money was probably a boon to daily existence. This action was not necessarily immoral, however. In fact, in cases like hers, we should seriously consider the positive benefits that the illness may have and perhaps decide *against* confrontation of continued symptom promotion. Removing the disease may remove the props, especially if a more appropriate all-consuming phenomenon is not available for substitution which could sustain interest in living.

This patient was, by all accounts, very passive. Such individuals are easy to treat because they don't argue, but it is difficult to help them down the alternative paths toward health. While they seem agreeable and placid, we suspect that they exhibit some apathy in following treatment regimens. For the patient in question, our experience told us she neither participated regularly in the exercise, nor in the biofeedback/ relaxation homework. These treatments benefitted her neither more nor less than her many drug regimens.

Interventions for such patients do not, in our experience, have a high probability of success. The patients are unlikely to give up their symptoms without monumental changes in living patterns. They are not likely to continue in therapy very long either, particularly if active involvement in the treatment is required.

The Profit-Motivated Patient. It is no secret to any practitioner who sees more than a handful of pain patients that if a litigation is pending, the probability of symptom removal or relief is likely to be inversely related to the perceived size of the requested settlement. Again, *perceived* value of settlement, not actual cash involved, is the key here. We are frequently amazed at the behavior of patients seeking a Social Security monthly pittance. They will hire private lawyers at great expense, fail to work for months or years, and ultimately lose money even if they are declared disabled enough to receive benefits. The investment may be an emotional issue, to "get back" at someone or to fight for justice, that clearly excludes much real attention to the dollars involved.

Several subcategories can be identified within this typology, which has been labeled the "Whiplash Rhymes with Cash" syndrome. One includes the true faker who has concocted symptoms. This is probably rare, since there is generally some medical support, even if it is tentative; otherwise, the litigation would be a meaningless exercise. Another consists of those persons who, perhaps at an unconscious level, recognize the tremendous amount of time and energy expended in a lawsuit yet sustain symptoms to protect against the cognitive dissonance which would result from suddenly getting well. If they got well, patients of this kind would then have to contend with feeling foolish for having so invested themselves in a now nonexistent cause.

One wonders, in fact, how many major malpractice or other litigations are dropped because the patient regains function or health. Probably few, indeed. So, even if the disease or disorder is real, little treatment progress is likely until the lawsuit or settlement is resolved. Either a positive or negative decision will then give the patient permission to quit hurting.

Roger K. is a prime example of chronicity sustained by pending legal action. He had experienced several traumas which were ancient history by the time he was referred to our service. His 6-inch medical file revealed surgeries of all kinds on arms, spinal cord, etc., to relieve pain. He had gone to many specialists, received Facet injections, acupuncture, transcutaneous electrical nerve stimulation (TENS), physical therapy, massage, and exercise programs. He wore a cervical collar and walked with a cane. He took pain killers, diuretics, tranquilizers, and sleeping pills.

Being undaunted and eager to try our approach where other more conventional modes had failed, we began a biofeedback program (EMG and temperature). Roger K. came for treatment day after day with a pained half-smile on his face and a quiet statement to the effect that, "I sure hope this works." It didn't. We learned after the biofeedback sessions had been completed that he had a half-million-dollar litigation for negligence pending against one of the hospitals he'd been in earlier.

A third subcategory of patient, typified by Jane L., presents a somewhat more tragic situation. She could have significantly profited from bodymind intervention strategies immediately, but would not avail herself of the opportunity because to do so could have meant that she would not qualify for a pension that would ward off starvation, if little else.

She had originally been diagnosed with cancer of the bowel, but during surgery to remove the tumor, her rectum and vagina were resected as well. In view of the small localized lesion, this could certainly be regarded as extensive and radical surgery. As a result, her boyfriend deserted her ("with no sex, what would he want to stick around for?"). She also lost her job, and, as a minimally skilled laborer, she could be considered for little other than rather strenuous positions. Her osteoarthritic condition, however, made this impossible.

Despite these manifest difficulties, she was primarily referred to us for problems with anxiety, belligerence, and a neuroticism that concerned her physicians, as she frequently swore and yelled at them. She received from us general acceptance, as much unconditional care as we could muster, neck and shoulder massages, and biofeedback and relaxation training.

As her third Social Security hearing approached, she got worse and worse until she had registered complaints about every conceivable health factor. (She'd been denied assistance twice and was appealing the decision.) She called the offices daily in distress, and even acknowledged that she'd had a nervous breakdown before and was feeling that way again. All of this was tempered by her good judgment, since she demonstrated affection for her psychologist, bringing in small gifts and declaring that she thanked God each day for the relationship.

One day she came in with a new hairdo, neatly dressed, and looking 10 years younger. Her eligibility hearing was over and she had received a disability settlement of less than $200 a month. She staunchly maintains to this day that the psychophysiological service, which we felt totally unsuccessful in relieving either anxiety or pain, was of primary importance in her remission. She later managed two emotional traumas without decompensating in her usual fashion and has continued improving physically.

The moral to this story appears to be that it is sometimes worthwhile to sustain a relationship, even when all overt behaviors indicate the futility of the service rendered.

Patients Who Want to Get Well

It is perhaps too easy to explain that people do not get well after exposure to all possible kinds of treatment, including our expertise, because they have other priorities and agendas. Many people who do want to get well both consciously and unconsciously, and who should be able to based on their medical diagnoses, have been unable to do so. Often they have not received adequate education about their problem and may, in fact, be responding to quite erroneous information. For example, 70% of the back pain patients who develop chronicity have come to believe that their backs are as fragile as china plates, vulnerable at any time to breakage and to sudden intolerable pain—perhaps even paralysis. Such thinking obviously precludes participation in the exercising, stretching, and strengthening activities required for recovery, since the patients try to protect themselves through inactivity. Other people appear to have tremendous voids in their understanding of the relationship between diet, habit, attitudes, and disease, responding almost as if the illness were independent of anything else they did.

People who *do* manage to recover or to significantly stabilize their conditions appear to do so by being sufficiently motivated to seek out answers. They do not expect the miracle cure to drop into their laps. If the answer were simple, the condition would have been corrected early in treatment. Often an extensive trial and error period may be required before people find the key to improvement. We are mindful, though, of the diabetic who was uncomfortable for 15 years, with blood sugar levels that swung dramatically back and forth each day. She repeatedly requested medical assistance but was dismissed as a "crock" who was not following her regimen properly. When someone finally suggested she divide her insulin dosage into two injections, giving herself two rather than one per day, however, her metabolism responded appropriately. Often, then, the key to reestablishing good health *is* uncomplicated but is simply not shared with patients.

In addition to being motivated to "not take 'no' for an answer," one of the primary characteristics of patients who significantly rehabilitate themselves is that of *flexibility*. The ability and willingness to change attitudes and habits is crucial. Much of the time, we see patients who react inappropriately to stress, in all of its broad definition of physical and psychological events, and whose tissue or vital organs deteriorate over time from the continued strain or irritation. The classic cases, of course, are the gastric reactions to stress, which eventually result in ulcers, or the repeated and sustained autonomic arousal which has been related to essential hypertension.

With insight and education, people can change their responses, but only if they are willing to make some major changes in lifestyle. It is not an easy task. Often it means changing eating habits which may have great cultural significance and offer tremendous emotional satisfaction. Sometimes it may mean leaving a position of employment in which years of time and untold quantities of effort have been invested. It may mean relearning ways of communicating or, in fact, deciding to end relationships which have continued to deteriorate despite all efforts at salvation.

We applaud the courageous voyage toward health and find repeated affirmation of the tendency for all cells and all systems to readjust so that both physiological and psychological integrity is maintained. "Readjustment" itself implies flexibility, movement, motivation, and ability to respond to the environment in new and different ways until homeostasis or health is achieved at every level of functioning.

We work on the assumption that everyone wishes to be healthy and that, given some realistic alternatives, they will choose a path toward health. We maintain that assumption until all evidence is overwhelmingly to the contrary because we have been intermittently rewarded for our persistence. In fact, two of the most perplexing people we have studied provided powerful reinforcement for this working assumption.

The first was a handsome gentleman, Max L., in his early 40s. He was well educated and well-to-do, able to spend large sums of money in his search for health. He referred himself to us, having experienced a condition resembling Meniere's Disease for over 15 years. It was a tentative diagnosis, however, even though he had been subjected to every diagnostic procedure available at several nationally known institutions.

He had been bounced from clinic to clinic, from department to department, and was finally told that psychiatric treatment was necessary, since no definitive physical diagnosis was forthcoming. Again, seeking out the best the profession had to offer, he underwent psychoanalysis three times a week for six years. His symptoms rarely changed and would periodically worsen until he required hospitalization. Throughout, he maintained a successful business, but his life became unbalanced because of his work and the visits to his analyst. No time was left for developing interpersonal relationships. Despite his protestations to the contrary, superficially he appeared to be someone depending on his disease in order to have a reason for existing. To remove the disease would have created a void in his lifestyle.

He specifically requested that we assist him in imaging, a process he'd read about in conjunction with cancer patients. We did so, combining it with biofeedback for his anxiety and some bioenergetics exercises. We also requested that he begin to taper off his tranquilizers if he felt comfortable doing so and if his psychiatrist would agree.

He was a model patient, a superb biofeedback subject, and most willing to carry through with any instruction. Despite all this, his condition only grew worse, and new symptoms erupted. The relationship with us also appeared to conflict with his loyalty and allegiance to his analyst, even though we collaborated on treatment. He finally terminated the therapy, all the while stating that he sincerely believed in our methodology, that it was the wave of the future, and that he would return when and if the loyalty issue were resolved.

Over a year later, he called to say that he had just returned from the leading specialist on his condition in the world, having once again undergone lengthy and uncomfortable tests. Here, too, he was asked to stop taking his tranquilizers prior to the examination. His symptoms intensified, he became photosensitive, and he developed chills and shakes. His physician, who had seen over 500 cases of the alleged disorder, recognized that this man was an anomaly. He was reacting very much like a drug addict would when withdrawing from narcotics. Indeed, he had exceeded the FDA's recommendation for taking his particular brand of medication by five years, even though no dire consequences had ever been consistently reported for excessively long usage. He is now going through the painful process of recovery, which may endure a year or more. However, he might not have ever reached this stage had he not had the perseverance to continue his search for health. Our role was minor in his treatment, but his influence on our belief that health is the natural and desired condition was monumental.

The second person, Anita G., deserves a book devoted to her experiences. She was referred by another psychologist for a persistent painful condition which, for all practical purposes, could be called temperomandibular joint (TMJ) pain. For this disorder there are successful somatic psychological treatments which focus on the joint and surrounding musculature, so we decided to accept the referral. However, her whole complicated history sent up red flags to the effect that this was probably an impossible case.

She was an engaging woman whose previous experience with both meditation and charismatic groups intrigued us. This was particularly so in view of the fact that she appeared at first glance to be a typical 60-year-old Texan who might be uncomfortable in any "consciousness-raising" movement. She was very "gutsy," having raised five children single-handedly, while working for 20 years to support her family. She had been widowed when her youngest was an infant.

On the negative side, she had been hurting for six years. During this time she had been to the dentist every single week to have her dentures altered in some way. Needless to say, several dentists had become frustrated and finally referred her to the chairman of the school of dentistry, who patiently continued to treat her. She repeatedly stated that "if only I could get rid of this pain, then all my other problems would disappear." We were aware of the current belief that pain which has persisted for such long periods is permanent if it is "real" to the patient (i.e., believed to be physical). If the pain is "unreal," in the sense of an hysteria, the patient would only be expected to symptom substitute.

All pain is real to a patient who has it, however. She was no exception. All of the major muscles in her neck, face, and shoulders were in constant spasm, probably in an unconscious attempt to 'armour" against the painful sensations from her dentures. The armouring has serious consequences which only exacerbate the pain, as the whole jaw becomes rigidly held in an unnatural position.

We eventually arrived at a mutually satisfactory explanation of the cause of the discomfort, which was that her first set of dentures fit poorly. Being a stubborn and determined woman, she kept them for several years until she ultimately developed something akin to phantom pain, which persisted long after the bad dentures had been replaced. The phantom pain, combined with the muscle spasm, provided a reasonable explanation for her physical condition.

Like Max in the previous case, Anita was a superb candidate for behavioral intervention, responding rapidly and becoming an expert at achieving physiological control. She incorporated relaxation and imagery into her lifestyle, and proved to be one of the most creative and thoughtful women we know.

As she became more confident of her ability to control her physiology and trusting of our judgment, she shared more of her complex life. She was a devout Catholic who had married eight years previously an ex-priest, who was also an ex-alcoholic. The problems encountered in that relationship were so involved that our heads spun as we attempted to understand both the religious implications as well as the difficulty her husband had had learning to be a husband after years of being a philosopher/priest. Her pain was put into perspective by her own insights. It had developed less than two years after their late-life marriage and was, she believed, a necessary ingredient heralding the beginning of their profound relationship.

In this kind of interpretation, the pain is not considered as a "tool" she could use against him for her own best interests, but rather as something that would allow him to learn to give, to feel, and to take husbandly responsibility. It also allowed her to learn to be cared for and to receive graciously after years of independence. From their point of view, both religious and in terms of historical expectation, the man was to be head of the house. Both wanted that, yet neither knew how to accomplish it; thus, they struggled for eight years, often feeling ostracized by other Catholics. Consequently, a support system was never established.

In our treatment, Anita G. learned all we could teach her about her muscle tension, and prepared to have a new set of dentures made. She and her husband, after several joint sessions with us, also attended a Catholic-sponsored couples' therapy weekend. Slowly but surely their relationship turned the proverbial corner. We now maintain contact by phone only, since a side benefit of the therapy has been the discovery of a group supporting Catholic couples in social, interpersonal, and religious ways. During the last conversation, the pain was not mentioned, so it has obviously lost priority in their lives. Not only did she want to be well physically, but she continued to seek out a fuller expression of total health in her life, which her pain, paradoxically, allowed to happen.

A Search
for Identity

In our practice and research, we tried several of what might be generically called "transition movements in medicine." These endeavors were an attempt to find a supportive community, a professional group to which we could pledge allegiance, a home that would offer a ready-made trellis upon which we could hang our ideas in an orderly fashion. Our experiences in this quest were undeniably positive. We repeatedly found not only reinforcement and constructive critique, but also the kind of stimulation that encourages creativity, excitement, and gumption. Nevertheless, we did not find a home. After debating jokingly about beginning our own transitional movement, we concluded that most psychologists who seriously pursue this area of study will derive their own personalized blend of philosophical implications and applications based on their needs and experiences.

Holistic
Medicine

From the holistic medicine group, perhaps the most broadly creative and accepting of all, we experienced our greatest stimulation of new ideas and frontiers in healing. We frequently were invited to speak to holistic groups, but we were usually anomalies on the program because of our emphasis on hard data. Spiritual and ethnic healing are hard acts to follow; we had to resist the encouragement to sensationalize our findings, a somewhat uncomfortable position for academic psychologists.

Without attempting to define "holism" (or, as is being promoted by one group—"wholism"), holistic medicine is currently an all-inclusive group of individuals offering alternative approaches to health care. They attempt to treat the whole person and to strive for new levels of mental, physical, and spiritual wellness. The alternatives range from acupuncture to Zazen. Although a group of holistic physicians have created the American Medical Holistic Association, and though continuing education credit was offered to physicians attending a course on holism at AMA meetings last year, the movement itself has had some distinct problems integrating to the medical mainstream.

A recent editorial in the *Journal of the American Medical Association*, entitled "Holistic Health or Holistic Hoax?"

(Callan, 1979) represents a turning point. The movement has attracted enough attention now, and is apparently threatening enough, for the writer to state that "It would behoove physicians to learn more about it." He describes it as "an uncontrolled nuclear reaction" whose advocates plan to make it "a top national priority" and indicates that it is already well funded by its membership and by foundation grants. The cynical, condescending tone belies any objectivity, indicating rather that holistic health ought to be watched carefully as an enemy to the integrity of medical practice.

Holistic health practices, nevertheless, offer ideas which occasionally bear fruit when subjected to scientific scrutiny. Interestingly, holistic health was the theme of the American Medical Students Association meetings in Texas, May, 1979. That, probably more than any other event, is a harbinger of *future* medical involvement.

Humanistic
Medicine The humanistic medicine group, sometimes distinguishable from holistic advocates (and sometimes not), has as its obvious focus the humanization of health care, but seems to concentrate rather heavily on issues of death and dying. One can apparently be humanistic without subscribing to alternative or adjunctive protocols, but one can *not* be holistic in perspective without being humanistic. In some areas, academicians who have taught traditional medical ethics now include themselves in humanistic medicine. Many, however, would scarcely consider deviations from AMA or FDA guidelines. Nonetheless, medical ethics has a valuable philosophical tradition and an "inside track" to the hearts of physicians (Who, after all, wants to be *un*ethical?). To psychologists, it offers an inroad which facilitates an understanding of medical obligations.

Behavioral
Medicine This movement seems to be the most logical group with which to seek alliance from a psychologist's standpoint. It is data oriented, within the embrace of both government and academia, and solicitous of *all* behavioral sciences (not just psychology) which have an investment in the anthropological, sociological, ecological, or ethical aspects of disease. In truth, behavioral medicine is currently being spearheaded by the "old guard" in psychological circles, i.e., those psychologists who have not deviated significantly from the mainstream of

psychological orientation and who, in many cases, have courted governmental agencies to support their research and training programs. One "elitist" group has organized to decide not only what behavioral medicine is, but also *who* should be invited to join the Academy of Behavioral Medicine. Still another organization, the *Society of Behavioral Medicine*, was formed to include those with a more clinical orientation than the research constituency of the Academy. Within three months, 500 membership applications were received. The membership is truly multidisciplinary and includes psychologists, physicians, physical therapists, social workers, and other practitioners within the general spectrum of allied health care.

Another group with interest in behavioral approaches to health and disease are the individuals who are involved in the newly created Division 38 of APA—Health Psychology. Also in APA is Section 2 (Health Research) within Division 18 (Psychologists in Public Service). Division 22 (Rehabilitation Psychology) has perhaps the longest history of active involvement in physical disease, but its future seems currently uncertain as its functions seem to be duplicated by the new Division 38. There are also ongoing "networks" of psychologists unified by such common interests as biofeedback, imagery, behavior modification, or just medicine in general.

There seems to be some merit to all these movements in seeking a professional identification. Certainly a variety of goals is necessary at first for establishing credibility, stimulation, debate, and for achieving a clearer notion of the state of the art. Currently, however, we are merely amused by the jockeying for position that is taking place among the groups as they vie for the ultimate plum of granting definition and direction to the role of psychologists in medicine.

Our own approach to patient care lies somewhere in between the all-embracing holistic movement and the hard-nosed behavioral scientist. We intend to be sensitive to the directions of our discipline, nevertheless, anticipating that truly creative approaches to treatment and research of disease will be conducted on a broad scale as a professional obligation.

CHAPTER II

IMAGERY
The Golden Thread

A golden thread has run throughout the history of the world, consecutive and continuous, the work of the best men in successive ages. From point to point it still runs, and when near you feel it as the clear and bright and searchingly irresistible light which Truth throws forth when the great minds conceive it.

Walter Moxon
Pilocereus Senilis and other papers, 1887, p. 4

The integrated effect of conscious and unconscious levels of functioning and the coordination of the physical with the behavioral domains of life are the bases for our approach to health and disease. These bases find expression in our principal method of treatment—imagery. In this chapter, we present two kinds of evidence in support of its authenticity and utility: historical anecdote and modern clinical doctrine. In several instances, case histories from our files or those of our colleagues are presented to illustrate the application of the technique.

**Imagery
Defined** Imagery is one of the first recorded treatments for disease. It has continued in one form or another throughout the history of medicine and may well represent the epitome in health maintenance once the parameters are thoroughly understood. Imagery, or visualization, or fantasy, might be thought of as the internal *experience* of a perceptual event in the absence of the actual external stimuli. The IMAGE is to be contrasted with a PERCEPT evoked by actual physical stimuli.

Images are usually thought of as involving the visual sense, but may well involve any other sensory modality associated with the image, including audition, olfaction, or even kinesthesis. The most extreme or clearest form of imagery is *eidetic imagery*, or *photographic memory*, in which total scenes can be recreated down to the smallest detail. For individuals who exhibit this skill, it is as if the memory storage and retrieval process, which is normally altered by time or imperfect perception or emotional stimuli, remains stable. An eidetic system parallel to that observed in the visual modality no doubt exists in all senses, but has been less thoroughly studied. Musicians, for example, who can "hear" total scores after one session certainly fall into this category of "imagers." Those who create complicated musical works in their heads, and who later proceed to play them without hesitation, even more effectively demonstrate the storage and representation of phenomena in the absence of actual auditory cues.

Imagery should be distinguished technically from retrieval of stored memory. The latter will conform somewhat to reality (given the distortions of time, etc.), but imagery need not be in line at all with any previously experienced stimuli. During the imagery process, loyalty to external reality is suspended and inhibitions on the creative process are released. Images of mind pictures, or sounds, or feelings which have *never* been PERCEPTS for an individual can be brought forth. The images of people that occur in dreams, as a case in point, are often composites of several individuals: the physical appearance resembles someone familiar, yet it is subjectively regarded as some other person. The symbolism that is observed in dreams or states of reverie, in which a concept or event is manifest in a representative object, is also characteristic of images which are not loyal to perceptual reality.

Imagery, as thus distinguished from stored memories of experience, has a certain freedom connected with it that plays an important role in discovery, invention, and creative artistry. Imagery has also been described as an important variable in learning and retention and has been studied extensively as an aid to verbal learning (Paivio, 1971).

Imagery and Medicine Before the Twentieth

Century In tracing the role of imagination, or imagery, in medical protocols, we found we were actually tracing the history of medicine itself. The "new medicine," which has imagery components as a prominent focus, practiced by progressive physicians today, is certainly not of recent origin; it has a recorded history of over 3,000 years. In fact, with the exception of the middle decades of this century, imagery has been acknowledged by the great physicians of each era as a powerful and undeniable variable in healing. It has only been since the advent of increased specialization and automation of medicine that this most distinctively humanistic component of patient/physician relationship has been occluded.

Ancient Healing: Egypt. The Hermetic principles, which originated in ancient Egypt, asserted that everything, including disease, was created from mentalistic phenomena. Ill health, it was believed, could be overcome by visualizing good health or by imagining the body in a perfect state or by envisioning a healing god.

Those ancient Egyptians who ascribed to the Hermetic philosophy and who integrated magic into the healing process were regarded as fine practitioners both in terms of diagnostic acumen and in pharmaceutical development (Binder, 1966). Many drugs and techniques were used, but medical effects were judged to be primarily magical. Aid and guidance were sought from a supernatural force when medicine failed (not unlike today!).

The ancient Egyptian god of medicine was Imhotep, whose name means "he who cometh in peace." Around the third century, B.C., temples were erected to Imhotep in which patients found relief through visualizations or dreams induced during sleep. This practice, later called "Incubation Sleep," has had a most fascinating history extending from Imhotep worshippers through Christian sects of the 19th Century. Hamilton (1906) reports that evidence of the practice was noted in Christ Church in Monmouthshire, Great Britain, in the 1800s.

Remnants of the ancient Egyptian tenets can still be seen in some modern movements. The notion of visualizing perfect health as a way to deal with disease remains an active concept in various vitalistic groups and permeates the Christian Science doctrine. During this century, Mary Baker Eddy, founder of the Christian Science Church and author of *Science and Health* (1934), expressed similar ideas related to techniques for overcoming disease: "To prevent disease or to cure it, the power of Truth, of divine spirit, must break the dream of the material senses.... Mentally insist that harmony is the fact, and that sickness is a temporal dream. Realize the presence of health and the fact of harmonious being, until the body corresponds with the normal conditions of health and harmony" (p. 412).

Ancient Healing: Greece. The cult of Asclepius provides an explicit example of the use of images in healing. The cult, if it can be called that, grew hand in hand with Greek scientific medicine. Asclepius was represented in Homer's Iliad as an aristocrat, a tribal leader, and a physician. Legend that developed around him and his accomplishments eventually resulted in his being elevated to a status of diety, or rather "half-god." He was then considered the product of a romantic encounter between the god Apollo and a mortal woman. His daughters were Hygeia and Panacea, who symbolized aspects of his profession. Ultimately, Asclepius was killed by the great god Zeus because he was said to be able to revive the dead—a perogative reserved to the gods themselves.

Some 200 temples eventually were erected throughout Greece and Italy to honor the practice of medicine associated with Asclepius. These Asclepieia were, in reality, the first recorded holistic treatment centers. They were located in lovely areas and contained baths or spas, theaters, and places of recreation and worship. Rich and poor alike were accepted. This policy agreed with the basic teachings of Asclepius who was believed to be "a kind sympathetic god, a physician first of all, to whom anyone, in suffering or in trouble, might turn." (Binder, p. 41). The only requirement was that the patients should be clean and think pure thoughts.

Incubation sleep, in addition to the rather utopian-like attention to material aspects, was the standard practice of the Asclepieia. At night, patients went to the temple or outlying buildings to await the gods. In preparation for this event, "The priests take the inquirer and keep him fasting from food for one day and from wine for three days to give him perfect spiritual lucidity to absorb the divine communication." (from Phillimores *Apollonius of Tyans*, Book II, Chap. XXXVII). Dreams were suggested while the patient was sleeping or, more probably, during the most susceptible and sensitive period immediately prior to sleep. Asclepius purportedly then appeared as a handsome, gentle, and strong practitioner. He either healed or advised treatment. He held a rustic staff with a serpent entwined about it, the symbolic caduceus originally associated with the god Hermes. The snake as a partner in healing has played a continuous symbolic role throughout history and it was also reported to be part of the incubation experiences; the serpent would heal patients by licking wounds or eyelids.

Many, many cures were ascribed to this process. The recipients of the cures, in fact, would leave stone images of the healed body part to adorn the walls of the temples. For whatever reasons, the methods appear to have been successful where other treatments had failed. Asclepius, though, might be considered a representative of a higher consciousness in healing. The staff and the snake continue as the symbol of medicine today and remind us of the art of the ancient practitioners.

Physicians and priests had utilized imagery for centuries, both in the Asclepieia and in Shamanistic rituals recorded in early civilizations of Sumeria and Babylonia. The elucidation of a mechanism for the process was not clearly stated, however, until Aristotle did so. According to Aristotle, the emotional system did not function in the absence of images. Images were formed by sensations, taken in and worked upon by the *sensus communis* (collective sense). These images were causal in altering body functions and in the production and cure of disease. Aristotle also held that the special images which occurred in dreams were valuable information for the physician and others, stating: "Even scientific physicians tell us that one should pay diligent attention to dreams, and to hold this view is reasonable also for those who are not practitioners but speculative philosophers." (Aristotle; *Parva Naturalia*, Oxford Ed., Vol. III, 463a).

Post-Aristotleian philosophers continued to define images as emotions and acknowledged their affect on the equilibrium that was health. The Stoics, for example, prescribed the following formula for preventative medicine: "Wipe out imagination; check desire; extinguish appetite." [1]

It is also interesting to note that the influence of the Asclepieia was enhanced historically by Hippocrates, the "Father of Medicine" and an Asclepiad himself. Medicine based on naturalistic, rather than mystical principles, has been symbolized by the life and teachings of Hippocrates for over 2,000 years. He believed that the physician's role primarily was to understand and to assist nature, saying: "A healer must be skilled in Nature and must strive to know what man is in relation to food, drink, occupation, and which effect each of these has on the other." Not unlike Asclepius, he was characterized by gentleness and concern, love and dignity. He stated: "Where there is love for mankind, there is love for the art of healing."

Galen, whose practices and dictums influenced the practice of medicine for 45 generations, was the last important "pillar" in the millennium of Greek medical pre-eminence. His approach was based on the Hippocratic theories of the four humors, on the concept of critical days (forerunner to biorhythms), and on erroneous theories of pulse and urine functioning. He understood psychophysiological relations well, however, and recorded his impressions of causal aspects of emotion in apparent physical disease.

Galen reported the use of imagery as a diagnostic of humoral imbalance. In the absence of laboratory tests, images offered what was felt to be clinically important information. Patients were queried about dream content, and if certain images were reported, the extent and type of imbalance was determined. For example, images of loss or grief related to an

---

[1]These text statements and the following information from the Pre-Descartesian era are secondary citations from McMahon (1976). The interested reader is sincerely advised to read the review of imagery in medicine during this period in toto and to examine the following: Osler (1921); and Binder (1966). The latter source is an especially good reference of historical texts on medicine.

excess of melancholy (black bile), and terror or fright reflected a predominance of choler. Galen emphasized the circularity inherent in excessive humors which nourished corresponding images, which in turn produced more elaboration of humor. He acknowledged implications of the cycle for therapy.

Dark Ages. According to Osler (1921): "The Greek view of man was the very antithesis of that which St. Paul enforced from the Christian world. One idea pervades thought from Homer to Lucian like an aroma—pride in the body as a whole. In the strong conviction that 'our soul in its rose mesh' is quite as much helped by flesh as flesh by soul the Greek sang his song—'For pleasant is this flesh.'"

As expressed in this sentiment, Christianity can be seen as a factor contributing to the stagnation in medical understanding characteristic of all thought during this period. While Christ certainly can be regarded as one of the greatest healers of all time, his early followers were more preoccupied with Judgment Day, the afterlife, and the attainment of spiritual perfection. The routine care and feeding of the body were neglected functions. As a matter of fact, physical needs were often denied or even abused in order to reach religious enlightening. Perspectives other than those espoused in early Christian fundamental thought did survive, however. Prodicus made a rather remarkable statement which implies a principle of unity and which lends to the Greek healing arts a metaphysical truth and goodness consonant with Christ's teaching, if not early Christian practices: "That which benefits human life *is* God" (5th Century B.C.).

Asclepius survived the Christian purge of pagan gods— probably because he was unique in his goodness. As Asclepius resembled Imhotep, so did Jesus Christ embody the spirit of Asclepius; the parallels between the old god and Jesus were too many to overlook. Further, incubation techniques continued to be used in the temples, since the practice of healing through sleep images appeared successful. The names of more modern saints (St. Cosmos and St. Damian, in particular) instead became associated with the miracles that occurred.

Middle Ages Through the Renaissance. The role of imagination a la Galen persisted through the Middle Ages. It was restated and embellished by physicians of the Renaissance, but lost none of its vitality, as evidenced by the following statements attributed to Agrippa (1510): "So great a power is there of the soul upon the body, that whichever way the soul imagines and dreams that it goes, thither doth it lead the body. . . . The passions of the soul which follow the phantasy, when they are most vehement . . . can thus take away or bring some disease of the mind or body. For the passions of the soul are the chiefest cause of the temperament of its proper body. So the soul, being strongly elevated, and inflamed with a strong imagination, sends forth health or sickness."

According to McMahon (p. 181, 1976): "The key to an understanding of such pre-Cartesian theory lies in recognizing that imagery was understood to be as much a physiological reality as it is today regarded as a psychological reality. When an image became an obsession it pervaded the body, bound up the heart, clutched at the sinews and vessels, and directed the flesh according to its own inclination. Soon its essence became manifest in its victim's complexion, countenance, posture, and gait. Imagination had greater powers of control than sensation, and thus, anticipation of a feared event was more damaging than the event itself; horror of death killed with the same authenticity as an externally inflicted wound. A strong imagination of a particular malady, such as fever, paralysis or suffocation was sufficient to produce its symptoms."

One of the most colorful physicians of this era was Paracelsus, variously called the Luther of Medicine, the arch-charlatan, the drunken quack, the founder of modern medicine, and the Renaissance Christ of Healing by his contemporaries and biographers. He cured and quarreled and made men think, stirring "the pool as had not been done for fifteen centuries." (Osler, p. 187). He lectured in German instead of traditional Latin. He built a bonfire and then burned the *Canon*, the bible of medicine, speaking out boldly for independent judgment among physicians. His contemporaries railed against him, but his patients adored him. He was credited with numerous cures and with giving the original impetus to the development of pharmacy. His philosophical treatises, however, inspiring the Rosicrucians among others, probably have had a more enduring influence than any of his medical writings. That is because his ideas were transcendental and generally regarded as difficult to comprehend by the less than intellectual reader.

Paracelsus frequently reiterated the theme that three principias controlled his conception of everything related to men: the spiritual, the physical, and mentalistic phenomena. Stoddart (1911) paraphrases him by stating: "Man is his own doctor and finds proper healing herbs in his own garden; the physician is in ourselves, and in our own nature are all things that we need" (p. 213), and Hartman (1973) quotes: "Man has a visible and an invisible workshop. The visible one is his body, the invisible one is imagination (mind). . . . The imagination is sun in the soul of man. . . . The spirit is the master, imagination the tool, and the body the plastic material. . . . The power of the imagination is a great factor in medicine. It may produce diseases in man and animals, and it may cure them. . . . Ills of the body may be cured by physical remedies or by the power of the spirit acting through the soul. (p. 111-112)." In short, Paracelsus believed that imagination was the creative power of man.

McMahon chronicled pre-Cartesian medical thinking as invariably holistic or psychosomatic. In her opinion, it was replaced by a mechanistic physiopathology because the psychophysiological approach was logically inconsistent with the Cartesian concept of dualism. In the core practice of medicine, imagery lost its status.

Nevertheless, healers or shamans in many primitive and modern cultures have continued to use imagery both diagnostically and therapeutically (Service, 1958). Both Canadian Eskimo and Navaho Indians use visualization in healing. The shamans of these tribes maintain contact with tribal spirits through dreams and visions, and consult with the spirit world while in a trance-like state. The herb healers, too, visualize correct herbal preparations for patients' disorders.

Besides Indian cultures, other schools of thought which emphasize visualization in the treatment of disease have persisted in one form or another throughout history. Many have been an integral part of a culture's folk medicine, such as the healing arts practiced among the Cuendaro of Mexico. Others have been associated with philosophical or metaphysical movements such as the Rosicrucians, a most enduring group whose visualization practices might be studied with profit by psychology and medicine alike. However, these various schools are really tangential to the practice of modern medicine *at the present time.*

Mind/body dualism has persisted in the current medical model of practice, though much lip service has been given to holistic concepts. Regardless of the influence of Descartes, however, clinicians have continued to take note of the relationship between imagerial system and disease. Attempts have been made to treat disease using imagery processes, particularly when all else has failed. Even so, empirical tests of psyche/soma interactions will no doubt be required before medicine recommits itself to the mutually important roles of physical and mental factors—particularly "images"—in the causation and course of physical disease. This need to demonstrate a relationship which was taken for granted until our current epoch of rapid technical growth in medical techniques puts a new burden of truth on the "mind" advocates which must be addressed.

The Golden Age. The comparative "Golden Age of Medicine" conceptually began with the renewed query of the

Renaissance. The grand discoveries of this age largely concerned the functioning of the soma. With increased understanding of somatic functioning, the successful combat of infectious disease and the development of anesthesias, finer surgical techniques became possible. One has only to look at longevity tables to decide that physically we are more advantaged now than at any time in history.

Credit should go where credit is due, however: much of the advantage we have in maintaining good health stems from vastly improved sanitation. The filth and grime that harbors disease has been significantly reduced; the occurrence of infectious disease has diminished therefore as well. Descartes reportedly said: "We could be freed from an infinity of maladies both of body and mind if we have sufficient knowledge of their causes and of all the remedies with which nature has provided us." (Source unknown). The development of sanitary living conditions has helped to make that prophesy come true for infectious disease, at least. As one sage put it, "The development of cheap cotton undergarments which can be changed frequently, and the existence of glass windows in houses has done more to eliminate disease than all of the medical discoveries put together."

Even though medical developments of the golden age were almost exclusively discoveries of the purely physical aspects of disease, the mental and spiritual features of man's tripartite unity were not totally ignored.

Outstanding physicians admonished their students to "observe the whole patient"; in this sense there was a continuing respect for the role of an individual's internal experiences in the treatment outcome. However, the understanding of nonphysical involvement in disease was not advanced to any significant degree. The humanistic element in treatment suffered generally from the intensive concentration on tangible cause-and-effect relationships.

We believe that the wisdom of Sir William Osler will serve as a beacon to guide the rehumanizing of medicine which has begun with changes in medical school curricula as a response to patient demands for respect and dignity. We recommend Osler's original works, both for their description of the fundamental practice of medicine and for their historical perspective. His book and papers are beautifully and poetically written, capturing the essence of scientific medical practice as it was conceived at the turn of the century with an altruistic concern for patient well-being. An attitude reminiscent of the Grecian belief in the divinity of healing, and a concern for the welfare of mankind permeate his philosophy. The all-encompassing nature of this concern prohibits an exclusive concentration on the damaged tissue, the tumor, or the failing heart, per se. It promotes instead a type of practice that places *patient* needs before tools and techniques as the primary focus of care. He admonished physicians to observe their patients, saying, "*They* will tell you the cure."

Osler's kind of thinking embodies the long-intertwined history of imagination and disease. There is a respect for the information offered by the patient from both conscious and subconscious sources. In his historical treatment, Osler himself discusses the use of imagination in medicine and reports cases of its successful use in his time. One of his most frequently quoted statements, "It is much more important to know what sort of patient has a disease than what sort of disease the patient has," indirectly acknowledges the mental and spiritual, or psychological, aspects of medical care to be greater in their importance to the physician than the treatment of disease itself. He seems to imply that physicians should first and foremost have an understanding of the unique psychological makeup of each patient.

Modern
Medical Practice
There are obviously two ways to assimilate the historical information on imagery just presented. One can accept it in a spirit of understanding the roots of medicine, but having no particular relevance to modern practice. One can also accept the information as representing a "thread of truth" which comes from the common experiences of our professional predecessors. If one assumes the latter posture, that imagery was and is an integral part of medicine, then it is reasonable to seek out sources of information which might guide research and practice.

While the use of imagery in the healing arts has a timely flavor as well as a venerable tradition, no truly *acceptable* research has ever been conducted on imagery as a viable medical intervention per se. This situation is somewhat peculiar. Even in the absence of appropriate statistical evidence to support its efficacy, imagery has been utilized by physicians of this century, and clinical support has been found for its validity.

In the context of contemporary medical practice, imagery can be discussed in terms of the "placebo effect" and also in conjunction with some creative innovations in *treatment*.

Placebo. Imagery, we believe, is the basis for the so-called placebo effect. The word "placebo" is derived from a Latin word meaning "I will please." It is a medically inert preparation given to a patient when no appropriate treatment is available, or when a patient requests medication though none is believed necessary. Notwithstanding these inert properties, however, its use often occasions a dramatic pharmacological effect. It has been reported to account for healing in from 30 to

70% of the cases tested, even for repair of tissue damage (Frank, 1973). The placebo effect may be induced by any number of manipulations, real and symbolic, in addition to the traditional sugar pill or water injection. It no doubt accounts for any beneficial effects of inappropriately prescribed medicine and perhaps even for a portion of the observed effect of appropriately prescribed treatment.

According to Frank (1973), the beneficial effects of the placebo lie in its symbolic power: "It gains its potency through being a tangible symbol of the physician's role as healer. In our society, the physician validates his power by prescribing medication, just as a shaman in a primitive tribe may validate his by spitting out a bit of bloodstained down at the proper moment." Shapiro (1959, p. 303) states that the "history of medical treatment until relatively recently is the history of the placebo effect." People, of course, did overcome disease prior to the 20th Century. Spontaneous remissions and dramatic cures have been reported throughout the chronicling of medicine.

While the precise mechanism of the placebo is unknown, it would appear to be a *product of the imagination;* it is enhanced by all those factors that contribute to the peculiar contents of the imagination. The hopes and fears, expectancies, the previous learning experiences, and archetypal and current belief systems—all form the basis for the quality and degree of the response.

Frank (1973) asserts: "Study of the patients' reactions to pharmacologically inert medication is a means of investigating effects of their expectations, mediated by the doctor-patient relationship, on their physical emotional state." We propose that the effect on the physical system occurs in the same fashion as that suggested for imagery. Positive or negative mental images concomittantly lead to emotional reactivity which, in turn, creates equilibrium or disequilibrium in the total system.

The placebo effect is not simple. It is not innocuous nor trivial. It cannot be dismissed as "purely mental," but can involve every system and cell in the body. In the words of Freud (1953, p. 289): "Expectation colored by hope and faith is an effective force with which we have to reckon in *all* our attempts at treatment and cure."

The power of the placebo response has been demonstrated experimentally as well as historically. Active medications were compared with inactive medications (placebo) in double-blind studies to determine the "pure," or uncontaminated, effects of the medicine. In one study (Lorr, et al., 1962), psychiatric patients improved on a number of mood and behavior indicators as long as they received a capsule, regardless of its contents. Ah, the power of symbols!

Other studies support the variation in response that can be obtained by preprogramming expectancy in the absence of any pharmacologically active agent. For instance, Volgyesi (1954) reports on patients hospitalized with bleeding peptic ulcers who were given water injections and told either: (1) that the injections would cure them; or (2) that they were experimental and of undetermined effectiveness. Seventy percent of the first group showed "excellent" improvement in their condition which was maintained for a period of over a year. Only 25% of the second group, however, showed a remission in symptoms.

The constellation of expectancies surrounding treatment may not always be neutral or positive. We frequently find patients who regard treatment as more destructive than the disease itself. These individuals rarely respond well, but instead respond in a way consistent with their thinking. This idea is demonstrated anecdotally by the increased number of side effects patients report after becoming aware of them. Experimental evidence also indicates that paradoxical effects from drug preparations are observed when the patient expects those effects rather than typical reactions. One case study (Wolf, 1950), using ipecac, involved a pregnant woman who was told that ipecac, a well-known emetic, would cure nausea. She indeed experienced a cessation of her discomfort, although vomiting and exacerbation of nausea had occurred when she had previously been given the drug without these instructions.

The placebo effect, conceived as the manipulation of a patient's imagings with a symbol, is undeniably the most valuable universal aid to health. By virtue of training and tradition, it is the *psychologist* rather than the physician who has the skills to manipulate the combination of conscious and subconscious memories, motives, and beliefs necessary for achieving this effect. Paradoxically, the psychologist is handicapped by virtue of the Zeitgeist that proclaims healing to be the bailiwick of M.D.'s and, *sometimes*, D.O.'s. Therefore, the *power* to transmit to the patient the belief system requisite to overcoming disease rests in the hands of those trained in traditional medicine. Rarely can the psychologist, or other allied health professional, imbue the magic to the symbol— whether drug, surgery, or simple admonitions to eat well and exericse properly.

Autogenics. A German neurologist and psychiatrist, J. H. Schultz, developed techniques in the 1930s to affect psychophysiological processes which were collectively called autogenic therapy. His work, reported in a seven-volume series by

Luthe (1969), is the most thoroughly described and documented of any in the area. Whether the careful clinical descriptions of outcome for some 2,400 case studies constitute
adequate evidence in lieu of carefully controlled experimentation must remain an individual matter. In Europe, the techniques have been accepted for decades.

Schultz employed six standard exercises which were done
with patients sitting or lying in a state of relaxation. Preliminary instructions were given to imagine being in mental
contact with the part of the body on which concentration was
centered, to repeat a special phrase visually or verbally, and
to have a causal attitude toward the results. This notion of
imaging the physical part or process and "letting" the exercise
take effect (passive volition)—rather than trying to *force* a
change—is very much in accord with current thinking on the
mechanism of imagery as a mediator of physical change.

The six exercises generally seem to serve two functions:
(1) to relax, and (2) to train some autonomic control over
vascularity. These functions are virtually identical to current
clinical biofeedback tactics. They compose an activity
sequence which consists of directed behavioral responses
gained through repeated utterance of suggestive phrases. In
the first exercise, patients begin by stating over and over "My
right arm is heavy." Then they proceed to feelings of warmth
in their extremities with the second exercise and continue on
through such instructional control of the body systems as
"Heart beat calm and regular." The fourth exercise focuses on
breathing; the fifth on warming of the solar plexus; and the
sixth on cooling of the forehead. Supplementations and alterations of the exercises to more specifically treat various disorders are also reported in the several volumes; Volume II is
perhaps the most useful for behavioral medicine.

Two aspects of Schultz's work should be pointed out: (1)
his specificity of treatment, and (2) the extensive use of verbalizations. Regarding the former, Schultz recognized both
the power of the techniques, if used appropriately, and the
damage that could be produced by inappropriate verbalizations or visualizations. For example, one phrase used in conjunction with relaxation of the abdominal muscles is "My solar
plexus is warm." This phrase should not be used with gastritis
patients who already are suffering from gastric motility.
Increased blood flow in that area could be contraindicated.
Indiscriminate use of the techniques not only are therefore *not*
benign, but could aggravate a physical condition. We stress,
again, the necessity for psychologists to understand as thoroughly as possible the nature of their patient's disease.

With respect to the second point, the emphasis on both
verbalization and visualization is an integral part of the
process. The patient is chanting phrases to himself and, at the

same time, visualizing a related image. The more advanced meditative exercises, in fact, are complex imagery or visualization practices which are intended to gain access to information that is not at the conscious level. The verbalizations, in our experience, are a kind of mantra. They may serve many of the same functions of the mantra; i.e., centering and gaiting out external stimuli while allowing the body to relax in a "wakeful, hypometabolic state," as Wallace, et al. (1971), termed it in research on Transcendental Meditation. Because the autogenic phrases are specific instead of nonspecific in terms of bodily function, unlike the classic "Om" mantra for example, they program the patient to expect or allow certain responses to take place.

In our work, the phrases seem to be useful at an early stage of imagery training, but for many patients they are disruptive. Such patients prefer to use other tactics for controlling physical response such as visual imagery or kinesthetic, proprioceptive imagery. We know of no patient who, after becoming adept at physiological control or at attaining an altered state of consciousness, continued to use the verbalizations. They are a valuable first step, however. They often serve as an interface for people, typically left hemispheric, who require a concrete verbal approach before accepting or allowing the symbolic abilities of the right hemisphere to function. There is a variety of research to be done in this area, including studies to determine *which* individuals are more likely to respond to verbalizations in assuming psychophysiological control as opposed to those who can more readily image in a visual sense.

Autogenic training, in conjunction with standard medical treatment, has been documented as successful in a myriad of acute and chronic situations including asthma, headaches, diabetes, arthritis, low back pain, gastritis, surgical procedures, and dentistry. Depending upon the exercise, physiological responses induced by the training have included changes in EMG response (muscle potential), skin temperature, blood sugar levels, white blood cell counts, blood pressure, heart rates, hormone secretions and EEGs (brain waves).

By way of understanding these phenomena, we may speculate that a "body wisdom" or other homeostatic mechanism naturally allows the return to a normal state of health if a person is once relaxed and in mental contact with his or her physiology.[2] Research supports the notion that relaxation is an optimal state for healing to occur. Sympathetic nervous system functions, which are usually activated by stressful conditions and which tax the body's resources, are decreased

---

[2]Health *is* the normal state; disease the abnormal.

during relaxation. Vital energy required to fight disease is thus conserved.

Yet, if relaxation is all that is required to become attuned to body needs, then it should not matter much whether the autogenic phrases are inappropriate for a given condition. On the other hand, the patient is likely to become confused between body signals and the therapist's instructions when the instructions or phraseology are inappropriate, distrusting one or both. We feel there is, most definitely, a body wisdom that reveals itself in images which is capable of defining both cause and cure for disease.

Observation of animal behavior indicates that the healing power of relaxation is not exclusively a human characteristic. When ill, animals may retreat, quit eating, and sleep a lot. This process allows a slowing down of overall body function and creates an optimal situation for cleansing and balancing. In many, maybe most, humans this wisdom is a dormant ability which requires re-education, however. Perhaps the answer is to provide the patient with the best possible "autogenic phrases" to produce a healthful response and, at the same time, to respect the patient's own bodily signals and symbols as being of therapeutic value.

In summary, we acknowledge the usefulness of the autogenic approach. In its most basic form, it helps those patients who require such a verbal interface. The standard exercise has initial efficacy for many patients who require some concretion in order to "get started." We question, though, which aspects (verbalizations, relaxation, education, communication, imagery, etc.) are most vital and for whom they are most effective. The major drawback seems to be that the autogenic exercises are incredibly tedious and patients complain vehemently about this aspect. We assure them that all forms of meditation and autonomic control are conceptually "boring" to a population supersaturated with external stimuli. The tedium is worth the effort because the results of the awareness eventually attained will change their lives for the better. If they don't trust this article of faith, they obviously drop out.

Natural Childbirth. Possibly the most interdigitated area of imagery and medicine is in obstetrical practice. In particular, the methods of natural childbirth proposed by Dr. Grantley Dick-Read (1953) are relevant to this discussion. Patients who have experienced these methods and nurses in obstetrics who have taught them have been among our best supporters and "informants." The mind/body connection, mediated by imagery, is no surprise to any of them. Neither are the important breathing exercises which we teach all patients in order to help them begin their understanding of conscious control over their bodies.

Dr. Dick-Read recognized the negative programming or negative imagery most women in our culture have about the natural process of birth. He also recognized how this negative imagery contributed to the "fear-tension-pain syndrome." He said: "The visualization of an incident may surround a natural and physiological function with an aura of pain or pleasure so vivid that normal reflexes are disturbed." So fear of childbirth, perpetuated by negative images, results in pain and distress. Removal of the fear and the old programmed thoughts, "desensitization" in psychological terminology, can effect a more positive and pleasurable event. Many thousands of natural childbirths all over the world bear witness to this phenomenon.

Cancer Imagery. The contributions of Dr. O. Carl and Stephanie Simonton in assisting the integration of psychological, including visualization, techniques into the treatment of disease are discussed in the cancer chapter. Our reluctance to go into detail either there or here is because our knowledge of their practice is historical, not current. Their thinking changed dramatically throughout our acquaintance with the technique and no doubt has continued to do so. Dr. Simonton has played a key role in this subject, however, because he is a well-trained physician and because he is vocal and adamant about his position. Regardless of how his practice or his beliefs have changed, his commitment regarding the importance of imagery in cause and cure of cancer has not changed.

We doubt if any modern physician has as extensively polarized the medical profession as has Carl Simonton. From our vantage point in one of the most conservative medical institutions in the United States, we know full well with what skepticism fellow academics regard his work. The major objection seems always to be the attraction which the mass media had for the Simonton approach (and vice versa to some extent). A comment by a member of the local county medical board, however, may be "closer to the bone" of current medical feeling toward Simonton's work than is the blanket rejection at the medical school. In an interview with the medical writer of a local newspaper, the gentleman said that he really saw nothing terribly wrong with what Dr. Simonton was *doing.* In fact, he extended a backhanded accolade, stating that work with "dying" patients depressed him personally. To the "undying credit" of Dr. Simonton, this work did provide patients with a sense of comfort and hope in that gentleman's opinion.

We believe it is because of the extensive publicity received by the work and because of the Simonton appeal to laymen that the concept of imagery finally will be researched and scientifically manipulated to the patient's advantage. That kind of impetus could be offered only by a physician and only in conjunction with the ultimate in physical diseases—cancer.

General Practice. Michael Samuels, an author of *The Well Body Book* (1973) and coauthor with his wife, Nancy, of *Seeing with the Mind's Eye* (1975), has the dubious distinction of writing books which disappear more often than any others from our shelves. We heartily recommend his work as a lively introduction to the field and as a continuing reference. Based on his writing, he appears to have a better understanding of imagery, both in terms of historical focus and of current application, than any other physician in print.

Trained as a physician at New York University, Samuels has worked at San Francisco Hospital, on the Hopi Indian Reservation, in a county public health setting, and in an innovative holistic clinic. Working with these varied populations, he became dismayed at the lack of understanding people had about their own bodies. He believed that only with the proper kind of information could they learn to care for themselves.

In his books he describes how to diagnose via discussions of symptoms as well as fantasy trips, sensing disharmonies and imbalances in each part of the body. At the same time, Samuels does not compromise himself on good medical procedure. He is always advising when diet or de-stressing techniques are inappropriate and when medical advice should be sought. Unlike authors of many home medical books, however, he does *not* recite, "For this condition, promptly see a physician," after discussion of each symptom.

He does share "sacred" medical knowledge about such things as vaginal exams. Indeed, he gives step-by-step directions on how to conduct one and what to observe. One of our physical therapists responded, after reading his section on vaginal exams, "He can't do that." But he does, making the mysterious information commonplace and simple. His work is easily 20 years ahead of its time, inasmuch as it provides a viable health maintenance system that is available for the entire population. This availability is important, since one-half of the population cannot afford medical care in acute situations, much less in the absence of disease or in chronic conditions.

Samuels's other interest is photography; he appropriately provides a very visually oriented experience for his concepts through his own excellent photographs, his creative choice of classic works of art, and his medical drawings. He makes an important distinction between *receptive* and programmed visualization, offering training in both forms. Receptive imagery involves relaxing, deeply tuning in, and allowing spontaneous images to occur which can serve in a diagnostic capacity. These images also can help to determine treatment.

Programmed imagery reflects the treatment or healing component of visualization. He suggests the images of healing can come from books on medicine and biological science, or from x-rays and laboratory results. He provides examples for many conditions.

Samuels's work should provide a helpful beginning for anyone interested in the art of imagery intervention. He does not, however, offer any evidence on the effectiveness of the methods he describes, such as for whom they do and do not work or whether they have been tested at all. Essentially, he provides those not having his skilled background with a wealth of information on which to build and test theory.

Orthopedic Surgery. In an article in *Today's Clinician* (1978), Robert Swearingen, an orthopedist practicing at Summit Medical Center in Colorado, reported on a humanistic approach to the management of bone fractures which includes visualization as a cornerstone of the treatment. He recited an initial impression of the differences in pain medication requirements he had noted among patients brought in by ski patrols. Those who were relaxed required less medication; significantly, they had all been picked up by the same few members of the patrol who focused on the patient as a total human being and intuitively used relaxation techniques.

He further justified the use of relaxation throughout the healing of fractures because lowered excitation levels facilitate mending. He says: "Part of the technique of maintaining relaxation during convalescence is to respect the patient's ability to understand his injury and to influence healing. . . . I show him x-rays, explain the fracture, describe the procedure I'll use to reduce it, and discuss how long it will take to heal . . . . I draw pictures of the injured bone and show the healing process in four stages." The four stages, redrawn and paraphrased, appear in Figure 2.1. Swearingen prescribes whichever meditation technique the patient can best benefit from, whether TM or eclectic approaches and with or without an instructor, suggesting the pictures he has drawn can be used as healing visualizations.

Swearingen is evidently collecting data but does not present it. Like Samuels, he provides a backdrop for creative research efforts. Far from being one of the typical young maverick physicians, however, Swearingen is a published and respected member of his profession. That makes his approach doubly exciting. On many occasions, we have used his work to describe the potential uses of imagery to conservative physicians. His approach, for some reason, has a facility for bridging the gap between holistic and traditional procedures.

Figure 2.1

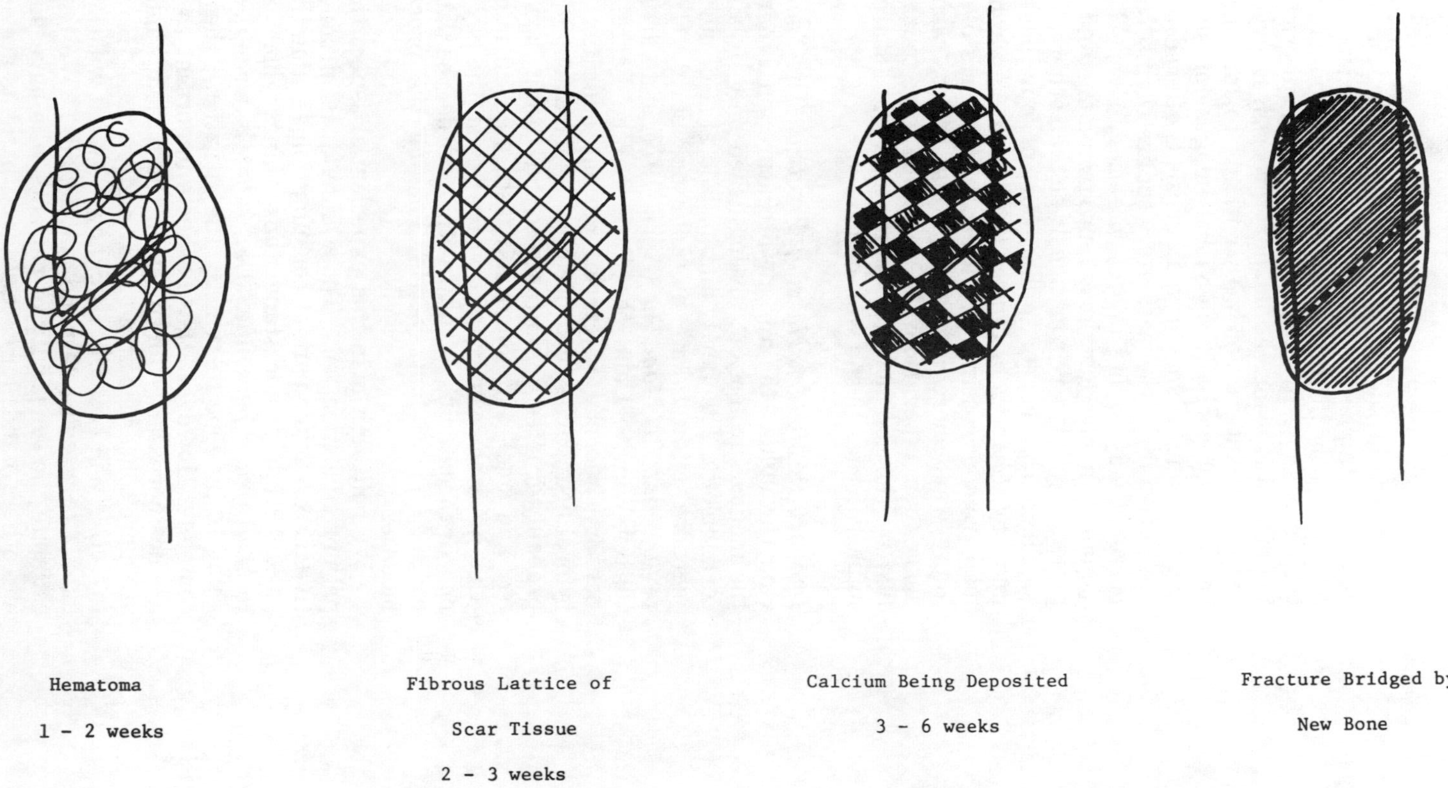

Hematoma	Fibrous Lattice of	Calcium Being Deposited	Fracture Bridged by
1 – 2 weeks	Scar Tissue	3 – 6 weeks	New Bone
	2 – 3 weeks		

The use of Dick-Read, Samuels, Simonton, and Swearingen as examples of 20th Century physicians who have re-
discovered the historical golden thread should in no way imply
they are alone in their efforts. Every physician who uses
hypnotism is using the imagery process. Everyone who uses
the human interaction with patients to influence attitude is
also relying partially on visual images for success. On the
negative side, whenever a diagnosis is offered with respect to
life expectancy, the patients visualize themselves, in a very
personal way, dying or deteriorating. Every health professional is involved in image programming and reception of
patients, some more consciously so than others.

Since the earlier publication of our book on cancer
imagery, *Imagery of Cancer* (*IMAGE-CA*), we have received
mail from practicing physicians in all parts of the country.
Many want more information, but others write simply to
share their experiences. We continue to be touched and grati-
fied by the common quickening and the future direction it
implies for health and well-being.

Imagery in Modern Nursing Practice. The "golden thread"
runs throughout the nursing literature, on a course similar to
the medical profession, distinguished only by a difference in
terminology. This newly emphasized area of nursing is called
"sensory information" by Johnson, et al. (1978), and is
reviewed in *RN Magazine* (April, 1977) in an article called "A
Better Way to Calm the Patient Who Fears the Worst."
Sensory information carries patient education beyond the
typical boundaries of procedural explanation. It provides, of
probably greatest importance to the patient, how it's going to
feel and smell and sound and taste, i.e., an indication as to
what he or she can expect to *experience* (the key word) in the
new or threatening event. In other words, the patient is taken
on an a priori fantasy trip, imaging the process with all
faculties.

We believe it is in this experiential aspect that the usual
patient education fails. Those individuals producing instruc-
tive materials for patient consumption assume that when the
patient crudely understands those things which are important
to *health care personnel* (i.e., what is wrong, and what is
going to be done to remedy the situation), the education is
complete. However, those aspects important to the treaters
are not necessarily foremost on the patient's mind. Patients
are more concerned about their experience—"How am I going
to *feel?*" "Will I *hurt?*" "If so, how?" "What will the device look
like?" "How will I respond emotionally?" We tend to under-
estimate the sensitivity of patients who have put their lives
into others' hands for cure. In fact, patients are acutely sensitive to their environment apparently even in coma or when

under anesthesia. Therefore, a gentle discussion of procedures and events seems justified under most circumstances.

A good case example was a patient we saw with long-standing phantom breast pain. She had had a radical mastectomy and postsurgical radiation two years prior to her referral for pain which she vividly described as a torturing hand reaching around her chest wall and grabbing her in the night. Early in the course of therapy, she was encouraged to examine the reason for her pain. She said immediately it was "the radiation machine." Apparently, a new cobalt machine had been installed in the middle of her treatments which made a different sound from the previous one. She attributed the "funny" noise to something being wrong with the machine. She also related that she saw the radiation therapist duck away quickly when the new machine came on. She did not mention her fears then but continued to believe the machine had "cooked" her, causing persistent pain. When we went back to the radiation therapist to discuss the strange sound, we learned it was merely a soft clicking characteristic of that brand of equipment when turned off.

Whether the fear had anything to do with the patient's phantom pain is irrelevant. (It did *not* go away after the explanation.) What is important is the fact that, had the sensory aspects been explained even though they were inconsequential to the treater, two years of erroneous attribution could have been avoided. However, in all fairness to the health profession, it is not possible to second-guess a patient's perception of all stimuli. It becomes the responsibility of the patient then to ask for an explanation of disturbing sights and sounds.

In looking experimentally at the effects of sensory information, Johnson and her colleagues provided a variety of convincing data. The techniques were used in controlled experimentation with patients about to undergo cholecystectomy, laboratory-induced ischemic pain, cast removal, pelvic examination, and endoscopy. By a variety of dependent subjective and objective measures, the sensory conditioned patients responded better to treatment, even to the extent of significantly decreasing postoperative hospital days. Interestingly, those patients who received relaxation instruction plus sensory information were consistently superior. Relaxation thus appeared to be a vital prelude to physiological change.

Johnson's work offers a necessary translation of a practice virtually identical to Swearingen's and Simonton's into basic, palatable, noninflammatory medical and nursing terminology. For many of us, "meditation" and "healing visualization" are a stable part of the professional vocabulary. For others, though, these terms still retain vestiges of Eastern mystical hocus-pocus. One of the survival tactics we have learned is to communicate like a chameleon: conceptual truisms can be called many things and yet retain their "essence." "Sensory information" connotes something well within the ongoing paradigm. How much more acceptable to state, "I would like to provide your patients with sensory information as part of their educational process, as well as to teach some relaxation exercises," than to state, "I would like to help cure your patients with healing visualizations." While both imply identical procedures and outcomes, the former is more likely to result in a professional being led to the patient instead of the door. The sensory information notion is perhaps philosophically closer to our feeling that the teacher/pupil relationship is the direction which must be taken in the future by medicine rather than the traditional treatment relationship which implies patient dependency.

We are currently studying the effect of sensory information on one of the most devastating treatments, the debridement and grafting of major burns. For our study, we have loosely followed Johnson's guidelines in developing sensory information, including the following specific suggestions:

1) Identify the salient sensory features of the procedure to be used;
2) Ask patients how *they* perceive the process (We attempted to cover all sensory processes, whenever possible, and to structure our interviews so that we maintained informational consistency.);
3) Select *typical* experiences for illustration (atypical experiences are only confusing);
4) Choose words that most patients will understand (This always provides a challenge for us with our low-socioeconomic, racially mixed population.);
5) Use synonyms for "pain," such as "discomfort," that do not have the emotional impact of that word.

Sometimes "discomfort" is not appropriate, and "pain" is the only word which can be used. In such cases, Johnson advises against discussing the severity to be expected or how much sensation can be felt. One of the major problems hindering treatment of iatrogenic pain, however, is the patient's feeling of helplessness and loss of control. In our experience, for finite pain such as that which occurs during debridement, telling the patient the expected *duration* allows some measure of prediction over the procedure. Predictability attenuates that helpless feeling at least somewhat, because the patient knows when the pain will start and stop. If this sense of control can be extended to the point of allowing the patient to participate in the determination of a reasonable schedule, the helplessness is further dissipated.

Johnson stresses some other aspects of sensory information that have been important in her applications. For one thing, this technique does not take the place of discussion of procedures, exercise, ambulation, etc. She also emphasizes that patients should not be told that the sensory information will reduce distress or enable them to cope more effectively. By just teaching the sensory information, better coping will naturally follow.

Application
of Imagery
We have moved away from the traditional psychology which has its heart in mental health approaches. Personally, we grew disenchanted with basic academic research, as did Barbara Brown, seeing "the security blanket of traditional methodology smothering the vital mechanism of a 'new' mind" (1975). In its place, a new model is being pioneered which has as its focus the personal responsibility of individuals in maintaining natural health of body systems. Imagery, by whatever name, is among the participative techniques that has found a home in the new dimension.

In exploring the uncharted territory of mind/body relationships to health and disease, we have found nurses to be our spiritual colleagues. However, whereas nurses are already in a position to practice psychological intervention skills, psychologists have a difficult road ahead creating their niche. Moreover, while nurses are already comfortable and knowledgeable about health care practices, psychologists, for the most part, will have to re-educate themselves. Most importantly, patients trust their nurses and still associate psychologists only with the treatment of "crazies."

In summary, we expect the initial alliance between the nursing and psychology professions to continue developing as we learn one another's skills, but we suspect psychology will remain in the background, polishing and refining its tools before turning them over to the nurses for application. We also envision a new breed of specialists, trained in behavioral medicine, who have both nursing and psychological skills. This specialty will not, by any means, be like psychiatric nursing, which still owes allegiance to mental health. In fact, some of the more promising aspirants to this field are those master's level nurses who return for an advanced degree in psychology, or vice versa.

One such individual is Pat Heidt, a psychotherapist who completed her Ph.D. in nursing at New York University, and has used imagery extensively in conjunction with "Therapeutic Touch." We value her comments on application because they indicate a synthesis of experience and skill apart from our own; we quote from a paper she presented at the Second Annual Conference on Imaging and Fantasy Process (November, 1978) about a treatment format modeled after our

IMAGE-CA approach. Using what she calls *Image Disease/ Discomfort* to explore with patients in a general hospital setting their feelings about being ill and hospitalized, she found that the use of creative imagery served three main functions. It:

"(1) helped the investigator to form a close relationship with the patient in a short period of time;

(2) facilitated expression of patient's feelings about being in the 'sick role'; and

(3) indicated patients' beliefs about their own ability to take part in the healing process."

Her format, like ours, consists of tape recordings designed to help the patient relax each body part and to take a mental journey through the body. The patients are then asked to draw their imaginings about the disease/discomfort, how they imagine getting rid of it, and how their treatment assists in the process. An interview is designed to explore further the three themes. While there are, as yet, no predictive studies on the efficacy of this format for treating general discomfort, she has found it to be useful clinically, stating: "My growing experience is that patients generally want to tell their 'stories' to health professionals who manifest a sincere interest in them. As I became more skilled in eliciting detail about the drawings, i.e., a more accurate description, the patients unfolded much information about themselves and a feeling of closeness and trust developed between the patient and myself in a short period of time. It seems that they want, either consciously or subconsciously, the health professional to understand how they 'see' their own illness and to start the treatment plan from these perceptions."

With Dr. Heidt's permission we present synopses of four dialogues she had with individuals hospitalized in a large New York City medical center. Her comments appear as part of this discussion.

Case #1 Mr. John R. was a 60-year-old pastor, married, who was hospitalized for the first time with what he described as a "heart attack." Figure 2.2 is his drawing. A part of the dialogue follows:

PH: Describe how your discomfort looks in your mind's eye.

Pt: Here is a black light—I am in the dark so to speak. I am an active gymnast and thought nothing like this could happen to me. I've always been active in Scouting—so why me? The rubber band you see is around my heart—tightness and swelling in the larynx, so much it wanted to burst. I didn't want to take a chance, so I came for help. Something said this

Figure 2.2

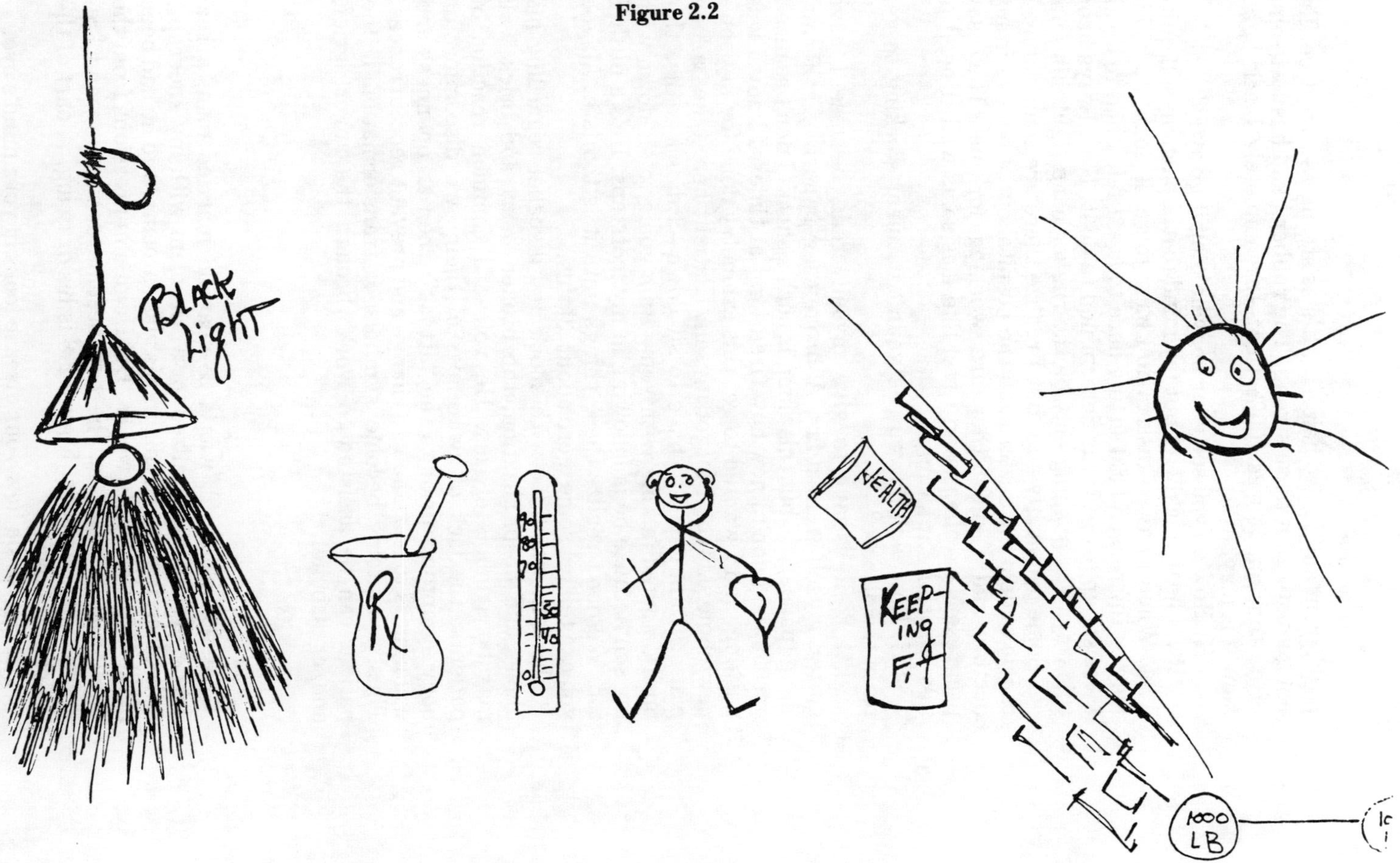

is different and I need help. . . . It's as strong as I let it be. I'm
not going to let it be so strong. The rubber band has lost some
of its tension. It was 100% tight—a completely black light.
Now it is maybe 30.

PH: How do you see your body helping it go away?

Pt: I heal quickly if I put my mind to it. I push myself quite
a lot. When I have a task to do I have to get it done. . . . This
may be the reason I am sitting here today. I felt I had to do all
I was set up to do. I was determined to do it. I've always been
this way. The pushing may be the rubber band tightening up.
. . . Some people give up, but I realize there are some things I
can do to help the doctors and the hospital out. I believe in my
doctors and I know they are working for me. They say
progress is excellent, and I feel like it is so as well. I need to
take one thing at a time. . . .

PH: How well do you see your treatment working to get
rid of the disease?

Pt: Well, I have to give myself credit because I have
gotten myself well so far. A broken leg is sort of a normal
thing (pause) . . . but this thing is such a shock. I don't realize I
am 60; and I don't know how tired I get at times. I know I was
pushing, and I wanted to get this cabinetry done for my son's
new home. Maybe I forgot myself. (Patient here takes a long
pause.) I am going to have to sit down—I didn't realize this
until I started talking with you—I am going to sit down with
my son because he is following in my footsteps. He's a pusher
too. We don't realize these things until it is too late. Maybe
you can tell me some more about all this. . . .

John R. was filled with shock and disbelief regarding his
illness and hospitalization; the broken heart and brick wall
may be symbols of this. He voiced a common reaction of
patients: the lack of awareness of their own discomfort or
body symptoms prior to the "attack"; then an openness and
willingness to learn how to change and prevent reoccurrences.
Thus, symptoms become symbols of transformation if the
patient can be assisted to work through the anger, grief,
and/or disbelief.

Case #2 Eddie T. was a 28-year-old married man, a real
estate broker, hospitalized for a "problem with my kneecap,"
as he described it. His diagnosis was sarcoma, and he had been
in the hospital for six weeks. Dr. Heidt's impressions from the
nursing staff were that he had become demanding and "re-
gressed" in his needs. Figure 2.3 is his drawing. A part of the
dialogue follows:

PH: Describe how your disease looks in your mind's eye.

Pt: There are clumps of disease trying to destroy my

Figure 2.3

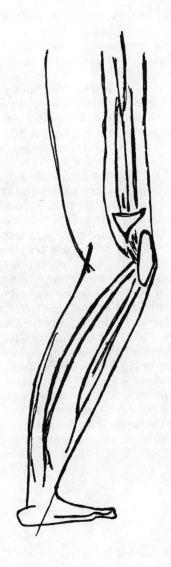

kneecap—little beads of disease, like in a petri dish, in the joints, causing pus, and destroying the knee. I don't know what is going on. Everyday there is something different, because the doctors disagree on the treatment. I'm insecure because my arm is swollen and my temperature is way up and . . . . (Patient begins to cry, and it is several minutes before interview continues.) I don't know how strong it is. I can feel just great and then the doctors turn around and say "but we have to operate."

PH: How do you see your body helping it go away?

Pt: I don't. I am out of it . . . you know, lacking confidence. I know I could try—maybe it would help. Do you believe in all that mind stuff? I feel just terrible . . . .

PH: How is your treatment working to get rid of the disease?

Pt: I'm taking antibiotics. I don't know what they do . . . (Patient begins to cry again; end of interview.)

Some patients, such as Eddie T., have weak imagery in describing how effectively they see their bodies getting rid of illness. There is a marked contrast between how they view the illness itself and how their treatment and their own defenses can get rid of it. In the interviews, there is also a confusion of belief about their own ability to fight off the disease. It seems that these patients have very concrete imagery instead of more symbolic ways to represent their feelings (Figure 2.2). In the case of Eddie T., I returned a second day to finish the interview, because his sadness had terminated the first prematurely. On this occasion, he spoke about his mother, who was interfering in his new marriage, and his fear of facing a confrontation with her. He stated, "Finally, I just had to put my foot down." He gave no indication of "seeing" any relationship between his drawings and the material of which he spoke during the interview. I asked him to use some imagery to picture how he would like his body to be and to draw this (Figure 2.4).

Figure 2.4

Case #3 Mary M. was a 23-year-old hemiplegic hospitalized for a "kidney infection," as she put it. She underwent an ileostomy at age 14; this was the first time she had had an infection causing hospitalization since. She was also a full-time student in Journalism. Figure 2.5 is her drawing. A part of the dialogue follows:

PH: Describe how your discomfort looks in your mind's eye.

Pt: That's me in a relaxed state. The antibiotics are like Black Flag® , killing off the bugs. The bugs are put to sleep and pass out of my system. . . . There are a lot of bugs, and they are very strong—I had 106-degree temperature. However, there is no infection left—I am getting ready to leave here; so I guess you could say there are just a few bugs left. We have to take precaution because there is always a possibility that some bugs may wake up, and I have to be on the lookout for them.

PH: How do you see your body helping it go away?

Pt: I might decide to carry a can of that stuff around inside of me. I had to call the armed forces out this time to help me. There is a little cabinet there below my ribcage—germs live in there all the time. . . . When it gets too bad—I mean the pain, or temperature, or headache, I'll know whether I should get some help or not. . . . If I have pain in the waist area, I might pick up the signals sooner the next time. (pause) You know, this was a fluke accident. I have not had any problems before. This was a bad summer for me. I don't know, maybe it had something to do with emotional strain. I've had to overwork emotionally, trying to keep up with everything. . . . (Patient goes into a long story of a "relationship that has broken up," and after this, interview is terminated.)

This case illustrates how a rich imagery could be the basis for an ongoing treatment plan. Although Mary M. drew a body which appears asexual and without feet, there is some activity going on in terms of the effectiveness of her body in getting rid of the illness. She took the opportunity during the interview to talk about personal concerns that may have contributed to her illness, and suggested she was returning to therapy until she felt better.

Figure 2.5

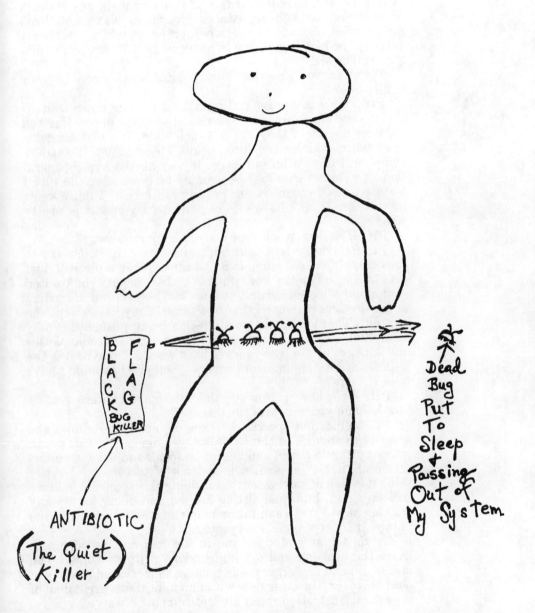

Case #4 Mr. Erwin C. was a 62-year-old man, hospitalized for symptoms of a "heart attack." He said he was hospitalized for a series of tests to see whether he should have "heart surgery" or not. Figure 2.6 is his drawing. A part of the dialogue follows:

PH: Can you describe how your disease looks in your mind's eye?

Pt: This is my heart and my throat leading down to it. It shrinks and closes up. The arteries are closing down—instead of being one inch, they are 3/4-inch wide. It's like a garden hose with a kink—the kink needs to open up instead of dripping. I want it on full force. It may need a bypass operation. . . . The arteries may be opening up now; since the 16th I feel better. Of course, I am getting more rest. I don't know how strong it is. I have lots of pain, so I guess it is pretty strong.

PH: How do you see your body helping it go away?

Pt: Relaxation lets your body run freely. Rest lets it run smoothly. It's like a pump in a fish tank. When a piece of dust gets into it, efficiency goes down. . . . Stress gets you excited so the pump works harder. It does feel better, but according to the doctor I may need that operation. They have to cut the root out. There is an obstruction—it's being pushed down by something—I wish I knew what it was. . . . (Patient pauses and wipes eyes.) Maybe years of hard work . . . maybe it is the letdown after stopping work early . . . maybe I shouldn't have done it. . . .

PH: Well, how do you see the treatment you are getting now helping you get rid of the disease?

Pt: Medication speeds the flow of blood and allows the arteries to enlarge to their regular size again. (At this point, patient picks up pencil and begins to speak and draw an interaction of "lines," as shown in bottom of picture 4.) I really think it is lack of hard work that is doing this to me. It is like a balloon again. I am just sitting around and doing hardly any walking now. I was a sanitation man and walked a lot. For the past year I just stopped everything. . . .

Erwin C. later stopped me in the hall and asked me to share the drawing and my impressions with his family. The idea of impending surgery was causing an increased anxiety in him; however, the interview with him indicated a great deal of anger and frustration about his "retirement" life style.

Figure 2.6

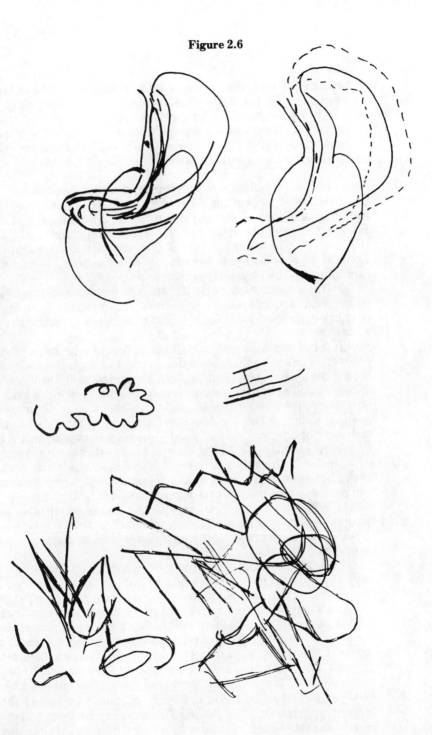

Basic
Guidelines By now the reader should have a feel for the basic concepts behind the bodymind treatment. At this point, we feel it is appropriate to present some guidelines for using imagery in conjunction with physical disease. In the following discussion, a step-by-step procedure is outlined for applying the technique to clinical situations.

Preparation. (1) Begin by understanding as thoroughly as possible the aspects of the patient's physical disease itself. Get the chart and/or call the physician regarding medical history. Look at previous and current treatment; find a PDR (Physician's Desk Reference) if drug names are unfamiliar. Look at effects and side effects. In other words, become as familiar with the physical symptoms as possible.

(2) Interview other patients, such as friends and relatives, or personal acquaintances, who have the disease. Just listen to them describe how it feels to have diabetes or arthritis, or whatever.

(3) Find *superior* patients; that is, those who have either recovered from the disease or done remarkably well in view of their prognoses. Ask them how it happened that they are so different and about their experiences of getting well. Find out how they pictured disease and treatment and their own healing ability. The "exceptional patients" have been the mainstay of our work; the "good" imagery comes from them. People frequently ask, "How do you know whether imagery is good or not?" The only way we can know is to study the correlation between type and disease response. Superior patients and patients who deteriorate rapidly anchor the findings.

(4) After becoming familiar with the disease, attitudes and images peculiar to it, and to a variety of patients who have that diagnosis, begin structuring an approach to diagnosis and intervention.

The effect on the researcher or clinician of this kind of exploratory activity is profound. It imbues a sensitivity for the disease that can come from no source other than the patients themselves. It has been suggested that only those individuals who have had, or still have, a particular condition are sensitive enough to counsel with others about it. Such, of course, is the premise of many volunteer-staffed organizations like abortion agencies, cancer groups, and Alcoholics Anonymous. There is truth to their premise; most of us *cannot* know what it is really like to be epileptic, diabetic, or spinal cord injured, much less all of these. The imagery process offers a more intimate kind of understanding than any other procedure we have found.

Diagnosis. (1) Guide the patient through relaxation procedures. This is an essential first step. Symbolisms which reflect subconscious material do not spring forth readily. They are inhibited by external stimuli, by tension, and by other noises in the system. It is what we call quieting and/or centering in order to listen to one's own physiology. Our own relaxation instructions are printed in the example which follows Step 2. There is nothing unique about them. In fact, we encourage therapists to use whatever technique they are comfortable with to relax patients.

(2) Instruct the patient to take a "mental journey," merely observing these factors:

    (*a*) the disease or disorder,

    (*b*) the treatment,

    (*c*) any personal defenses or ability to fight disease.

Very often the patients are ignorant of any factual information on (*b*) and (*c*) so that suggestions of mechanisms of action are necessary, without actually programming the images themselves. The taped "graft take" script, below, is an example of this step.[3]

* * *

BURNS: PRE-GRAFT

This tape is designed to help you understand the treatment you are about to undergo which includes grafting your wounds. Before I begin to talk about it, however, I would like for you to get very relaxed so that your body will feel a little better and you will be more able to concentrate on what I am saying. First of all, I would like for you to begin concentrating on your breathing: inhaling, exhaling completely, thinking to yourself, "relax." Inhale, exhale. Again. And again. Whenever you feel tension or anxiety or pain during this tape, I would like for you to breathe deeply and say to yourself, "relax." Inhale, exhale. Now, gently close your eyes and, as I count downward from 10, think of yourself getting more and more relaxed, letting all of the tension and the pain flow out. Ten. Nine. Eight. Seven. Six. Five. Four. Three. Two. One. Very good.

Now, let's take a mental trip through your body so that we can identify any remaining tension or anxiety. Begin with your feet, thinking of them getting very heavy, relaxing, sinking down. Mentally imagine all of the tension flowing out of your feet, allowing the muscles to become very loose and very smooth. Think for a moment about your legs and your calves, particularly. Think of them, too, becoming very heavy. All the tension leaving them. Upper legs, abdomen and your hips. Now, at the count of three, I want you to concentrate on

---

[3]The tape recordings for this script, as well as others cited in this book, are available through Medisette, Inc., 2225 Beltline Rd., Carrolton, Tx.

making the lower half of your body feel twice as good and twice as relaxed as it is now. Just let it happen. One. Two. Three.

Think of all the muscles up and down your back and let them relax. Now the muscles in your neck and in your shoulders. See the knots unwinding, anxiety and fear flowing out. The muscles in the upper part of your arm, the lower part of your arm, and your hands: let them go. Let the tension dissolve. Now, think for a moment about your head, remembering there are a lot of muscles and a tendency to store tension in your head; see them relaxing, the muscles around your eyes, around your jaw, your mouth. Let them go and become very, very loose. Just let that happen. Remember that when your body is relaxed, like it should be now, the pain is less and you are better able to participate in the healing process.

Now, in your imaginary journey, go to the area where you have been burned and, if you know where you are going to be grafted, I want you to particularly think about that place on your body, forming a mental picture of the process as I describe it to you. Remember, whenever you feel anxious about the pain, take a deep breath and say to yourself, "relax." In surgery, while you are asleep, the area of your burn which is to be grafted will be cleaned very well and the graft will be gently placed on the open wound and covered with a thick layer of dressings. Okay, now I am going to tell you about the first three days after you have your graft. I want you to try to listen very carefully and again to see or feel this process happening, all the while remembering that the body is a magnificent machine which has built-in means for repair and for healing and for returning to health.

The first day, I want you to imagine the wound itself secreting a kind of a glue. This glue is very important because it latches on to the graft, helping it to stick and to become part of your body. It is very important for you to remain very still and not move the area of the graft. Any movement of the grafted area will cause the graft not to stick. Please spend some time letting this happen. Okay, on the second day after you receive your graft, I want you to imagine your body sending nutrients into the area of the graft itself. Tiny blood vessels begin to sprout, sending oxygen and nourishment to the cells for survival. This is a very important time, and, again, you must stay still so that the tiny new vessels can grow properly. Remember to relax during this time, too, so that your muscle tension does not impair, in any way, what is taking place. Now, I would like for you to spend a few seconds thinking of this happening. . . . On the third day, your own blood vessels actually connect to the blood vessels in the graft, and, if all goes well, on this third day—or perhaps shortly thereafter—the graft will be permanently adhered to your body. It becomes another part of your body and begins to heal like any other tissue. Imagine this happening.

Again, let's go back over the three events that will be happening: the wound secreting its own glue, your body sprouting new little vessels in the direction of the graft so that nutrients can be supplied, and, lastly, the blood vessels connecting to the blood vessels in the graft so that healing can be complete. If skin was removed from one part of your body for the graft, you may be feeling some discomfort from that area. Remember that healing takes its natural course here, too, especially if the wounds are kept clean and dry. Now, continuing to stay very relaxed, very calm, and mentally alert, begin to open your eyes whenever you feel ready.

* * *

The diagnostic component begins an educational process which continues throughout. It is important, however, that the patient not *force* images, but rather let them occur spontaneously. (This is comparable to Samuel's discussion of "receptive imagery.") We want to know the true imagings, not the fancified versions of how he or she wishes things to be, nor socially approved versions. A baseline is the goal.

(3) We then ask the patients to draw, in some fashion, the three essential parts of the imagery: disease, treatment, and healing ability. The drawings serve to clarify the concepts for the patients as well as for the clinician. Be prepared for resistance! We assure them that drawing ability is unimportant, but that we need to know in something other than *words* what they are sensing. We find most people feel very lonely with their symptoms and desperately want someone to understand how they *really* feel. They usually will cooperate if they understand the intention.

(4) The patient is interviewed on the content of the drawing, again focusing on the three aforementioned factors and the relationships between them. The *IMAGE-CA* contains a standardized protocol which is scorable for cancer diagnosis. Interview questions of a somewhat different nature (i.e., relating to treatment) appear in the Burn Graft protocol below.

* * *

IMAGERY OF BURN-GRAFT EVALUATION

Instructions: After the patient has listened to the tape-recorded information, offer the following comments.

"Now that you have heard about some of the events that will take place during the next three days, I would like for you to describe any thoughts or mental pictures or feelings that you may have had during the tape."

Then allow the patient to express himself/herself for two or three minutes at this time. Ask the following questions specifically, if they have not been discussed.

1. Describe the wound, the glue, and the secreting as you imagined it in your mind's eye.

Vividness	1	2	3	4	5
Activity	1	2	3	4	5
Effectiveness of description	1	2	3	4	5

2. Describe your body sending nutrients into the graft.

Vividness	1	2	3	4	5
Activity	1	2	3	4	5
Effectiveness of description	1	2	3	4	5

3. Describe the graft becoming part of your body.

Vividness	1	2	3	4	5
Activity	1	2	3	4	5
Effectiveness of description	1	2	3	4	5

Total Score   _____

Note: 1 = poor; 5 = excellent.

*   *   *

(5) The most fundamental dimensions to recognize for all conditions are described below for each factor.

Disease. The vividness and process, as well as its strength or ability to persist over health.
Treatment. The vividness of the description and effectiveness of some mechanism of action.
Healing Ability. The vividness of the process, effectiveness of the action.

All of these factors are described in some detail in the *IMAGE-CA*. The dimensions are fairly straightforward. However, it is very often the *interaction* the patient describes that may be most important in interpreting the imagery.

Very, very few patients have difficulty describing or drawing the disease, regardless of their creative bent. It is the counter-disease action that they cannot visualize well. Thus, therapy begins.

Therapy. (1) After the imagery has been collected in a non-judgmental framework, it is carefully studied as a diagnostic interview, or scored if a scoring system is available. Symbolic constructs and investment in the factors are compared with the information offered by exceptional patients. Questions we try to answer are:

(*a*) How is this patient coping with disease?

(*b*) Are disease constructs denied?

(*c*) Is the disease visualized as strong, all consuming?

(*d*) Are the visualizations consonant with medical fact? (For example, does a man with low back pain visualize a smashed vertebra when medical records reveal no pathology?)

(*e*) Can an avenue of treatment action be expressed?

(*f*) Is treatment imaged as inert, negative, or positive?

(*g*) Can *any* defenses located within the body be identified?

(*h*) Are they effective?

(*i*) In regard to locus of control, which are the more powerful, treatment or internal factors?

(*j*) Which appears to be the most vivid and powerful construct—disease, treatment, or self?

Finally, and most importantly, given the *assumption* that imagery is correlated with subsequent disease status, is this individual likely to deteriorate, stabilize, or get well? If getting well does not seem to be predicted, what factors lead to that decision? We do not expect novice therapists to be very accurate at answering this question. In fact, the first time we made these decisions on a group of low-socioeconomic patients, even though we had worked for several years with patients suffering similar disease, we failed miserably to predict outcome. Nevertheless, it is valuable to ask the question and strive for good judgment.

(2) Both positive and negative aspects of the imagery are discussed with the patient. For example, the therapist might begin by saying:

"You do not seem to be too clear on how your treatment works. Let's talk about that."; or

"You describe your condition as steadily deteriorating with no repair taking place. But repair can occur—here's how. . . ."; or

"Your description of treatment is very clear to me. I can tell you have a lot of faith in it. But you do not seem to think your body has a built-in healing ability that helps treatment along. Let me describe it to you. . . ."

This is patient education in its true form, based on the age-old adage that understanding of the disease is the beginning of health.

(3) We then actively *program* imagery. Using drawings by other patients, tapes, textbooks, lab reports, and stylized presentations, we attempt to show not only the disease itself but also the healing principles. The drawings used in conjunction with the graft-take imagery appear in Figures 2.7, 2.8, and 2.9. We have created our own materials for one simple reason: the usual instructional materials designed for patients show only the disease, *not* how the body fights it successfully. Planting the notion of recovery requires all possible visual aids, especially when patients have been programmed for failure by other sources. There is a less-than-subtle difference between this process and building up "false hope." We are showing patients how the action occurs so they can be prepared to interact mentally with the natural process of healing.

(4) Because relaxation appears to be a vital preliminary to imaging, we offer instruction in some form. Typically, the taped instructions previously described are given; the patients are able to obtain copies of the tapes if they wish. We find that many already have participated in Yoga classes, hypnosis or self-hypnosis sessions, or in some kind of counseling that provides such training. Many are also quite adamant about continuing their own methods. We usually agree but suggest, particularly if the disorder is stress related or stress aggravated, that perhaps they ought to try another method, since they were obviously not gaining as much relief as they wished using their current procedure.

There are many ways to skin the cat. We prefer a method that allows the individual to concentrate mentally on specific muscles as a sensitizer for the imaging. Benson's relaxation response (1975), Transcendental Meditation, Zazen, or other forms of meditation geared toward altered states of consciousness are certainly useful under many circumstances. They are particularly useful later in training when spontaneous as well as programmed images may be valuable. However, they do not serve the initial purpose of *conscious* muscular relaxation.

We normally deliver the general relaxation instructions in person at the beginning of treatment. Attention is in time directed to specific body parts which are involved in the disability. Often, though, research considerations and time constraints require the use of pre-recorded instructions, at least

Figure 2.7

Figure 2.8

Figure 2.9

after the first session. Another important issue here is the emphasis placed on *independence*, as opposed to *dependence*. We have observed that continued personal guidance in relaxation and imaging by an instructor defeats the goal of independence. In a teacher role, we find we can more productively allow the patient to participate in the relaxation exercises alone, or using a tape, discussing problems and insights afterwards.

Most of our work is done using biofeedback-assisted relaxation. The modality of feedback (usually temperature or EMG with frontalis or forearm placement) varies according to the patient. Once patients are given the relaxation instructions, they spend 10-15 minutes maintaining the relaxed state. It is during this time that guided imagery is proposed. The specifics of training in the biofeedback response are admirably described by Gaardner and Montgomery (1977). It is beyond the scope of this book to reiterate that information; the "how to" of biofeedback cannot be grasped in a single chapter, perhaps not in a single book. It is a highly complicated, intricate, and powerful technique if *used skillfully*, and we in no way wish to gloss over the importance of learning it from competent sources.

Biofeedback is certainly not essential in relaxation training; patients can learn to relax and image without instrumentation. It is helpful because it speeds the process along and gives feedback to the *therapist* on patient progress in learning to relax.

(5) The nature of the guided imagery training is contingent upon the information gleaned from study and diagnostic sessions, the patient's disease and disease history, and the baseline ability to image as determined in earlier sessions. Above all, it is a creative experience between therapist and patient. Several practical reasons for using a guided imagery process are outlined in the following paragraphs.

    (a) Many patients tell us, "The worst thing is the fear —that's what kills you." For patients with a significantly severe diagnosis, even tangential and fleeting thoughts of the disease may engender a fear response. This response is increasingly probable as they have these thoughts in the night or when isolated from companionship and reassurance. On a theoretical basis, however, there is reason to believe it is impossible to experience fear in a relaxed state. Images of a feared stimulus are therefore provided in a state of physiological relaxation. The effectiveness of this type of procedure as a means of conditioning new physiological responses to aversive thoughts, such as disease-related stimuli, has been well documented for phobic reactions. This type of counter-conditioning is intended to ameliorate those fearful events. In no way does it constitute the training of denial defenses.

(b) From a pragmatic standpoint, compliance with medical regimen is more likely if the treatment is seen as effective and trusted. Side-effects, too, are more likely to be mild or well tolerated if the treatment is looked upon as a friend rather than a demonic invention. One of the understated aspects of imagery intervention is the effect it can have on cooperation with standard treatment. A more positive attitude toward treatment and outcome is frequently engendered. Often an opposite reaction to treatment—rebellion—is anticipated by the medical profession. Also, when patients have a positive outlook toward their ability to live well with or without illness, they can begin to do very different kinds of things with their lives. Healthy thoughts quite naturally lead to healthy behaviors and to living life in ways that are adaptive and satisfactory.

(c) Another benefit of guided imagery is the training in physiological sensitivity which patients receive. Once people begin to form the habit of mentally traveling through their bodies, a type of awareness develops that otherwise does not occur when internal stimuli cannot be discriminated. This is particularly important in cases such as diabetes, arthritis, epilepsy, and headache patients, where subtle body signals can provide information on steps to take in order to alleviate an acute situation. All such patients receive cues when the system is stressed or unbalanced. If heeded, proper procedures, such as rest or cessation of some activity, can be initiated at an early point and an "attack" can be averted.

(d) Finally, while somewhat more speculative, it is our firm belief that imaging or visualizing a response can actually produce the desired change. We realize this can be achieved readily with biofeedback procedures. There is additional evidence, though, that the biofeedback is not necessary. Visualization has been shown to be sufficient for differential hand temperature and pupil changes (Luria, 1968), gastric motility changes (Luthe, 1969), and salivation changes (White, 1978) to take place. Whether or not blood factors can be altered or other biochemical changes controlled by specific visualizations (for example, imaging sugar being utilized in the cells of diabetics rather than remaining in bloodstreams) is an open question at this time.

The effects of imagery are obviously general, leading to increased relaxation and re-establishment of homeostasis for all systems. At the same time, the extent of the specificity presents a challenging area for research. We hypothesize that all tissues and cells are capable of being changed by visualization, but that those with the more obvious relation to "voluntary" muscular control will be the most easily learned. The primary inhibitor to determining effectiveness in the more specific systems at this stage of development has to do with the lack of appropriate instrumentation for taking continuous measures of blood, tissue, and organ change.

Technique Despite the potential advantages which were outlined above, it would be a contradiction to advocate a universal approach to such highly variant subject matter as imagery. Nevertheless, certain pitfalls and insights from our experience may be helpful to the reader.

a) We carefully listen to the patient's usage of words to determine their favored modality for imagining (See Grinder & Bandler, 1976). We assume that, with repeated statements such as "I can see how that could be," or "I see myself as a . . . ," they may rely primarily on the visual sense. Hence, they are likely to be visualizers. Other patients may be "feelers" or rely on more kinesthetic, proprioceptive (non-visual) images. Visualization may then be a less-favored modality. Grinder and Bandler call the favored sense the most highly valued representational system; it is the system a person typically uses to bring information into consciousness (1976). There seems to be an advantage in working initially with the favored sensory modality, and then extending imagery to include less readily used senses.

Regardless of the patient's chosen system of sensing and directing internal stimuli, there appears to be a hierarchy of maturation in the ability to image. This hierarchy follows roughly from *verbalizations* (talking to oneself in Autogenic-type exercises) to *visualizations* (which may also be vivid enough to recapture sounds, smells, and kinesthetic cues attached to the imagery), to a state of *nondirected reverie* (a feeling state nearly impossible to verbalize). For most of us, the feeling state is a moment or two of ultimate dissolution of the consciously established boundary between mind and body. Visual images are denied; in fact, once patients become adept, visualizations are usually considered only a way-station in achieving this state.

b) The drawings are vital. An expression of the imagery in some nonverbal way to the therapist has been necessary for all but the most enlightened patients. To apply a verbal structure to nonverbal affects is, in a sense, an artifact for communication. The images seem to be given substance and made real when they are expressed as the pictures the patient "sees." Periodically, and always to our regret, we have backed away from requesting the drawings of images. Not only is the image made real to the therapist and researcher, but also to the patient who is frequently grappling with ill-formed notions of these representations. Other therapists have patients sculpture images in clay, or dance them, or act them out in pantomime; but, again, the mode of expression needs to be a mutual decision, based on beliefs and skills, between the therapist and the patient.

c) Patients require time, patience, and encouragement in recapitulating their internal image structure. Rarely are they able to describe imagery immediately. It often takes days, sometimes weeks, for the concept to "jell." The insights attained at the end of the interminable wait are well worth the time invested.

d) Because the initial elicitation of imagery constructs requires several sessions over a period of days, we recommend the time between sessions be used for dreamwork. (Shades of Asceplius!) We give to the patient a suggestion to dream about symbolizing the disease and counteractive forces, requesting that the dream contents be written down as soon as possible after awakening. It is not at all unusual to hear reports about how the disease was attacked during dream sleep and also some message involving a psychological etiology. Dream sleep, when symptoms and symbols blend and creative tendencies are unleashed, is an ideal state upon which to capitalize in imagery training. One of the greatest challenges to us, and to psychology in general, is the multitude of people who can scarcely comprehend mind/body issues except in terms of folk wisdom or religion. Our usual response is to begin very simply with breathing exercises to show that there is mental control over physical processes. We may also do massage to achieve a centering effect and to bring areas of tension to the conscious fore. In addition, for these individuals, we have found it is useful to break the guided imagery into two sessions. The first is intended to focus on the pain or disease itself. After this step has been accomplished, suggestions are given at the following session to identify an image which can counteract the pain or disease. For example, if fire is imaged as the pain, we might suggest dousing it with water. If spears or arrows are imaged as pain, we may suggest dissolving the points. The main consideration is to continue to support the patient in the identification of counteractive images. Some patients are one step ahead of us and have very useful, creative counter-images. Other patients feel comfortable with our suggestions and adopt them readily. Whatever their orientation, most eventually adopt a personalized version. As a case in point, one particularly good patient decided that his fire (pain) would be best resolved by removing the sticks of fuel, rather than dousing it with water.

e) One approach that we feel is extremely helpful for soliciting imagery material is to explain that bodies understand and respond to images much better than words. We dramatize this by identifying a phobia (snakes, heights, closets) and then asking the patient to repeat three times meaningfully, "I'm afraid of snakes (or whatever)," noting any physical fear response. Generally, of course, there is none. We then ask the patient to form images while being guided through an imaginary encounter with the feared stimulus. Again, the response is noted. It is usually more intense. Conversely, we have the patient repeat out loud, "I am relaxed," several times. An imagery procedure is then presented, using soothing scene descriptions for response comparison. The result is similar.

f) Before imagery can be accepted by many people into a therapeutic regimen, an explanation of how it relates to psychophysiological response mechanisms is usually necessary. For this purpose, detailed explanation of the mechanism is given in the next chapter. Much of the information is of academic interest only. The following series of pictures and an accompanying explanation has usually provided a sufficient rationale. Figures used for education are numbered 2.10-2.17.

Figure 2.10

As most of us are aware, whenever we are nervous or anxious or frightened, our bodies respond in certain disturbing ways. We may quiver or shake, our palms become sweaty, and we may feel very confused. Seeing a snake close by, for most of us, produces these and other responses.

Figure 2.11

At the same time that these bodily responses are taking place, certain other responses that are beyond our awareness are also happening. For example, the image of the situation is being registered and processed in our brains, and signals are being transmitted to all parts of our physiology.

Figure 2.12

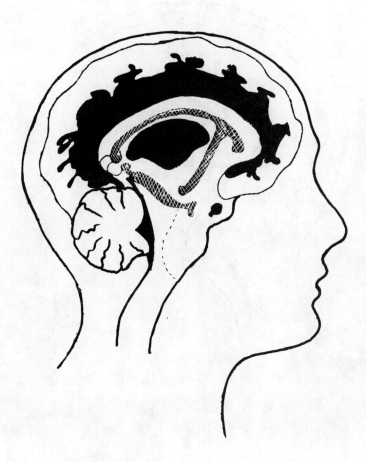

Some areas of the brain are known to be quite involved in processing these emotional situations. One such area is the limbic system (shown here in crosshatch).

Figure 2.13

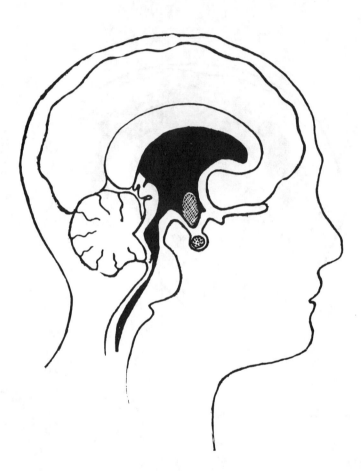

Two other structures involved in processing emotional situations are the hypothalamus and pituitary (shown here as the crosshatch and dotted structures at the base of the brain, respectively.

Figure 2.14

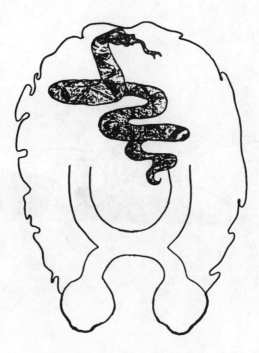

Interestingly enough, though, we don't have to be in the actual presence of a feared situation (a snake, a boss, a plane) to *imagine* being in that situation. These images—or imaginings—can involve the same structures in our brains and bodies; that is, the limbic system, the hypothalamus, and the pituitary, as well as every organ, cell, and tissue. The same fear response can thus occur simply by imaging the situation vividly. If fearful thoughts continue to plague us, it is a well-known fact that both mental and physical disturbance can occur.

Figure 2.15

Fortunately, though, this business of imaging in order to experience a body response can have a positive effect as well. Lying on an air mattress in the middle of a soothing body of water, for example, produces a restful sensation for most of us.

Figure 2.16

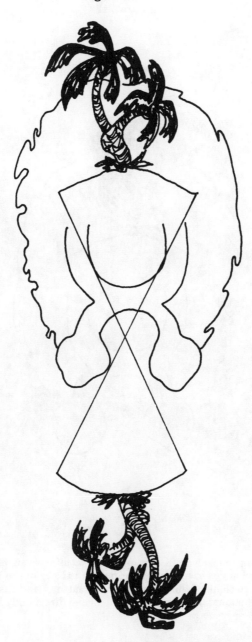

Our brains respond and process the information similarly, and mental structures are activated as in the fear response, except in a more health-ful direction.

Figure 2.17

Merely imaging oneselves in this pleasant situation can also produce
physiological changes in every cell, organ, and tissue of the body. Many
people prefer to think of this as "mind over matter," and that is exactly
what it is: using mental processes to control and direct body function.

CHAPTER III

BRIDGES OF PSYCHOPHYSIOLOGY

As the 1980s begin, we are in the process of picking ourselves up and dusting off after receiving a near-mortal blow from dualistic mind/body thinking more than 200 years ago. The shattering of the interrelationship between mental, physical, and spiritual phenomena, which reverberated into all scientific disciplines, has lost momentum. Many of us have likewise reached an impasse in our approach, regardless of that portion of the segregated being which we have within our province of study. This impasse, and the resultant pressure for consideration of all of the needs of an individual in striving for total health, could not have emerged prior to now. We have to exhaust all resources within our private domains of influence, and reach a plateau of understanding, before taking the next step. That is, a need was aroused to consciously establish a bridge between the hypothetical divisions of being. The bridges, of course, did not disappear several hundred years ago when they were denied existence on the intellectual basis of Cartesian dualism. Interest in them from a standpoint of scientific study simply waned.

In keeping with the division of human totality, the 19th century saw the physician taking charge of physical problems which theretofore had been cared for by any number of disciplines, including preachers and butchers. Psychologists, on the other hand, assumed the study of mental phenomena, as textbooks of the late 19th century claimed "psychology is the study of consciousness." At the same time, spiritual matters continued to be restricted within the bounds of religion and philosophy. Curiously, most of us continue to regard ourselves as having some skills as armchair philosophers, as curbside consultants in psychology, and certainly as lay experts on religious issues—not to mention politics! Yet we maintain a "hands-off" policy with regard to health care topics, having abdicated decision making in that area to the physician.

By the 20th century, even the broad divisions of practice and study mentioned above had been drastically altered within domains. Medicine followed a natural course of increasing specialization, capitalizing on new pharmaceutical and technological advances. The care of the patient was finally relegated to the care of a very special *portion* of that patient. Who could question the merit of this shift to greater specialization? We daresay a high proportion of people, given a choice, would seek out a heart specialist in matters of coronary disease, or an oncologist if the diagnosis were cancer. Hence, not only was the trend to increased specialization a natural result of progress in other fields, but it was also a desirable development in that certain individuals came to have skills in special areas which demanded complicated task performance and advanced technical knowledge.

In psychology, too, drastic changes in emphasis occurred early in the 20th century. The study of consciousness was dismissed as an inappropriate area of research, probably to a large extent because technical advancement was slow. Instead, psychology became the study of behavior or, as an introductory textbook would put it, "Psychology *is* the science of human behavior." Mental concepts were not considered an appropriate subject matter for psychology. They were considered by some not to be appropriate concepts for any kind of study at all; under the Watsonian influence within psychology, consciousness was denied existence completely.

In more recent times, the development of a field of study known as physiological psychology has brought about a return of interest in "mental" phenomena. Like the new developments in medicine, it was not possible to conduct investigations in this area until technical advances had occurred in related disciplines. The brain was mapped and areas associated with behavior were identified. More importantly, physiological psychology allowed mental concepts to be given prominence once again. Previously intangible events such as reinforcement, pleasure, and punishment became "real" instead of hypothetical constructs as they were identified with neurochemical activity at specific sites in the central nervous system. Loci for sensation, emotion, and memory were defined and repeatedly verified. Behavior and cognition were reduced to neuronal firing in the brain, just as disease had been reduced to the study of a finite complex of cells.

A similar retraction from global, diffuse function to a narrowly defined core of influence can loosely be traced in the spiritual domain. The result can be observed in the increased separation of church and government, of church and school, and of church and everyday institutions such as marriage, birth, or death. The churches, from Luther and Calvin forward, reduced spiritualism to doctrinism. The church also lost out in Western healing practices, even though healing and religion were inseparable components of the Judeo-Christian tradition. Religion was relegated to a time, a place, and a building, as it no longer served an integrating function for the majority of people in our culture. Perhaps the "ecumenical spirit" and the charismatic movements of the 1960s and the current interest in Eastern religions represent the beginning of a synthesis in spiritual thought—a turning away from spiritual reductionism.

What we are now witnessing in the approach to medicine is a rebound phenomenon known as holism or humanism. Having reached as basic an understanding of medicine, psychology, and religion as our current yardsticks and microscopes will allow, we have recognized the importance of the Gestalt—that the whole is truly more than the sum of separate entities. We recognize, too, that it is now time to consolidate the expanded understandings from medicine, from psychology, and from religion in our evolutionary process. We view this trend as timely and inevitable, but by no means permanent. In our opinion, it will continue until a certain degree of satisfaction with the process has been reached. At that point, a desire to return to fundamentals may become manifest once more.

The Physiology of the Bridges of the Body/Mind

There are only a limited number of ways that so-called mental processes can be directly observed. Most, if not all, require an artificial situation because the operations required do not only affect the system to be studied, but may throw every other system in the body out of balance as well. Observation is further complicated by the fact that many areas of the mammalian brain appear to have similar functions in order to maintain response patterns, stimulus receptivity, and processing of information in cases of damage.

Early in the development of physiological psychology, the search for the "engram," or the location of specific memory, failed. It was instead determined that the cortex has a property of "equipotentiality" of function, a term coined by Lashley (1950), one of the pioneers in this area. This means that any given mental process, or thought, or memory is stored in multiple cells, perhaps in every cell within a very large area of cortex. Lashley and others have provided further support for this back-up storage theory of memory; failure to perform previously learned tasks has been found in animals to be a function not of the particular location of cortex damage, but rather of the *amount* of damage sustained. Lashley has termed this the principle of "mass action." These findings have necessitated proposals of brain function that do not conform to the previous belief of an isomorphic relationship between site and function. An example is the notion of holograms espoused by Pribram (reviewed by Ferguson, 1978) and others.

Hologram Theory. In the search to understand the interaction of millions of living cells, a physical theory based on holography has been generated. Initially, the concept was developed by a Nobel physicist, Dennis Gabor, in his studies of three-dimensional photography. However, Karl Pribram of Stanford University has extended these principles into a focus on brain function.

The term "Holograph" was adopted by Pribram in response to the failure to find any single group of cells (or the engram) in the brain cortex responsible for specific memories or perceptions. He has demonstrated that the viewer can see a replica of an object in a three-dimensional space by providing two separate images at once. The brain thus integrates the interfering wave forms into a holographic "image." A lengthy study needs to be undertaken before the specifics can be fully appreciated, but a brief summary will suffice to make the point of bodymind integration.

For example, when cortical areas associated with specific types of responses (such as muscle groups in body move-ments, EEG frequencies, or eye movements) are repeatedly activated together, there begin to be predictable patterns. Mathematically, these patterns are much like continuously oscillating sine waves, and they can be expressed in what are known as Fourier transforms. By breaking up compound waves into their simpler components, a perspective on the encoding mechanism of information and memory, as well as the retrieval and decoding process, is gained. The principle of hologram theory points out the cortical property of storing whole perceptions in a variety of perceptual faculties (hearing, seeing, touching, etc.). By association, each perceptual component is capable of regenerating the whole perception. Pelletier describes the process simply:

> Through the use of Fourier transforms and two concepts borrowed from laser physics, the perplexing problem of long-term memory storage and retrieval becomes resolv-able. A stimulus such as sound, smell, or an image triggers an individual's short-term memory, which then resonates through the infinite complexity of stored holograms until an association is triggered in long-term memory. Any pattern or pattern-set of long-term memory can be elicited selectively. (1978, p. 118)

To illustrate this phenomenon, consider the separate wave images created on the surface when two rocks are thrown into a pond. As the two waves collide, they may gain a greater magnitude of intensity if they are similar in pattern (i.e., the troughs are complementary). On the other hand, they may also cancel one another out if there is a lack of any pattern matching. The degree to which they combine their forces determines what the eventual overall pattern will be. As Pribram (Goleman, 1979, p. 70) explains:

Imagine what it would be like to learn a tennis serve if you had to extract every feature of what you were copying, and to describe every move to yourself, feature by feature. You never think about doing it that way—you just watch how it's done, then go ahead and try it yourself. You'd never be able to imitate the subtleties of the serve piece by piece. But if the whole configuration is transmitted and analyzed by virtue of its component wave forms—if the brain does a Fourier transform and activates the appropriate holographic motor pattern—then the entire movement can be readily imitated.

The integrity of the continuous exchange between reaction and action, encoding and decoding, conscious and unconscious, or autonomic and voluntary processing is the pre-requisite for health. Any failure or abuse at any point in the system resounds and reverberates, altering each and every cellular complex. The notion of health which we are now proposing is a synchrony of the body and mind.

A Wealth of Data Sources. Regardless of the state of the art, one must eventually cease speculation and look in "the horse's mouth," as the philosophers years ago discovered after arguing incessantly about the number of teeth the creature might have. One of the usual methods for studying mental processes consists of brain stimulation in patients who are undergoing surgery with only local anesthesia, which allows them to report on their experiences. From this kind of procedure, a map of the brain has been constructed, identifying areas which may be related to functions such as memory, cognition, learning, reinforcement, and emotion. Other techniques for mapping consist of observing brain-injured patients who exhibit certain behavioral or functional deficits. In cases where the locus of the lesion is known, assumptions can be made about that area having "something" to do with the observed dysfunction—even where there may be other factors complicating the picture of the total organism. Thus, though the picture may be muddied by edema, general debilitation, or drug effects, repeated observation in large numbers of individuals can provide correlative information on site and mental function. Damage incurred as a result of tumor, injury, or stroke has provided information about the nature and location of specific central nervous system processes in this manner.

Additional information has been gleaned from animal studies designed to detail functioning of the mammalian nervous system. A large number of techniques are available for the study of site/function relationships: electrocoagulation and laser damage to specific areas; stimulation; ablation; severing neural connections between areas of the brain;

observations of retrograde degeneration after neuronal damage; chemical implants; and "spreading depression," which involves temporarily anesthetizing large areas of the cortex. Another approach involves examination of brain tissue for chemical and structural change or aberration after the animal has been subjected to such predisposing conditions as organ and gland removal, deprivation, enriched environmental experiences, and nutritional alterations.

Even with such a variety of laboratory methods available, physiologists seldom agree on how the brain "really" functions. For example, in one of the most overworked, overpublished areas of physiological psychology, the role of hypothalamic mechanisms in hunger and satiation, theorizing has continued 40 years after the modulation areas of the brain were first identified. All of the above methods are vulnerable to criticism and the findings open to interpretation. To date, however, neither technology nor human ethics has come forth with anything more acceptable or more accurate in terms of operations and manipulations which might aid our understanding of cognitive function. In order to create a physiological framework for the discussion of imagery effects in disease process, the rest of the chapter ties together experimental findings from several fields of endeavor in brain research.

Perception vs. Ideation. We begin with the initial proposition that images, whether mental pictures or cognitive representations of some other sort affect physiological reactions both directly and indirectly and in turn are affected by them. For this reason they are of particular concern in the consideration of health and disease. The images, if visual, occur without the stimulation of light waves; if auditory, without the input of sound waves; and so forth for the other sensory modalities. To this extent, they are crudely differentiated from the perception and processing of external stimuli.

One of the first tests of visual experience without light stimulation—and, in fact, one of the first empirical studies of mental imagery—was conducted by Sir Francis Galton in 1883. Much to his dismay, he found many colleagues skeptical of his idea that simulation of the visual perception experience occurred when historical events were scanned from memory. Since Galton's pioneering work, other evidence has been uncovered concerning the similarity of physiological involvement in imagery and in perceiving external stimuli. For example, the Rapid Eye Movements (REM's) which are noted during dream sleep have been found to correspond occasionally (but not always) to reported dream content (Dement & Wolport, 1958). For example, on one occasion during a sleep study, five upward eye deflections were noted by the above investigators just prior to the subject's awakening and describing a dream about climbing five stairs.

Other information pointing to the similarity between internal response states of events perceived and events imaged comes from the scattered literature about "Eidetikers." People who fall within this classification have the ability to re-capture past happenings in astonishing detail—as if the images were more perfectly engraved than usual into their memory banks. When asked to describe a previous visual scene, eidetikers exhibit scanning motions, as if the picture were projected in front of them. Luria (1968) reports on a most unusual individual with such eidetic imagery ability who was able to increase his heart rate by imagining himself running. He could also differentially alter the temperature of his hands by imaging himself placing them on a stove or squeezing ice. Even the size of his pupils and cochlear reflex could reportedly be altered by imaging sights and sounds.

One of the most interesting reports on the use of eidetic imagery in medicine is that of the courageous studies of Dr. Henry Head (1920), reported more recently in an unusual book entitled, *Body Image and the Image of the Brain* (Gorman, 1969). Head, a famous neurologist who practiced in London during the early years of the 20th century, was an eidetiker. He was struck by his own ignorance of the physiology of peripheral nerves, particularly as they are involved in sensation. Head recognized the need to study the nerves closely in a patient with discrete damage; but such an individual would be extremely difficult to find, since trauma or disease was seldom so specific. Believing that the subject must be otherwise healthy and also a trained member of a medical team in order to report sensory findings, he chose to undergo an operation on himself. The cutaneous branch of the radial nerve and the external cutaneous nerve were first surgically divided. Then a small segment of each nerve was removed before the severed ends were sutured back together. This resulted in a loss of skin sensitivity over a large area on the outer half of the fore-arm and the back of the hand.

Head carefully monitored his sensations to various stimuli and charted the return of function. Commenting on his per-formance during weekly examinations, Head noted that he always was more accurate when not required to think about what was going on and responded better on those tests which required no introspection. He would sit with closed eyes and let his attention wander over "internal images." Sometimes he would become sleepy, but his accuracy at discriminating certain levels of sensation actually *increased* during these periods. This was puzzling to Head, but very much in line with the notion of a more open communication and awareness between body and mind during deeply relaxed states of near-sleep.

Head wrote that his own mental processes were based on visual images to a large extent; even abstract concepts such as virtue or cowardice were associated with images of colors. He also recalled musical tones by "seeing" the notes—which indeed classifies him as a singular sort of imager. Because of his remarkable ability to image, Head was able to develop a detailed picture of his own anatomy:

> With my strong powers of visualization I rapidly developed what may be called a visual map of the affected area. I had but to close my eyes to see a picture of my hand with the affected area marked upon it, as clearly as in a photograph. As soon as a spot was stimulated, I saw its position on this map and at once described the neighboring landmarks. I could even give approximate measurements; for instance, I would say that the point stimulated lay in "the interosseous space about one inch from the head of the first metacarpal." Occasionally, I was allowed to point with the index finger of the right hand; but, since this in itself acts as a stimulus, it should be rarely permitted and should be reserved for special occasions. (Quoted by Gorman, 1969, p. 44).

While eidetikers possess an unusual quality in the vividness and precision of their imagery, certain aspects of the process are relevant to the general population. In reciting a demonstration suggested by Julian Hochberg of New York University, Neisser (1968) recommends trying to remember how many windows there are in one's house or apartment. If one has not considered the answer before, active looking and counting are usually necessary. He states that even people who claim to have no visual imagining ability can develop an internal representation of the walls and count off windows as they are scanned. He concludes that imaging seems to involve mechanisms similar to those used for actually seeing and counting; therefore, images themselves are constructs, *not* copies.

Work from animal laboratories supports the notion that imagining may well involve some of the same neural channels as vision, and involve similar behaviors. John and Killiam (1959) conducted an elaborate experiment to record neural activity in many parts of the cat brain in relation to acquisition and extinction of an avoidance response. Briefly, the cats were trained to jump from one box to another whenever a light flashed 10 times per second. Later a differential stimulus was introduced—a light flashing seven instead of 10 times per second. As the animals were learning to discriminate between different cues, they would frequently perform the avoidance response in the presence of the seven-flash-per-second cue. However, in recording activity from the visual cortex, it was apparent that a 10-per-second evoked potential was present. In other words, the animals were responding to cortical cues, or internally generated constructs, and not to objective "fact." Indeed, the visual system was active but did not correspond to external reality. The hallucinations had neural representation, though, and triggered an imperfectly learned behavior.

Gazzaniga and LeDoux (1978) disagree that the visual cortex is chiefly involved in imagerial experiences of a visual nature. They attribute the persistence of the belief that imagery is intimately related to the process of perception to the lasting influence of the British empiricists on psychological thought. The empiricists maintained that *all* mental phenomena were derived from sensory experience, and that images were nothing more nor less than weak sensations. Instead, Gazzaniga and LeDoux suggest a more mentalistic concept of images. These authors postulate a separate neurophysiological mechanism for images, which may involve codes that transcend perceptual experience. Their theorizing is based in part upon intensive study of a patient who had an intact anterior commisure, but a sectioned corpus collosum. (These two structures both serve to bridge the left and right halves of the brain.) When the anterior commisure is intact, visual information can be transferred between hemispheres. However, visual *imagery* did not transfer in their reported case. On the basis of this and other case studies, they suggest that the frontal cortex, instead of the visual cortex, is crucial in the imagery phenomenon and that damage to this area results in decreased ability to image or fantasize. More evidence for this position is provided later.

There is also a vast amount of literature documenting the effects of visualized scenes—pleasant or fearful—on the musculature and autonomic system, though the content of the imagerial process itself has not been studied systematically and related to physiological change. A specific example is the production of saliva reported by White (1978). This investigator found that salivation rate was affected by what was imagined. Furthermore, control was enhanced in those individuals reporting the presence of vivid imagery. The study is an important one, in that it offers correlational support for the role of imagery in autonomic control.

Wolpe (1958) and others (see Kazdin & Wilcoxin, 1975, for a review) report on the use of imagery during a type of psychotherapy called desensitization, or de-conditioning. As part of these procedures, people are asked—during a state of deep relaxation—to imagine various objects and situations which have been unpleasant for them. The rationale is to assist the subject in overcoming fears or phobias by conditioning those thoughts to a physiological state of relaxation instead of anxiety. Theoretically, one cannot feel physically anxious and relaxed at the same time. There are over 150 reports of studies using this technique, thus making it one of the most extensively tested and documented approaches in psychotherapy.

While certain forced images undoubtedly produce variable physiological responses, the reverse must also be true, in that induced physical states will change or alter images. A direct test of this hypothesis was conducted by Wolpin and Kirsch at UCLA (1974) where subjects were asked to imagine eight different scenes in states of : (1) muscle relaxation, (2) muscle tension, or (3) the usual muscle state. Greater muscle tension resulted in images described as more active, frightening and out of proportion, less friendly, less attractive, and containing louder sounds and poorer solutions.

The existing data, then, point to certain physiological correlates between sensory and imaging processes. However, on logical grounds, as well as on the basis of limited empirical evidence, some additional or differential neurochemical involvement can be assumed to operate in the latter instance which distinguishes it from routine sensory activity. Minimally, some type of coding process yet to be demonstrated, but which would allow for multiple, redundant storage and an elaborate retrieval of the image itself, can be hypothesized. Once the retrieval of the construct occurs, the processing from that point would follow the pathways of sensation.

On a more fundamental level, images occur in the absence of sensation and, as such, have considerable effect on emotional response. For example, during dream sleep, or daydreams, or meditative states, cortical and autonomic mechanisms can be selectively aroused by the images experienced. The physiological responses elicited in this way can linger, changing and enhancing moods later on in the wakeful state. Further, electrical stimulation of the cortex in conscious patients undergoing brain surgery supports the view that both sensations and images can occur without the stimulation of receptors (Penfield & Rasmussin, 1950).

In summarizing the current findings on imagery in brain/behavior relationships, it seems fair to conclude that:

1) images *do* correlate with certain physiological states,

2) images may precede or follow physiological states, suggesting both a controlling and reactive role,

3) aspects of the behavioral response (as well as the physiological response, if one cares to distinguish between the two) to the image may simulate the response to an external stimuli, and finally

4) images are "real" in the sense that they can

    a) be induced by certain conscious, deliberate and subconscious acts (electrical stimulation, fantasy, and dreaming), *b*) be measured by instrumentation (although limited) and self-report, and

c) have some measurable *consequences* on physiology.

Beyond these antecedent and consequent conditions, and related to the very limited ability to measure directly, the study of imagery is fraught with the same difficulties inherent in any attempt to measure intrinsic, phenomenological events. But, regardless of how elusive the actual measurement of its activity, the importance of the construct is that, for disease, imagery can be conceptualized as the hypothetical bridge between *conscious process* and *physiological change*. Prior to tracing the proposed circuitry related to the phenomena that serve to bridge mentalistic and physical function, a brief recapitulation of the nervous system is necessary.

An Overview of the Nervous System

A diagram of the nervous system components appears in Figure 3.1. The nervous system itself is arbitrarily divided into two major, but vastly interrelated components: the *central nervous system* and the *peripheral nervous system*. The central nervous system is subdivided into two major components: the *brain* and the *spinal cord*. The function of the cord is to conduct impulses to and from the brain. The importance of the spinal cord lies in the fact that it is the only route to the brain from the rest of the body. It is a complicated integrator of all functions of the body.

The brain itself consists of a number of divisions which may vary, depending upon the relative emphasis placed on cellular structure and system function by a particular discipline of study. The difficulty in achieving universal agreement in naming structures and systems, and in segmenting the brain into reasonable divisions, arises because the brain itself is a jelly-like mass. Hence, much labeling is purely arbitrary. We will use one of the simplest approaches here, dividing the brain into *forebrain, midbrain,* and *hindbrain* structures. The forebrain consists of the telencephalon and diencephalon. The telencephalon areas with which we will be concerned are the cerebral cortex and many of the limbic system structures. The diencephalon includes the thalamus, the hypothalamus, and the pituitary, among other things. The midbrain, like the forebrain, is divided up into several structures which include visual and auditory pathways (called the *corpora quadrigemina*) and the substantia nigra, an area which is related to muscular control. The hindbrain contains the cerebellum, the pons and the medulla oblongata—areas which are rich with neural pathways (such as in the reticular formation) and which have a widespread influence on priming cortical mechanisms, but which are beyond the scope of the current discussion.

Figure 3.1

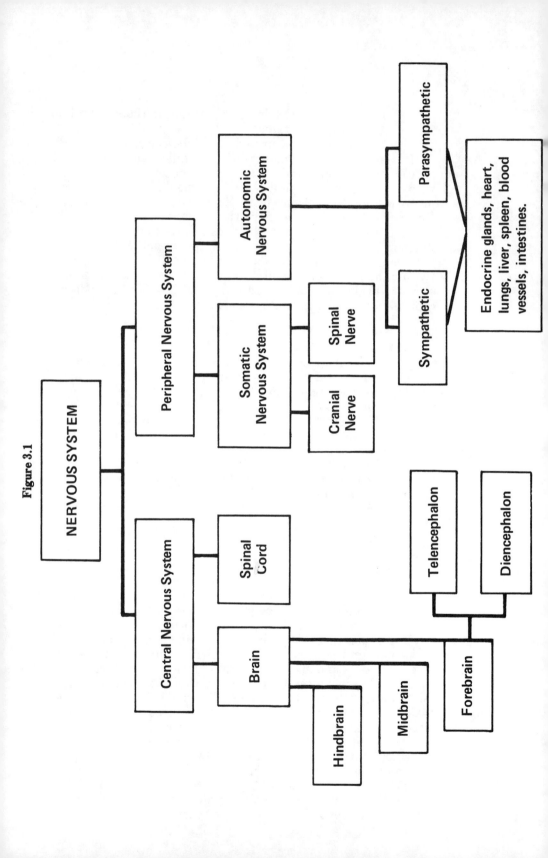

The peripheral nervous system consists of the *somatic nervous system* (SNS) and the *autonomic nervous system* (ANS). The SNS structurally consists of 12 pairs of *cranial nerves* and 31 pairs of *spinal nerves*. The function of this branch of the peripheral system is to assist one in maintaining contact with the outside world. Messages are received from the sense organs, and transmitted to the spinal cord and the brain. Impulses are delivered from the central nervous system via these pairs of nerves to striated muscles. Very discreet types of voluntary action can be effected under conscious control of the individual through this somatic system.

The ANS, on the other hand, was believed for years to be involuntary and beyond the reach of conscious control. Now we know that this is only partially true and that, with certain techniques such as biofeedback, we can learn to alter the response of target areas innervated by the ANS. The heart, the liver, spleen, and pancreas, intestines, blood vessels, glands, and the urogenital system are all influenced by ANS.

The ANS is generally responsible for the maintenance of the internal environment of an individual, whereas the SNS is primarily involved in reacting to stimuli in the external environment. Thus, we have a ready-made physiological dualism that conforms to a notion of higher (i.e., cortical) control vs. lower (subcortical, or more primitive) directive influences. The distinctions between the two systems begin to blur as our understanding increases, however, and as we become cognizant of the massive integration existing between them.

The ANS can also be divided into two systems—the *sympathetic* and the *parasympathetic*. A simple conceptualization is that the former system takes over when action is demanded, while the latter serves as a balancer to maintain homeostasis within the many physical systems. Factually, the two systems do not operate as if in separate milieus, but rather serve the body simultaneously, continuously, and in a coordinated manner. The activation of both systems of the ANS is facilitated by "releasing" factors, or hormones, apparently manufactured in the hypothalamus. These factors, for example, send messages that signal the release of anterior pituitary hormones that control the secretion of the endocrine glands. The secretions of the adrenal cortex, the thyroid, the testes, and ovaries are controlled by similar means. In addition to the chemical control exerted by components of the central nervous system, neural connections have been identified. In particular, those between the posterior aspect of the pituitary and the hypothalamus are involved in controlling fluid and electrolyte balance and in the "let-down" of milk and uterine contractions during nursing. The adrenal medulla is also controlled by neural fibers of the sympathetic nervous system.

In referring back to Figure 3.1, it is apparent that it is an organizational flow chart, merely designed to show categories and subcategories of systems. What is not obvious on the chart is the cross-influence between and among categories, such that the ANS is under the control of diencephalon structures, the SNS is responsive to telencephalic structures, and so forth. As we continue in the text, we hope to clarify somewhat the nature of the interrelatedness, because it is that point that is critical to the understanding of the psychophysical bodymind response. We will begin with a discussion of the most advanced cognitive system in the brain as it relates to hypothetical integrative mechanisms which we call images, or "bridges." We proceed downward through the more primitive areas that evolved earlier in the species, concluding finally with the peripheral nervous system, so that we move from brain to body in an orderly and systematic fashion.

Role of the Cortex
Left Hemisphere/
Right Hemisphere
and Representation

of the Image The cerebral cortex consists of multilayers of neurons, or nerve cells, distributed in several types of neural tissue which are distinguished by the recency with which the tissue evolved. The communication within the cortex is characterized by a general vertical direction of information processing—from cortex to subcortex and then to cortex—in a U-shaped flow. The cortex itself is made up of two hemispheres connected via a large bundle of nerve fibers called the corpus callosum (Figure 3.2). Cortical areas involved in sensory and motor functions of the left side of the body tend to be located on the right side of the cortex and vice versa. Communication is maintained between both sides by the corpus callosum and also by two other fiber bands that bridge the thalami called the anterior and posterior commissures.

There is an abundance of recent evidence leading to the conclusion that the right and left hemispheres have evolved certain specialized functions as a consequence of either phylogeny or ontology development. Perhaps, as Gazzaniga and LeDoux (1978) suggest, specialization was necessitated by the expanded demands of verbal development on the cortex, and the ultimate competition for synaptic space. While overgeneralizations are cautioned, for the majority of the population, language function is lateralized in the left hemisphere of the brain. On the other hand, the right hemisphere (previously thought of as the nondominant hemisphere) has specialty components relevant to an understanding of the physiological paths of image storage and retrieval. The major

Figure 3.2

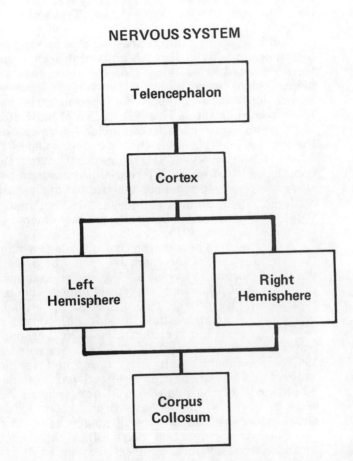

NERVOUS SYSTEM

differences in right and left hemispheric function include: (1) the right hemisphere tends to use nonverbal images in thought processing, and (2) the right hemisphere uses an oppositional, nonlinear, and relatively less analytic style than does the left (Bogen, 1969; Levy, Trevarthen, & Sperry, 1972).

The hemispheric differences have been supported in part by studies of individuals with unilateral brain damage. These were reported as early as 1861 by Broca, when left hemisphere lesions were identified in two patients with severe speech loss. Other support for specialization has emerged from the significant and careful studies of individuals in whom "split-brain" surgery was conducted—surgical severance of the connections between the two hemispheres (Gazzaniga, 1970; Wilson, Reeves, Gazzaniga, & Culver, 1977). Other techniques for study of differential processing modes have included various electroencephalographic analyses (Buchbaum & Fedio, 1969; Dumas & Morgan, 1975; Ornstein & Galin, 1976) and studies of lateral eye movements (Schwartz, Davidson, & Maer, 1975).

A parallel area of research that offers a few more pieces to the puzzle is that of the cognitive mode, or *preferred* hemisphere, of normal individuals. The major assumption behind this work postulates that one type of information processing is typically favored over the other (e.g., verbalization vs. imagerial). Supportive data include differential responsiveness to imagery and verbal strategies in therapy, depending upon preferred hemisphere (Tucker, Shearer, & Murray, 1977). Even though results only approached significance, they suggest that treatment is more effective if it employs the cognition mode of the nonpreferred hemisphere. Additionally, tests of cognitive mode have been shown to discriminate between occupational groups of people believed to exercise one hemispheric function more often than another, e.g., ceramicists vs. lawyers (Galin & Ornstein, 1974).

Taken individually, these pioneering endeavors suffer under the "critical spotlight" of scientific appraisal. None are definitive in regard to hemispheric specialization; nor should they be expected to be so. They do, however, represent successive approximations to an understanding of the function of the bisected, as well as the integrated, brain. As such, they offer support for the position of imagery as the bridge between the more conscious levels of functioning and changes at the physiological level. An outline for that relationship follows, based on some logical inferences from previously cited investigators together with additional substantiating material.

1) The left hemisphere generally is the locus of speech or linguistic function and, hence, can be considered more evolved, at least phylogenetically.

2) The lateralization of speech during development seems likely to result in a competition for synaptic space in the one hemisphere, while allowing other functions to expand their neural and synaptic territory in the nonverbal hemisphere.

3) The importance of the right hemisphere to the concept of imaging extends from the typical findings of manipulo/spatial specialization, and the use of nonverbal or imagerial processes in problem-solving, to synthetical or holistic approaches in cognition.

4) Not only are nonverbal images an area of right hemispheric specialty, but *body image* itself seems to be generally lateralized here. For example, lesions in the right parietal lobe result in a syndrome characterized by a disorder of body image in which the patient may fail to recognize part of his own body, denying it to the extent that it may not be washed, covered, or otherwise cared for.

5) The right hemisphere appears to have a predominant role in processing emotional information. Several studies have discerned a right hemispheric relationship with emotional responses and judgment (Safer & Leventhal, 1977; Schwartz, et al., 1975) and also with cognitive processing during stress and anxiety conditions (Tucker, Roth, Arneson, & Buckingham, 1977). This function apparently remains intact even after the corpus callosum and/or anterior commisural connections have been severed. Whether this tendency reflects merely a relative inactivity on the part of the more verbal, rational left hemisphere during emotional behaviors or greater adaptivity of the holistic, spatial-manipulative processing mode of the right hemisphere to emotional states is unclear. From an evolutionary standpoint, certainly the latter seems more apt to have survival value.

6) Because of the role in emotional response, the right hemisphere modalities appear to have a more direct input into the autonomic functions of the body. In other words, the verbal functions of the left hemisphere are one step removed from the autonomic processes of the PNS. Therefore, messages may have to undergo translation by the right hemisphere into nonverbal, or imagerial, terminology prior to affecting any physiological change.

7) The left hemisphere, on the other hand, does have some command over musculoskeletal processes. Except in the case of sustained muscular spasm, pathology, or injury, conscious and deliberate control can normally be exercised over these body functions.

The verbal hemisphere may also be conceptualized as an interface between ourselves and the external milieu, both by virtue of language interchange and conscious musculoskeletal movements. The imagery of the other side of the brain is the medium of communication between the conscious levels of cognitive function and the internal environment. For these reasons, we focus on images as the transition between external and internal, conscious and unconscious.

We admonish patients who persist in verbalization and in intellectualizations to realize that their bodies do not understand those—but understand instead pictures, sounds, and feelings. Seldom can one manage to leave a physiological state of wakefulness by acclaiming "I must go to sleep." Peripheral body temperature rarely, if ever, arises on verbal command alone. Changes *do* occur when pleasant scenes are imaged or body pictures of a special nature are brought into focus. On the other hand, arms lift when we tell them, eyes blink, and toes wiggle. So we are possessed of dual systems in a sense, activated by differing procedures, but both integral to the maintenance of physical well-being.

The dualism is an oversimplification, as we well acknowledge, and there is continued "cross-talk" between specialty areas of the central nervous system. Words trigger images, and images induce verbal labelings. Nevertheless, there appears to be a format and order for translation of information that must be respected in order to consciously affect the so-called nonvoluntary or autonomic processes. That format is schematically described in Figure 3.3. The remainder of this section focuses on the role of cortical components in that format.

Frontal Lobes. The left and right hemispheres of the cortex are divided into four lobes: the frontal, temporal, parietal, and occipital. As we attempt to define with more specificity the neural circuitry involved in bridging conscious mental processes with physiologic systems, it appears that not only is the right hemisphere of the brain implicated, but also that research on the frontal lobes of the brain can add to our emerging model of psychophysiologic function. In particular, the right frontal lobe seems to be important. The frontal lobes are larger in humans than in any other animals, and are involved in motor control. The function of the *prefrontal,* or anterior most aspect, remains somewhat a mystery, but tentative findings indicate a relationship to memory storage and emotion.

For many years, the frontal lobes were believed to be the most evolved structure, containing the functions which separated *Homo sapiens* from less intelligent animals. That notion has not been supported with any degree of consistency, perhaps primarily because evidence from both surgical and intelligence testing procedures shows highly variable results (Gross & Weiskrantz, 1964). However, in the 1930s, the investigation of the function of the frontal areas was pursued

Figure 3.3

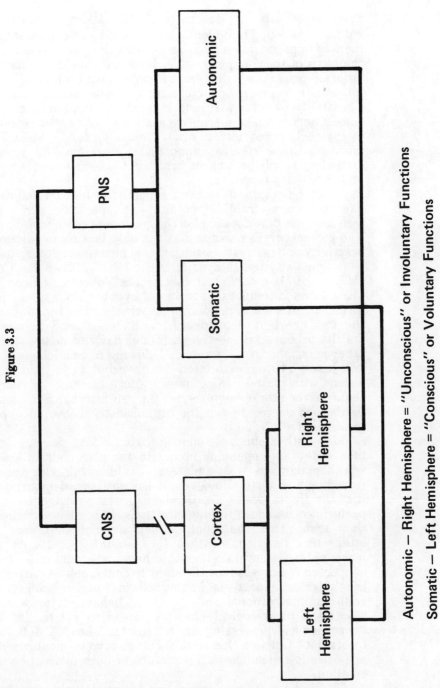

Autonomic — Right Hemisphere = "Unconscious" or Involuntary Functions

Somatic — Left Hemisphere = "Conscious" or Voluntary Functions

more rigorously by Jacobsen (1936). Using primates as subjects, he found that frontal lesions produced consistent and marked impairment on tasks requiring a delayed response. On the basis of these experiments, Jacobsen concluded that the anterior aspect of the frontal lobes was necessary for immediate memory, or for use by symbolic memory images. The ability to delay a response requires the maintenance of some internal image or representation of what that response ought to be, and under what circumstances it should be emitted. Other studies support the idea that this area is virtually the only part of the brain that is *indispensable* to the ability to delay response.

Similar findings have been reported in humans following psychosurgery—frontal lobotomy—an operation performed frequently in past decades for the treatment of mental illness. The patients were described as not only lacking in emotional reactivity and motivation, but also seemed unable to fantasize or imagine a future (Meyer & Beck, 1954). Milner and Corsi (Milner, 1971) established that frontal lobectomy produces disruptions in temporal ordering of events. The type of performance affected depended upon whether the lesion was in the left or right hemisphere, with verbal and nonverbal deficits produced respectively. Milner has also demonstrated other hemispheric asymmetries following frontal lobe lesions, left lesions being associated with verbal tasks and right lesions with maze-learning ability. Maze learning, of course, requires the storage and retrieval of an internal representation which serves to cue the organism to choose an appropriate path.

Many other changes following frontal lobe damage have been observed, depending upon size and placement of lesion, whether damage was unilateral or bilateral, the species tested, and so forth. However, it has *not* been demonstrated that the frontal areas are involved in the skills required to perform on standard intelligence tests. It must be concluded then that either the frontal lobes are not the "seat" of intellectual function, or that the usual I.Q. tests do not measure intelligence! On the other hand, what continues to be supported is the fact that the right frontal lobe—in particular the anterior aspect—is implicated in imaging ability. In addition, motivational and emotional behaviors, as well as associated physiological changes, are also related to the neurochemical processing of the frontal lobes. A definitive frontal lobe function therefore seems to involve modulation of activities in the subcortical structure of both motivation and emotion.

The findings of functional deficits in emotional and motivational behaviors are to be anticipated on the basis of neuroanatomical connections of the frontal lobes. Nauta (1964) and others have suggested that the frontal lobe may well be considered part of the limbic area, constituting *in toto* a "fronto-limbic" system. The limbic system, discussed below, is considered the subcortical area of emotional response integration. Nauta proposes that the anterior frontal regions constitute a neo-cortical extension of the limbic system, the dorsal portion being affiliated with the hippocampus, and the more ventral aspects associated with the amygdala (both structures within this system). There are many known fiber connections between frontal lobe and limbic structures, including projections from the anterior frontal cortex to the head of the caudate nucleus, hypothalamus, thalamus, and midbrain tegmentum.

On the basis of these findings, then, it appears that the cortical structures repeatedly implicated in the ability to form internal representations, particularly in relation to body images, converge structurally in the area of the right anterior frontal cortex. This is an area where collateral fibers are relayed to limbic systems implicated in the autonomic response so integral to maintenance of homeostasis. Figure 3.4 presents a diagramatic representation of these pathways.

The Limbic System. In tracing the transduction of images, or internal representations of events, into physiological change, the role of the limbic system cannot be ignored. We have previously referred to the finding that the frontal lobes both send and receive collateral fibers from the limbic structures. Hence, it has been proposed that the two areas constitute a single "frontolimbic" system. We must assume that both right and left frontal lobes are similarly rich in neural connections with limbic areas (having no neuroanatomical evidence to the contrary), but it is the right lobe that is of particular concern in our theorizing, since *body* images appear to be stored or elaborated here.

Debate continues among neuroanatomists as to the precise structures which should be included in the limbic system itself, since there are no hard and fast rules governing inclusion or exclusion from such a massive and cytologically diverse system. We will consider the amygdala, the hippocampus, the septal area, and the cingulate cortex as falling within the limbic system. Typically, the hypothalamus is singled out as being a "system" of sorts that is only partially involved with limbic function and deserving of a more unique classification scheme. However, as Isaacson (1974) points out, the hypothalamus has strong interconnections with all other limbic regions. From a functional point of view, many, if not all, of the effects produced by stimulation or lesions to the other limbic structures can be attained by similar operations on the hypothalamus itself.

Figure 3.4

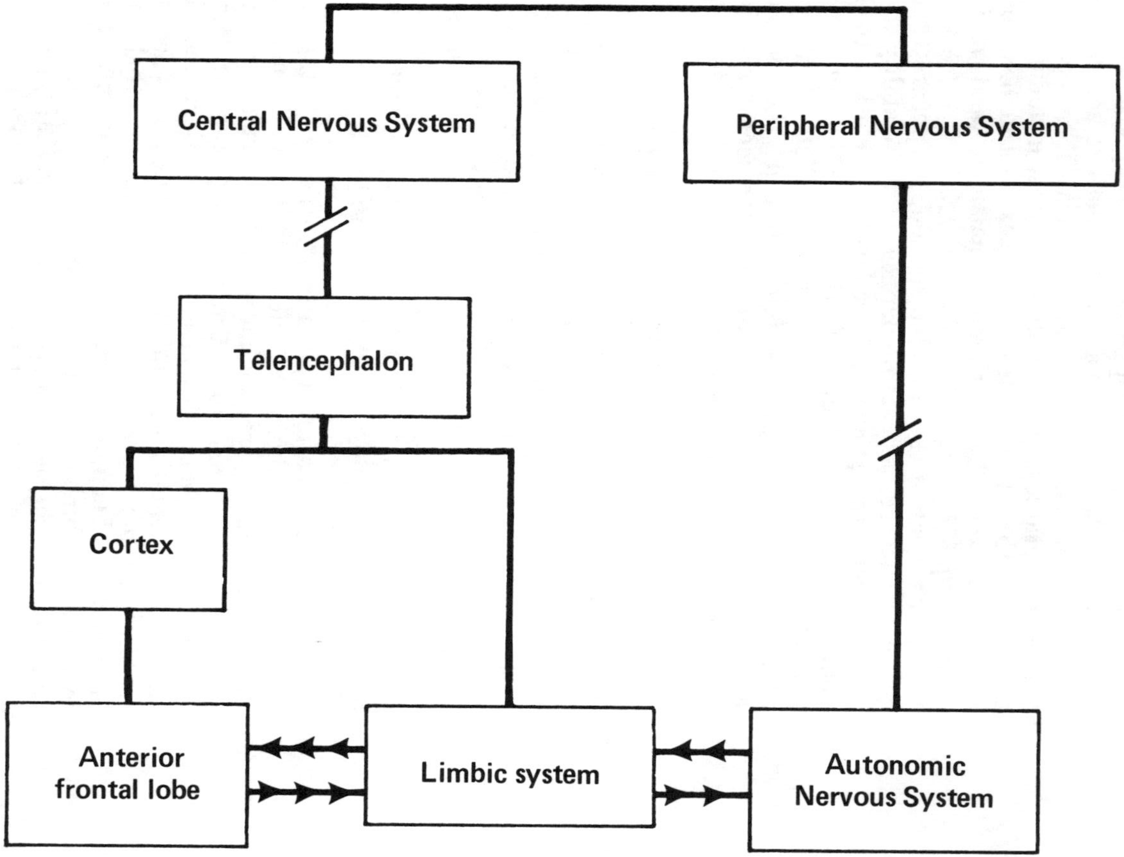

A Fronto-Limbic System Which Integrates ANS Function

Earlier conceptualizations of limbic function, particularly as posited by Papez (1937), focused on it as the neuroanatomical locus of the emotions. Papez proposed a circuit which provided some initial understanding of how mental experience or psychic activity might be translated into the physiological correlates of emotion. Much research has continued to validate the relationship between limbic function and emotional experience, if not the actual circuitry proposed by Papez. This circuit included emphasis on activity of the neocortex, followed by neural activity in the hippocampus fornix, mammillary bodies, anterior nuclei of the hypothalamus, and finally in the cingulate cortex. For our purposes, it is sufficient to note that anatomic change associated with emotion has been produced (or inhibited) by lesions or stimulations to these areas.

Far from being exclusively related to olfaction (as limbic structures apparently are in nonmammalian brains), experimentation has demonstrated relationships between brain activities in the limbic area and experiences of pleasure or reward (Olds & Milner, 1954; Olds & Olds, 1963) and of pain or punishment (Delgado, Roberts, & Miller, 1954), social interaction changes (Bunnell, 1966), and even violent behavior characteristic of the criminally insane (Mark & Ervin, 1970). The physiologically sophisticated reader will recognize our omission of a vast library of findings on the limbic system. The curious reader will wish to seek the original sources cited above for more detailed information. It is apparent, however, from this partial cataloging of findings that emotional responses originating in the limbic areas, in addition to the obvious effect on behavioral components of fighting and fleeing, also elicit profound reactions of the autonomic nervous system—a system previously thought to be primitive and beyond conscious control.

Hypothalamus. To attain a glimmer of understanding into the control of the autonomic nervous system, we focus now on the hypothalamus, remembering that many of the functions of the nuclei that compose this structure seem to be replicated by the limbic areas—exemplifying the brain's marvelously redundant "back-up" system. Structurally, and perhaps even functionally, the hypothalamus *is* related to neural areas where conscious processing occurs and images are formed. It is by no means isolated nor relegated to the status of reflexive or vegetative functioning.

The hypothalamus has been implicated in the physiology of nervous reactions. Disruption in these reactions can reliably produce disease or disorder in the homeostatic balance of the individual. Representative activities include neural and/or chemical involvement in the behaviors of eating, drinking, sleeping, sexual function, physical activity, and generally in the establishing of body rhythms or circadian patterning. Other effects are noted on heart rate, respiration, blood chemistry, and glandular activity. Activities of a broader scale include those generally categorized as motivational as well as emotional.

The hypothalamus even seems to be involved in the degree, or quality, of reaction to external stimuli; damage to it has been associated with underactivity or overreactivity to stimulus cues. Most recently, it has been demonstrated that hypothalamic activity is involved in the immunological response to disease (Lambert, Harrell, & Achterberg, 1979), in that stimulation to certain areas could produce decreased activity of the macrophages (a certain type of white blood cells). Results from other investigations have suggested that other adjacent areas of the hypothalamus are also involved in the enhancement of the immune response (Korneva & Khai, 1963). This is one of the body's most important responses to infectious disease, as well as cancer. The fact that there is central nervous system involvement—quite obviously through hypothalamus activity—places the control of disease in an entirely new perspective.

Pituitary. The next area of consideration in tracing the circuitry of imagery phenomena is the pituitary—the master-gland of the body, as it has come to be known. The hypothalamus is intimately connected with the pituitary through demonstrable neural and chemical pathways (Figure 3.5). Hypothalamic activity has been shown to alter every hormonal system, presumably through these neural-chemical interconnections. Affected systems include hormones involved in sexual behavior, growth, metabolism, and preparation for the stressful situations of flight and fight. Not only are the glands which elaborate hormones affected (i.e., ovaries, testes, adrenal, thyroid, parathyroid, etc.), but so, conceivably, is every organ, tissue, and cell.

Role of the Autonomic Nervous System

In tracing pathways of psychophysiologic response, we now consider the two branches of the autonomic nervous system that are under direct control of the brain. The hypothalamus again plays a critical role. The branches, with their target organs, are illustrated in Figure 3.6.

Perhaps more than any other glands, the adrenals have received attention in this age of studying the effect of psychic function on physical disease. A cursory discussion will be

Figure 3.5

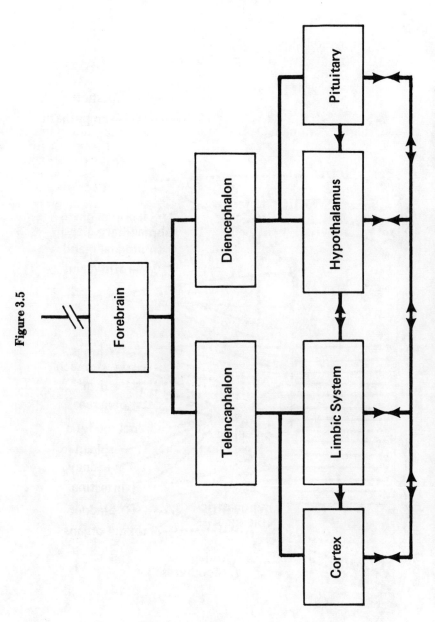

Interrelatedness of Cortical/Sub-Cortical Systems via Neurochemical Pathways

Figure 3.6

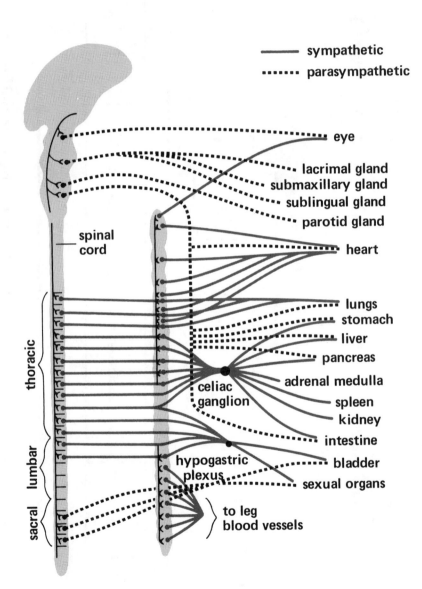

sympathetic

parasympathetic

eye

lacrimal gland
submaxillary gland
sublingual gland
parotid gland

spinal
cord

heart

lungs
stomach
liver
pancreas
adrenal medulla
spleen
kidney
intestine
bladder
sexual organs

celiac
ganglion

thoracic

lumbar

sacral

hypogastric
plexus

to leg
blood vessels

included here, merely to trace with a bit more exactness the paths of cognition or images through to the final end organ. While all glands involve similar pathways, the effect of mental processes on other glands has been less well studied. It is widely agreed, however, that all endocrine output is under a certain amount of emotional influence. Conversely, secretions from these glands affect emotional tone.

Walter Cannon (1934) and, more recently, Hans Selye (1956) have studied carefully the effects of emergency-type stress reactions on the organism, as well as the long-term adaptations demanded by prolonged exposure to stressful situations. In emergency reactions, the sympathetic nervous system predominates, acting in concert with the adrenal medulla. The hormones secreted by this gland, adrenalin and noradrenalin, have diffuse mobilization effects on the body, preparing it for fleeing or fighting, or other prompt action. Heart rate increases, sugar is released from the liver to provide quick energy to the muscles, pupils dilate, and blood tends to clot more quickly, while blood cell activity increases and blood flow is directed away from the peripheral vessels and organs to the muscles and the brain. This kind of stimulation not only prepares for emergency movement, but also for emergency repair—calling forth the analogy of a well-trained infantry battalion followed by a crack crew of medics. However, in our modern society, the troops seldom find a war once they arrive on the scene and must somehow dissipate without destruction.

Such reactions might be thought of as "acute" stress reactions. As with disease, the acute stress stage eventually approaches a chronic or long-term status if not ameloriated. Then the mechanisms involved also become permanently changed. Selye has described chronic stress in terms of a general adaptation syndrome. The emphasis is no longer on SNS/adrenal medullary action, but rather on the activities of the adrenal cortex. The hormones secreted by these glands (mineralocorticoids and the glucocorticoids) are under the control of other hormones released by the anterior pituitary called the adreno-cortico-trophic (ACTH) hormones. Again, the hypothalamus—that focal point for the conscious and unconscious function—influences ACTH release, bringing about diverse influences on the branches of the autonomic nervous system.

Under prolonged stress, it is apparent the glucocorticoids (hydrocortisone, corticosterone, and cortisone) try to continue the job of maintaining an organism fit to fight and repair. Nonsugars are transformed into sugar, and blood vessels are "sensitized" to the adrenal medulla hormones, so that action can take place even in a fatigued system. However, to the ultimate detriment of the long-stressed individual, the primary action of the ACTH and the glucocorticoids is to *reduce* inflammatory activity. While perhaps adaptive in the get-away, short-run, this leads to a decrease in the activity of white blood cells that fight disease. The massive changes sustained during prolonged stress go beyond immune activity to affect every system targeted by pituitary action, including reproduction, growth, and integrity of the organism at the cellular level.

In summary, we have traced a sophisticated network, emphasizing that the integrated nature of the central and peripheral nervous systems is such that every function is directly or indirectly related to every other function via neural and/or chemical pathways. We have repeatedly focused on the hypothalamus as the moderator of psychophysiologic response. Because of the known anatomical pathways between the hypothalamus and other areas of the limbic system—together with the interconnections of the limbic areas to the frontal lobes of the cortex—we also suspect that the anterior aspect of the right frontal lobe is one of the primary loci for body imagery. We are proposing that conscious or subconscious body images have a physiologic effect via these CNS channels upon the organs and glands which comprise the autonomic nervous system.

Unfortunately, as we have traced the imagery process within a psychophysiologic framework, two important aspects have been neglected. First of all, we must assume that the process is a full, unbroken circle with influences working on the mind as well as the reverse. A healthy body certainly promotes good feelings, just as the impact of disease or trauma changes a person's mental outlook. The street must be two-way. Secondly, we have repeatedly used examples of destructive influences—negative images and emotions, and prolonged stress, and damage to the system—rather than examples of hope and repair. Any biologic system designed to strive toward health could not respond only to negative, damaging events. Therefore, from a logical standpoint alone, we must assume some degree of conscious control in a return to and maintenance of health. And that is precisely what requires demonstration to the skeptic within us. Few would question that the bridges of the bodymind are passable when it comes to making ourselves sick, but the notion of getting ourselves well requires some massive shifts in belief. Descartes lives on within the innermost reaches of even the most enlightened of us.

CHAPTER IV

CANCER
The Ultimate Mystery

Our long-time interest in cancer, above all other diseases, stems from a multiplicity of complicated events in both of our lives. We have persistently invested more energy in that direction because, just when we were ready to move on to other vistas, new developments occurred which encouraged us to take another look at the issues. Furthermore, we feel that the confused cell, purposelessly growing, holds clues to the life process itself. Once both the biochemical properties of the cell and the properties of the host that promote or allow proliferation are understood, mysteries that extend far beyond the malignancy will be solved. For scientists, this presents the foremost challenge.

Cancer is remarkably unlike most other diseases, in that it represents a natural process gone awry. This destruction, induced by one's own life forces, leads to death in two of three cases despite all modern medical know-how. Very little has changed statistically in 25 years, with the exception of higher cure rates for a few select sites which either respond well to certain types of treatment or are prevented from reaching an advanced stage by early detection and treatment. As a result, some cancer patients may be living longer, while cure rates are not much improved.[1]

Other chronic diseases, such as rheumatoid arthritis, can also be categorized as an instance of the host attacking from within. But, unlike cancer, the drama of life and death does not usually accompany these debilitating conditions. Cancer, then, is the ultimate challenge and the ultimate frustration.

It is also for personal reasons that our interest in cancer has been sustained. Like many cancer researchers, we became interested out of a sense of mission, having had many family members succumb to the disease. The research and treatment activity is not unlike counter-phobic behaviors: becoming involved in a feared event in order to quell the anxiety

---

[1]Cancer statistics can be obtained from the National Cancer Institute, HEW, and from the American Cancer Society. Most useful publications are *End Results Tables* and *Cancer Prognosis Manual* from those respective institutions. Cancer incidence tables appear in *Vital Statistics for the United States.*

surrounding that event, flying in order to diminish the fear of flying, turning around and shaking hands with the bogeyman behind you to get a first-hand look at his (or her) awfulness.

Psychological research related to cancer, as Bernard Fox phrases it in a recent literature review (1976), is a "most difficult kind of research." In dealing with the psychological aspects of the disease, limited funding is available, and whatever studies are conducted may be subjected to the most hypercritical review. The existing scientific paradigm in this regard is steely with invested interests. It has been our experience that there is a striking contrast between the review given studies on psychological aspects of cancer and other, more innocuous topics in our discipline, regardless of the rigor affiliated with the conduct and analysis of the research. Some papers seem to "get lost" on the reviewer's desk. A case in point is one study we conducted in which a sophisticated, statistical technique called "canonical correlational analysis" was used to interrelate data on blood measures and psychological factors (Achterberg & Lawlis, 1979). The manuscript was reviewed and declared sound by two national experts in statistical methodology. In addition, it was presented for critique at a regional meeting of statisticians and was favorably received. Nevertheless, upon submission to an "appropriate journal," the reviewers—obviously ignorant of multivariate statistical techniques—called it statistically inappropriate and suggested that our computer program might be wrong since our correlations were so high! The supreme indication of active resistance to attitude change is the use of irrational arguments where rational ones do not exist.

In the past, major contributors to the literature on cancer have presented their findings with the hope that they would affect the treatment of the patient and shed understanding on the course and etiology of the disease. But, when their theses were irrationally rejected, they pursued new career directions instead. This has been the case with Beatrix Cobb, Eugene Blumberg, and Bruno Klopfer—all of whom originally stated in the 1950s what a new group of researchers are saying again now: i.e., that the course of cancer is related to psychological functioning. At a conference in 1954 (Gengerelli) where cancer researchers offered their findings, it was predicted that the information presented would alter the course of cancer therapy. Obviously, that prophesy was not immediately fulfilled. So we are merely reinventing the wheel as the 1970s come to a close, but with impunity and with the knowledge that replicability is the cornerstone of validity. Yet it does not promise to be an easy task, for, as a physician told an early researcher, "Even if you *prove* psychological factors have something to do with cancer, I won't believe you." (LeShan, personal communication.)

**Historical
Perspective on
Cancer Research** The history of cancer research with a psychological
emphasis is ancient, and it varies greatly in the degree of
scientific rigor associated with findings. The trends have been
recorded in a classic article by LeShan (1959) and in a recent
and thorough rendition by Fox (1976). Holden (1978) has
summarized the state of the art in *Science,* and an annotated
bibliography has been prepared for professionals and paraprofessionals interested in the field by Achterberg,
Matthews, and Simonton (1976). To briefly recapitulate the
trend of research in this area, it stretches from anecdotal evidence handed down by the fathers of medicine (e.g., Galen), to
crude descriptive analyses of the last century (Snow, 1893), to
the intuitive and experimental expertise of Larry LeShan
(1966), and finally to the new group of researchers armed with
computer storage and analysis capabilities, standardized
psychodiagnostic tools, and the insights of their predecessors.

Classification of Cancer Research. Psychologically oriented
cancer research may be conceptually divided into three basic
types: (1) that which deals with psychological attributes of
people who are ultimately diagnosed with cancer (i.e.,
etiological focus), (2) investigations of the relationship
between cancer site and personality, and (3) those studies
relating outcome of disease to psychological functioning. The
major findings of each division are discussed below.

Etiology. Etiological studies have generally been conducted on a retrospective basis and have been done with a clinical flavor using few, if any, objective measures. Characteristic in this regard is the work by Elida Evans (1926) which
discussed the cancer patient in a Jungian context. We feel her
monograph has superb clinical utility, even though substan-
tive data are lacking. Other studies, which are well covered in
the reviews mentioned above, generally compared patients
already diagnosed with cancer to healthy individuals or other
disease groups. Virtually all studies showed significant differences, but comparison among the studies to find "kernels of
truth" is difficult because of the variance in populations
studied, inconsistency in testing instruments used, and decisions which may have been based on subjective interview criteria. A literature summary of factors related to cancer
appears in Table 4.1.

One of the more productive approaches involved an analysis of responses obtained from people at the time of the examination for cancer. Patients eventually found to have carcinoma
tended to express more helplessness and hopelessness than
those who were diagnosed with benign conditions (Schmale &
Iker, 1971). This type of study is particularly valuable in

Table 4.1

LITERATURE SUMMARY OF PSYCHOLOGICAL FACTORS RELATED TO CANCER

Author(s)	Year	Instrumentation	N	Psychological Factors Related to Cancer
Walshe	(1846)	observation	unknown	"woman of high color and sanguinous temperament"
Paget	(1870)	observation	unknown	deep anxiety, deferred hope and disappointment
Snow	(1883, 1890, 1893)	observation	250	depression
Evans	(1926)	psychotherapy progress	100	the last of a major catharsis
Foque	(1931)	observation	unknown	sad emotions
Miller & Jones	(1948)	observation	6	frequent occurrence of emotional difficulties
Bacon, Renneker, & Cutler	(1952)	case history	40	masochistic character inhibited sexuality and motherhood, inability to discharge anger
Greene	(1954, 1966)	interview	20	loss of significant other
Jacobs	(1954)	observation	unknown	self-destructiveness
Greene, Young, & Swisher	(1956)	observation	32	unresolved attachment to mother
Inman	(1964)	case study	1	guilt over masturbation
Muslin, Gyarfas, & Pieper	(1966)	questionnaires	74	separation from significant other
Greene	(1966)	observation	100	sadness, anxiety, anger, or hopelessness
Paloucek & Graham	(1966)	observation	88	psychosocial trauma and poor childhood
Kissen	(1967)	interview	930	disturbed relationships in childhood, ongoing adverse life situations
Blumberg	(1954)	MMPI, Rorschach	50	defensiveness, anxiety, low ability to reduce tension
Ellis & Blumberg	(1954)	case studies		low ability to reduce tension

Author	(Year)	Instrument	N	Findings
Bugental	(1954)	MMPI (Blumberg's sample)		brooding, useless, lacking in energy
Wheeler & Caldwell	(1955)	Rorschach	60	labile, preoccupation with sexual body, inhibited with early sex experiences, close attachment with mother
LeShan & Worthington	(1956)	Worthington Personal History	152	loss of important relationship, inability to express hostility, anxiety over death
Kissen & Eysenck	(1962)	Maudsley Personal Inventory	116	extraversion, neuroticism
Coppen & Metcalfe	(1964)	Maudsley Personal Inventory	47	extraversion
Nemeth & Mezei	(1954)	Rorschach	50	few M, lower 4%, passive hostility
Booth	(1964)	Rorschach	93	rigid guilt feelings toward others
Evans, Stern, & Marmorston	(1965)	adjective checklist	56	submissiveness
Netzer	(1965)	Taylor Manifest Anxiety Scale, Neuroticism Scale, DAP	50	body image distortions, denial, fear of loss of control, neuroticism
Kissen	(1966)	interview, MMPI	150	incidences of child behavior problems
Koenig, Levin, & Brennan	(1967)	MMPI	36	depression
Tarlau & Smalheiser	(1951)	interview, Rorschach, DAP	11	mother-child relationship
Cobb	(1952)	Rorschach, interview	100	anticipatory fears and underlying dependency
Reznikoff	(1955)	TAT, sentence completion	50	birth order and family domesticity, sadness, negative feelings
Bahnson & Bahnson	(1964b)	Rorschach	12	superficial extraversion, low empathy, "flattened" affect, rigid, constricted
LeShan	(1966)	Worthington Research Life History	450	early childhood relationship problems, recent adult event, loneliness
Bahnson & Bahnson	(1966)	interview	49	denial and repression of impulses
Achterberg & Lawlis	(1978)	Image-Ca, MMPI, Firo-B		denial, imagery, negative self-investment
Thomas	(1976)	questionnaire		early neglect

understanding the psychological responses immediately prior to the diagnosis. However, research programs with a longitudinal perspective are required to determine with more certainty whether specific personality traits manifested early in life can be harbingers of the ultimate diagnosis. In one such project conducted by Thomas and her colleagues (Thomas & Greenstreet, 1973; Thomas & Duszynski, 1974), medical students were tested and interviewed. Records of morbidity and mortality were maintained, and it was found that individuals who were diagnosed with cancer later in life were psychologically distinct from other disease groups, particularly with respect to feelings of isolation or neglect as children. These differences were evident as many as 20 years in advance of the diagnosis.

Similar studies funded by the National Cancer Institute are presently underway to determine the extent to which stress may be a precursive factor in carcinogenesis. In one of these projects, Ralph Paffenbarger, of Stanford University, will investigate the relative occurrence of cancer and heart attacks among two groups of men from whom psychological test results were obtained while in college. It should be noted, however, that the investigator apparently entered the study with a bias, since he was quoted in Holden's *Science* article as saying, "My guess is there is no relationship between psychological factors and the risk of getting cancer."

In summing up studies of the psychological etiology of cancer, it is fair to state that the relationship remains largely retrospective or intuitive. With the exception of the sources cited, it is often based only upon the subjective experience of clinicians who listen to their patients. However, what we assume to be a retrospective bias may not be as formidable an obstacle as once deemed. Thomas's findings do, after all, substantiate the "after-the-fact" work of LeShan (1966) of Bahnson (1966), and of Greene (1966).

Site and Disease. The second type of study within our taxonomy attempts to relate site of malignancy to personality functioning. These studies are interesting, but again suffer from the "retrospective bias" imposed on the work. We do recognize that different *lifestyles* are associated with different disease sites; i.e., the relatively infrequent occurrence of cancer of the cervix among nuns, contrasted with the elevated rate among women who were sexually active from a young age. Also, there is evidently some influence of culture on the location of malignancy. Women in industrialized countries are much more susceptible to cancer of the breast than are women in the underdeveloped countries. Lifestyles which include high tobacco and alcohol intake are more likely to predispose one to cancer of the larynx. On the other hand, some lifestyles are characterized by a remarkably low incidence of cancer of any kind. In the general population, Mormons are a notable example of this fact. Among clinical groups, it has been reported that catatonic schizophrenics are not likely to be diagnosed with cancer (Scheflen, 1951; White, 1929).

Singling out the variables which are most contributive to the disease in general, or to the site in particular, has been difficult, and it is easy to attribute causality where none may actually exist. For example, do diet and nutritional factors play a major role in the development of breast cancer, or is a more basic contributive cause the stress which women face in an industrialized and technological society? Massive personal adjustments, changes in role assignment, and new directions chosen by women themselves may produce significant psychophysiological impact. Psychological researchers have begun to attempt the resolution of these issues by differentiating among characteristics of the various disease sites. Breast cancer patients, for example, have been described as significantly different from cervical cancer patients (Wheeler & Caldwell, 1955). The women with cancer of the cervix, for one thing, reported having suffered significantly more deprivation of affection as children. Other careful, long-term studies of the lung cancer population by Kissen (1966, 1967) have established an inability on the part of these patients to discharge emotions, as compared to healthy individuals or other lung disease patients.

Other differences among groups of cancer patients remain in the realm of clinical impression, lacking any solid objective justification. Nevertheless, it is our belief and experience that the psychological variance associated with different types of cancer is valid. Like so many other issues in this field, we have faith that the relationships will eventually be documented to the satisfaction of the researchers. For the purposes of this book, however, it will be helpful to at least briefly consider these impressions since they can provide a springboard for subsequent research or therapeutic intervention.

As a case in point, it has been our experience that women who present with cancer of the colon are quite different from breast cancer patients. Colon patients are more likely to be assertive and even demanding. While they no doubt exist, we have never seen a passive woman with primary cancer of the colon. In fact, the county hospital patients we observed with this diagnosis, to a woman, were flamboyant and outgoing. In contrast, the breast cancer patients were more likely to be "sweethearts"—gentler, quieter, more comfortable in the traditional passive female role (or at least more likely to *assume* that role), and expressing more dependency needs. In this regard, it is interesting that Drs. Derogatis and Abeloff of Johns Hopkins Oncology Center found those women diagnosed with metastatic breast cancer, and who did *not* exhibit these passive traits, lived longer (Derogatis, Abeloff, & Melisaratos, 1979). Their results, first reported at the American Society of Clinical Oncology in 1977 further indicated that survival time was positively correlated with patient attitudes, with level of vigor, and with the posture that was adopted by patients (i.e., the extent to which they became actively involved in treatment).

These suppositions offer valuable insights, especially in terms of therapeutic application. For example, interventions geared toward assertiveness training would probably be of more value for treating breast cancer patients than for treating women with cancer of the colon. With colon patients, we have frequently noted compulsions and overcontrolled behaviors very much like the ulcerative colitis patients reported in early psychoanalytic literature. When identified in a specific patient, they can often be redirected as very powerful sources of energy in the fight toward a return to a productive life. The site of the disease, then, may have significant value in guiding the psychotherapeutic approach, particularly if sensitivity is used and if the patient is not pigeonholed by virtue of the diagnosis.

Another broad speculation concerns the Hodgkins Disease patient. Even the name seems to protect the patient from the social revulsion that typically is felt by the cancer patient, even though Hodgkins is considered a form of malignancy. More like the TB patient of previous centuries, the Hodgkins patient appears to languish or simply fade out of life. The prognosis for this particular disease is fairly good (approximately 50% chance of five-year survival), and improving all the time. Often, though, patients who are controlled and symptom free appear to "fade," to remove themselves from the mainstream of vocational and social activity. A case example was a young neurosurgeon whom we interviewed and tested. He had no symptoms at the time of testing, other than periodic fatigue. He had left a profitable practice and for the past seven years had stayed at home, living with the aid of health insurance payments. The medical benefits were comfortable, but by no means permitted many luxuries. At the opposite extreme was a 37-year-old man from quite another social strata. His disease allowed him to gamble at neighborhood bars eight or more hours a day, but he could not work, nor could he hold his infant son.

Greene (1966), in reporting on case studies of leukemia and lymphoma (of which Hodgkins is one of several types) spanning a 15-year period, found that the disease seemed to develop in an environment where a significant loss had occurred. Such a loss might include a loss of self-esteem related to injury or operative procedure, retirement or change of work, as well as loss of close family members. The knowledge of some type of loss, followed by a pattern of giving up or retirement from the mainstream after the diagnosis, may certainly be of use in the therapeutic encounter with the patient. Not all Hodgkins patients may fall in these categories —perhaps very few do, and we saw only a select sample. Nevertheless, it was impressive enough to bear recording. The alternative explanation, of course, is that the disease makes one "semi-sick"—like a lingering influenza, as has been reported by several patients. If so, the fading out or languishing might be predictable.

We elaborate somewhat on these aspects merely as a reminder not to ignore the previous work nor the clinical impressions scattered throughout the professional literature on site and personal functioning. We also encourage more rigorous data collection on these issues. After all, good research is generally the verification of things clinicians knew all along.

Disease Outcome. The third type of study, the identification of psychological factors related to course of disease, would seem to have more treatment utility, since the prevailing emphasis of medicine is on post-diagnostic intervention rather than preventive health. Our own work in this area was inspired by that of Blumberg, West, and Ellis (1954) and Klopfer (1957), who were able to predict certain aspects of the course of disease using psychological protocols. Klopfer, using the Rorschach, developed a scheme to evaluate the relationship between ego defensiveness and loyalty to reality. Patients who had slow-growing tumors were characterized by a nonchalant attitude toward reality and were also lower in energy investments for defense of their egos. The fast-growing cases were people who tried to be loyal to reality, who invested too much ego defensive energy in an attempt to be good, and who were characterized by the "Prince of a Fellow" syndrome. It was concluded that when energy was so diverted in this direction, there would be too little left to protect the individual from the ravages of disease. The same idea reverberates also in the literature on stress (Selye, 1956; Cannon, 1934; Holmes & Masuda, 1970).

Blumberg and his colleagues, too, were successful in predicting whether tumors would grow rapidly or slowly. His criteria were based on a combination of MMPI scales: F minus K, Hypomania, and Depression (in relation to Hypochondriasis and Hysteria). The patients with faster growing tumors were more defensive, had a greater motivation to appear good, and appeared less disturbed than they really were. They were described as having more tension as a result of emotional conflict, with a concomitant inability to adequately defend themselves against anxiety. They also appeared unable to reduce tension through actions. Both Klopfer and Blumberg were able to predict degree of tumor growth with approximately 80% accuracy using these rather similar criteria, but differing instruments.

The most recent contribution to this type of research is that of Derogatis and Abeloff, mentioned earlier, who found in 35 women with metastatic breast cancer that there was a significantly different attitude among those women who lived longer. For one thing, expression of anger, or at least the *ability* to express anger (even toward disease, physician, or treatment) was more likely to be a characteristic of the women who survived longer. The women who succumbed earlier to the disease were more likely to be pliant and cooperative.

While all of these studies were conducted with small numbers of individuals, they seem to arrive at a common conclusion that the inability to express anger is detrimental to the patient's health. There are other sources for support of this position:

1) In virtually all psychotherapeutic models, the ability to express anger is considered important for the patient's *mental* health. In fact, much therapy is geared toward allowing a patient to find an acceptable outlet for repressed negative emotions. The cancer patients who have this ability apparently live longer, so that the advantage of open expression seems to enhance physical as well as mental health.

2) In C. B. Thomas's work mentioned earlier, one of the precursive characteristics which served to distinguish those medical students eventually diagnosed with cancer was their generally "low-gear" interpersonal style with little propensity to express emotion. A major question that can be posed of these data is whether such patients are really repressing strong emotions, or whether they are truly only moderately reactive. In other words, the possibility exists that they really never "felt" much emotion. The way the clinician interprets the basis for this so-called "low gear" will determine the therapeutic approach.

3) In accounting for the relationship between modern stressors and modern diseases, the inability to discharge negative emotions has been frequently singled out as the culprit. Through the normal process of evolution, which includes the premise that the fittest survive to reproduce, humans who have the most well-developed systems for fleeing or fighting are more likely to contribute "overtime" to the genetic pool. We might then assume that, for reasons having to do with survival of our ancestors, we are magnificently equipped to physically react to situations which affect us emotionally. Unfortunately, the direct physical channels for dissipating emotions are seldom available now. Once upon a time, the real tiger could have been slain, but punching out

the paper tiger (the job, the boss, the spouse, the traffic) is maladaptive in today's society. So, strangely enough, the members of the species who may have been the most likely to survive in a more primitive surrounding are precisely the ones most likely to be victimized by the stress of civilization. The tension and the anger turned inward become self-destructive. The physiological mechanisms involved have been described elsewhere (Selye, 1956; Solomon & Moos, 1964), and include descriptions and information about the occurrence of the usual "psychophysiologic" conditions such as ulcers, as well as the autoimmune disorders and cancer.

4) From a common sense standpoint, patients who express anger and appear to be fighters are more likely to have that fight reflected at the basic cellular level. Conversely, it is difficult to imagine the passive, dependent patient as having a powerful immune system. The components of holism—physical, mental, and spiritual—are not likely to follow a grossly different set of rules.

The Superstars. In an attempt to understand the psychological resources exhibited by cancer patients who have managed to significantly outlive their predicted life expectancies, a series of standardized tests was administered to approximately 70 patients (Achterberg, Matthews, & Simonton, 1976). The patients were middle to upper class and advantaged in terms of receiving treatment at major medical centers. The date of diagnosis was noted for each patient, and those patients who died within 13 months after diagnosis were compared with patients who had lived at least two years past diagnosis. Those who were still alive, but had not yet lived for two years past diagnosis, were dropped from further analysis. This procedure yielded two small groups with well-matched diagnoses in terms of predicted disease outcome (see Table 4.2).

Table 4.2

DIAGNOSTIC COMPOSITION OF TWO OUTCOME GROUPS

**CATEGORY I: Patients who lived in excess of two years
past incurable diagnoses**

---

2 Colon with liver metastases
1 Lung with brain metastases
1 Undifferentiated carcinoma spread to inguinal,
   pelvic, and peri-aortic nodes
1 Breast with lung metastases
1 Ovary with stomach metastases
3 Breast with bone and chest-wall metastases
1 Kidney with lung metastases
1 Advanced pharyngeal and esophageal extension
1 Breast with lung and bone metastases

---

12 Total patients in Category I

Table 4.2 (Concluded)

**CATEGORY II: Patients who died within 13 months
after incurable diagnoses**

1 Melanoma with lung metastases
2 Breast with lung metastases
1 Stage IV lymphoma
3 Lung cancer
1 Kidney with lung metastases
1 Pancreas
1 Breast with liver metastases

10 Total patients in Category II

The patients who outlived their expectancy had significantly different scores on scales of the MMPI, the FIRO-B,
and Locus of Control which, taken together, describe a
composite profile characterized by:

Refusal to give up
Flexibility
No physical decompensation when under stress
Rejection of the invalid role
Noncomformity
Aggressiveness, assertiveness
High ego strength
Self-reliance
Creativeness
Past history of success
Limited belief that "powerful others" were in
    charge of their well-being
Insightfulness

Clinically, the patients who fit the above description were
open to new ideas, would not take no for an answer, and were
highly individualistic and egocentric. They sought out the best
specialists they could afford and demanded the newest techniques in therapy, including even those of a less orthodox
nature. They were generally feisty individuals who acted out
with both their medical consultants and one another—not
quite the stereotypic picture of the cancer patient. Most of the
traits are not usually considered desirable in social circles,
particularly in women who, in our society, are typically reinforced for humbleness, graciousness, and nonconfrontiveness.
The thought occurs that we may be setting ourselves up for an
unwelcome outcome in which subsequent generations contain
large numbers of women who exemplify these traits. This
would be the case if a selection process exists whereby those
females in traditional passive roles are the primary child
bearers. The assertive, androgynous women who, genetically

or as role models, can offer their daughters the characteristics of the superstars may marry less often (or later) and have fewer children because of their own professional needs. On the other hand, of course, they may transmit to those daughters they have some other disease pattern, such as coronary heart disease—an increasing fact of life for the assertive, ambitious, Type "A" woman. After all, habits and behaviors *are* related to disease patterns.

Low Socioeconomic Breast Cancer Patients. In order to better understand the ramifications of psychological involvement in cancer, we studied several populations which resembled our earlier, well-educated, and enlightened group in terms of clinical diagnosis. Individuals in one group were women who had been treated for breast cancer at a county hospital which was the teaching facility for Southwestern Medical School. They were primarily indigent, black, and poorly educated. We studied them with a purpose in mind similar to the previous group: to determine what factors relate psychologically to good disease outcome, as measured by *quality* of life criteria. *Quantity* of life was not a reasonable criterion, since breast cancer carries with it a lengthy life expectancy; indeed, there is at least a 60% chance of being alive 10 years later, for all stages. The women were tested at the time of diagnosis and follow-up monitoring was conducted for a year after testing. Even though over a hundred patients were treated initially, many dropped out: some died and others could no longer be located. Nevertheless, the conclusions based on the results of 18 patients for whom we had complete data, were that psychological test results correlated with current functional status and were predictive of rehabilitation status at one-year follow-up for these individuals. However, the characteristics related to good treatment response were somewhat different from those of the other, higher socioeconomic patients, though essentially the same types of testing instruments were used (modified in format to compensate for the lower reading level of the patients).

A modified version of the Patient Status Form (PSF) by Izak and Medalie (1971) was filled out by a physician and a social service worker *or* a psychologist at the beginning for each patient to determine quantitatively both (1) physical status and (2) subjective functional abilities. These two scales, as well as several of the individual items comprising them, were then used as criterion variables. At follow-up intervals, a physical therapist recorded information about strength, range of motion, and other measures relevant to the status of the mastectomy. We found, surprisingly, that women who scored *high* on scales of the FIRO-B which indicate sociability were the ones who had a better chance of being functionally sound at follow-up testing. (The opposite was true of the higher socioeconomic group.) Also, items on the PSF which related to activity outside the home were effective measures of physical strength at one-year follow-up. Psychological scales on the MMPI Mini-Mult that were predictive of ability at follow-up were Hypochondriasis ($r = -.75$), Depression ($r = -.63$), Hysteria ($r = -.77$), and Psychasthenia ($r = -.48$), indicators of bodily preoccupation and repressive defenses. In this latter respect, the patients from both socioeconomic levels were similar. However, a concurrent elevation in Psychopathic Deviate ($r = -.61$) was related to functional difficulties in the low socioeconomic group; in the exceptional group this scale, which may be interpreted as nonconformity, was predictive of *good* progress. It would therefore seem that acting out can be conceived of as healthy at one end of the socioeconomic spectrum but not at the other. (See Cromes, 1978, for a more complete discussion of these particular results.)

The imagery obtained with the IMAGE-CA technique was also predictive of rehabilitation potential: it was correlated with objective physical measures at one-year follow-up. (See *Imagery of Cancer* for more complete data on these individuals.) It is important not to overinterpret these data since patient numbers were so small. However, the results are offered as interesting and useful observations for the clinician who deals with such populations.

To summarize, the patients in the lower socioeconomic status who led active, socially involved lives (and in this group this usually meant extensive church or family involvement) and who had positive attitudes (reflected in their imagery content) toward disease, treatment, and their own ability to heal, were the ones who functioned better physically a year or more after surgery.

Cancers with Good Prognosis. Many types of cancer carry rather good prognoses. For some sites, in fact, the patients may more often than not expect to survive surgery and live long enough to die from other causes. Life after surgery, however, may be fraught with adjustment difficulties. Two such types of cancer are of the larynx and of the bowel (or colon). For the former, even with regional node metastasis, fully one-third may be expected to live past the magic five-year survival point. For the patients with cancer of the colon, 10-year survival rates are even higher (60% for Stage I or II). Both groups carry with them a heightened probability of a full return to life, work, and recreation—provided psychosocial factors permit doing so.

Larynx. The patients with this disease may have had significant adjustment problems prior to diagnosis. Heavy drinking and smoking are known behaviors in a high percentage of cases. The cancer itself is believed in many instances to be related to the trauma of these toxic substances. The wide variance in quality of life maintained after surgery no doubt correlates to pre-surgery adaptive behaviors, but also hinges on how well the individual can learn to communicate after surgery, since the usual laryngectomy produces loss of speech. Because the most widely accepted and optimal method of learning to communicate after surgery is through esophageal speech (as opposed to learning to make sounds with a mechanical device), we used this as a criterion in our studies (Gibbs & Achterberg, 1979).

An exhaustive survey of the literature revealed that re-establishment of speech was not consistently related to morphological features of the patient, but rather to such psychological factors as motivation, energy level, and fortitude. We also became aware of a characteristic which interfered with group therapy among these patients, and even with individual interviews and presumably with communication generally; that is, many wives (and indeed the majority of such patients are male—hence the masculine gender is usually appropriate when discussing them collectively) were so verbal and so ready to speak for their husbands, that they had to be specifically requested to stay quiet and allow the patient to express himself. We investigated this factor, predicting that the spouse would be vitally important in degree and quality of speech attainment. We recruited subjects through the Lost Chord Society—a group of well-motivated patients who meet at regular intervals for education and social purposes. Our results may be skewed due to the fact that they did exhibit interest and enough concern to meet together; however, in attempting to recruit subjects from our county hospital population, not one patient responded.

A large volume of data was gathered from each of 10 patients and their spouses. The research procedure involved study of the nature of the marital relationship both pre- and post-surgery, together with an examination of such characteristics as interpersonal need patterns, communication methods, social activities, disease education, drinking and smoking patterns, etc. A timed story-telling situation (which actually served as a projective technique) was used to assess communication styles between patient and spouse.

We found, as predicted, that good speech was not related to demographic data. It was, however, related to the amount of disagreement on the story telling; i.e., those patients who argued more, also spoke more clearly! It was further

discovered that, when both marriage partners had mutual
affectional needs met, speech was likely to be of higher
quality. The expanded importance of the spouse's role in facilitating communication and adjustment in the long run can, and
should, be readily pointed out to the patient. For example, the
spouse can encourage the patient to talk more by asking
questions in such a way that longer sentences are required for
a sensible answer, for example, "What would you like for
dinner?" rather than, "Hungry for chicken?" Additionally, a
little counseling in the immediate post-surgery interim by the
nurse or physician (or whoever is responsible for discussing
the physical dimensions of rehabilitation) can be of benefit.

Encouragement to relearn communication skills as quickly
as possible, together with an explanation of *why* this is felt to
be important for adjustment, can be given soon after surgery.
The spouses at this time can also be encouraged to stand back,
resist the temptation to communicate for the patient, and to
stop interpreting the sounds for those less familiar with the
esophageal speech than they. "Practice makes perfect" can be
an ever-present motto regardless of Good Samaritan
tendencies. The dynamics of interpersonal behavior,
particularly in regard to familial interactions, may be of
concern also. Since a high percentage of laryngectomees have
a long history of heavy drinking and smoking, one might
assume that the spouses might resemble the "alcoholic's wife"
in that they mothered and protected the "weaker" partner for
many years of marriage. Requesting that they suddenly
reverse such tendencies and allow the partner to struggle for
a time in order to regain some communication skills may be a
difficult task—far more so than for partners who have adopted
a different pattern of interaction.

Ostomates. The second group of patients, those with bowel
cancer who underwent ostomy surgery (creation of a new
opening or "stoma" for bowel or bladder elimination), were
not unlike the laryngectomees. We studied 306 ostomates (103
of them with a diagnosis of cancer) who were attending con-
ventions of the United Ostomy Association. We wondered of
them, too, what would determine a successful return to daily
living. A five-page, 106-item questionnaire was administered
to them. It was divided into sections as follows:

1) Demographic data (age, education, sex, geographic
   information);
2) Rehabilitation history (for example, date of surgery,
   type and from whom ostomy information was received,
   exposure and awareness of ostomy and services,
   opinions on the value of information and service, length
   of hospital stay in weeks, postsurgical complications,

work and activity records, perceived pain, irrigation information, and other "quality of life" variables);

3) Personal adjustment before and after surgery (change in marital status, sexual and functional relationships, dependency needs, mutual respect for mate); and

4) Attitudes regarding ostomy (dealing generally with truths and myths surrounding ostomy together with real and imagined disabilities).

Patients were also asked to fill out a Fundamental Interpersonal Relationships Orientation (FIRO-B scale)—a standardized instrument designed to measure interpersonal relationships on the three dimensions of affection, control, and inclusion (Schutz, 1967).

The data were then analyzed using pain postsurgery, return to work, and return to leisure activities, as well as sexual activities, as criteria for successful re-entry into life's mainstream. In all cases, including physical pain, the results included either educational or psychological variables exclusively. Table 4.3 contains those results.

Table 4.3

REGRESSION EQUATIONS OF OUTCOME CRITERION

Criterion Variable	Variables of Greatest Independent Prediction	Overall F-ratio
Pain	1 High wanted Inclusion (FIRO) 2 Low expressed Affection (FIRO) 3 High express Inclusion (FIRO)	3.95*
Leisure	1 Knowledge of tax deduction for appliance 2 High wanted Inclusion (FIRO) 3 Low expressed Inclusion (FIRO) 4 Low wanted Affection (FIRO)	4.03*
Sex Activities	1 Number of Enterstomal Therapist visits 2 Belief that recovery was speedier with Entersomal Therapist 3 Acknowledgement of good ostomy care at discharge 4 Desire for more Enterstomal Therapist visits	3.86**
Work Activities	1 Low wanted Control (FIRO) 2 High wanted Inclusion (FIRO) 3 Low wanted Affection (FIRO)	3.45*

$*p < .05$
$**p < .01$

Additionally, in a final, open-ended question ("What would you like to have changed if you had to go through surgery again?"), the majority of ostomates asked for more counseling regarding the adjustments ahead of them, and 35% specified the need for counseling and/or education to occur pre-operatively. Only nine patients complained of the surgery itself.

The patients were not asking for psychotherapy, adminis-tered by a special practitioner; rather they were asking for (1) facts on psychosocial adjustment processes (i.e., what to expect), and (2) some reasonable ways of coping with the inevitable adjustments. They were anxious, particularly post-diagnosis and presurgery, and full of myths and erroneous information (such as "no swimming," "no travel," "no sex" after surgery). The usual therapeutic skills psychologists use are certainly applicable for these patients, but only in a context that includes significant amounts of medical informa-tion that can be shared with the patient. For example, in order to do any sexual counseling, a preliminary conversation with the surgeon would be advisable to determine whether any impotency was likely to be primary or secondary, temporary or permanent (probabilities vary depending upon type of surgery and extent). We found the local United Ostomy Asso-ciation to be a storehouse of information that could be integrated with patient counseling. The Ostomy Visitor program is another resource which provides an invaluable service to new ostomates. In this program, patients are typically visited by another ostomate—usually of the same sex and approximately the same age— to provide information on adjustment problems in a supportive, but believable fashion.

We were obviously dealing with an elite group of ostomy patients who may have motivations similar to the Lost Chord Society membership. It is precisely for those reasons that we respect their comments, regardless of whether they general-ize to the population at large. In their comments, test scores, and direct answers to questions, they were saying that their psychological functioning was intimately involved in their recovery, yet that aspect had been most sorely ignored in their treatment. Additionally, we might infer from their comments that it was from nurses that they expected to get this information. Fully 21% specified the inadequacy of the education of the nursing staff as a source of dissatisfaction, asking for "more knowledgeable nurses" and stating "nurses on units should be educated."

In summary, we have evidence for a significant relation-ship between the ostomy patient's socialization (or need to belong), affectional needs (or close personal relationships), and quality of life postsurgery. There was also an expressed need to be informed and counseled on these adjustment aspects at the time of surgery. None of this comes as a surprise. What is astonishing (yet somewhat difficult to relate) is the massive amount of nonsignificant physical and demographic data in predicting treatment outcomes—as judged by both lack of statistically significant correlations and by the patients' own failure to mention these in their comments. They are not requesting new and improved surgical techniques, but rather heightened levels of awareness and understanding.

Treatment Implications

Our intention in this chapter is not to describe a step-by-step treatment program. We intend, rather, to broadly specify treatment implications based on findings reported in the literature and our own experiences. Our bias is that treatment must be as well grounded in a data base as possible but that to withhold psychological intervention until "all the facts are in" is unethical. The facts may never be "all in." However, there are sufficient data currently available to warrant pursuing a psychological approach, together with medical treatment, in the best interests of patients with malignancy.

As we have reiterated throughout this book, psychotherapists may not find goals and objectives which were developed for a model of mental health totally appropriate for the cancer patient or for any patient with disabling physical disease. For that reason alone, the research on psychological aspects of cancer can be a valuable guide as we begin to develop intervention models that are effective, problem specific, and appropriate to the type of patient treated. Writing from our own clinical perspectives, we have attempted to categorize this research into three treatment models for use with particular groups of cancer patients.

Disease Intervention Model. This type of program has at the heart of its philosophical approach the idea that cancer can be caused, and the growth influenced, by psychological and stress phenomena. The issue of carcinogenic substances is generally managed by pointing to the exceptions—not all smokers get cancer, neither did all chimney sweeps. Surveillance theory is involved here: cancerous cells are frequently present in an organism, but only become manifest in clinical malignancy when inhibitory factors are deficient. This can occur under stressful situations, judging from the results of analog studies (Riley, 1976). Additional studies are currently underway to determine whether stress is a viable precursor in humans, and theoretical models for the mechanism involved have been developed (Solomon, Amkraut, & Kasper, 1974). If, in fact, the cancer cells are naturally present, as proposed by the surveillance theory, yet cancer is not typically diagnosed until stressful events occur, then what is the cause of cancer—the stress, or some mysterious virus or alteration in processes? As Selye said, if microbes are ever present, yet do not cause disease until stress, what is the cause of disease—the microbe or the stress?

Given these factors, the disease intervention models acknowledge that if the patients once become aware of, and take steps to relieve the stressors or the events that caused life to lose meaning, whether through attitude change, behavioral alterations, or spiritual growth, or if they can program their minds toward health rather than disease, then the *soma* will follow suit. The model is exercised by a growing number of organizations, most of them outside the mainstream of the established medical profession. This is not to say that they do not receive acknowledgement, and even referrals, from the more traditional core of medicine, for in some cases they do. More typically, however, they depend on self-referral and work tangentially rather than in close concert with the primary physician or oncologist.

One of the forerunners of this intervention model was Wilhelm Reich, who maintained, among other things, that cancer was the result of a blocking or damming up of sexual energy (stasis). After laboratory experiments, Reich developed his model of energy systems by which individuals with cancer were theorized to have a significant loss in energy resources with which to combat disease. He felt that, with efforts to free up the patient's natural forces, the disease could be reversed. He thus formulated a "bioenergetics" psychotherapy. Although he reported success with 22 patients, Reich became involved in legal issues, and later died before extensive evaluation of the procedures were completed. Reichian-like groups continue to seek specific strategies for integrating the "bodymind" (e.g., bioenergetics, Radix, and primal therapies).

The most completely developed system currently in operation designed specifically to manage the psychological aspects of cancer is the Cancer Counseling and Research Center in Fort Worth. Its directors, Dr. Carl and Stephanie Simonton, have pioneered in treating the emotional needs of cancer patients and have in recent years expanded a training program for professionals interested in their work. Much of our original data and the conceptualization for future studies was based on our contacts with their exceptional and well-motivated patients. To attempt a thorough description of their methods would be an injustice to the reader, since we are familiar with it only from an historical perspective.

During our acquaintance with the Simonton organization (one of us as Research Director), the practices were in a state of flux. They encompassed, at one time or another, elements of Jungian analysis, behavior modification, Gestalt, Arica, massage therapy, Transactional Analysis, self-hypnosis, exercise therapy, and spiritual emphases. The amount of time devoted to each trend largely depended on the interests of the professionals and paraprofessionals who were affiliated with the organization. As is usually the case in fluid, developing models, elements of each new direction were maintained if they proved useful. However, two features of the approach were (and presumably still are) invariant: (1) a very confrontive type of psychotherapy which has as one of its main goals to convince a patient to assume responsibility for the cause and the course of disease—a process which usually requires painful self-examination; and (2) regular relaxation and mental imagery focused on positive attitudes toward treatment and disease. The latter process was shown to be correlated with the physical course of disease and published as a diagnostic, the IMAGE-CA (Achterberg & Lawlis, 1978).

The Simontons describe their own practices in a recent book (*Getting Well Again*, Simonton, Simonton, & Creighton, 1978). The interested reader is encouraged in that direction. Another, briefer, description is provided by Pelletier (1978), who additionally presents beautifully marshalled evidence and a rationale for the necessity of considering the mind in its full capacity to affect both health and disease. We will not attempt a duplication of that material here.

Disciples of the Simontons and other professionals who have integrated aspects of the approach into their own practices are scattered across the country. Some combine the Simontons' technique with hypnosis (e.g., Newton Center for Clinical Hypnosis in Los Angeles), with biofeedback (Gladman Memorial Hospital in Oakland), and with what we call "creative" therapies, i.e., therapies which rely on expressions of art, dance, or music in healing rituals. The creative groups have proliferated on the West Coast and are active in the Holistic Medicine Movement.

The major question at this point is whether such strategies work, at least in the sense of changing the course of disease. No one really argues much that psychological strategies "work" to improve the quality of life, but quantity is another issue entirely. In any event, if they work to prolong or improve life in any measure, are we not morally obligated to strive to make them available to all cancer patients? Are we not, in fact, remiss in a medically unethical fashion if such care is omitted? A parallel might then be drawn between ignoring a patient's emotional needs (allowing them to take their "natural course") and allowing a cancer of the lung to grow through its natural course. Treatment for cancer of the lung is only minimally effective in prolonging life, and seldom results in a "cure." Yet, to withhold even this basically ineffective treatment would be medically unthinkable.

On the other hand, if there is contrary evidence, i.e., that psychological intervention strategies are basically impotent in warding off or halting tumor growth (disregarding for a moment the improvement in quality of living), what kind of quandry are practitioners in who allow their patients to receive (and pay for) these services with the promise—explicit or implicit—that the disease course can be altered via such strategies! Is the quandry so dissimilar to medical situations which divest patients of all financial resources for treatments which have limited effectiveness, at best offering a few more months of living? The latter instance is further confounded because the last few months may be of *lesser* quality because of drug side-effects.

The ethical paradoxes are faced by everyone in the cancer treatment field, not just the johnny-come-lately holistic interventionists. A great deal is made of "unproven cures" which smack of quackery, yet where are there any "proven cures"? The "cure" (defined as an arbitrary number of years alive without recurrence) has changed very little during the past 25 years—perhaps longer, though the records are unclear on this point. We do know that many "spontaneous" remissions are documented, that people do get well, and that patients are surviving longer than ever before. Thus, the factors that pose significant issues and paradoxes in cancer treatment, and with which the psychological intervention models, in particular, must concern themselves, are: (1) Virtually all medical cancer treatment is best thought of as an avenue for increasing longevity, not as a cure for disease. Interventions which the public *perceives* as cure, or which claim cure rates, are regarded with great suspicion. (2) Many medical protocols exist, and are practiced despite statistically questionable advantages over other treatment (or even over no treatment at all), being maintained by tradition alone. But psychological intervention methods do not have such a history of tradition and will probably not be accepted unless they offer *dramatic* results. (3) Nonmedical intervention is faced with having to justify its existence, presumably on the same bases as medical treatments, with the same scientific scrutiny and rigor, consisting of clinical trials conducted under controlled conditions. Yet the massive funding for the required clinical trials generally comes from federal sources or drug companies—neither of which has the appropriate vested interests to support studies of psychological intervention. Even with minimal evidence that a drug or surgical protocol is, or will be effective, a secondary financial support for its application occurs in the form of patient or insurance company (third party) payments—a luxury seldom afforded the groups offering nonmedical interventions. Finally, the majority of individuals who offer these adjunctive psychological interventions do not have finances or resources available for adequate research. Therefore, most have little inclination or ability to do so—much as the physician in private practice seldom does, or can, research the response of the patient clientele to treatment.

So, in rhetorical answer to a question previously posed, there are no tests proving the utility of the psychological intervention methods via rigorously controlled clinical trials, and none are likely to be conducted for some time. The evidence *does* exist, and has been previously cited, that there is a *correlational* relationship between the individual's psychological functioning and the course of cancer. We, and others, have repeatedly provided documentation in a variety of populations. Rarely will a physician argue with the idea that some patients give up and die after a diagnosis of cancer, regardless of stage or severity, while others determinedly fight against the most hopeless odds. Even one or two patients out of every 100 diagnosed with liver cancer are alive after five years, though the majority die within three to five months. Those alive are different psychologically as well as immunologically. They are winners, not just survivors.

Now, the real issue is not whether these patients—these superstars—are different, for we know that on an objective basis. Rather, the question to ask is whether there are psychological strategies capable of changing people who are *not* winners or fighters or stars into those things? It might further be asked whether the winners and fighters would not get well *anyway?* As one physician told us, after we described the exceptional patient study: "I have a few of those patients in my practice. Most physicians do, and there is no doubt that their physical progress is extraordinary. But I didn't have anything to do with it. I just listened and respected their courage." Perhaps therein lies a rather simple answer.

In studying the Simonton patients for two years with every possible strategy except the nebulous "control" group, it is fair to state that their patients do live longer than the median life expectancy for the population as a whole. However, we know that tables of longevity are often based on low socioeconomic populations, who have a *shorter* life expectancy after diagnosis than more affluent groups (Berg, Ross, & Latourette, 1977). The Simonton patients are economically privileged and should be expected, on this basis alone, to exceed the median—which may *already* be falsely and negatively skewed. Many of the patients had in fact exceeded that mark long before presenting to the practice. Furthermore, obviously passive, noncompliant patients who distrusted the methods were screened out altogether and thus did not contaminate the data. If we matched psychological profiles of the Simonton patients with patients at a major cancer treatment center, such as Sloan-Kettering or M. D. Anderson, would we get the same results in terms of treatment responses? Maybe. There are indeed very unusual recoveries that occur after exposure to the practice. How do we account for these? Would they have been as likely to have happened had the patient latched onto a grape juice cure? Or a faith healer? Or an Orgonne box? Our feeling is no, not unless the patients *believed* in these aspects as curative. We are left with the powerful belief system of the patient as a key factor in disease course determination.

The point should be emphasized, however, that there are patients who subscribe to certain psychological modes of treatment and are able to recover or stabilize against all odds. They have belief systems attuned to the notion of self-responsibility and self-healing, and they seem naturally to collect around therapists who also have those ideas. They deserve continued study and recognition as do populations where cancer is seldom a cause of death. We learn from the anomalies, the exceptions to the rule. We learn why people die from cancer by studying those who die. Perhaps in order to understand why people survive we must study the survivors.

This seems like a logical focus, but to date the data are sparse. Nevertheless, the psychological intervention groups are here to stay. Furthermore, they are growing and publicized to the extent that the names associated with them are becoming household words. They offer promise and an alternative to patients who feel they are confronted with little of either from the established medical model. And they offer undeniable evidence that patients who subscribe to the methods fare better than the national average. So it is not *whether* but *why* they live longer that remains open to interpretation.

The Rehabilitation Model. Our professional involvement in cancer has in several ways been characterized by unusual and opportune happenstance. At the time we were analyzing our cancer data from the Simonton patients, and wondering how generalizable any findings could be in view of the specificity of the population, we were offered the opportunity to co-direct an evaluation effort for a cancer rehabilitation demonstration project. It was funded by the National Cancer Institute for three years and was in the final year of operation, with no previous systematic attempt at data collection having been attempted. Virtually all of our work, then, had to be retrospective, and our impressions were colored by having to recapture the essence of the project at a time when staff was being terminated and enthusiasm had all but ceased. Evaluation teams are always threatening, so much of our time was spent in establishing some degree of trust in order to elicit cooperation.

The program was to have served as a prototype for other rehabilitation efforts with cancer patients. The objective was to demonstrate that cancer patients, the majority of whom live for some time after the diagnosis, could be treated in a framework of rehabilitation. This constituted a rather innovative approach in comparison to the traditional tendency to treat them as hopelessly terminal, with little potential for living. The patients for whom this particular project was developed were racially mixed, the majority being black and—for the most part—dependent upon the charity facility for medical care. A total of 385 patients were seen over the three-year period. While many disease sites were represented, the greatest number of patients were those for whom the practice of physical medicine was appropriate, i.e., mastectomy patients (126), gynecological (61), gastrointestinal (54), head and neck (43), and others (101).

The "Team" concept was utilized with teams comprised of a physiatrist (an M.D. with specialty in physical medicine), social workers who served as "patient advocates," psychologists, nutritionists, an enterostomal therapist, occupational and physical therapists, a nurse, and a speech therapist. Weekly clinics were conducted where patients were appointed at intervals as needed and seen by the appropriate team members. Additional programs and groups in nutrition and exercise were offered, although most were restricted to the sizable number of mastectomy patients. Some follow-up was also available when the patients were admitted into the hospital for further treatment. Weekly team conferences were held, and it was believed that these "staffings" were the necessary ingredient for the team concept to work.

The patient's psychological needs were recognized and dealt with in what has come to be recognized as the "usual" fashion in rehabilitation settings. It embodied a two-edged strategy of determining: (1) what problems the patient was encountering in dealing with the diagnosis, treatment, and subsequent lifestyle; and (2) playing a supportive role in helping patients develop coping strategies for whatever outcome appeared inevitable. From our vantage point, the psychological approach could best be classified as rational/reality therapy. Patients were encouraged to discuss their fears, and the real vs. the unreal were sorted out. This process provided the emotional relief which comes from voicing anxieties and from hearing that many do not necessarily have to come to pass (Cromes, 1978).

Undoubtedly, this type of multidisciplinary approach represents a decided improvement in cancer care. We advocate its adoption in whatever piecemeal measure possible for any given facility. The sham of the many well-funded Comprehensive Cancer Care Centers across the country, which largely ignore the psychosocial (and rehabilitation in general) components of care, is a testimony to the fact that the model is not yet widely applied. Financially, of course, there are problems. The inclusion of many team members in after-care is frightfully expensive (the three-year demonstration project cost approximately $1,000,000). Even if the patients have medical insurance, which most of the county patients obviously did not have, most coverage for adjunctive expense is stingy or nonexistent. And, finally, many cancer patients have already encountered massive expenses; their earning power is diminished and their financial resources are depleted, so that paying for allied health services is not possible. The total team approach almost always will require subsidy—but then perhaps part of the 12 billion spent annually in the war on cancer could be earmarked for these support services.

The following is a condensed summary of findings from our evaluation of the Cancer Demonstration Project, as they pertain to psychosocial services (and not necessarily to the many other services offered in conjunction with the project):

(1) Psychosocial team components (i.e., services rendered by psychologists, social workers, patient advocates, or other cancer counselors) worked effectively only when the team head (a physician in this project under discussion) recognized and respected the validity and necessity of dealing with the patient's emotional needs, and additionally acknowledged that it was more appropriate for those who had been specifically trained in such services to do so. There also appeared to be advantages in allowing the psychosocial components to determine whether or not their *own* services were necessary after interviewing the patient (otherwise referrals might be sparse or inappropriate). Without this kind of autonomy in decision making, the team members become handmaidens to the physician who autocratically refers, based on personal judgment. The gist, then, is that respect for each specialty is of utmost importance in providing a contented team as well as good treatment.

(2) While a control comparison group did not exist within this particular demonstration project, it did seem valuable to have a physician as team leader. It was felt that only with a physician could an appropriate liaison be established with the hospital, the medical school, and community medical resources. Treatment of physical disease, after all, is done on the physicians' territory. Regardless of what administrative skills a nonphysician might bring to the situation, communication difficulties might be expected to occur.

(3) The patients low on the socioeconomic scale seemed more likely to accept the social worker rather than the psychologist as their emotional mainstay. And why not? Social workers have always been the friends of the indigent—assisting with clothes, the welfare check, and whatever other basic necessities of life are required. Psychologists, and most definitely psychiatrists, are regarded in many instances with suspicion and distrust because of the common association with mental health rather than physical health models. This principle was reinforced by our previous experience with the economically well-to-do patient, who felt cheated if anyone other than the team M.D. was the primary source of psychological support. The moral of this story is to consider carefully the clientele in choosing the professional most agreeable to their needs.

Psychologists, by training, are better qualified to meet these needs at a higher level (as in Maslow's hierarchy) but seldom have skills for offering the concrete social services which have to take priority over the development of self-esteem. Psychologists, nevertheless, have a great deal of expertise to offer the multidisciplinary approach in terms of (a) communication and administrative needs, (b) psychological and vocational testing, (c) tactics for stress intervention, and finally, but perhaps of greatest interest to the medical field, (d) skills requisite for program evaluation and research.

(4) In a rehabilitation program, where patients generally are appointed to services (as compared to the intervention model, which is self-selecting), a diversity of motivations and expectations for recovery are encountered. A need for flexibility is therefore indicated. While some opportunities exist for using stress-reduction techniques, self-help interventions, and psychotherapeutic practices, most of the support in this project was geared toward meeting more basic needs, assisting with return to some semblance of physical function, and strategies for coping or learning to live practically with cancer. Also, since the patients may have extensive disease and little reserve to withstand more treatment, death is an ever-present reality for many. Counselors who intend to support their patients beyond the rehabilitation stage will require sensitivity in understanding the needs of the dying patients.

The ultimate fate of the particular program in question—and probably many more like it—was that once goverment funding ceased, major changes were forced upon the sponsoring department. Either some new sources of subsidy would have to be identified or the program would have to be abandoned altogether. Fortunately, the personnel involved in this project had sufficiently demonstrated the usefulness of their approach so that many were absorbed into the larger medical school/county hospital system. The format for holding the Cancer Rehabilitation Clinic became part of the standard county hospital procedure and was implemented on a 2-day basis every two weeks. The patient response, however, was disappointing: fewer and fewer kept their appointments. Many were bewildered about why they continued to be appointed since they no longer had active disease. Others who were being seen concurrently in a tumor clinic where they received medication and x-rays sensed a duplication of services. Staff enthusiasm had dwindled in the absence of a concerted team effort, formerly held together by federal support. Few new patients were picked up because of the lack of adequate manpower resources. Integration with services that provided acute treatment of newly diagnosed patients was also restricted. Good intentions, in the absence of considerable monetary support, are not sufficient to maintain a broad rehabilitation program.

The Hybrid Model. The intervention model and the rehabilitation-multidisciplinary model in the forms described are really exemplary programs. Yet, because of the expense and lack of accessibility, they are not likely to be widely adopted in their entirety. What is more likely, however, is the adoption of a hybrid model—a mixture of the two basic philosophies—which can be readily adapted by the private clinician who may see only a handful of patients. The hybrid model is likely to be appropriate for application by allied health personnel (psychologists, social workers, rehabilitation counselors) and nurses who encounter a wide variety of patients with many special needs, and who work in settings which may or may not be supportive of aggressive psychological intervention. It is the conceptualization of practice which we favor as currently being the most practical. The following assumptions form the basis for the model:

(1) The patient has a set of beliefs regarding cancer, life, and death, and is entitled to act out and express those beliefs.

(2) Any treatment, psychological or otherwise, is more likely to be successful if it fits in with the patient's belief system (i.e., if the patient has a chemotherapy "consciousness," use that approach—it's likely to be the only thing readily accepted).

(3) Patients are entitled to grieve and to die "with dignity." They are also entitled to try to keep themselves alive in any way that makes sense with the same dignity. This does

not overlook the important medical issue of providing the patient with all the "facts" and then allowing free choice.

The hybrid method, while largely patient and situation dependent, follows a more or less typical flow from assessment to treatment.

Assessment. Patients are studied or assessed for one of two reasons: Either they are part of a research endeavor in which particular questions are being investigated (i.e., Is there a relationship between site and personality factors?), or they are to be offered psychological services, and the assessment provides some insight into their specific needs. Hopefully, assessment findings can also be communicated to the physician for use in the consideration of treatment plans (see Krug, 1978, for numerous examples of instances where psychological information can be a viable part of treatment decisions). Since we are most concerned with the psychological intervention applications here, we will deal exclusively with the latter aspect.

Regardless of the criteria chosen for assessment, systematic testing is preferable to diving into a patient's psyche without any kind of agenda. The luxury of in-depth psychoanalysis may not often be appropriate for this purpose, and more cursive methods will probably have to be chosen. The following guidelines are offered to assist the allied health professional in deciding upon the most appropriate course of action.

(1) Select an instrument to examine the patient's mood state, since that is likely to be a major issue in counseling or supportive therapy. The Profile of Mood States, State-Trait Anxiety Inventory, and Beck Depression Scale have all been used with cancer patients, and data have been published.

(2) Select a standardized instrument which describes something about basic personality traits in order to facilitate understanding of the patient's typical response patterns. Both the 16 PF and MMPI have been widely used in this regard. The latter was found to be predictive of disease course when combined with other instruments.

(3) Interpersonal behavior styles are worth investigation (FIRO-B has been useful for us). Social or affectional behaviors emanating from these aspects are very important in the response to serious disease. This may be thought of as the perceived quality of the patient's support system.

(4) Study the issue of *control.* Control has cropped up repeatedly as an important factor in disease and treatment response. This is not surprising since cancer can be thought of as control gone haywire at the cellular level. The extent to

which one feels out of control may well be reflected in the "giving up" syndrome we frequently see, even in the face of minimal disease. MMPI Control and Ego Strength subscales, Locus of Control Scales, and FIRO-B Control Scales are all valuable indicators of patient feelings about this vital aspect.

(5) Read the literature on psychological findings for differing sites of disease, for example, Kissen's (1966) work on Introversion-Extraversion and lung cancer. The particular instruments may no longer be available, or at best obscure, but the research findings may fit the patient and help both patient and therapist deal with the situation.

(6) Finally, a disease-specific inventory provides the most solid basis for a behavioral approach to medicine. It is a frequent clinical observation that patients who present with physical symptoms expect those symptoms to be directly addressed and respected. A typical individual is not likely to respond well to the insinuation that diseases of the body are manifestations of mental imbalance. Patients also do not react well when a psychiatrically based diagnostic (such as the MMPI) is administered without the explanation that it is to determine lifestyle patterns, *not* schizophrenia.

The instrument which evolved out of our need to understand the disease-specific response was the IMAGE-CA, which is described briefly below. Details of administration, normative data, reliabilities, rationale, and applications are discussed more completely in the manual accompanying the test (Achterberg & Lawlis, 1978).

In preliminary work, we administered a large battery of psychodiagnostics together with a blood chemistry assessment to a group of 126 cancer patients with a common diagnosis of incurable disease and approximately a 5% chance of five-year survival. Interestingly, factor analysis of these data indicated that psychological factors were the best predictors of two-month follow-up disease status, with something we termed as disease imagery being by far the most powerful predictor. Thus, we turned our focus toward the image variables and standardized the procedure for data collection, scoring, and interpretation. The imagery included a patient's attitude about three basic factors: the disease, treatment, and his/her ability to overcome the disease (i.e., immunological properties). The imagery of cancer is administered by having the patient initially listen to tape-recorded relaxation instructions, a prelude that appears necessary to induce and attend to body images. Following the relaxation information, a type of disease education is offered which informs the patient and instructs him/her to image or visualize tumors, immune system or white blood cell activity, and any current treatment. Following this guided, but nonprogrammed imagery, the patient is asked to draw these three factors. The aspects of the drawing are then elucidated in a structured interview which is comprised of such questions as "describe how your cancer cells look in your mind's eye," and "how do your white blood cells fight disease in your body?" The interview protocol, together with the drawings, are then scored on the basis of the 14 dimensions which include vividness of the cancer cell and white blood cell, activity of these two components, as well as perceived effectiveness of the treatment. Symbolism, reported frequency of images, imagery ability, and clinical impression of disease outcome are also scored. The weighted and summed total score reflects something we loosely call "quality of disease-related imagery," or the attitude or expectancy the patient holds regarding the disease process. More concretely, the score has been shown to predict state of health two months post-administration; it predicts the degree of establishment of the esophageal speech in laryngectomee patients and functional or rehabilitation qualities which involve return of range of motion and muscle strength in mastectomy patients at one-year post-administration.

The format for the test was derived after listening to approximately 200 cancer patient sessions during which the disease and treatment were discussed. Various attitudes and emotions were repeatedly brought up, and these clinically seem to be related to the patient's physical response. Then, two normalization studies were conducted. The first group of 58 patients with metastatic diagnoses were highly unusual in that they were exceptionally well educated and had chosen to receive a type of psychotherapy that included using relaxation and guided imagery in addition to medical treatment. The criterion variable for them, i.e., state of disease, was predicted with 93% accuracy for favorable prognoses and with 100% accuracy for unfavorable prognoses. A second normalization group was comprised of indigent, racially mixed patients who presented to a county hospital for treatment. The imagery, while certainly more difficult to elicit from this group, nevertheless proved a valid indicator of functionality.

Intervention. One of the questions most frequently asked of us is what we do, step-by-step, when we see a cancer patient? That very question at an American Psychological Association presentation provided the impetus for the current book. It may still go unanswered to some extent because of the state of the art and the necessity for many kinds of intervention, depending on the orientation of the therapist, the medical milieu encountered, and the patients involved. However, taking all these factors into consideration, we stress (1) a process of understanding the available information on psychological and medical aspects of cancer *before* taking on the responsibility of a cancer patient, (2) understanding the patient's belief systems, (3) providing a mechanism whereby the patient can explore or sample other mindstyles, (4) respecting whatever decision is made regarding the struggle for life, and (5) regarding the therapy as teaching rather than healing. To that end we offer whatever alternatives we ourselves have in our awareness, realizing that those we greet with the most enthusiasm are likely also to be those most appealing and effective for the patients. (A case in point is the finding by Taub (1977) that a biofeedback response could vary as little as 9% or as much as 80% in individual patients, depending upon whether the therapist believed in the treatment or not.) We also emphasize the responsibility faced by any teacher to keep up with new developments in the field, to present pros and cons, and to allow students (patients) to judge for themselves, in light of their own values, what they wish to accept or reject. They will do that anyway. Such a release from the need to control attitudes is an exhilarating experience for the therapist/teacher in and of itself. Forthwith, several composite cases are presented to illustrate our own method of intervention, based on the capacity of facilities and our pattern of referrals.

Case #1   Marge N. was a 46-year-old woman with breast cancer who called in for an appointment because she had heard that we were cancer researchers who might be able to help her. The disease had metastasized, but her condition was stable, and she was, for all practical purposes, in good health. An appointment was made, and, during the initial interview, she presented as a very psychologically aware woman who had been in a therapy group that used Gestalt techniques. She was also familiar with, and anxious to use, imaging techniques in order to feel more a participant in her return to health. She readily acknowledged that she had "let things get to her," including her own frustration that she had neglected her personal development. She and her husband were trying to redevelop some' common interests other than two children who were away at college, and they both wanted intensive professional help in restructuring their lives. She was very positive about the outcome of her treatment, based on IMAGE-CA testing. She was, in truth, an exciting and unusually well-motivated patient who would have been a delight to work with. However, in what we believed to be her own best interests, we referred her to an "Intervention Model." There she and her husband could spend an intensive week together with other patients having similar needs. We felt that she would benefit most from such an aggressive psychological approach.

Case #2   John H. was a private patient who chose to go to the medical school teaching hospital because he believed it more likely that he would receive expert treatment there. Diagnosed with malignant melanoma, he was 35 and a steamboat captain by trade. The first time we saw him, he was virtually incapacitated. He had massive infections around drainage tubes, and his doctors would find a new lump almost daily. Two metastasized tumors had been removed and a third was biopsied and found benign. We visited him for two days in a row, checking his progress and establishing a basis for a relationship. On the third day, our researcher, Ms. Harriett Gibbs, asked if he would be willing to listen to a tape of relaxation and mental imagery instructions, and then answer some questions. He agreed. He was left with a pencil and paper and asked to think about and draw how he saw his tumors and treatment, as well as his white blood cells or immune system. Within 48 hours he presented a magnificent series of drawings, further requesting that the tape and tape recorder be left there with him. Within a week he had improved enough to be released from the hospital. To our delight, he took full credit for his remarkable condition, stating that "attitude is everything." He also clipped articles from newspapers which discussed new protocols for treatment of his particular condition and shared these with his doctors. Subsequently, he was transferred to M. D. Anderson Hospital, where one of the treatment programs was ongoing. He received a very aggressive series of chemotherapy and immunotherapy, which he and other patients have appropriately called "Shake and Bake."

The drawings of his perceptions at the earliest stage of treatment, explained in the accompanying dialogue with Ms. Gibbs, are presented in Figures 4.1-4.7. A second series of drawings completed a year later for one of the authors, along with clinical impressions registered at that time, is presented in Figures 4.8-4.10 for comparison. We were never sure where he obtained his accurate information on the mode of action of his medications—and neither was he. He seemed to have pieced together odds and ends of comments into a coherent system. He apparently was the blithe spirit of the ward when he went for a treatment—encouraging, cheering. Even though he was receiving a type of chemotherapy that is noted for toxic side effects, he had none of the usual reactions such as excessive hair loss. His "Afro" got a little thinner, but not noticeably so. He had also convinced himself to keep food down during his nauseous days for at least three minutes to allow carbohydrates to digest. He felt this was necessary in order to keep his energy level high. He also *gained* weight during treatment. This most unusual patient was by no means psychologically oriented, and, therefore, discussions of mental participation in the development of disease would have been inappropriate. Nevertheless, he was strong, and he believed that his treatment was effective. More than that, he believed his own attitude kept him alive. He was also very opinionated and argued vehemently when we said his cancer cells were weak and confused. "Not mine," he said, "they are strong buggers, and need a strong treatment." We assumed this was a probable reason for his enthusiastic participation in the treatment itself. He stayed long enough to charm all the single women on our staff during his periodic visits at our clinic, and then would leave again. Last time we saw him, he said he was starting to "kick up his heels a little" and had decided to live a full life. Even in his worst days, though, he "lived." He would go fishing out in a heated barge on the lake and even drink a little beer out there. He never caught much in the way of fish, but felt that the activity helped somehow, just by staying involved in "well" behaviors.

John's Imagery
Dialogue with Harriett Gibbs

H: Describe these to me. (Figure 4.1)
J: This right here is the cancer cell.

Figure 4.1

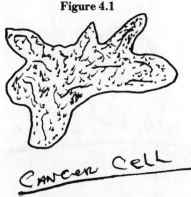

H: What are these black dots here?
J: The cells inside the cancer cells. These here, I don't know what that would be.
H: These arm things? Do they move?
J: Oh yes, all are movable.
H: Does it move right now?
J: All the time.
H: Does it travel?
J: Travels?
H: Can it go anywhere?
J: Of course. This would change to different shapes and sizes.
H: Like jelly?
J: Sure.
H: Does it have a color you associate with it?
J: No, no color.
H: When you were sitting there thinking about the tape, what did you see in your mind's eye?
J: Let me explain it to you this way. The cancer they found at the first surgery has roots and it will travel—it can travel anywhere. And the way I have in mind, mine traveled up this way.
H: Each little individual cell?
J: Yes. It also can be stored. It's stored away also. I believe this.
H: What is it made of? Is it gooey, jelly-like? Is it brittle?
J: No, it's like a blood cell to me. Kind of soft.
H: This changes shape?
J: Yes, it can. I believe when it moves it goes to a different shape.

H: Now tell me about the white blood cells. (Figure 4.2)
J: That's a white blood cell.

Figure 4.2

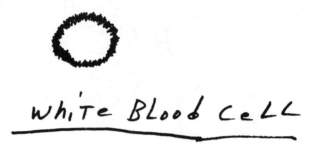

white Blood cell

H: Not scientifically, but what *you* see and what *you* feel.
J: It fights off your diseases and it attacks and kills your cancer cells, your viruses, leukemia, etc.
H: Is the cancer cell bigger than the white blood cell?
J: No, I wouldn't think so.
H: Do you think in your head that there are more white blood cells than cancer cells?
J: Yes, there are more white blood cells than cancer cells.
H: Describe what they look like, what they are made of, what color.
J: They would look like caviar. That is what I think.
H: Are they sticky?
J: I would not think so.
H: Are they colored?
J: I believe they would be white.
H: Whereas the cancer cells are clear?
J: Of the cancer cell, I would say it would be a brown. Yes, I think it would be more of a brown.
H: So these white blood cells are white, and there are more of them than the cancer cells, and they may be larger. What is the fuzzy edge to the cell?
J: That is the way I saw it, a long time ago.
H: Does it move?
J: Of course. It moves constantly all the time.
H: Does it go anywhere it wants to go?
J: Yes, I believe so. I believe it could be fast and slow.
H: How about yours?
J: Mine must be slow.

H: Now the picture down here, cancer of the lymph glands. Describe what this is for me. (Figure 4.3)

J: These are lymph glands here.

Figure 4.3

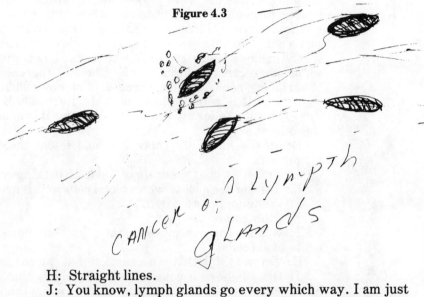

H: Straight lines.

J: You know, lymph glands go every which way. I am just drawing you a lymph gland. I believe these are little bitty cancers.

H: These black things?

J: Yes.

H: What are they doing here?

J: They are moving. Well, they are just going. I am saying that this is inside the lymph gland.

H: So they are just shooting along there?

J: Yes. Like little cells in your veins.

H: They look smaller here than this one here. (refer to Figure 4.1)

J: Yes, that is because this is a lymph gland.

H: What about the shape?

J: That's the way I see them moving. Something like a blood cell. I believe these move slowly.

H: When it's moving like this, is it a hard cell or a soft cell?

J: This is a hard cell here and a soft cell. Stored is hard.

H: Where are the white blood cells here?

J: I did not draw that. If it attacked all the little cells, it would come like this. (refer to Figure 4.2) I see the white blood cells; these are really smaller, and these (refer to Figure 4.1), larger, than the white blood cells. They (the white blood cells) surround them and they come in on the kill. I think it would be like a poison. I think that there would be a poisonous type stuff that smothers it out and stabs it.

H: Do they win?

J: Sure they win. That's the diagram right there (Figure 4.4) of what is happening under my arm. When I drew it this morning, I was not feeling too good; I sketched them out as best as possible. This is from my other surgery—when I had my first surgery. Here is my rib cage (at bottom), and this is just a small skin flapped over here. I believe it started up this way. I believe there are different spots. I believe there are some in here, too, and that is why I believe there are some up towards my neck. This is where it is at now. This is what I think it is. It is going to look like this. I actually believe it is this. The knot under my arm is one of them. It is enlarged, like this other one.

H: In the knot, are there a whole lot of these, or just bigger ones?

J: Yes, it's a conglomerate of these little things right here.

H: Do you see a lot of white blood cells in this area?

J: Well, no, . . . no, I don't.

H: How come?

J: I think the cancer cells have won out more than the white blood cells.

H: Do you think that is a situation that can change?

J: Oh, I believe it could change. I believe that the white blood cells—with the treatment and everything—if you remove the main source, I believe your metabolism. . .the white blood cells, I believe they will take over and start on the job. They are the soldiers in armor. . .the infantry for us.

H: Do you see them as infantry? How come you did not draw soldiers?

J: Well, I don't know.

H: Isn't that funny? We had a client once who drew an army of white knights fighting an army of black knights. That's what he saw.

J: I saw mine in medical terms.

Figure 4.4

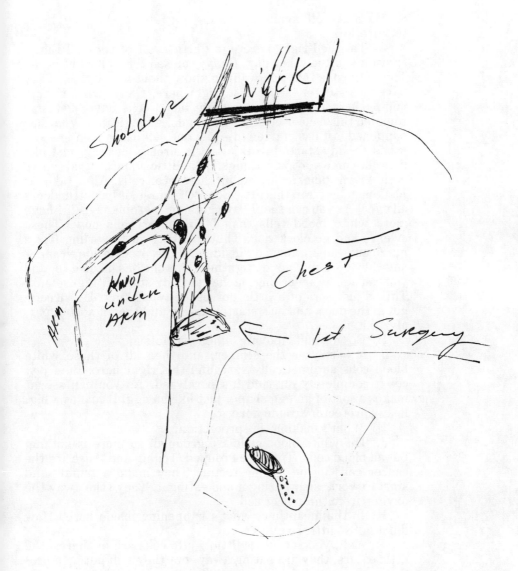

Imagery — 5 days later

H: Start off again by telling me about this cell here. (Figure 4.5)

J: This cell right here is a particle off of the cell that I showed you the other day. Okay, you see this cell right here? This is the one that you want to know about how it dies. They have this stinger, as I call it, right here. Okay, what is happening here is all of these white blood cells have just surrounded this cancer cell like a tornado, a hurricane. What has happened is it has started in—just one cell has gotten in—and it has already started working. It is already healing, just like little lawnmower-type things, just little mouths that go to eating right quick, chewing up the cancer cells. All it takes is just one to get into this little door. Of course, it has little doors all over. As you can see, I have got more; I think myself I have more white blood cells than I do cancer cells now. These swerve and go clockwise. They are both just swirling like a hurricane—one a tornado inside and the other a hurricane—and they both just get on fighting. This one has made it in, and you can see he's working, he has already started (Figure 4.6). This is just sort of a little horseshoe-type thing. He already got in the door, and he's started eating and then it sort of paralyzes it.

H: So this quits moving, when one gets in.

J: It paralyzes the stinger, and then all of these white blood cells automatically surround this right here; they just cut it completely off, and it's paralyzed. As you can see, it makes a sort of an egg shape, just like an egg. It makes a big, heavy protector around here.

H: What's making this protection?

J: The white blood cells are grouped, so there is nothing but all blood cells. They are grouped around, and these are the cancer cells inside the protector. They make a bubble and start to work; smothering it and eating it. They take away the oxygen from the cancer cell.

H: In the meantime, what's happening inside here? How did it get so little so quick?

J: Well, you see, your little white cells are in there—the little eaters, they are eating away, but they still put up a protector. Because it [the cancer cell] is so great, because this is so dangerous, they have to put it in a tube—like an egg—to keep it from going anywhere while they finish it off.

H: Yesterday you were describing how that looks, how that happens so quickly, and you said it was sort of like acid.

J: I still see acid, like you might take a test tube and put a drop of acid on there, and it starts eating. Just eat, eat, eat, eat. If you put a drop of acid on there, it would just start eating it away. It's melting away; it's forming a jelly on your stingers. These little stingers here are automatically

Figure 4.5

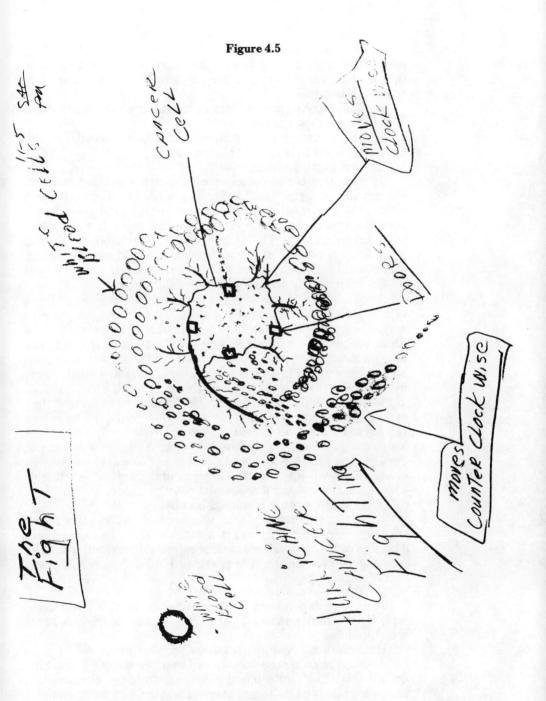

paralyzed, and, as you see in the next one, it is the same thing—it is just getting smaller and smaller. . .they are paralyzed. . .eating away.

H: This barrier here seems to be getting darker, thicker. What's happening here?

J: This is giving more protection. In other words, it still don't [sic] want to let any particle out.

H: Is it getting stronger?

J: Yes, this is the stronger one. But it's getting smaller; the smaller it gets, the harder it gets. Like a muscle or a clamp, the more that it works, the harder it would get. Then it gets down to the next one: very rigid; just thick, like muscle— we'll say muscle. Well, I would think that it would be like some kind of plaster of Paris. I think it would get that hard, that it would be something like plaster of Paris.

H: Is there any chance of that breaking open?

J: No. That's the reason they formed this plaster of Paris type stuff around this; that's the reason it is not going to give way. It forms one complete, say, plaster of Paris with all of these white blood cells surrounding it. But you even have your backup men inside here, just in case. And then you have your men in here working—your little eaters. They are inside here, but this is a three-stage type of thing. It takes that much to get this little thing down; I call it the little devil. And see, they even get closer in this shell, or whatever you want to call it. It's harder here, and it really makes it real hard, and it just keeps on, just smothering him to death. And this goes on and goes out the final stage, and it's just going to go. It will be discharged. It will go to your kidneys, and they screen it out. This is the trap where it screens it out right here.

H: Is there ever a chance this could fail?

J: No, it won't fail. Once this barrier makes the round capsule—I would rather call it a capsule—this will never fail. This one can, though. This cancer cell could win, but after the white blood cells once get in there and build this, it will never fail; it will always win.

H: Does the cancer win very often?

J: It only depends on if you can help it [white blood cells] win. If you think positive all the time. . .look at me now, how well I'm doing.

H: You're not seeing any failure in this right now.

J: No, I'm doing too good to say that the cancer is working on me now. The white blood cells are working, of course. It takes a while for this to get there; they have to work one at a time.

H: They are attacking your tumor, one particle at a time?

J: Right. As you would see back here on the other drawing, this is the original cell. This is the original cancer, and

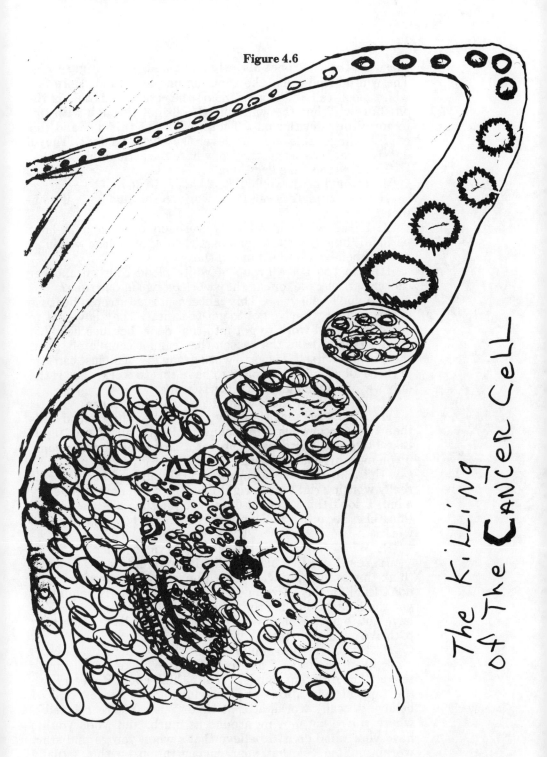

Figure 4.6

The killing of the Cancer Cell

these are the same ones in the lymph glands here (Figure 4.7). The white blood cells take them on one at a time. Here is a white blood cell and it goes inside the cancer cell; this is the one I drew. When the white blood cells get through with this in here, they get this one. Then they'll get this one and this one, they'll get this one—however they want to do it. They'll do whatever they want; they go where the action's at.

H: Does this take very long?

J: I would say it would take 24 hours to do it.

H: So your eaters can go to work on this and have it completely out?

J: If the white blood cells were doing it in a 24-hour period, I think it can take one particle of that cancer within 24 hours; I believe it can eat one of these up.

H: Can you get a group of white blood cells on another cancer particle, too, or can they work on two at one time?

J: I don't believe so. This cancer cell is so strong, because of this stinger, they've got to get to it first. They have got to surround it and work to get into that door, because he's just going so fast. That's the reason they cannot completely go at the whole cell itself. It has to work gradually. You just can't go in there all at once. You have to have this to work; that is the only way, in my mind, that it has to work.

H: Do you have more white blood cells than these?

H: At the present time, I've got more white blood cells than I do cancer cells. I'm feeling real good about this fight. Like I told you yesterday, I've got a new knot that has come up on me; this could go away too. It could go away, but like I say, this [the process] is working on this surgery here. This is really working right here, right now. This will never leave my mind; I don't think I could draw you another picture of anything else because I believe this is the only way that it could work.

H: When you think of the cancer, do you see this?

J: Yes, I do. I've planted this in my mind to see it, and I think this is the only way you will ever help yourself. If you don't think of this, if you don't think something is helping, if you think negative all of the time, you will never make it. You have got to have will power; you have got to have something to thrive on, and that will kill it.

H: Do you do this regularly?

J: With the tapes I use for relaxation. Like I say, during the day I do different things. I really think about it when I use the tape of relaxation—the chewing of the cancer cells. I believe it really works at that time. When you're relaxed— where you're not moving around as much, and when you do have your mind on it, I believe that's when you go and start working. You feel that your concentration on this actually helps to fight. If you did not think that it would work, it would never work. If you think sick long enough, you will be sick. If you think this is killing, it will kill it. It will get it; it's going to be there to get it, and nothing ever will change my mind.

Figure 4.7

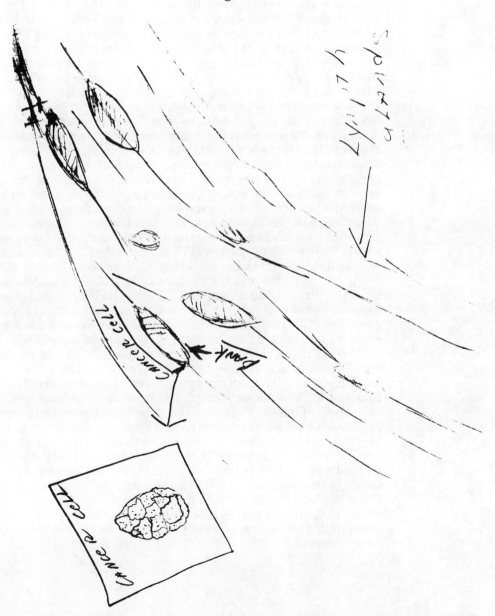

John H.,
Clinical Notes   May, 1977

John maintains that his cancer cells are embedded in the cavity like a tooth. They are surrounded by three and possibly four walls. We all have cancer cells like this, he says, but the difference between his and other people's is that his move around and therefore need to be destroyed. Chemotherapy breaks down these walls surrounding the cancer cell like "dynamite." He said they are extremely powerful acting in his system and that is the reason that the drug makes him so nauseous. The chemotherapy acts as a helper for the white blood cells, but in most people the white blood cells will take care of the problem. He needs a "little kick." The top drawing (Figure 4.8a) is enlarged significantly. The smaller insert (Figure 4.8b) more closely reflects what he believes to be the actual size of the cancer, the white blood cells, and the chemotherapy. He said he simply enlarged the cancer cell in order to show details. On this drawing are shown both the droplets of chemotherapy and the white blood cells. The chemotherapy, as with his past descriptions, enters the cavity in a counter-clockwise direction. The cancer cell moves in a clockwise direction. On the cancer cell are small doors. The chemotherapy droplets must enter those doors, and once they do, that is the end of the cancer cell. This is really a very beautiful description of the mode of action of cytotoxins. Once the chemotherapy gets into the cancer cell, it kills it by attacking all of the little capsules inside of it. What he describes as the capsules could well be nuclei, mitrochondria, etc. When I told John that the task that he had set out for himself was in reality a lot simpler than he made it, he did not believe me. I told him that the cancer cells were really confused and weak, and that was the reason they were so susceptible to the chemotherapy. He really did not accept that explanation. I told him to think about it for a couple of days and we would talk about it later. I asked John if he thought he had any control over his white blood cells and his chemotherapy action. He said that yes, it was all mental and that the response that he was having was the result of a positive attitude. He began to recite stories of people at M.D. Anderson on the same protocol who had died rapidly. He reiterated that it was all in the attitude. I also asked him if he went through a process of seeing the action of the chemotherapy and he said yes he went through this when he was lying in bed and the medication was being injected.

Figure 4.8

a.

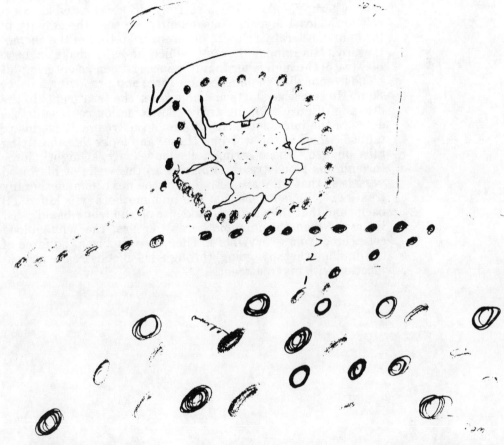

b.

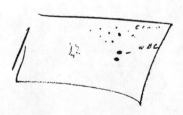

John's protocol for malignant melanoma (metastatic) involves a complicated series of immunotherapy, followed by chemotherapy, followed by a resting period repeated at intervals for at least a year. Consequently, he sees the activity of the immunotherapy as quite different from that of the chemotherapy. His immunotherapy, which he calls shake 'n bake because of the high fever that it induces is seen as entering his bloodstream with an unbelievable force and producing a fierce fight. He says this starts one hour after the treatment. In the drawing (Figure 4.9), the arrow-like depiction represents the entry of the immunotherapy in his bloodstream. It begins to diffuse (which is the word he chose) and looks like the string tails on fish. These string tails move with a mighty force through his bloodstream, adhering to the walls of his blood vessels so that they are active until the next immunotherapy treatment. He is aware that the immunotherapy is killed TB bacilli and that they activate and stir up the white blood cells. He says when the immunotherapy enters, the white blood cells come from everywhere. Then, he visualizes the force of the immunotherapy going through his bloodstream in conjunction with his treatment.

Figure 4.9

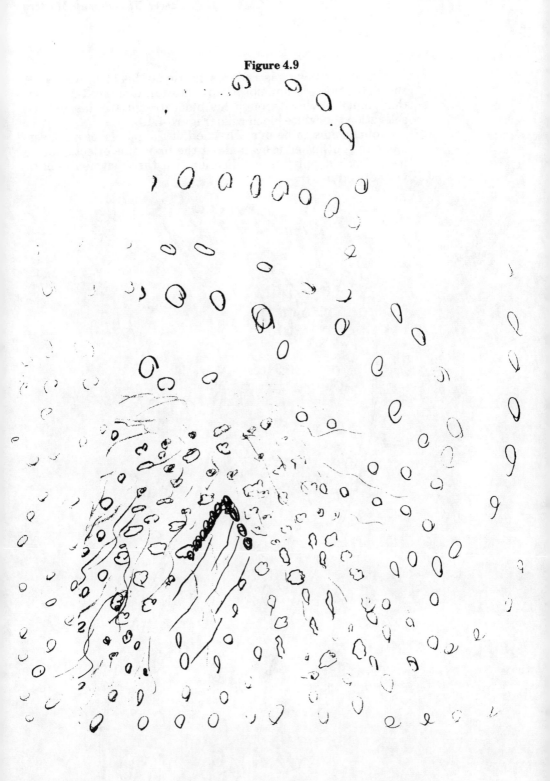

The final drawing is a representation of his blood vessel. It shows the tide of immunotherapy (most of it string-tail-like at this point) moving through his bloodstream stirring up and activation the white blood cells (Figure 4.10).

John seems to be overwhelmed at the power of his treatment and enthusiastic even about the toxic side effects, for he feels that is simply more indication that the treatment will be very effective.

Figure 4.10

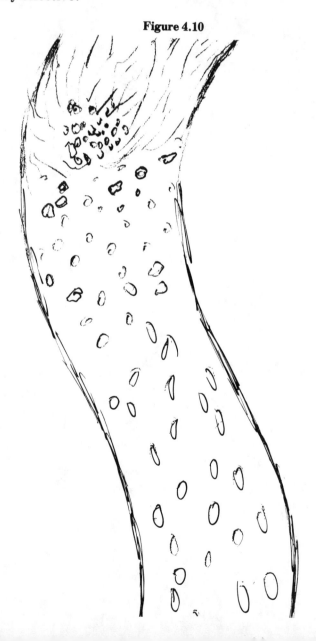

Our interactions with him, after his first desperate days, were primarily of a supportive nature. We feel we assisted him in finding a path for a return to health, but, beyond that initial effort, his own ego strength was sufficient for the task at hand. He has been *our* teacher, as a matter of fact, supplying us with words and concepts that help in the translation of medical information to patients.

Case #3 Al F. was another patient who was referred to our county teaching hospital for a special treatment/experimental protocol. He was diagnosed with glioblastoma—a brain tumor that carries a grim prognosis: an 18-month survival is anticipated for only 10% of all patients. Typically, treatment involves surgery to remove as much of the mass as possible, and then radiation is conducted. The treatment for Al, however, involved the use of his own immune capabilities. Blood was taken at intervals, and then the white blood cells were infused through a pump implanted in his skull. Al was 37, married to a lovely, supportive woman, and had within the last two years risen in his company to district manager. It was somewhat of an Andy Hardy story in that he had not received any education beyond high school, and his professional status was attributed to his own determination. He had been turned down four times for the position and was accepted on the fifth bid. He was a "most pleasant fellow," we all agreed. The nurses adored him because he never complained or argued, and was one of the few patients we have had who insisted on hearing how *our* day had been before doing much talking about himself.

Due to either his brain tumor, the medication or edema, he was experiencing some memory loss. A referral was therefore made to do psychological testing. He was tested using the WAIS and the MMPI, among other things. Despite a left hemisphere lesion, he had no speech problems and all but visual-motor functions appeared intact. His memory loss was definitely exacerbated by tension and fear of losing a faculty, and there were other indications that anxiety was an ever-present problem (i.e., sleeplessness, ruminating over upcoming treatment).

Biofeedback was recommended, and portable units were taken to his bedside. Autonomic relaxation appeared to be indicated, so he was asked to listen to relaxation instructions and then to begin to practice elevating his temperature. He was remarkably good at this task and said he he imagined being in his boat in the summer. Four weeks after our first encounter, he called from his room and said elatedly that the tumor was *gone*, that he "saw" it exit in a cone shape during his radiation. Our reaction was mixed: shared joy with him because of beliefs that patients do have these experiences, and they do have substance, and concern that he would crash emotionally if tests revealed the tumor's continued presence.

He was administered the IMAGE-CA on a Wednesday, shortly thereafter. His protocol reiterated that he refused to consider any further remaining cancer cells and that the white blood cells never did have a part in his treatment, while surgery and radiation had been effective. This had been a pattern, in that when asked each day how his WBCs were doing, he would avoid answering. Instead, he would discuss how the radiation was pouring in and killing the cancer cells. He was given beautifully clear pictures of macrophages in action, articles and tape recordings—all emphasizing immunology. He was shown other patients' drawings that he quite accurately assessed as being good or not good. But as far as changing his own conceptions, all the information truly fell on nonreceptive ears.

By Thursday he had developed meningitis from an infection around the infusion pump, seizured, and became paralyzed in the right upper half of his body. At this point, he and his wife were pleading for answers: "To continue or not to continue the treatment?" They both insisted the doctors ignored them whenever they asked how many people had survived the painful, experimental procedure. (No adult, by that date, *had* survived.) They claimed that they had never even been given statistical information on life expectancy for the particular site of malignancy. We encouraged them to ask repeatedly until they got answers with which they felt comfortable and to call in the trusted family doctor who referred them initially. Because Al was on Neurology, a service that was neither affiliated with our own service nor particularly craved our advice, the primary physician's intentions for the patient had to be respected.

After we were assured by the nurse that the patient *had* been given answers, we backed off—finding ourselves once again in a moral dilemma. To encourage him to continue in a treatment that debilitated him, was totally experimental, and in which he had no faith (indeed, felt "trapped" and helpless by his lack of understanding) violated our humanistic principles. Support for the opposite approach, i.e., "demand answers," "you have the right to the disposition of your own body," etc., would have assured us of never being allowed contact with another patient on that ward, and probably a severe and long-standing reprimand as well. (The participants in the Cancer Rehabilitation Demonstration Program had encountered a similar situation with another service which resulted in team members being barred from patient contact. Many cancer patients were denied access to the services of the Rehabilitation program because of the misunderstanding.)

We had encountered the medical model and temporarily lost the battle. Yet, the patient was in many respects like John in the preceding case: same age, so-called "incurable" disease, experimental treatment, same hospital. The difference was that John, unlike Al, "knew" all the answers—at least to his own satisfaction. He gleaned information from all his treaters, sorted and stored a remarkably accurate picture of both disease and treatment. He was not falsely positive; he knew he had a bad disease and would have a powerful and continuing fight with the aid of a treatment he trusted. Both John and Al had been told that treatment might go on the rest of their lives. In one of our sessions, Al stated that if it increased his chances for life only 30% it wasn't worth it. John, on the other hand, said he would do anything to stay alive.

Case #4   The final case was a 55-year-old woman, Florence L., who was seen as a charity patient. Ten months before we interviewed her in the clinic, she had a brain tumor partially resected. No other treatment was ever given because of the critical nature of the diagnosis. Prior to her admission, she had had several seizures, but had refused hospitalization for several weeks. Her 13-year-old son, with whom she lived, slept on the foot of her bed to watch over her. One of our researchers was doing an internship on the ward when Florence was finally admitted. She said Florence looked closer to death than anyone she had ever seen. From someplace the patient garnered strength, though, and pulled through. A recent CT (computer tomography) scan (two years postdiagnosis) did not reveal a trace of tumor, even though part of the mass had remained after resection. Her only residual effect is a mild paralysis in one leg. Otherwise, her doctors have told her she functions as if she never had a tumor at all.

Our interaction with her was to coordinate with the physical therapist (PT), using EMG biofeedback for muscle reeducation of her weak leg. It was an ideal situation: after the PT demonstrated which muscles were involved, we applied electrodes in such a way as to read microvolts of current as those muscles were contracted in the prescribed exercises. This procedure freed the PT and gave this most self-sufficient patient a treatment in line with her own thinking. She was also introduced to imaging; she was asked to mentally imagine those muscles working like they did previously and to see herself working and climbing stairs without the aid of a cane. Our purpose was to have her mentally rehearse the use of muscle groups—an exercise used by professional athletes in most sports.

She volunteered the information that she'd been seeing herself dancing again (which actually did come to pass several months later), and that she would like to marry again (which has not yet occurred!). She also stated that she knew precisely how much return of function she would have and what her gait would look like when she reached that point.

This lady stood out dramatically in our charity facility. Despite the fact that she had spent her younger years doing manual labor in the cotton fields, she was attractive, had pretty grey hair and unlined skin. She set goals for herself which we encouraged and respected. This last year these included planning an organic garden, planting, and harvesting it. No great psychological insight was ever verbalized, nor was any abiding religious faith expressed. Her close and continued relationship with her son was probably the most important aspect of her life. She was simply a strong and determined woman who conquered life again.

Lifestyle
Implications Every cancer patient has a story—the tale of the most formidable battle an individual ever encounters. An arch-enemy that attacks in the night, forewarns of death, sometimes "just when things are starting to go well." It causes what may be the very first encounter a patient may have with the ultimate destiny. Unlike wars or plagues, it is conceptually a disease from within, a failure of one's own body to protect itself; cannabalistic, eating oneself alive, confounded with treatment killing from the outside in. The severity of the conflict commands respect and reflection on the messages that the disease transmits. The charade of applying treatments to the lesion without acknowledging that cancer, psychologically, may well be the most important and devastating event in one's life, does the patient an injustice.

The fact that cancer is not respectable confounds the issue. One has only to visit the cardiac or thoracic units, observe the patients, and compare them to those in the oncology division to realize the difference in desirability of diagnosis. Cardiac patients may even be rather proud of the condition—battle scars from a life of stress and strife, ambition, and determination (all solid Yankee virtues). The cancer patient, on the other hand, appears somewhat ashamed of the diagnosis, almost like VD, it's something to shield from families and friends and colleagues. As Susan Sontag in *Illness as Metaphor* cites in a context describing cancer:

> Contact with someone afflicted with a disease regarded as a mysterious malevolency inevitably feels like a trespass; worse, like the violation of a taboo.

and

> Thus, a surprisingly large number of people with cancer
> find themselves being shunned by relatives and friends
> and are the object of practices of decontamination by
> members of the household, as if cancer, like TB, were an
> infectious disease.

On the other hand, for every patient who has expressed
the difficulty of living with the shame of the taboo—the "night
side of life" as Sontag puts it—there is at least another patient
who contemplates a positive message from the illness in the
broader scheme of things. This kind of attribution, believing
in some metaphysical principle that allows cancer to mean
something good, releases the patient from the victim's role.
That role can make the patient feel as if he or she were
attacked mercilessly without rhyme or reason. The attribution of a message to illness gives reason and hope that, once
the message has been learned, one can move beyond illness
into another state of awareness. Some of the possible
"messages" are described below.

New Lifestyle Messages. Most typical, perhaps, was a breast
cancer patient with organ metastasis, Joyce. Prior to her
diagnosis, she was feeling burgeoning pressures from her
career as a media specialist, and an on-again, off-again lover.
To her, cancer was a red flag that signaled "stop—change
directions—your life is killing you," much as a heart patient
may perceive a CVA. She began to resolve many issues, in
particular, the role difficulties which are inevitably present
when a woman becomes a top executive with many men in her
employ. Her problem with her lover was resolved when they
made love for the first time after her mastectomy. He left,
saying he could not handle the disfigurement. She has since
learned to manage the sensitive situation of the surgery with
potential lovers by first explaining her condition, and then by
leaving her bra on during love-making, unless her partner
requests otherwise. The first disheartening and abrupt
departure has never been repeated. She continued to feel that
she had made many valuable changes in lifestyle that she
would not have had courage to enact under any other circumstances, and that those changes have, in essence, saved her
life.

We are convinced that this kind of dramatic attitude and
lifestyle change may have the same physiological effect as a
so-called miracle cure from a seemingly inert treatment. (See
Klopfer (1957), for a discussion of a patient who remissed on
water injections because he believed they were a potent new

cancer cure, Krebiozin. He died within weeks after his beliefs were shattered by FDA reports repudiating the effect of the drug.)

Working with patients who identify messages in disease has a very potent effect on the therapist, particularly when those messages lead to desirable changes in lifestyle. In fact, we ask ourselves why people so frequently must wait until life appears to be over before gaining courage to examine and change the cares and responsibilities that have made them despair for so long.

Self-Punitive Messages. Other messages, which are less positive than Joyce's, include lessons from God to have more patience, to better understand the suffering of humanity, or to punish for long-ago "sins." Diseases of the primary or secondary sexual organs are likely to lead to the latter type of thinking.

Missionary Messages. A third type of message involves the interpretation that cancer has provided a second chance to lead a productive life. This opportunity is often fulfilled through helping other cancer patients to adjust. The "Reach to Recovery," "One Day at a Time," the "United Ostomy Association," and other volunteer agencies are populated with members who express this mission.

The first and last of the three messages, "New Lifestyle" and "Missionary," have in common behaviors which generally involve increased or redirected energy, and patients feel good about their enhanced productivity. The Self-Punitive Messages seem to be correlated with a more passive disposition and patients who give in or give up. In our interviews with dying charity patients, this attitude was occasionally associated with what now is popularly called a "good death"— one which was part of a divine plan and which was somehow deserved, with suffering to be expected and accepted.

We have found that early inquiry into the meanings of cancer within the patient's framework of causal and reactive events can be important for our understanding of their value system. It has also appeared to be important for the patient to mull over this issue and then verbalize it in a noncritical atmosphere. All patients we have interviewed, regardless of socioeconomic or intellectual status, have responded thoughtfully to this question. A useful response, it seems, is to ask those people who identify a lesson in punitive terms whether they must, in fact, maintain poor health in order to learn the lesson sufficiently, or whether they cannot once again pursue health with vigor and a new understanding.

Secondary Gains. The gains which occur from the loss of health may be greater from cancer than from any other disease. It is usually considered a death sentence which carries with it some time: time to forgive and to give, on the part of the patient as well as friends and relatives. The latter do just that—rallying with flowers, attention, and the visits we seem to crave from our children as a token of love and appreciation. For many people who have worked hard all their lives, or who may be feeling alienated from the mainstream of living, the benefits of the sick role may be overwhelming. In confronting this issue, we straddle the same kind of moral issue as when indigent, healthy patients seeking disability settlements from the state so they can quit working, ask us for assistance in making claims. Similarly, dilemmas arise when a large settlement is sought for an accident claim, not out of anger or actual loss, but because the money will solve some misery that faces the victim. Thus, the illness and its encumbent gains soothe a misery. Can the counselor suggest an adequate and rational replacement for disease which will permit the patient to reap the same benefits?

Major life changes may be required after a diagnosis of cancer. The therapist may well have to take more responsibility for suggesting and directing these changes than a more reflective type of psychotherapy would allow. Women who have the "empty-nest" syndrome—a prime time for cancer of the breast to be diagnosed—may have to develop new paths of emotional and intellectual growth. Men who are one or two years past retirement (also a common time for diagnosis of serious disease, regardless of age) may need to find new outlets for energy. It is a common clinical observation that when emotional and intellectual growth ceases, when creative processes halt, malignancy—which itself is a growth process—occurs, as in these lines from W. H. Auden's (1940) "Miss Gee":

> Childless women get it
> And men when they retire;
> it's as if there had to be some outlet
> For their foiled creative fire.

If creative pursuits are renewed, will the disease remiss? If new objects of affection are identified early in the mourning period after the loss of a spouse, will the individual escape the increased risk of dying from cancer during this period?

The secondary gains and loss aspects might be dealt with in the following sequence:

(1) Identify precursive conditions (through stress inventory or interview). Determine what kind of life the patient has led for two to three years prior to diagnosis.

(2) Identify, with the patient's assistance, the consequences of the disease; i.e., what changes have occurred both positively and negatively since diagnosis.

(3) Ascertain what behavioral changes would be required in order to maintain the positive (or secondary gain) aspects of being ill in the absence of the illness.

(4) Determine if a loss has occurred recently (either of a job, or a spouse, or children leaving, or retirement) and whether there is a reasonable path to replacement of that event or individual that could renew the patient's interest in staying alive.

We, as researchers and therapists, hopefully have grown past the conception that the study and treatment of cancer patients should be predominantly focused upon them as dying patients. The idea that their needs more frequently revolve around issues of living, not dying, presents a very different type of picture for study. It includes vocational counseling (a very rare and minimally funded area in cancer treatment), because old jobs may no longer be appropriate. The salesman with a laryngectomy has a very good chance of survival, but will have to learn a new vocation. Sexual counseling also becomes important, because sexual activity is a very fine indicator of how well the patient has returned to an active life and how good one feels about oneself. Life counseling, then, is vital. Even patients who ultimately die from the disease may live 5 or 10 years—years that can be the most productive and insightful years of a lifetime.

We advise all counselors in this field to become familiar with survival statistics (*End Results Tables*, HEW, *Cancer Prognosis Manual*, American Cancer Society, etc.). The interactions with a patient two months past a diagnosis of cancer of the pancreas would obviously be different from those with a woman diagnosed as Stage I or II breast cancer with no node involvement (the former's life expectancy is calculated in months, whereas the latter stands a 60% chance of living at least 10 years with no recurrence). It avoids the pitfall that one of our colleagues faced in designing a research project, using biofeedback for skin disorders. She had obtained permission to study skin cancer patients, but chose psoriasis instead because "Cancer is so heavy." Paradoxically, at that time, medicine was much more effective for skin cancer than on stubborn psoriasis. By the same token, counseling a stabilized Stage II Hodgkins Disease patient on self-image is probably more appropriate than assisting with a last will and testament. Consultation with the treating physician on these matters can be a determinant of the approach which should be used. However, if that is unsatisfactory or unavailable, the Tables mentioned above can be readily obtained and understood.

One final issue in regard to psychological intervention with cancer patients is whether or not to accept patients who have chosen to remove themselves from all medical intervention and wish to use "mental approaches" alone. Because of the relationship and communication that we believe is necessary with the medical community, and because psychological interventions offer at best a remote hope for recovery in their current stage of development, accepting such a patient has generally seemed unwise. Such decisions are often not without qualms and grief, however; particularly as we become aware of the negligible results of many protocols and as we see suffering from side-effects that obliterates all quality of existence, offering as a trade-off only a few weeks or months of life.

The private practitioner who does not choose to work in alliance with the medical profession, nor particularly needs physician sanction in order to function professionally, will still be faced with moral and ethical dilemmas in accepting and counseling patients who chose an alternative path. The dilemma is certainly not confined to cancer patients, although perhaps psychological interventions in that disease represent the most significant departure from traditional psychosomatic thought. Perplexities have arisen and will continue to increase in logarithmic fashion as we cross the boundaries of practice into physical disease. The professionals involved in health and disease will have to undergo significant self-examination in terms of roles and rights as health-care providers and face the ultimate responsibility for consequences of treatment. These areas of moral and ethical conduct are very, very grey.

Professional and public opinion is changing in regard to what constitutes adequate health care. The paradigm is shifting noticeably. Yet, guidance, and resolution of such central issues as who can offer what service to whom, under what circumstances, and with what expected outcome are not merely articles for endless debate. They require empirical tests. The fruitful methodologies for this kind of clinical research will no doubt need to be as nontraditional as the subject matter itself. We are no longer referring to the analysis of tissues, or blood, or cultures; we are concerned rather with total functioning human beings and with strategies that recognize and treat the many components of living. (Some suggestions for collecting and examining data of this kind are offered in the final chapter of this book.)

If cancer is really a disease of lifestyle, then behavioral specialties may have a broader and more exciting role than ever previously contemplated. The results of what has been termed the largest human biological study of life and death have recently been reported by the American Cancer Society at their annual meetings in New York. After a study of 20 years' duration—encompassing material from 1,000,000 subjects—it appears that behaviors are indeed vitally linked to cancer. Among the findings: (1) cigarette smoking (to no one's surprise) has been linked to many sites of cancer, not just lung; (2) obesity has been correlated to cancer of the uterus and ovaries in women, and colorectal and prostate in men; (3) statistical links were noted between "feelings" of fatigue and uneasiness (the nearest approximation, unfortunately, to psychological factors included in the study) and high cancer death rates. *All* of these behaviors have been well researched and treated using sound psychological principles in contexts other than cancer. For instance, hypnosis, relaxation and imagery, behavior modification, aversive conditioning, as well as a host of strategies for communicating, educating, and otherwise influencing attitude change, have been utilized with the cancer-correlated behaviors reported by the American Cancer Society. The potential for involvement in intervention and the efficacy of psychological applications pales by comparison to this expanded vista of the impact which the behavioral sciences could have on promoting freedom from this disease.

CHAPTER V

DIABETES MELLITUS
Learning to Think for an Organ

Physical Aspects of
Diabetes Mellitus Diabetes mellitus is a metabolic disorder which
occurs when the islets of Langerhans in the pancreas produce
an inadequate supply of insulin. The result is an increase in
excretion of urine, a high blood sugar level, and increased
urine sugar levels. Insulin causes the cells of the body to take
in sugar, or glucose, where it is converted into energy. The
liver normally stores glucose in the form of a carbohydrate
called glycogen, which is released into the blood when needed.
However, in the diabetic, an insulin lack results in low storage
of glycogen. Consequently, sugar is not taken into the liver
and other areas where it is needed. Instead, the blood sugar
level is high, and much sugar is excreted in the urine. Since
the body is unable to use glucose, it begins to burn fats and
proteins. When this process occurs, various poisons such as
ketones are released into the blood, which can eventually
result in coma and death. Insulin is often used to balance the
process and allow the liver and other cells to absorb the
needed sugar (Guyton, 1971).

According to the American Diabetes Association, diabetes
is the third cause of death in the U.S. and the leading cause of
new cases of blindness. Circulatory problems, kidney failure,
and higher vulnerability to infection are more likely to occur in
the diabetic. Although the physiological mechanisms are well
understood, the etiology of diabetes remains unclear. Heredi-
tary predisposition has been shown to be a factor in some
cases (MacDonald, 1974). The disease has also been linked to a
viral etiology (Nelson & Pyke, 1975), as well as obesity
(Alexander, 1950).

Stress and
Diabetes Since the endocrine system has been shown to be
involved in stress-related diseases, it seems plausible that
diabetes may also be influenced by psychological factors.
Slawson, Flynn, and Kollar (1963) suggested that precipita-
tion of diabetes was related to grief, depression, and object
loss. Hinkle and Wolf (1952a) stated that ketosis was produced
in severe diabetics as a result of stressful interviews. Even

nondiabetics can experience glycosuria, or an excess of blood sugar, when they feel fear or anxiety (Cannon, 1934). However, "the diabetic is metabolically vulnerable to stress to a degree varying roughly with the degree of insulin dependence" (Weiner, M., 1977).

What part stress may play in the onset of the disease and how it may be effectively managed are important considerations. Weiner (1977) states that anxiety may produce higher degrees of hyperglycemia in diabetics than in normal persons because the diabetics have a dysfunctional compensatory insulin response.

Other researchers suggest there is a relationship between diabetes onset and stressful life situations, and there may be certain psychological factors that lead to the development of the disease as well. In this regard, Lachman (1972) suggests diabetes may develop following *repeated* exposure to emotionally stressful situations. Physiologically, he proposes that the emotional response induces autonomic activation of the adrenal glands, stimulating liver breakdown of glycogen and, consequently, leading to a depletion of the liver-stored carbohydrates.

An earlier investigator, Alexander (1950), postulated the theory of "specificity" in relation to psychosomatic illnesses. This theory proposes that there are certain physiological responses to every emotion. Further, either an attitude of fight or flight accompanies an anxiety-producing situation. Concerning the sympathetic nervous system, Alexander (1950) suggested that diabetes may be related to unexpressed aggression and hostility. These unexpressed emotions lead to sustained sympathetic excitation that is not consummated in a flight or fight behavioral reaction.

Observing two diabetic patients from a psychodynamic perspective, Meyer, Bollmeier, and Alexander (1945) concluded that both had a strong need to have someone take care of them. When these dependency needs were not met, the patients reacted in a hostile manner. Diabetes then developed when these infantile wishes conflicted with the demands that were frustrated. Alexander (1950) noted that, in this case study, "withdrawal from the conflict into self-pity and passivity was associated with a decrease in glycosuria." (p. 198)

Hinkle, Evans, and Wolf (1951) and Hinkle and Wolf (1952b) also determined that diabetes onset often occurs during times of significant life stress. Agreeing with these findings, Grant, Kyle, Teichman, and Mendels (1971) describe the relationship between undesirable life events and a diabetic condition. Stein and Charles (1975) also recognized that stressful life situations affect the development of juvenile diabetes and observed: "Significant incidence of loss and severe family disturbance prior to the diagnosed onset of the disease was found, as compared with a group of chronically ill adolescents suffering from heritable blood diseases" (p. 238). Coming to similar conclusions, Hinkle, Evans, and Wolf (1951) found that insulin requirements for the juvenile diabetic tended to drop as family and marital distress was removed.

It has long been recognized that the hormones epinephrine, glucagon, and cortisol can interact and interfere with the production or the action of insulin. While these hormones are known to be elevated during stressful situations, the precise mechanism by which the hormones together may be related to the onset of stress diabetes has not yet been elucidated. However, Dr. Philip Felig, in an interview with a writer for *Diabetes Forecast* (Hoover, 1978), offered information on new research being conducted on this topic in his laboratory at the Yale-New Haven Hospital. The research team, sponsored by Felig and directed by Dr. Robert Sherwin, is involved in the production and reversal of stress diabetes in nondiabetics via an "hormonal cocktail" containing the three above-mentioned hormones. It is hoped that by studying the hormonal combinations that precipitate the disorder the occurrence of diabetes might be prevented.

Previous studies have revealed that emotional stress can significantly affect the course and management of diabetes (Baker, Barcai, Kay, & Hague, 1969; VandenBergh, Sussman, & Vaughn, 1967; VandenBergh, Sussman, & Titus, 1966; Weller, 1961). Also, blood glucose levels can be affected by emotional stress (Baker, et al., 1969).

The authors of a recent study (Minuchin, Rosman, & Baker, 1978) described the situation of three adolescent girls who had what was termed "psychosomatic diabetes," a condition that would not respond as expected to normal medical treatment. A most unusual occurrence—hospitalization—was required for these girls 10 to 15 times per year for diabetic acidosis. Each adolescent saw a different psychiatrist, and similar evaluations were made. All three patients were said to have difficulty in handling stress, were felt to be immature in coping with difficult situations, and also tended to internalize anger. It was concluded that there was a distinct psychosomatic component to their disease, and the emotional arousal led directly to physical decompensation.

Weekly therapy sessions with the girls had little effect on the need for hospitalization. However, when they were in a care facility, and therapy was continued, diabetic control was regained. The researchers concluded that the family environment was quite stressful to the patients because, in each case, bouts of ketoacidosis reappeared when the child was returned home. Later, in one case, family therapists were brought in to work with the entire family. The goal of therapy was to help the family deal with hidden conflicts, as well as to teach the child how to handle them. After several months of therapy, marked improvement in family interaction was evidenced, and the hospitalization pattern was broken.

Consequently, psychogenic factors and stressful life events not only seem to precede the onset of diabetes, but also exacerbate an existing diabetic condition. Effective means for dealing with these stressors need to be examined.

Treatment
Procedures Diabetics obviously require some type of supportive counseling to enable them to deal with what one diabetic called "a life-long negotiation with a limitation, a no-win, non-vacation assignment" (Sims, 1978, p. 13). Diabetics have unique problems imposed upon them by their disease which are not encountered by patients with other diagnoses. These special issues deserve consideration. If we do not treat all presenting patients as individual human beings, but instead use some blanket therapeutic approach, we may overlook the need to manage disease-specific problems. The pancreas of nondiabetics operates automatically. But diabetics must learn to *think* for a nonfunctioning, or moderately functioning, organ. This means that *constant* attention must be given to any energy expenditure or intake. The following thoughtful quote regarding the constant surveillance of body function is offered by Sims (1978).

> I have to stay in touch with what my body tells me. There is careful examination of the physical and psychological state, albeit subliminally, from moment to moment. This is especially useful when I am not sure whether I am angry, fearful, tired, frustrated, coming down with the flu, or hypo- or hyper-glycemic. They all feel somewhat the same, especially in the beginning, because of the release of adrenalin. It's good training in pulling problems apart and figuring what to do next without blaming the circumstances. There's a lot of practice in living with the tension between immediate gratification and restraint from long-term rewards. (p. 15)

In few other instances of chronic disease can a person be so totally in control of symptoms. Such control is, of course, based upon a thorough understanding of how the laws of physical health affect the condition together with some expertise in attuning to physical needs, so that proper adjustments can be made in diet, insulin, exercise, and sleep. The control of diabetic symptoms is not a problem that can be relinquished to the medical profession—for all a physician can do is prescribe and adjust insulin levels periodically, educate, and treat the symptoms that occur if the disease takes its toll on other body systems. Beyond the prescription, treatment is wholly dependent upon a patient's willingness to give himself or herself the aversive injections, and to otherwise learn to think for the pancreas. Any diminution in motivation to do this is accompanied by rapid physical feedback. The diabetic is given only moderate leeway in the amount of physical abuse, stress, and neglect he or she can tolerate.

Surprisingly few psychological interventions have been reported for these patients, whose well-being depends on psychologically related factors of motivation, and who could profit by techniques for stress management. The necessity for psychological treatment has been recognized for some time, however. A survey of the literature revealed that, as early as 1926, Gigon, Aigner, and Brauch used hypnosis with four diabetics and suggested to them that the pancreas would produce more insulin so that urine and blood sugar would greatly decrease. Both urine and blood sugar tests subsequently showed marked decreases in sugar (Dunbar, 1935). Luthe (1969) reports the positive effects of autogenic training with diabetics in lowering insulin intake.

More recently, a case study was reported using biofeedback-assisted relaxation with a 20-year-old juvenile-onset diabetic (Fowler, Budzynski, & VandenBergh, 1976). The patient was monitored for a baseline period of six weeks and then trained in relaxation techniques using EMG biofeedback for a second six weeks. During the training period, her daily insulin dose dropped to 59 units from the average of 85 units per day during the baseline period. The patient also reported a decrease in emotionality and in diabetic fluctuations. This study has been frequently cited with the warning not to work in ignorance of the potentially disastrous health problems that might occur as a consequence of biofeedback or other stress-reduction techniques. Patients should be warned that insulin needs may drop suddenly, so that they can avert a serious hypoglycemic attack. An improvement in condition may work against diabetic patients (and hypertensives, too) who have fixed amounts of medication, since improvement means less insulin is required. Hence, unless the dosage is reduced, the body may be overwhelmed.

A Bodymind
Approach Carol Kershaw, in both her private practice and research activity, has developed an interesting approach to

the psychotherapeutic management of diabetes.[1] She has integrated imagery of disease techniques with Gestalt Therapy. Gestaltists view the psychophysiological disturbance as a manifestation of some feeling's being stopped by muscular inhibition. Perls, Hefferline, and Goodman (1951) present an example of how an individual may thus somatize an emotion. That individual, instead of allowing himself or herself to cry, for example, cuts off the feeling and instead develops headaches, breathing problems, or other symptoms to prevent the expression of crying. As a result, symptoms of a disease develop and attention becomes focused on treatment. Yet the individual does not take responsibility for the "disease," nor does the person realize the headache, or slow and tight breathing, is a result of armoring the body through muscular tension.

According to Gestalt Therapy, the organism always moves toward self-regulation. Unhealthy functioning occurs when polarities are out of balance so that conflict occurs between "top dog" and "under dog." An individual experiences some parts of the self as acceptable and other parts as not acceptable. In order for the person to flow as a total process, that individual must accept all parts of the self and achieve a balance between them.

In relation to patients diagnosed with juvenile-onset diabetes, Dr. Kershaw has observed some imbalances that characterize such individuals. These clinical observations were based on interviews, results of personality tests (16 PF), and therapeutic sessions with 35 diabetic persons. The diabetic clients showed a need for control of their feelings and in their interpersonal relationships. They also evidenced a high degree of anxiety and were easily affected by stressful situations. Certain parental messages had been swallowed whole and were still operating in these patients. They used introjection and retroflection as defense mechanisms. Through retroflection, the person did to himself or herself what that individual would like to have done to others. The diabetics who were observed turned unexpressed anger and hostility inward and thereby influenced physiological dysfunctioning. Unlike other persons who also internalize their anger, these diabetics suffered from a malfunction of the energy system.

There seemed to be a theme of starvation present among this population of patients, in the sense of "starved" for love

---

[1]Authors' Note: Credit for researching much of this chapter goes to Carol Kershaw. She ventured into uncharted territory to conduct her dissertation, and in doing so has developed one of the few psychological treatment models for diabetes. Her frequent and repeated encounters with diabetic patients have given her some unusual insights which she shares in two case studies.

and affection from the family-of-origin. Once the disease developed, the patient received more attention, primarily from the parents, and they were set apart from others by having diabetes. The greater reward in their families was for illness rather than for health, a behavior pattern which may be culturally reinforced. The starvation theme was played out through a physiological response in which the body was starved of its life energy. One diabetic client stated, "If you are dying for something sweet, go ahead and eat it to kill that craving." The metaphor of "dying for something sweet" may be taken literally in the sense that the body was actually dying for nourishment.

Family-of-Origin Messages. The families in which these 35 diabetic patients were reared were similar, in that many clients reported much marital disturbance between the parents prior to the onset of diabetes. The mothers were often perceived as overprotective, while the fathers were seen as emotionally distant. Many of the patients felt unaccepted and desired more attention and nurturance than was received from parents before the diagnosis of diabetes.

Numerous messages were communicated to the diabetic persons from their families-of-origin, having to do with what values were important to maintain, how to gain love and affection, how to be successful, and what kind of relationships to have in the future. Many of these messages were seen in client imagery, which will be discussed shortly. Some of the messages that were delivered openly and through meta communication included the following:

1. Be in control.

   One diabetic female's mother was fond of saying, "A woman should be like oil on the water to smoothe out problems." Another diabetic person remembered being able to manipulate his parents easily to get what he desired.

2. Do not be angry or upset.

   A diabetic male client remembered his father's saying, "It won't help to get mad." Another man heard his mother comment, "Somehow everything will work out for the best. No matter what happens, keep your chin up." Still another woman client recalled her mother's anger-binding statement every time the client would quarrel with her siblings, "Love one another." Finally, one diabetic woman tells herself, when upset, "Whatever is happening is not important enough to bleed over." She recalled her mother suggesting to her that it was unacceptable to become angry. Now, blood will literally appear in her eyes when she becomes too upset.

3. Death will occur at an early age.
   One diabetic male expected to die at age 25. He was 24 when he made that statement. Also, he remembered his family talking about other members of the family who had died before age 30. It was their expectation, and his, that he would act out that message. His grandmother, though elderly, died shortly after she had her gallbladder removed. The client stated, "Now I'm having gallbladder trouble." He went on to say, "She and I have the same philosophy. We're all going to die anyway, so I'd rather die having enjoyed life than live by starving to death. There is no assurance of living longer if you're rigid about diet and exercise. I really don't have any control over it." This man had great difficulty in stabilizing his blood sugar. Part of his difficulty came from being lax about following a healthy diet. Also, he occasionally would omit his insulin injection. "Sometimes I just blow it off." Another diabetic man, when diagnosed at age 19 as having diabetes, was told by his physician that he could expect a 10- to 15-year life span. After much conflict, this person chose to believe that he had much more control over his life than he had been led to believe. Presently he is 39 and in good health.

Other messages that were communicated from the family-of-origin included:

4. There are strong and weak people in this world. Be strong and do not ask for help—except from mother.
5. You are special but flawed.

Imagery of Diabetes. In order to help persons suffering from diabetes better deal with the "stress of life," the use of imagery and relaxation techniques (in a Gestalt framework) was incorporated to the overall treatment strategy. Each client in this group was asked to listen to a guided imagery tape which suggested that the person visualize the diabetes, pancreas, the cells taking in the sugar needed for fuel, and the insulin treatment that was being received. Similar to the process used with the IMAGE-CA, the patient was asked to draw the visualizations. After the patient explained the drawing, the imagery was used therapeutically.

The imagery that diabetic patients described was indicative of the way in which they perceived themselves and their lives. For example, one woman visualized her diabetes as an octopus monster that had complete control over her life. Her insulin treatment was perceived as almost incidental and quite ineffective. Clinically, she was emotionally labile and chronically depressed. She expressed a sense of hopelessness and helplessness, and she believed she had little control over her life. Consequently, her diabetes was not well controlled. The image was an accurate view of her reality.

Another woman, aged 35, drew and described her diabetes as residing in a "dead stump," the pancreas, which was grey in color. She talked fearfully to the therapist about her expectations concerning the disease. She expected to die at age 42 from other medical complications and was making preparations for that event. Her family history indicated that four other members had developed diabetes and had often told her she would die at an early age. This client was not only suffering from diabetes, but coronary disease and cystic fibrosis as well.

One diabetic male, aged 50, envisioned his pancreas as a partially functioning pink organ. He saw the insulin treatment as a "river of life," which gently stimulated the pancreas to work better. He believed that he would not necessarily return to health, but that he would improve. His attitude toward life was quite positive, and he hoped that someday he would not have to take insulin.

One of the most creative images was furnished by a diabetic female, aged 16, who first visualized her pancreas as a flat water bottle (Figure 5.1). When the therapist suggested that little activity could take place in the image, the client later changed her visualization. She began imaging her body as a house that needed electricity. In her mental picture, she saw an electrician coming into the house and throwing an electrical switch. Energy from the currents, symbolic of insulin from her pancreas, flowed into every room. The rooms were symbolic of cells and organs in the body. In her imagery, the body began to function properly. During a 15-week period, this client listened twice a day to a relaxation and imagery cassette recording tape. She was asked to record her daily insulin units and also subjective units of disturbance (SUD) on a scale from 1 to 10. She reported that her insulin dose remained about the same, after having stabilized, but her mean SUD score dropped from approximately 8 to 2. She also reported that she was able to generalize her feeling of relaxation from the tape to other stressful events during the day.

In summary, the imagery in these examples reflects attitudes toward the illness and the treatment process, as well as family-of-origin messages, which were manifested in more or less adaptive behavior patterns. The imagery represents the degree of control that the individual felt he/she had over the disease and also the self-confidence associated with his/her ability to manage it. In working with the diabetic person therapeutically, this information was used to help the individual integrate polarities and become centered. Gestalt technique involved fantasies, dreams, the "hot seat," and—always—a focus on present awareness. Questions such as, "What are you

Figure 5.1

a. 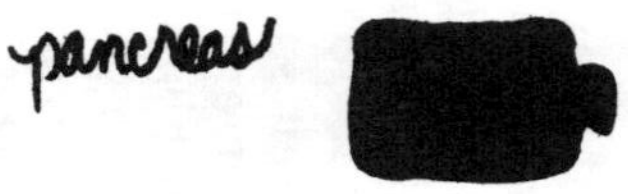 pancreas

b.

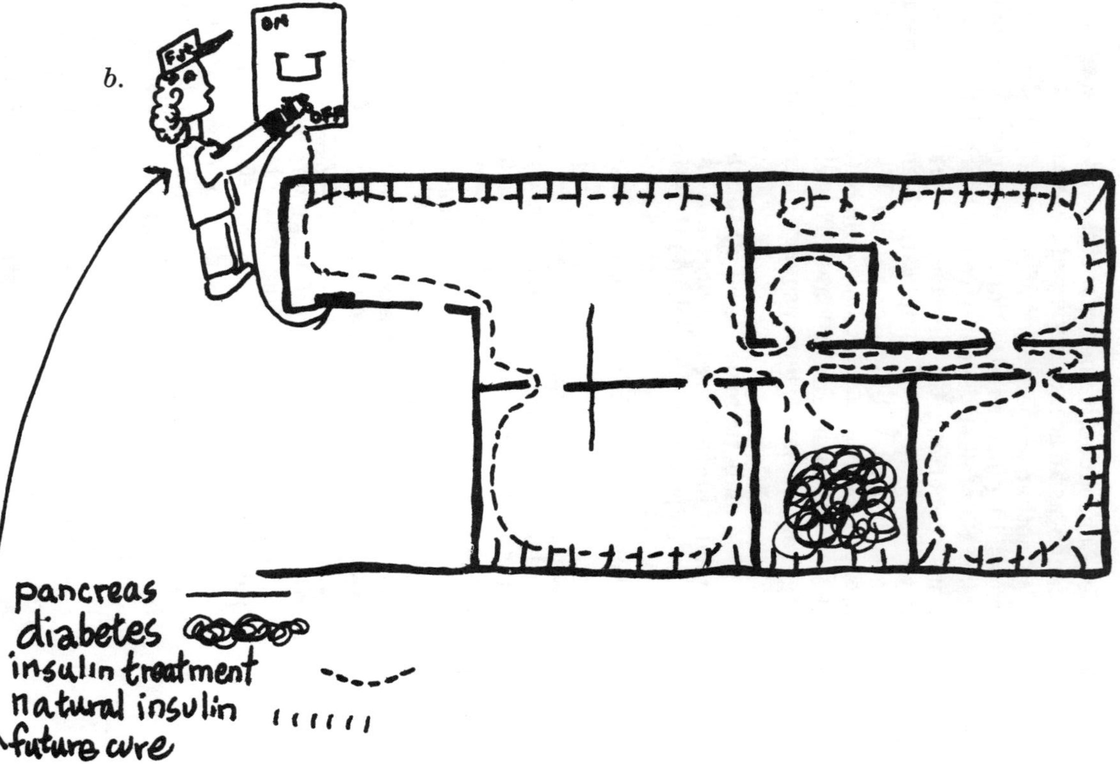

Pancreas ⌇⌇⌇⌇⌇
diabetes ⌇⌇⌇⌇⌇
insulin treatment ⌇⌇⌇⌇⌇
natural insulin – – –
future cure ⌇⌇⌇⌇⌇

sensing, feeling, doing? What do you want? What are you thinking?" were useful for bringing about present awareness. The therapist would begin by asking the diabetic person to imagine being each part and element of the process. Through the Gestalt experience, the person was required to observe the phenomenological aspects of his or her own behavioral and physiological functioning. Attitudes and expectancies about quality of life and death were confronted, as well as the message which the disease had to give the person. Some diabetic patients decided to change their beliefs about the disease process. Others made decisions to keep negative attitudes toward the disease and treatment process. However, after therapeutic intervention, these attitudes had been brought into present awareness.

Before Gestalt therapy was conducted with diabetic clients, the question was posed: "If your diabetes had a message to give to you, what would it be?" Following are several examples of responses that were given.

* * *

Client: It has created a mountain for me to climb and to have a victory. It didn't get the best of me. I'm learning something from it. You don't fight a problem; you change it into an asset.

Client: The message is that I'm not perfect. I'm vulnerable and fragile.

Client: Diabetes says I am here to stay. I won't leave you.

Client: Diabetes says to me exercise, eat light, and relax.

Client: Take care of yourself, you are important. And slow down and spend time—smell the flowers.

Client: OK, fellow. This is life. The only thing you were doing before me was being a custodian. Now that you've got me, you're getting financial assistance, and you're getting to some point in life. You're going to be more than a custodian.

* * *

Some individuals had dialogues with their disease, which indicated the ambivalence they experience.

Therapist: Would you be willing to pretend to place your diabetes in that chair and make some statements to your disease?
Client: (laughs) I don't want you. Go away.
Therapist: Now be the diabetes. How would you respond?
Client (diabetes): Well, I'm sorry. Whether you want me

or not, I'm here to stay with you, and it's up to you to take care of me.

Therapist: Now be your insulin and place your pancreas over there. What would you say?

Client (insulin): Why aren't you working? You're giving this kid a hard time. Work just a little harder (said pleadingly) so he won't have to take the shots.

Client (pancreas): I'm just going to sit here. I have other things I want to do. It's your loss and my gain.

Client (insulin): You're lazy. You are not doing your job.

Therapist: He has stopped himself from working, made himself alone, like you have withdrawn socially?

Client: (laughs) So to speak—yes. He doesn't want to work with the different parts of the body. I have excluded myself to the point where I don't socialize really with other people. The more I try, the more opposition I experience.

* * *

Another patient dialogue with the disease revealed the connection between family-of-origin messages and present behavior.

Client (diabetes): I've got your attention and I'm not going to go away just because you want me to make sure that you won't be spontaneous or irresponsible.

Client: It was unacceptable as a child for me to be spontaneous.

* * *

A third client dialogue with diabetes had several messages.

Client (diabetes): You dummy. Why do you do some things you ought not to do? Why don't you spend the necessary effort and time to make me happy before you go running off on other things. Don't begrudge the time it takes to take care of me, because the benefits outweigh the time. You'll spend less time at the doctor's office. Don't take yourself so seriously. You need to stay calm.

Client: Sometimes you do things without any rhyme or reason. Plus the medical world has confused ideas about what to do, so I get confused. I try to figure out what I have done wrong, but sometimes I can't.

Client (diabetes): You know that you need to take care of yourself. You know what the price-tag is for not sticking to your diet and exercising properly.

Therapist: You sound like a friend.

Client: I kind of feel that way. I can't remember not being a diabetic. Diabetes is me as much as that foot, and I like myself. That happens to be part of myself even though it hurts me at times. Diabetes also helps me because it's a reminder to take good care of my body.

* * *

Finally, another client dialogue demonstrated an intense personal struggle over the issue of death.

* * *

Therapist: Would you explain how you see your diabetes?

Client: My pancreas looks like a pinkish-grey shriveling, a demise of each organ, a dwindling of the body, a going away.

Therapist: You are going away?

Client: Yes (crying). We are struggling—my diabetes and I. I have a tendency to come on very strong with other people. I don't want them close to me or to love me too much.

Therapist: Because . . .

Client: Because I'm going to have an early death, and I don't want you to grieve. Don't get too close to me.

Therapist: I will stay as far away as you want. (Gets up and moves back from client) Is this far enough?

Client: Too far. (Therapist moves in closer) That's okay.

* * *

In working with the issue of death, this client decided not to change her decision about an early death. She did, however, change her style of living in some ways so that she began to really enjoy the present.

Case Studies In an intensive case study, Dr. Kershaw investigated the family life history, personality factors, locus of control, stressful life events prior to illness onset, and imagery of diabetes of five individuals diagnosed as having juvenile-onset diabetes. A clinical analysis of two of those cases is presented in the following pages. The clinical analysis consisted of summarizing biographical data, family-of-origin experience, diabetes medical history, religious beliefs, perceived causes of the disease, family-of-origin messages, data from the *Sixteen Personality Factor Questionnaire* (16 PF), *Internal—Powerful Others—Chance Scale* (IPC), *Social Rating Readjustment Scale* (SRRS), and an analysis of the subject's imagery.

* * *

Case #1 Gloria B. was a white female, 36 years old, married, and the mother of two daughters. She had graduated from college with a bachelor's degree in psychology, was now employed as an insurance analyst for an underwriter, and had worked only for three years. She went to work because of financial strain, which occurred when her husband lost his job.

The eldest of six children, Gloria was born in east Texas. She was reared in a family with two brothers and four sisters. A seventh child died at birth.

Family-of-Origin Experience. Gloria indicated that the family functioned fairly well, with the usual sibling rivalry. However, she did not respect her mother, who was perceived as a weak person. Her mother never disciplined her except by controlling her diet and giving injections on time. Instead of using discipline, her mother would cry whenever she misbehaved. Gloria believed that her mother was both overly affectionate and verbal and attempted to force a sense of closeness. She referred to her mother as "syrupy sweet."

In contrast, Gloria's father was distant and physically unexpressive. Although he never told her that he loved her, he demonstrated affection by making comments about her appearance and referring to her as "daughter." She perceived her father as being wise and more genuine and deserving of respect than her mother. He was not verbal, but when he spoke, he communicated a sense of wisdom.

As a couple, the parents were seen as experiencing much discontent between themselves. Gloria believed that her father was not supportive of her mother. Instead, he tended to withdraw from any conflict.

Presently, she said, she felt close to her siblings. She perceived herself as closer to her sisters than her brothers, and occasionally acted as a parent to her youngest sister. In relation to her parents, Gloria still felt somewhat disdainful toward her mother and admired her father greatly.

Diabetes Medical History. The age of diabetes onset was 4. Later, three of the sisters developed the disease. There was no diabetes on the father's side of the family, although he had been a juvenile diabetic. Her mother's father developed adult-onset diabetes at age 65.

The mother developed kidney disease, phlebitis, and had bouts with pneumonia. In comparison, the father had good health, except for his diabetes.

When a child became ill in the family, all usual activities stopped. The grandmothers were summoned and special treatment was administered. The extended family member would spend extra time with, and give special attention to, the child who was ill.

Religious Beliefs. Gloria remembered attending church with her family. Her mother spent much time with the children in teaching them to pray. At the time of the intervention, religion was quite important to this patient. She believed that God was active in her life; when she died, she expected that she would go to heaven. Gloria also said that she had beaten the statistics by outliving what medical authorities say is a normal life span for a juvenile diabetic. The possibility of death was an ever present one, but she did not believe that death would be the end of her essence.

Perceived Causes of the Disease. Gloria believed that her diabetes occurred because of a genetic flaw inherited from her parents. She also considered the physical structure to be related to having developed diabetes. In other words, those individuals in the family who had developed diabetes all had a similar build: short, tiny, with a tendency to gain weight.

Family-of-Origin Messages. Some of her mother's favorite sayings were: "You reap what you sow," "You get out of life what you put into it," and "You can do or be whatever you want." The last statement was made in the context of not asking for help from anyone else. Gloria's mother was also fond of saying, "Love one another," especially during sibling arguments. In relation to her father, she could only remember one favorite saying of his. He often stated that, "Honesty is next to godliness."

Based on clinical observation of these parental messages and others which were indirectly discussed during the interview, the following family-of-origin messages were revealed.
1. Death will occur at an early age.
2. There are strong and weak people in this world. Be strong and do not ask for help.
3. Do not be angry.
4. Be in control.
5. Life is beautiful and fleeting.
6. You are special.

Clinical Impressions. Gloria tended to greatly somatize her stress. From the interview, she indicated that she felt anxious much of the time. During a particularly high-stress period, she had experienced memory difficulties and immediately thought she had hardening of the arteries in her head. As reported by her, and confirmed by her medical history, the subject suffered from cystic fibrosis and coronary heart disease as well.

Although the interview dialogue was replete with laughter, she tended to be aggressive and explosive. Also, she covered a sense of insecurity with brashness and exhibited a desire to be in control of situations and people.

16 PF. On the 16 PF, Gloria exhibited higher than average scores relative to the general population on Factors A, B, C,

E, F, H, I, M, and N. This profile would indicate that the subject was quite outgoing and enjoyed being with people. She had much ego strength and could be accepting of difficult situations. While she was dominant, assertive, and competitive, she was also cheerful, venturesome, and drawn toward more intellectual and cultural interests. The high M score also indicated that she led an active fantasy life. Further, she was insightful in relation to herself and was socially astute. The high I score indicated the patient was sensitive and artistic, yet demanding, insecure, and attention-seeking. Finally, as a way of enduring stress, she had a tendency to develop psychosomatic ailments (Cattell, 1962).

I P C Scale. Gloria scored high on the Internal scale, which demonstrated that she believed she had control over her own life. A low score on the Powerful Others scale indicated that she believed powerful others did not have much control over her life. Finally, according to the low score on the Chance scale, she believed chance forces did not control her life (Levenson, 1972).

SRRS. Because of the early onset of diabetes, the SRRS was not reflective of significant stressful situations. The only two life events recorded on the SRRS were the death of a close family member and personal injury or illness (Holmes & Rahe, 1967).

However, in the interview, Gloria was able to recall several important events which occurred six months to one year before the onset of diabetes. She fell from a bicycle and later fell from a truck. Her family moved to a new house, and her mother became pregnant. When her brother was born, Gloria remembered feeling extremely frightened.

Imagery of Diabetes. The patient was able to visualize her diabetes, insulin treatment, and pancreas only in a vague manner. Her imagery was apparently influenced by a statement that had been made by her first physician; he told her that her pancreas would eventually resemble a tree stump. In her imagery, the pancreas was visualized as a tree stump that was in a state of decay. Gloria perceived her disease as very strong, her blood quite thick, and her cells as moderately permeable. She also viewed her pancreas as somewhat inactive.

In terms of treatment attitude, she had a fairly negative attitude toward the treatment process, and the description was not very clear. She believed that the treatment was not at all effective as a cure. She further believed that she would experience continued physical deterioration. The clinical impression was formed that the subject would experience continued active disease at a rapid rate.

* * *

Case #2 Ralph T. was a white male, aged 39, married for a second time, and the father of two sons. He had received a bachelor's degree in engineering and had been employed as an electronics engineer for several years. He was reared in Arkansas and resided there with his wife and two sons at the time of the intervention.

The eldest of two children, he was born 10 years prior to the birth of his sister. The two children were reared by their natural parents. Also, Ralph indicated that his sister was unplanned.

Family-of-Origin Experience. Ralph remembered much stress and conflict between his parents when he was growing up. His father was an alcoholic who was somewhat emotionally abusive to his mother. In some ways he admired his father, who had a positive attitude much of the time and was quite intelligent. His father seldom played with him, however, and there was little physical affection expressed.

The mother abused food and became obese as the years passed. She was quite protective of Ralph and was a companion as much as she was a mother. She expressed affection by being protective, and he enjoyed being witty to amuse her. They played, talked, and spent a considerable amount of time together. Ralph remembered being able to manipulate his mother very easily.

Because of the age difference between his younger sister and himself, Ralph felt like an only child. His sister was a "plaything" for him, and they were not close when they were young.

The relationship now with both parents was indicated as being positive. Ralph believed that he had successfully taught his father how to share affection. There was still distance between himself and his sister.

Diabetes Medical History. The age of diabetes onset was 19. There was no diabetes in the family on either side, with the exception of an uncle who developed the disease in his 60s. However, Ralph was unaware of his uncle's diabetes until he had developed the disease himself.

Basically, the parents had poor health. The mother developed emphysema and was overweight. She had little control over her eating. The father had a serious heart condition as well as alcoholism.

When a child became ill in the family, the mother was nurturing. The father was not supportive of any family member when that person was ill. Ralph did recall using illness in a manipulative way to gain attention from his mother.

Religious Beliefs. Religion was an unimportant concern in the family. The parents only attended church on special occasions, and the children were not required to attend. As a young child, Ralph had involved himself with a particular religious group. However, he was much more interested in socializing and in participating in the woodshop activities which they sponsored.

As an adult, he believed religion to be quite important. Social contact was no longer the prime motivation for church attendance. Rather, the most important element had become the personal sense of being connected with God. This spiritual connection was experienced through involvement in the church. Ralph believed in a life after death and conceived it as some kind of "spiritual transition."

Perceived Causes of the Disease. Ralph believed that his diabetes occurred because of a series of particularly stressful events. He and several friends stole a tire and were subsequently arrested. During this period, he was in the service and desired to be released from duty. The subject also believed that diabetes may have developed because of his need for caring and affection at that time in his life. He described the separation from his mother as being another stressful factor.

Family-of-Origin Messages. One of the mother's favorite sayings was, "Somehow everything will work out for the best." Ralph interpreted this statement as meaning that life is fatalistic, and the implied message was that he had little control over what transpired in his life.

The father had many favorite sayings that were cliches. However, one statement that stood out was, "Be careful, and don't let people take advantage of you."

Based on clinical observation of these favorite sayings and others which were discussed during the interview, the following family-of-origin messages were revealed.

1. Do not be spontaneous but be controlled.
2. Do not be angry.
3. Be perfect.
4. You are unable to take care of yourself. Let your mother take care of you.

Clinical Impressions. Ralph tended to be quite self-controlled in his speech and deliberate in action. He was intellectual and rational in his dialogue. Also, he had a good sense of humor and quick wit. He described himself as being quick to anger. He tended to be introspective and took responsibility for his feelings and behavior. He was optimistic, cheerful, and positive in his outlook.

16 PF. On the 16 PF, Ralph exhibited scores which indicated deviation from the average on all factors except L, N, and Q_2. This profile revealed that he was reserved, critical, distrustful of others, and preferred working alone. He tended to be easily upset and annoyed and changeable in his attitudes and interests. According to the profile, he was prone to psychosomatic disturbances. He was assertive, dominant, and competitive, as well as cheerful and enthusiastic. Being somewhat expedient, he tended not to be rule-governed. He was shy, timid, and especially sensitive to perceived threatening situations. Also, the profile showed that Ralph was dependent, overprotected, and felt insecure. He was experimenting, had difficulty with authority figures, and had an explosive temper. Finally, the score on Q_4 indicated that he was tense, unable to tolerate criticism, and somewhat anxious (Cattell, 1962).

I P C Scale. Ralph scored high on the Internal scale, which indicated that he believed he had control over his own life. A low score on the Powerful Others scale indicated that he believed that powerful others did not have much control over his life. Finally, he did not believe that chance forces exerted any influence in his life.

SRRS. Ralph's life-change score of 305 was reflective of significant life stress within the year previous to onset of diabetes. Holmes and Rahe, authors of the SRRS, said that a score of 300 points indicates that the individual has a 79% chance of developing a serious illness within the following two years (Dohrenwend, 1974). The patient recorded that during this time the following events occurred: jail term, personal injury or illness, change to a different line of work, beginning school, revision of personal habits, change in work hours or conditions, and a change in residence. There were no other important events not listed on the SRRS which were felt to be particularly relevant. However, he described his being drafted into the service, where he was forced to attend language school, as one of the most stressful times in his life.

Imagery of Diabetes. Ralph visualized his diabetes, insulin treatment, and pancreas poorly. He imagined his pancreas to resemble a cauliflower that was grey in color. The insulin resembled a molecule model which opened the door to the cells. However, he related that it must be magic as to how the insulin moves through the cell walls. He perceived his disease as somewhat strong, his blood as moderately thick, and his cells as moderately impermeable. He also viewed the pancreas as completely inactive.

In relation to treatment attitude, Ralph had a fairly negative opinion of the treatment. He believed that the treatment would be moderately ineffective as a cure. Further, he believed that he would experience continued physical deterioration but at a very slow rate. The clinical impression also was one of the subject's experiencing continued active disease at a rather slow rate.

* * *

Relaxation and Visual Imagery

Program The two patients described above were involved in a larger study that examined the effects of a relaxation and visual imagery program on insulin dose. A baseline of two weeks, during which the subjects recorded daily insulin dose and other variables, was taken. Each subject was then requested to listen to a cassette tape recording of guided imagery and relaxation for six weeks, twice daily. During this time, they continued to record daily insulin dose. Then, a two-week follow-up period was conducted during which the subjects did not use the tape recording.

The relaxation and visual imagery program had little effect on insulin dose over the six-week time period for both patients. However, both individuals indicated that they were able to generalize the feeling of relaxation learned from the program to other situations where they had previously responded by becoming tense. It is suggested that more research be devoted to the psychosomatic aspects of diabetes, particularly with respect to beliefs and expectations about health and disease that are part of whole family systems.

In the authors' joint experience, Dave P., a 38-year-old patient who was also a medical writer at the time of our first acquaintance, was a principal "teacher" in expanding the imagery concept of treatment from cancer to other diseases. A dialogue with him, together with pictures of his complicated images appears elsewhere (Achterberg & Lawlis, 1978). He had been diagnosed as a child with "brittle" diabetes—supposedly terminal and uncontrollable. His mother, in fact, was told by their doctor to keep him at home and not plan for him to go to college. He defied prognostications, however, and is alive and well without any complications. One of his chief disputes was with the danger and damage produced by the "scare" tactics of many diabetes educators. He felt he had been inundated all his life with warnings that he would be impotent, lose his vision, have his feet amputated, and so on. He adamantly has tried to counter this negative imagery by replacing it with a more positively visualized outcome.

His direction for imagery came from a lecture he attended on Silva Mind Control. The lecturer did not discuss disease as such, but rather talked about having a positive mental attitude and utilizing an imagery process to express that attitude. Dave later said he forgot the lecture until he went to his physician and the beginning stages of diabetic retinopathy were diagnosed. (Retinopathy is an occasional concomitant of diabetes that may eventually result in blindness.) He decided at that point to begin imaging regularly, a practice which in time led to a quite complicated series of images. Briefly, he envisioned Vikings traveling down a fjord, chipping out the channel, i.e., clearing his clogged vessels (See Figures 5.2-5.5). Other images included a power plant to keep his pancreas functioning and clear streams representing his clean blood vessels.

He began making some major changes in lifestyle, including a vigorous exercise program of jogging. He would image, in fact, while he was jogging. He admitted to earlier physical abuse of his body—drinking too much, sleeping too little, not eating properly. He seemed to describe, in our opinion, a kind of challenging of his body during his youth. We have observed this behavior in several diabetics; it is as if they were pressing their luck or testing their "limits." His medical condition in recent years has remained superb, and his insulin requirements have decreased over time. The disease appears to be under his control, not controlling him.

Another unusual patient we saw and studied in depth was Sarah L. She, like the journalist described above, was classified as a juvenile-onset diabetic. She was diagnosed when she was 8 years old, and was in her mid-30s when we saw her as a biofeedback patient. She had had a retinal hemorrhage earlier and recognized that she was acutely sensitive to stress, to the extent that her vision served as a barometer for her emotional condition. She was in a quandary, too, because the exercise she depended upon to "burn off" excessive sugar was exacerbating her visual problem via increased blood pressure. At the time of her treatment, she was undergoing several significant life changes. Her professional life was in turmoil: a grant she was working under was nearly finished and no job was in the offing, and her potential increasing loss of vision might necessitate learning drastically new and different working skills. She was divorced several years earlier, but was in love with and living with a very kind man. Her living situation had never been quite resolved with her socially bound family. An impending decision for her was whether or not to accept a placement in a school for the blind for a short period of training in the event she lost her eyesight. To top off her life-change encounters, she had discovered a breast lump just a couple of days prior to her first visit with us.

She was a magnificent biofeedback patient. She readily mastered autonomic control and evidenced all of the required

Figure 5.2

Figure 5.3

Figure 5.4

Figure 5.5

motivational indices that predict success in treatment. Her imagery is abstracted from her chart and appears in Figure 5.6).

The imagery drawings were not done at first with Sarah, since her vision was not terribly good. Instead, a structured interview was conducted. The interview was unusually detailed, since she was such a well-educated patient. In asking her what her diabetes looked like, she said that she really did not know. She did see the blood vessels as working extremely hard, restricting, constricting, and implanting impurities. The blood vessels were throbbing and contracting. The heart was having to work harder. She saw these vessels particularly around her eyes. The vessels got smaller as they went down to her feet. Her heart, though overworked, was still healthy because it was "young enough."

The impurities she described were more a heaviness in the vessels. She did not see the sugar as white granulated sugar, but rather as a heavy liquid which slowed down the flow of blood. It could gravitate to her feet, but it could not get back up. She assumed that the blood sugar was producing darker and thicker blood than normal. Percentage of sugar in her blood she estimated at 25% or under. Most of this information, however, was based on medical information. When asked how she saw the blood sugar moving, she said that the impurities were moving all the time and affecting every part of her being. She said this with some emphasis. Later she said that the diabetes looked to her like a wall, or a door, surrounding the cell. The cells took in the sugar when the insulin pressed a button; the sugar then was allowed into the cell, but only when insulin was present. When the insulin began to leave her system, the walls formed up against the cell.

Her pancreas she saw as working adequately. Now, based on some new information, she believed it might be actually functioning, but that the insulin was killed after release. She said it might also be that the islets of Langerhans had shriveled from disuse and had given up. The insulin she described as a warrior. However, she only *verbalized* this warrior image and said that they really had no form. The insulin did battle by starting the body functions that begin the balancing and rebalancing act that are required for her metabolism. She said that the insulin simply enabled something natural to happen. She said that, when she was about 12, she began imaging positively in order to get over giving herself injections in her stomach. She started verbalizing to herself that the insulin would save her life and was her friend.

When asked what else her body was doing to fight the disease, she said that her state of mind helped, but also alluded to how her thoughts harmed her previously. She said that exercise was also as important as the insulin she took.

Figure 5.6

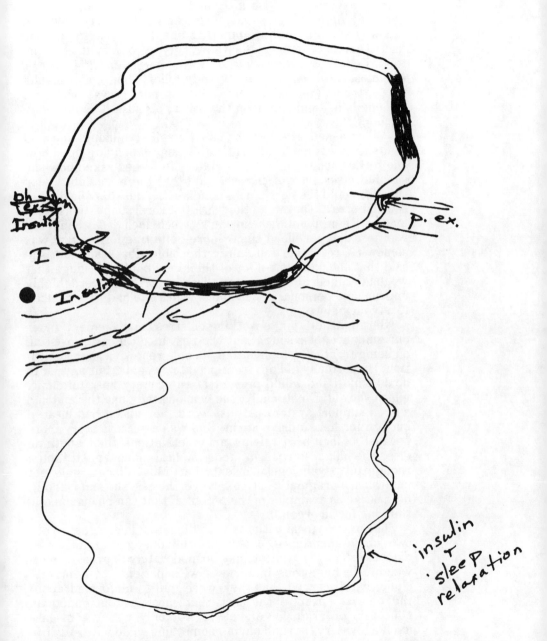

During exercise she also imagined warriors entering to help her body fight off the sugar. The warriors took the shape of arrows that went in, burning up and exploding the sugar. She had two sets of imagery for the two types of insulin that she took. Lenta® was more like a TV commercial for 24-hour cold capsules; there was slow and steady relief. The regular insulin was extremely powerful and could zap her. It was better on the one hand, and worse on the other, because it could really lay her flat.

When asked whether she saw herself stabilizing, she said that she saw a 75% chance of stabilizing, depending upon how she settled some other things in her life. When asked how she saw her disease reversing, she said that there was not a way that she could see herself as a nondiabetic, but that she did not see diabetes as the end of the world. Several suggestions were made to her about her imagery which included giving her warriors and her blood sugar more definitive forms. She was somewhat resistive, but, after the biofeedback session, she said that she had done a lot of thinking about the things that we had talked about. She realized that these were highly unusual and personal issues about which she had never talked to anyone before.

Sarah, in addition to working on stress management under our guidance, also sought out the best medical care, insisting on being treated by a physician of some renown at our institution. He normally did not treat private patients, but agreed to do so only if she would present at the county hospital clinic, which she did. Emotionally, she was basically healthy and had a good support system. At last word, her vision had cleared enough for her to drive again. She was a success story more because of her own talents and motivations than anything else. She balanced realism, good medical management, and a thoughtful psychological orientation. Most diabetics do not have such a pragmatic outlook. Nevertheless, she and Dave P. both serve as examples of the potential that can be attained in thinking for an organ.

The more typical patients with diabetes, in contrast to our two above-mentioned cases, are middle-aged, adult-onset diabetics. They very often may be moderately to grossly over-weight. In numerous interviews with patients at a private clinic, we discerned that they were quite uninformed about the disease, despite the fact that most had attended an education program for diabetics. Not only was the disease itself a mystery (beyond having something to do with sugar in the blood), but most regarded it as an accident. Further, they saw themselves as passively at the mercy of the disease and their doctors as merely responsible for monitoring it for them.

A most extreme example was a 50-year-old woman who was college educated, but chose to work as a housekeeper.

She was grossly obese (300+ pounds) and treated herself frequently to her own gourmet cooking. She elected to discontinue her insulin injections following surgery for ulcers, but at the time we interviewed her, seemed reasonably adjusted or under "dietary control." Additionally, she appeared to be an extremely active woman, which was particularly unusual in view of her girth. However, she encountered a series of situations which caused her anguish, including the loss of a daughter, repeated thefts, and other financial difficulties. Her health failed, an event that was attributed variously to depression, working too hard, and menopause. Her vision became blurred, and she had repeated infections on her extremities. Meanwhile, she was literally dragging herself from one situation to the next, consuming large amounts of carbohydrates, perspiring heavily, urinating frequently, and generally continuing on a downhill spiral. For a diabetic diagnosed 10 years previously, these health signs should have registered a warning immediately. They did not, and she continued until her family admitted her to the hospital in a near-comatose state. Later, we learned it was the third time she had been admitted under similar circumstances.

Denial of symptoms? Death wish? Ignorance? Probably all three intertwined if the truth were known. Whatever the reasons, "forgetting" to take insulin, ignoring diet and medical advice, and so forth, are not unusual. They go beyond simplistic explanation and intertwine into the whole complex phenomenon of mental health. Education is part of the answer, as that allegedly leads to compliance—although it is difficult to prescribe exact rules for compliance. Insulin, once or twice a day, and a careful diet may be sufficient *most* of the time, but allowance must also be made for the not infrequent circumstance in which stress is encountered, sleep is lost, or exercise routines change. The point is simply this: the only way a person seems to be able to live comfortably with a diagnosis of diabetes is by listening carefully and constantly to the body's changing demands—a highly individualistic prescription. When a patient chooses not to listen, as did the woman discussed above, then diabetes is usually only a symptom of the problem in living and not a disease in itself.

The peculiar needs of the diabetic are discussed in an article by John Muldoon (1978). In particular, he discusses the health system itself as a smoothly working institution when acute care situations are encountered. However, diabetics require ongoing attention, assessment, and treatment. They frequently feel that the system has forgotten their needs. Muldoon stresses that the only way a patient can get the required care is by assuming an active role in treatment—trying to understand the disease, the health care system, the physician, and the psychological aspects of having diabetes.

He further states:

> Because the biochemical aberrations responsible for the physiological difficulties underlying the diabetic condition are not understood, and manifest themselves uniquely in each individual, the diagnosis of diabetes requires close study of the illness as it manifests itself. This study is made difficult not only because of the uniqueness of each person's illness but also because the personality of each person seems to contribute to the manifestation and clinical course of the illness as well as to the treatment and stabilization of the condition. In a sense, there is no such thing as "diabetes." The term is an abstraction based on common laboratory information about a large number of persons.

and

> The unique quality of diabetes in each person has much more important implications for treatment than would be the case with an acute illness. Consequently, adequate care requires both the analytical competency of the technician and the integrative perceptiveness and adaptiveness of the complete clinician. Diabetes stretches the patience and talents of both the diabetic and the caring professional to limits unknown in the care of the acutely ill individual. (p. 349)

Diabetes necessitates the development of an exquisite internal biofeedback system—what we have been calling the formation of body imagery—in order to maintain health. Rather than a plight, the existence of this finely tuned sensitivity may enhance wellness. As Dorthea Sims (1978), a diabetic for over 20 years, stated in the *Diabetes Educator*, "I have a chance to look at and admire the great beauty and mystery of how the body works, to begin to appreciate the routes by which the warmth of the sun is now in my hand. It is especially important to count blessings when one is fighting a battle where there can be no victory in the ordinary sense. (p. 15)."

CHAPTER VI

BACK PAIN
The New Blue Collar Epidemic

Dynamics
of Pain Most patients seek medical or psychological treatment because of one generalized symptom—pain. Problems of the back—one of the primary sources of chronic pain—alone generated 18,824,000 physician visits from May, 1973, to April, 1974 (National Center for Health Statistics). Chronic pain costs Americans anywhere from 35 to 50 billion dollars a year in health services, drugs, and lost work days. There is little doubt that if pain was thought of as a disease entity instead of a symptom, it would be considered the major disease of the country.

Pain is usually considered a signal telling us something is wrong. However, once the signal has been noted, any sustained response to the pain can become maladaptive and detrimental to a total lifestyle. Pain can be a shield to hide our insecurities, an excuse for our lack of ambition (Oh, my aching back!), and even a retirement fund or money tree. It may even be a national resource or slogan—"Give until it hurts." Pain can be a sanctuary or haven, or perhaps a clock to pass the time. It can be a source of gratification, a sleeping pill, a codeine high, or—at the very least—a chance to give oneself permission to take a needed respite.

Interpersonally, pain can be a whip to control one's physician; a pulpit from which to preach a gospel. It can be a weapon to injure friends or family, or a conversational topic for friendly discussion. It can be a form of manipulation, either for the self-perceived victim of selfish children, or as an excuse to be selfish after a lifetime of giving.

Pain may be many, many things, depending upon one's background and culture. Pain, however, is *not* a defect in a column of dye, nor is it a configuration of electrical impulses on an electromyograph. Surprising to many, it may not even be reflected in pictures of abnormal bone growth or degeneration. It also may not show up on an MMPI profile or responses to an interview form.

Pain is a personal experience unfelt and unseen by anyone else in the world. No one else can objectively identify the quality and quantity of pain. To that extent, pain is purely an illusion and can only be understood as such. Up to now, no one has been able to satisfactorily objectify and discriminate pain as reported by patients, nor is there agreement on the outstanding psychophysical variables to feed into the pain formula. Pain etiology and expression mean different things to different professional groups, depending upon their special interest or field of interest. Orthopedists often visualize bone structure in their quest to ease or modify pain, whereas the neurosurgeon may focus upon nerve pathways as factors. The psychologist traditionally consults developmental, social, or personality factors as the outstanding determinants, while the psychiatrist may seek out possible psychiatric defenses to explain individual differences.

Despite the lack of agreement, a preliminary decision can be made about the disposition of a patient's care based upon whether the pain is classified as chronic or acute. This discrimination does correspond to major treatment protocols. The characteristics of the two categories are described below.

Table 6.1

DISCRIMINATION OF ACUTE VS. CHRONIC PAIN
(Summarized from Gorrell, 1978)

	Acute	Chronic
Cause:	Injury or inflammation	Resultant problems from surgery, psychological, social, cultural, and other interactions with environment.
Diagnosis:	Medical (physical)	Combination of physical, psychological and social with secondary diagnosis.
Duration:	1 day to 2 months	2 months or greater
Therapy Considerations:	Routine protocols	Experimental protocols, primarily behavioral and social. Drugs never cure pain and may be addictive. Surgery may worsen situations.
Effects of Pain:	Transient changes in personality. Vocational prognosis is good. Family and interpersonal relationship disruption is minor.	Personality temporarily or permanently changed. Vocational prognosis is poor, often loses job. Interpersonal relationships often disintegrate
Prognosis:	Good	Poor

In this chapter and the next, we present models of pain management designed for two specific conditions: low back (or spinal) pain and rheumatoid arthritis. Both are chronic pain conditions which have eluded traditional medicine. Back pain continues to be the most costly type of discomfort in the country, and management of rheumatoid arthritis is still in the stage of an experimental science with no known causes nor cures. Both conditions are aggravated by stress and have a distinctive reputation for involving a psychogenic component.

The prototype programs are those that worked well for us, given the patient population and facilities to which we had access. In focusing on back pain, the present chapter presents a far more comprehensive program because it is based on an inpatient, multidisciplinary effort. The rheumatoid arthritis model of Chapter VII was derived, on the other hand, from a series of smaller studies, the conclusions of which were extrapolated and then put into practice in a larger program. The more fragmented effort in developing treatment programs for arthritis may continue to be a national reality except in a few well-appointed centers. The monetary facts in this country are such that financing (primarily through workmen's compensation payments) is generous for back pain treatment; those patients with arthritis may be largely left to their own resources, or to Medicare/Medicaid support, which does not include broad-based treatment. Arthritis patients are, of course, generally older, and the disorder is nonwork related. Therefore, the goals for the two groups are divergent: a rapid, intensive program that allows the back pain patient to return quickly to a productive lifestyle vs. inexpensive techniques that can be conducted at home to relieve arthritis for an indeterminate length of time.

Pain as a Personal Experience

Any experience is an existential perception, especially pain. Whether the person attributes the sensations with positive or negative connotations is a matrix of factors, beginning from the first stimulation of birth and its associations to situational reinforcement of pain/pleasure behaviors. Several investigators support the notion that pain behavior is largely determined by social determinants (Craig & Best, 1977; Newfeld, 1970) and modeling (Craig, Best, & Ward, 1975; Johnson, 1973). In these studies, the perception of the intensity of pain related to whether or not a social reinforcer could be inferred. Chaves and Barber (1974) as well as Melzark, Weisy, and Sprague (1963) have shown that even experimental pain can be influenced by suggested attributions.

The connotation of pain experience can be characterized as much more negative among chronic pain patients than other medical patients (Pilowsky, Chapman, & Bonica, 1977). As a group, the chronic pain patients have developed, either from a reactive or an otherwise premorbid personality, an emotional response to pain as homogeneously negative and self-restrictive (Leavitt, Garron, Whisler, & Sheinkop, 1978; Graffenried, Adler, Abt, Nuesch, & Spiegel, 1978). The emotional response, while not labeled as depression, has been termed a defensive mechanism to negativity on MMPI profiles (Sternbach, 1974; McCreary, Turner, & Dawson, 1977).

The most provocative personality research has been with the MMPI with studies that have shown differences of chronic pain patients from more organic pain patients (McCreary, et al., 1977), but that discrimination becomes less distinctive when later investigators have shown the chronic pain patients to be far from homogeneous (Bradley, Prokop, Margolis, & Gentry, 1978; McGill, 1979).

The conclusion of all research in pain dynamics is that these patients are undergoing stress in one form or another. Stress not only has a negative impact on the emotional adaptation to pain, but has been reported as inhibiting physiological response on the body's natural pain opiates (Levine, Gordon, & Fields, 1978).

The picture of the pain patient as influenced by negative thinking may not necessarily relate to a bleak prognosis. In fact, since these patients are so affected by the emotional response, it stands to reason that psychological treatment would have a positive possibility (Barber, 1963; Sternbach, 1978; Swerdlow, 1974). Psychotherapy is no panacea to all pain. Patients' attitudes are well crystallized by the time we see them. But the components of patient courage and clinical sensitivity have confirmed that many patients can change both psychological and physical goals.

Back Pain   Insurance companies pay out far more for low back pain treatment than for any other type of medical care. According to Dr. Norm Shealy of the Shealy Pain Clinic in LaCrosse, Wisconsin, only 3 percent of all Workmen's Compensation cases in Wisconsin were disk related; yet, these cases received 75 percent of all claims payments (*Medical World News*, 1976). More than 110,000 spinal disk operations are performed each year in the United States, and low back pain is believed to affect about 80 percent of all individuals at some time during their active lives. Although the condition usually subsides within a month, it is episodic by nature, and is a common cause of absenteeism.

In view of these figures, it is likely that back pain will eventually affect each of us in either a direct or indirect manner. The challenge of dealing with chronic low back pain is therefore a formidable one for the health-related professions, and no one discipline is objective enough or broad enough to consider all aspects of the phenomenon. Moreover, the rehabilitation of chronic back pain depends primarily upon the motivations of the patients themselves. Any treatment approach will only be successful to the extent that it facilitates patient goals and also reflects their level of personal responsibility for health.

Back pain, in our experience with chronic patients, is usually the result of injury sustained either in lifting, falling, or an automobile accident. That is to say, none of our patients would be described as having psychosomatic onset. After the initial muscle strain or tear, and perhaps disk rupture, the patient has typically had a recurrence of pain. Sometimes the surgeon returns the patient to the operating room one to five times in an attempt to remedy the source of pain. Finally, for those patients who have not experienced any relief, our multi-disciplinary behavior-oriented procedures are recommended.

A Broad Physiological Perspective. A brief explanation of the psychophysiological aspects of back pain is presented in order to gain a perspective on treatment protocols. There are four basic factors that contribute to the syndrome from a *behavioral* point of view: muscular tension, bone structure, internal narcotic production, and emotional response to stress.

Muscle systems. The human muscle is complex in mechanical structure, but very simple in function. It can only contract or relax. By contracting, it becomes shorter, allowing a physical leverage to develop via bone connection and body movement. There are two critical conditions to be considered in this action: (1) the muscle knows one and only one reaction to *any* stimulation—i.e., to contract; and (2) each joint has at least two opposing muscles for its control. Thus, tension in one muscle does not occur without relaxation in another. In fact, there are more than 600 muscles that control the body in a complementary system of coordinated movements.

The muscles supporting the upper half of the body are strategically located around the backbone. In Figure 6.1, the principal muscles involved in torso stabilization are illustrated by groups A, B, C, and D. Muscle group A carries the burden

Figure 6.1

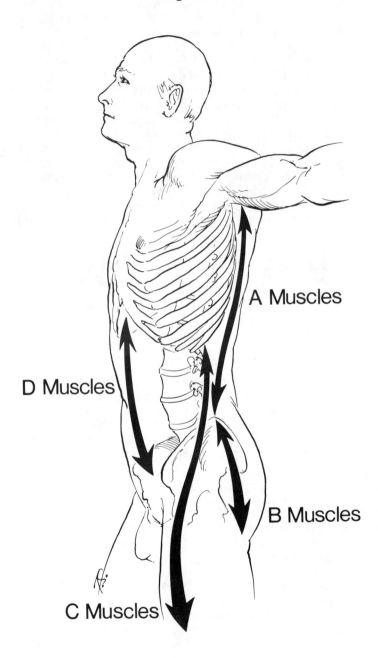

of leverage and reacts to any injury imposed on the bone structure. Moreover, these muscles may be injured directly through trauma or indirectly through surgical procedures. Consequently, it is a commonplace for most back surgery patients to experience pain in this muscle group. Many confuse this natural pain with bone stress or nerve damage. Although it is true that scar tissue and nerve pathways can be intertwined, this condition can be corrected with stretching exercises.

Muscle group B often contributes to back pain because the shorter leg muscles pull at the A muscles and create stress at the overlap in the lower back and hip contracting point as well. We once treated an executive who literally had to be picked up off the golf turf twice because of severe back pains. Upon examination, we found six "knots" in one leg and seven in the other. Through massage, the pain eventually dissipated, and he was able to return to his golf game. At one-year follow-up, he was playing golf without any physical distress.

Group C muscles are particularly important to the balance of the pelvis and are involved in the condition of lordosis, or "sway back." Occasionally, these overstressed muscles can chronically pull the pelvis forward, creating strain on the bone structure and nerve irritation.

Group D muscles, the stomach muscles, usually balance the upper body structure so that weight is evenly proportioned on the bone structure. The problems these muscles create are not usually through stress or tension, but rather through lack of use. Over the years, individuals use these muscles less and less, relying on the rigidity of the backbone to support their weight. It is interesting to note that most children and athletes utilize these muscles very effectively to keep their bodies flexible. Consequently, one of the treatment goals for many back patients is strengthening these particular muscles while, at the same time, relaxing or stretching the A, B, and C muscle groups.

Skeletal systems. The bone structure related to back pain is usually the domain and focus of the surgeon, because this aspect primarily involves the functional relationship between vertebrae. Briefly stated, the backbone is made up of a series of joints, called "facets," which allow only a limited range of motion. Cushions, commonly referred to as disks, between each pair of vertebrae support the weight of the individual and allow some flexibility to the backbone while protecting the spinal cord. Nerves associated with regulation of the body leave the spinal cord through rear openings of the backbone. If the distance between the vertebrae becomes restricted, the nerve is "pinched," creating pain. This condition can be caused by the narrowing of the vertebral space as a result of either diseased disks or an imbalance of bone structure (see Figure 6.2). Consequently, treatment strategies focus on widening the spaces between vertebrae. The widening may be attempted by means of a combination of techniques, including surgical restructuring, exercise to change bone alignment, and relaxation to relieve undue pressure on the nerve points.

The body's system of drugs. In acute medical crises, such as surgery or trauma, the administration of narcotics is deemed important for shock management and for humanistic considerations. However, it is intriguing to note that the body has many chemical reactions of its own for combating pain.

In order to understand the mechanics of pain control, it is important to understand the current theory of chemical transactions within the body. The body has millions of nerve cells within it, usually within patterns. These nerve patterns consist of nerve fibers passing impulses from one to another at synapses. The synapse is the junction of the tail-like ending of one nerve cell and the body of another nerve cell. When nerve cells pass impulses along in communication with one another, one releases a chemical called a *neurotransmitter* from the nerve ends. The neurotransmitter crosses the synapse and transfers its energy to the outer membrane of the next nerve cell. Messages, including messages of painful stimuli, are sent in this fashion by certain ascending pathways to the appropriate structures in the brain for decoding.

The thalamus is the principal subcortical structure involved in transmitting pain signals. It is a large, oblong structure which is divided into two parts, the lateral and medial thalamus. The lateral thalamus processes information regarding touch, light pressure to the skin, and sharp, prickly pain. The medial thalamus processes deep, chronic, burning pain (Snyder, 1977).

Pain medication impinges on the pathway between the thalamus and the source of irritation by blocking the transmission of pain messages at the level of the synapse. On the molecular level, the narcotic agents attach themselves to areas of high receptivity, thus blocking other chemical transactions that may occur.

Recently, John Hughes (1978) and his coworkers at Aberdeen found two structures, both termed *peptides* (due to their property of being chains of amino acids) which appeared to be the body's own chemicals for managing pain. One was termed methionine and the other, leucine. There is a chemical difference between the two, although they act in an identical way. For example, when the body communicates a severity of irritation beyond discomfort, the perceived pain is deadened by modulation of the so-called pain threshold. At the point where one begins to perceive a stimulus as painful, specific

Figure 6.2

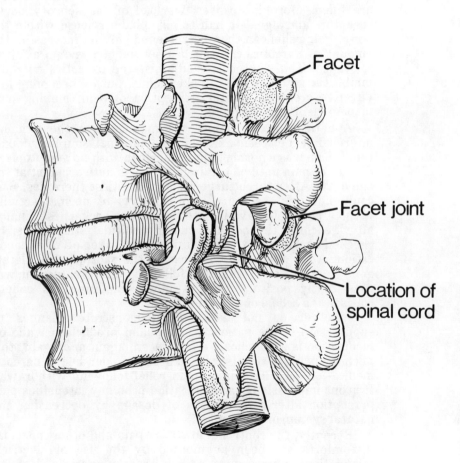

Facet

Facet joint

Location of
spinal cord

pain killing molecules composed of these peptides (currently called enkephalins) are released.

This discussion is rather academic until one begins to discriminate between artificial narcotics and the body's manufactured narcotics. Under normal circumstances, enkephalins probably fill a specific number of receptor sites as an ongoing surveillance for pain management. With the addition of morphine or some other narcotic, the rest of the receptor sites are filled. Morphine causes overload of the sensory nerve receptors and signals a halt to enkephalin release within the body. Pain relief can then be achieved only by increasing the amount of narcotic, creating a phenomenon known as drug tolerance. Thus, externally administered narcotics not only inhibit the manufacture of enkephalins, but by becoming less effective create a greater perception of pain, making pain management more complex.

A patient by the name of Sam illustrates the dynamic interchange between external and internal sources of pain relief. Sam was a normal, ambitious man with no symptoms of disease or pain until he was involved in an auto accident at the age of 20. After three surgeries and countless therapies, Sam could not tolerate more than 10 days of normal activity without having to have bedrest for severe backaches. Finally, after reaching the point of making suicidal statements, he checked himself into the hospital and was taken off of all medication. After a week of withdrawal, the pain was completely gone from consciousness, and follow-up after six months was consistently positive. Sam is now completing his college courses at a school on the West Coast.

Whether or not we could demonstrate changes or suppression of the patient's enkephalin production while on medication is academic. We have seen, again and again, this phenomenon of patients who had been under heavy narcotic medication actually gaining pain relief following withdrawal. It is our impression that medication probably intensifies pain perception after two months of dosage by decreasing the natural system of pain control.

Recently, the control of low back pain and other muscular discomforts has been augmented by the use of electrical stimulation, a procedure called Transcutaneous Electrical Nerve Stimulation (TENS). The source of stimulation is a little electrical transformer about the size of a cigarette package with two, or more, pairs of electrodes. These electrodes are placed on the surface of the body over the location of the perceived pain. When the transformer is turned on, a current ranging from 1 to 50 milliamps pulsates at a frequency of 2 to 110 pulses per second. The determination of settings for amplitude and frequency are typically based upon clinical trials.

TENS is based upon the Gate Control Theory of pain perception (Melzack & Wall, 1965). In principle, pain impulses go from the peripheral to the higher levels of consciousness on two different kinds of nerve fibers, one larger in diameter (highly myelinated) and the other smaller in diameter (little or no myelination). Stimulated large fibers are perceived as general sensation, whereas the stimulated small fibers relate to more specific perceptions.

Although the fibers communicate different pain senses, they compete with each other for attention. The model predicts that when a specific sensation is present, its perception will be blocked at the neurological gates by the "quantitative" superiority of a more general stimulation to the large nerve fibers. The electrical pulse of the TENS serves as the overpowering sensation to the large fibers that tends to "block out" pain perception.

Zimmerman (1978) relates pain relief achieved through the action of TENS to more classic neuropsychological principles:

1. Suppression of ongoing discharges which are initiated in peripheral endings of regenerating proprioceptive afferents.

2. Pre- or postsynaptic inhibition of spinal neurons which are involved in the processing of noxious stimuli.

3. Repression of denervation supersensitivity of neurons in the central nervous system.

4. Long-lasting hyper-polarization by postexcitatory active ion transport.

Campbell and Taub (1973) suggest, however, that TENS relieves pain by inducing some neurons to produce enkaphalins, the endogenous opiates which interact with receptors to produce analgesia as described earlier.

We have found that 71 percent of our back patients acknowledge some relief (10 to 50 percent) of their pain as a result of TENS treatment. Effective electrode placement appears to vary widely. We allow patients themselves to try different locations, strengths, and pulse rates to determine what combination works best for them. Some patients with low back pain place the electrodes on their legs, some on their hips, some on the lower or upper back. Some patients even place the electrodes on their shoulders! Yet, if the previously discussed models of TENS action are correct, the most effective placement of the stimulation should be between the area of injury and spinal cord, thereby either blocking out the fiber connection or raising the level of enkaphalins at that particular location in the spine. In this regard, it should be mentioned that we do find transcutaneous electrical stimulation to be helpful for spasms when specific "trigger points" can be located with the instrument.

The emotional response. Emotional response to pain is largely a learned response and, thus, amenable to relearning. Most of our back pain patients have a similar developmental background. They usually are from poor families and have had to work very hard for their survival. The fact that their companies are often footing the bill confirms the general hypothesis that they have been relatively successful in their work habits. For these reasons, it seems reasonable to assume that their value systems include a positive regard for the work ethic and a desire for rehabilitation. However, there are implicit values and reactions which actually defend against successful pain relief.

One of these negative emotional responses has to do with the attitude that, if some problem exists, one can overpower it with muscular activity. Unfortunately, this strong motivation to overpower the pain does not usually help. By reacting to the pain with muscular stress, the body often works against itself, more stress is built up, muscles may be reinjured, and a pattern of defeat is soon created. Mary, a 30-year-old patient, was an airline stewardess and had suffered from back pain for two years. After the first six months of constant pain, she decided she would "beat it or it would beat her." She bought a bicycle and rode it incessantly to a state of fatigue, then she spent the next month in agony. Her motivation to attack muscular pain with muscular stress was correct, but her technique was erroneous. We attempt to teach responsibility for health tempered by respect for *both* relaxation and proper exercise.

The second emotional response which magnifies physiological pain response is fear. This involves a learned attitude that pain is a "nasty, terrible thing" which must be localized and not allowed to spread. Behaviorally, this response can be observed in the patient's physical reactions of not breathing and of restraining the muscles around the painful area. It is not unlike the response of many dental patients who hold their breath, restrict their throat muscles, and grip the chair in anticipation of pain. Obviously, these kinds of reactions are antagonistic to rehabilitation in a treatment setting. An injured area needs oxygen for repairs to be accomplished; the muscles need to be relaxed to facilitate this process, and fear of pain must dissipate for muscle relaxation to occur.

We attempt to teach patients that pain is normally a friend who warns and protects us against physical insult. We explain that chronic low back pain patients are *not* experiencing normal pain. What they *are* experiencing is a maladaptive reaction to early pain, which hurts much worse. Just as the athlete understands and listens to his or her body in order to control it, the pain patient is taught to allow natural resources to cope with the stress. This is *not* to say that the patients resign themselves to a life of passivity. Instead, patients are encouraged to adopt a positive lifestyle of reacting to the pain by initiating the *relaxation* response instead of the fear response. The newly acquired consequence to the pain, then, is to relax the muscles in a systematic fashion and thereby employ pain management techniques. Such techniques are actually very active and require concentration as well as internal drive.

A Psychological Perspective. The physiological origins of back pain are fairly straightforward. However, the influence of other individual factors on prognosis is more subtle, though no less important. From a psychological perspective, three separate considerations must be taken into account: the behavioral response to low back or spinal pain, the personality traits associated with the perception of pain, and the interpersonal dynamics related to the management of the case.

Behavioral. The behavioral response to pain is divided into two large categories of observation: habitual behavior and stress response. Habitual behaviors tend to fatigue back muscles and create situations of greater pain intensity. They can be easily observed in leisure and work activities. In order to determine the impact of poor response habits, we often ask our patients to carry out their usual routine in a mock environment. A checklist is utilized, a modified version of which appears below.

Checklist of Postures Related to Various Behaviors in Low Back Pain

Behavior	Negative Habits
I. Posture	1. Locked knees
	2. Head carried forward
	3. Round shoulders
	4. *a.* Prominent abdomen (pelvis tipped)
	b. Exaggerated lumbar (curves forward)
	c. Protruding buttocks
II. Lifting	1. Unbent legs and hips
	2. Entire load is pulled from back muscles
	3. No leverage is apparent
	4. The body twists in transport
	5. Objects are carried away from body
III. Sitting	1. Forward slump
	2. Feet do not reach floor
	3. Exaggerated lumbar curve

IV. Lying   1. Head on high pillow that strains neck, arms,
                        shoulders
                     2. Lying flat on back without bending legs or hips

The behavioral response obviously goes beyond these simple postural considerations and patient self-report. Therefore, the behavioral diagnosis should include observations in the midst of activities which typically cause discomfort. Some behaviors that often correlate with intensified pain are:

1) Holding one's breath or taking quick, shallow breaths at the onset of pain,
2) Tightening a set or sets of muscles,
3) Showing other fear responses (dilated eyes; quiet, shallow breathing),
4) Showing flight response (becoming agitated, trembling)
5) Decreasing temperature of extremities.

Personality assessment. There are two aspects of personality diagnostics that we have found to be useful: (1) to determine the perception of the pain as it impacts emotionally on the patient's life, and (2) to ascertain how well the patient will do in the program.

1. Emotional Involvement. With respect to the first diagnostic consideration, our patients are usually administered the *Minnesota Multiphasic Personality Inventory* (MMPI) and a diagram with which they pictorially describe their pain (Figure 6.3). The drawing is scored along five dimensions:

1) How "real" the pain is, based on what orthopedists believe to be anatomic localization of pain pathways. Any "unreal" pain pathways cited by the patient count 2 points each. The following are some examples of "unreal" pain:
   a. total leg pain
   b. lateral whole leg pain (trichenturic area and lateral thigh allowed)
   c. circumferential thigh pain
   d. bilateral tibial area pain
   e. circumferencial foot pain
   f. bilateral foot pain

2) Extent to which the drawing shows "expansion" or magnification of pain (2 points for each inclusion), i.e.,
   a. back pain radiating to ilium crest, groin, or anterior perineum
   b. anterior knee pain
   c. anterior ankle pain

3) Extent to which pain is overly dramatized (1 point each), i.e.,
   a. additional explanation notes
   b. pain drawn outside the outline
   c. circling painful areas
   d. lines to demarcate painful areas
   e. arrows

Figure 6.3

NAME:

Mark the areas on your body where you feel the described sensations.
Use the appropriate symbol. Mark areas of radiation. Include all
affected areas. Just to complete the picture, please draw in your face.

```
          ====                    oooo              xxxx                  ////
Numbness  ====  Pins and Needles  oooo  Burning     xxxx  Stabbing        ////
          ====                    oooo              xxxx                  ////
```

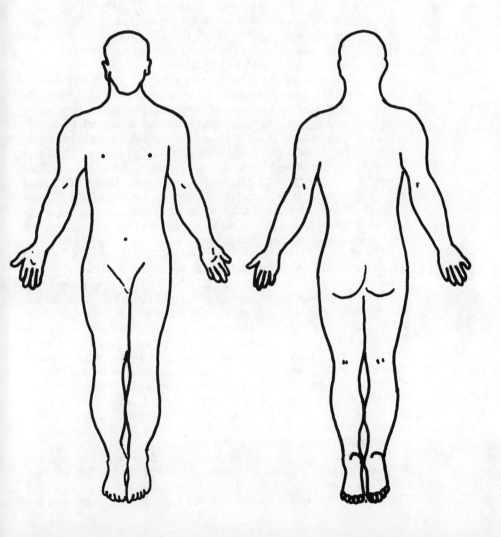

4) Extent to which additional areas besides the back area are drawn in (upper trunk, head, neck) (1 point each):

5) Lack of specificity of pain (the roving pain) (2 points).

Our work was stimulated by, and reaffirms the results of, an earlier study by Ransford, Cairns, and Mooney (1976) which reported that MMPI profiles were related to the drawings. Their study found that 93 percent of the patients (70 percent in our study) who had Hs and Hy scale scores of more than 70 —the traditional hysterical reaction—also had scores of 3 or more on the pain drawings. At the same time, 79 percent (55 percent in our study) of the patients who exhibited no hysterical pathology on the MMPI had scores on their drawings of 2 or less. With our patients, we have found overall that 66 percent of those with pathological MMPI profiles have scores of 2 or more on the pain drawing, 73 percent of those with normal MMPI profiles have scores of less than 2. These results are revealing with respect to communication between physician and patient. We feel that the patient is saying, "I hurt emotionally as well as physically."

As indicated above, some subjects in the pathological group were the classical hysterics who used pain as a neurotic defense against reality. In the present context, they were usually creating pain in order to avoid some aspect of themselves. For example, Kay was a 41-year-old woman who was quite average both mentally and physically, except that she had severe pain in her back. The pain was so bad that she had to go to bed every time she had an episode. Her MMPI and Pain Drawing are presented in Figures 6.4A and 6.4B. Her pattern of elevated Hs and Hy scales, together with a Pain Drawing score of 4, are indications that she had a great deal of psychological investment in pain.

The clue that her symptoms might be serving as a defensive mechanism occurred when we noticed situations that appeared to precipitate the pain. She would have more pronounced pain whenever her 18-year-old daughter attempted to interact with her. As the dynamics later revealed, the patient resented her daughter with a fierce intensity because of a history of embarrassing behavioral acts, such as a premarital pregnancy and numerous problems with school officials. Quite possibly due to her need to see herself as an adequate mother, she avoided awareness of this resentment by using pain to focus on her physiological needs rather than her emotional conflict. Once she was able to express her resentment, she was freed of the necessity of using pain as a shield, and a rapid recovery followed.

The conversion "V" profile and pain drawings are similar for patients who are not always using hysterical defenses, but could be more aptly described as socialized pain patients. These patients' social environments have been structured by their family and friends so that their pain is almost necessary for communication. Joan, a 51-year-old woman who had a very close family unit comprised of seven grown children, their spouses, and five grandchildren, was a good example of this type. Her MMPI and Drawing are presented in Figures 6.5A and 6.5B.

Joan's family activities centered entirely upon her pain. The family gatherings occurred because of the condition or status of her pain. At a treatment conference, the family members openly admitted that if their mother had no pain, there would be very little else with which to relate. Interestingly enough, although they acknowledged their role in reinforcing the pain, they were unwilling to change. There was unanimous agrèement that they preferred a continued close family interaction at the expense of the mother's pain. Joan's case may be unusual but by no means unique, for we have encountered numerous family clusters who have grown up together around the pain or illness of some family member.

Other patients can be found as victims in the legal reinforcement of lawsuits, social security hearings, and divorce negotiations. There is also an overlap with patients who get caught up in a love-hate relationship with the physician. This particular syndrome reflects the patient's perception of a physician's care, in which any failure of medical treatment is projected upon the physician with vengeance and hostility. However, when confronted face to face by the physician, these emotions are converted almost completely to seductive statements of admiration and compliance. It is suspected that this syndrome is based upon the patient's attitude that the "powerful doctor" is responsible for cure, combined with the fear that physician's care will be withdrawn if that wrath is tendered. In the face of any condition which gives no promise to be self-limiting, such as low back pain, the threat of withdrawal of medical care can be fearful indeed. The love-hate relationship victimizes the patient to the point that a role of chronic passivity combined with hostility is created which can only be uncomfortable for both patient and the health care professionals.

2. Program Prognostics. The MMPI and Pain Drawing records are useful for understanding the chronic pain patient's *involvement* or psychological investment in the pain experience. However, we have not found these records to account for predicting success in a treatment program of pain control. Instead, the *Sixteen Personality Factor Questionnaire* (16 PF) has provided the basis for evaluating the potential of patients to improve with treatment. Since each patient is considered for continuation or discharge after only a week of treatment, the predictive equation for probability of success is a major consideration. For parsimonious reasons, we have developed

Figure 6.4A

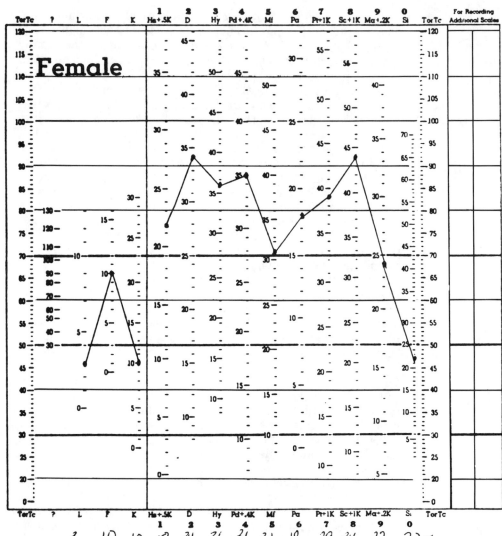

	?	L	F	K	**1** Hs+.5K	**2** D	**3** Hy	**4** Pd+.4K	**5** Mf	**6** Pa	**7** Pt+1K	**8** Sc+1K	**9** Ma+.2K	**0** Si		
Raw Score		3	10	10	18	34	36	31	31	18	29	34	22	22		
K to be added					5			4			10	10	2			
Raw Score with K					23			35			39	44	24			

Female

Figure 6.4B

NAME:

Mark the areas on your body where you feel the described sensations.
Use the appropriate symbol. Mark areas of radiation.   Include all
affected areas.   Just to complete the picture, please draw in your face.

Numbness ==== Pins and Needles oooo Burning xxxx Stabbing ////

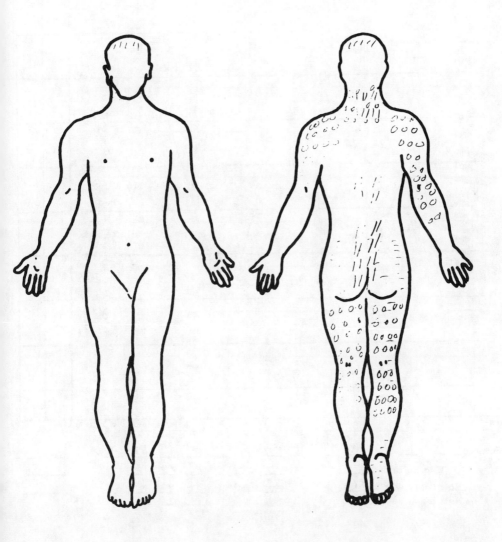

Figure 6.5A

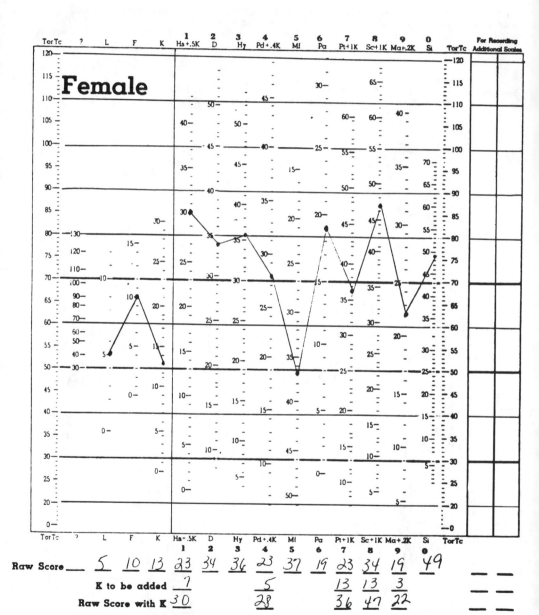

Raw Score	5	10	13	23	34	36	23	37	19	23	34	19	49	
K to be added				7			5			13	13	3		
Raw Score with K				30			28			36	47	22		

Figure 6.5B

Mark the areas on your body where you feel the described sensations. Use the appropriate symbol. Mark areas of radiation. Include all affected areas. Just to complete the picture, please draw in your face.

Numbness ▪▪▪▪ Pins and Needles οοοο Burning xxxx Stabbing ////

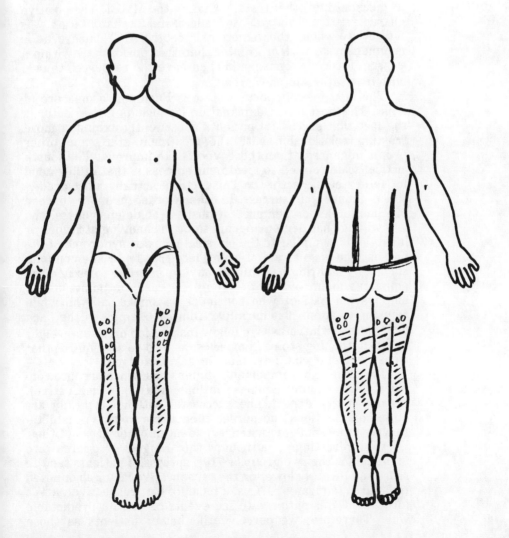

an empirically based "poor man's" equation that does not require extensive calculation. Clinical interpretations of the results are provided below. Because many readers may be unfamiliar with the dynamics of the 16 PF scales, only basic generalizations which appear to have clinical utility in pain management are discussed. Scores, means, and standard deviations are available from the authors upon request.

The prediction method is based on seven of the scales from the 16 PF and is clinically logical. The most predictive index is a combination between Factors C and Q_4. Factor C, a measure of ego strength or coping strength, depicts the reserve of emotional resources available to deal with stress. Factor Q_4 is a measure of tension similar to a generalized level of anxiety as measured by other tests, including the MMPI. The positive characteristic, relative to successful rehabilitation, is indicated when the emotional control (C) measure is commensurate with or greater than the tension (Q_4) within a person. Basically, one should then have the resources to deal with frustrations as they arise.

The next most important scale is Factor L, a measure of trust. The most direct explanation for including this factor is the fact that successful patients consistently exhibit a more trusting relationship with the treatment staff, and other people in general, than those who fail to improve. The fourth critical scale related to treatment success is that of low need for self-esteem, Factor Q_3. This factor is actually more predictive of failure than success. In other words, the more concern one has for his or her pretentiousness or defensiveness, the less willing that person appears to be in changing attitudes or lifestyle. It is similar to the classical neurotic syndrome of the person who is so afraid of losing face that he or she commits suicide by ignoring healthful behavior, in order to escape the embarrassment of being wrong. A case in point is the emphysema patient who continues to smoke, all the while refusing to admit it is harmful. Another example is the back pain patient who refuses to follow instruction on losing weight or strengthening stomach muscles, as if to do so requires that a basic defect in character must be acknowledged.

Two minor, but important, dimensions which are also considered are Factors G (conscientious) and Q_1 (conservative). As one might expect, the successful patients typically are quite conscientious and pursue their drive toward rehabilitation with the same persistence evident in other areas of their lives. Interestingly, although the ranges of scores are identical for the two groups (3-10), successful patients tend to score significantly lower on the conservative factor as opposed to failures (a mean of 4.7 vs. a mean of 6.1, respectively). We interpret Q_1 as patience to see events occur in a predictable way. Therefore, we perceive the better patients as those exhibiting patience and conscientiousness, as opposed to those exhibiting impatience and incontinence.

As a bonus, we find that Factor B, labeled Abstract Thinking, can be a very useful factor. Not surprisingly, successful patients have usually been higher on this factor than unsuccessful patients, but the ranges were identical and the predictability not particularly powerful. As a general rule, it is our interpretation that the smarter the patient, the better prognosis for change.

To apply the empirical findings mentioned above, we developed a decision model to predict the potential for treatment. For each of the 16 PF criteria discussed above which are met by the individual, a predetermined number of points are awarded. No points are given for any unmet criteria. The points are then cumulated to get an index of treatment motivation. The model is outlined below.

Decision 1: If Factor C is equal to or greater than
Q_4 ($C \geqslant Q_4$) $= 4$ points

Decision 2: If Factor L is less than 5 ($L < 5$) $= 3$ points

Decision 3: If Factor Q_3 is less than or equal to 5
($Q_3 \leqslant 5$) $= 2$ points

Decision 4: If Factor G is greater than 5, or
($G > 5$), or if Factor Q_1 is less than 5
($Q_1 < 5$) $= 1$ point

Decision 5: bonus: If Factor B is greater than or
equal to 5 ($B \geqslant 5$) $= 1$ point

$$D_1 + D_2 + D_3 + D_4 + D_5 = \text{motivation index}$$

The resultant score will range from 0 to 10 (omitting the bonus if the sum is already 10). The range of scores is approximately equal to 10 percentile intervals. A score of 5 is roughly the mean; also, 50 percent of the cases fall below and 50 percent of the cases are above that score, so that it is the median as well. As a score deviates from that mean, the chances of "success" vary accordingly (1-3, poor; 4-6, fair; 7-9, good; 10, excellent) (Lawlis, Mooney, Selby, McCoy, in press).

Because of our attitudes regarding rehabilitation and potential change in people, we may allow a trial period in the program of 2-5 days despite a poor showing on the prognostic device. A score of 4-6 reflects only fair potential for rehabilitation, but with regular staff evaluations to determine amount of progress, the individual may benefit enough to justify participation in the program. A score of 7-10 is considered to be one of high motivation for success and certainly worthy of continuance in the program.

As an illustration of how the system works, two examples have been chosen from our files. John presented the 16 PF profile in Figure 6.6. It is apparent that John had high Q_4 factor and low C factor scores, indicating that although his frustration might be mild, he did not have the emotional strength to deal with the stress. Clinically, he showed perseveration in his worries about his future. Although trusting (L), he was impatient (Q_1), not conscientious (G), and not an abstract thinker (B). A total score of 3 indicated a poor prognosis for rehabilitation outcome. He worked with us for three weeks but could not see himself in any role other than that of a failure. Although relatively successful on the biofeedback equipment, in terms of learning muscular relaxation, he could not break his pain lifestyle upon returning home. He continued to remain unemployed, even though his reported pain had been reduced to negligible levels.

Another patient, Jill, was a 65-year-old female who complained of severe pain in her back and legs. Although her MMPI and Pain Drawing indicated a strong emotional investment in her problem, her 16 PF motivational score was 9. Her C factor was greater than Q_4 (4 points); her L factor was less than 5 (3 points); and although her Q_3 was not 5 or less, the G was greater than 5, and also her Q_1 was less than 5 (1 point). Her overall score of 8 plus a bonus of 1 point for Factor B greater than 5 yielded a motivation index of 9. In other words, she had good emotional control, trusted the staff, was conscientious, patient, and bright. Her need for self-esteem did not convert to defensiveness and was used in a constructive way for self-growth (Figure 6.7). Not only did Jill demonstrate a strong will to rehabilitate herself after a year of convalescence and two operations, but she became a very vocal inspiration for other patients in the clinic.

Group Techniques
of Treatment
Techniques utilized in the Spinal Pain Program are based on the principles of developing awareness through confrontation of attitudes and pain behaviors and of restructuring these in ways that are more likely to be related to a healthy, productive lifestyle. They may appear mechanistic when described generally, but in actual practice the techniques are quite subtle. General descriptions are offered only as basic guidelines.

Imagery. Imagery in the treatment of pain is largely a combination of therapist practice, sensitivity, and creativity, paired with patient receptivity, motivation, and ability. We have used a variety of transcripts with success. One such program

Figure 6.6

Name: John

Comments:

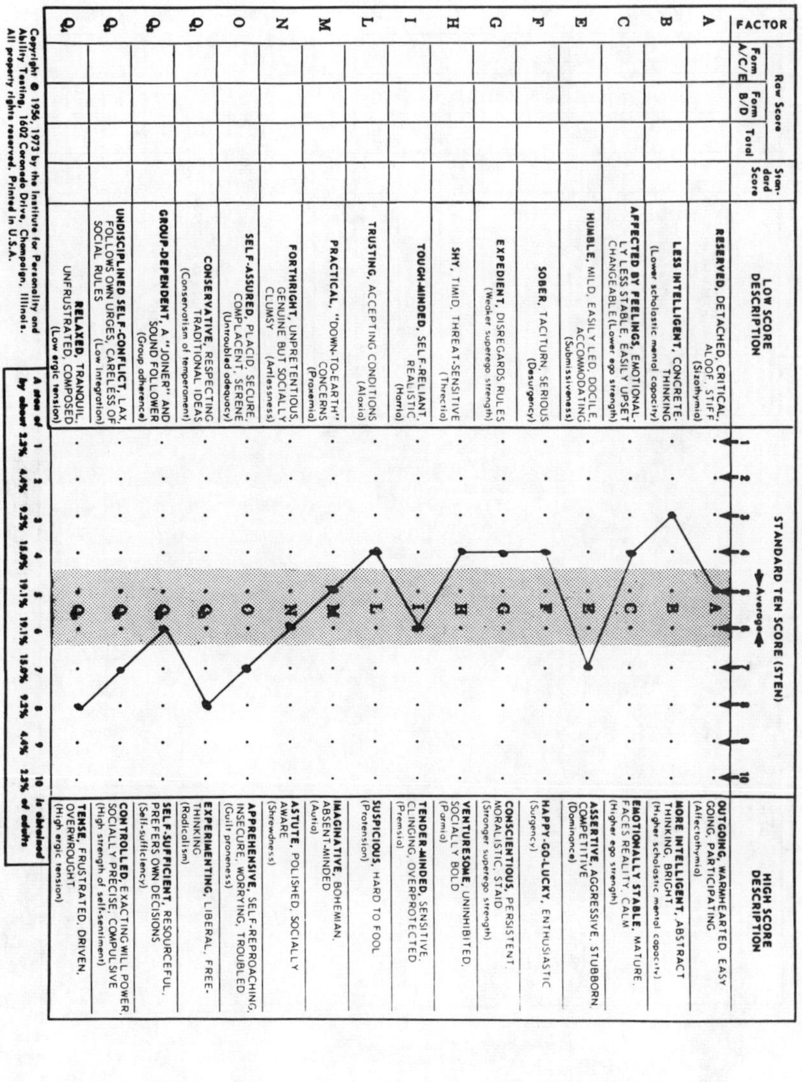

16 PF TEST PROFILE

STANDARD TEN SCORE (STEN)

FACTOR	Row Score Form A/C/E	Form B/D	Total Score	Standard Score	LOW SCORE DESCRIPTION	HIGH SCORE DESCRIPTION
A					RESERVED, DETACHED, CRITICAL, ALOOF, STIFF (Sizothymia)	OUTGOING, WARMHEARTED, EASY GOING, PARTICIPATING (Affectothymia)
B					LESS INTELLIGENT, CONCRETE-THINKING (Lower scholastic mental capacity)	MORE INTELLIGENT, ABSTRACT-THINKING, BRIGHT (Higher scholastic mental capacity)
C					AFFECTED BY FEELINGS, EMOTIONALLY LESS STABLE, EASILY UPSET, CHANGEABLE (Lower ego strength)	EMOTIONALLY STABLE, MATURE, FACES REALITY, CALM (Higher ego strength)
E					HUMBLE, MILD, EASILY LED, DOCILE, ACCOMMODATING (Submissiveness)	ASSERTIVE, AGGRESSIVE, STUBBORN, COMPETITIVE (Dominance)
F					SOBER, TACITURN, SERIOUS (Desurgency)	HAPPY-GO-LUCKY, ENTHUSIASTIC (Surgency)
G					EXPEDIENT, DISREGARDS RULES (Weaker superego strength)	CONSCIENTIOUS, PERSISTENT, MORALISTIC, STAID (Stronger superego strength)
H					SHY, TIMID, THREAT-SENSITIVE (Threctia)	VENTURESOME, UNINHIBITED, SOCIALLY BOLD (Parmia)
I					TOUGH-MINDED, SELF-RELIANT, REALISTIC (Harria)	TENDER-MINDED, SENSITIVE, CLINGING, OVERPROTECTED (Premsia)
L					TRUSTING, ACCEPTING CONDITIONS (Alaxia)	SUSPICIOUS, HARD TO FOOL (Protension)
M					PRACTICAL, "DOWN-TO-EARTH" CONCERNS (Praxernia)	IMAGINATIVE, BOHEMIAN, ABSENT-MINDED (Autia)
N					FORTHRIGHT, UNPRETENTIOUS, GENUINE BUT SOCIALLY CLUMSY (Artlessness)	ASTUTE, POLISHED, SOCIALLY AWARE (Shrewdness)
O					SELF-ASSURED, PLACID, SECURE, COMPLACENT, SERENE (Untroubled adequacy)	APPREHENSIVE, SELF-REPROACHING, INSECURE, WORRYING, TROUBLED (Guilt proneness)
Q₁					CONSERVATIVE, RESPECTING TRADITIONAL IDEAS (Conservatism of temperament)	EXPERIMENTING, LIBERAL, FREE-THINKING (Radicalism)
Q₂					GROUP-DEPENDENT, A "JOINER" AND SOUND FOLLOWER (Group adherence)	SELF-SUFFICIENT, RESOURCEFUL, PREFERS OWN DECISIONS (Self-sufficiency)
Q₃					UNDISCIPLINED SELF-CONFLICT, LAX, FOLLOWS OWN URGES, CARELESS OF SOCIAL RULES (Low integration)	CONTROLLED, EXACTING WILL POWER, SOCIALLY PRECISE, COMPULSIVE (High strength of self-sentiment)
Q₄					RELAXED, TRANQUIL, UNFRUSTRATED, COMPOSED (Low ergic tension)	TENSE, FRUSTRATED, DRIVEN, OVERWROUGHT (High ergic tension)

A score of: 1 2 3 4 5 6 7 8 9 10
by about: 2.3% 4.4% 9.2% 15.0% 19.1% 19.1% 15.0% 9.2% 4.4% 2.3% is obtained by about 2.3% of adults.

Figure 6.7

Name: _Jill_

Comments:

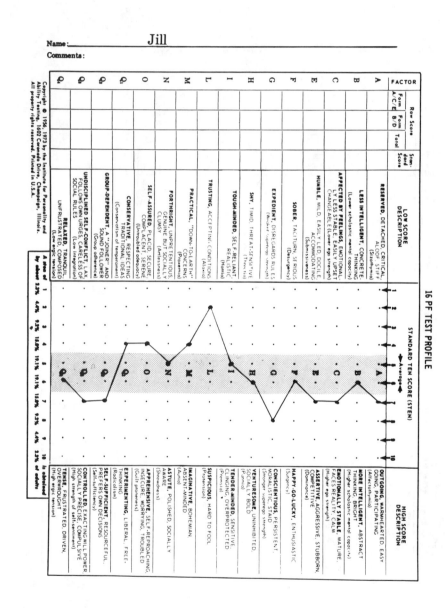

involves a focus on enkaphalins and health; another one is on general relaxation as it relates to muscle tension.

The use of imagery is very powerful on a number of levels: cognitive and behavioral, as well as physiological. We believe that through relaxed communication of the imagerial events we can discover the basic belief system of the patient with regard to his or her pain control. Particularly with people who have chronic pain, direct questioning about such a belief system usually yields little information. Typically, we ask the patients to draw the images they had while they were in the relaxation phase. We are interested in three aspects: (1) the vividness of the images, (2) the pain itself, and (3) the dynamics between the perception of the pain and how the body can intervene to combat its effects.

Vividness. If the patient can reach a depth of visualization wherein there is concrete vividness, that individual has taken the first step in demonstrating some reliability in pursuing a goal of awareness and change. This level is analogous to the determination of suggestibility in hypnosis. We assume, too, that motivation to cooperate and trust are major factors in the accomplishment of this phase, even though there are certainly individual differences in inherent ability to perceive, to achieve, and to relate vivid internal representation. Characteristics that are usually used to ascertain the vividness of the imagery are:

1. The specificity of the drawings;
2. The colors used;
3. How the components would feel if touched;
4. The projected motivational aspects of the elements (such as angry animals or evil weapons, like spears or arrows).

The variety of forms which symptoms may take in the images is fascinating. Figure 6.8*a* is the picture of a "cloud" of pain, pervasive and ominous. (Incidentally, clouds are not good predictors of successful outcome and may be related to the perception of vagueness.) Figure 6.8*b* shows pain around the shoulders as emanating from pickaxes and a knot, whereas Figures 6.8*c* and 6.8*d* are fairly typical in showing spikes or knives impaling the tissue.

Pain. The second component to be evaluated in the dynamics of pain imagery is the specific nature and source of the pain itself. For example, there have been patients who have seen the pain as a little man with intentions of hurting them, as a thorn that gets angry, as a snake with the mission of biting at regular intervals, or as an amorphous pillow.

If the image appears to involve other humans, we believe that the individual has real-life emotional conflicts that can be confronted on a concrete level. In our experience, suggestions

Figure 6.8*a*

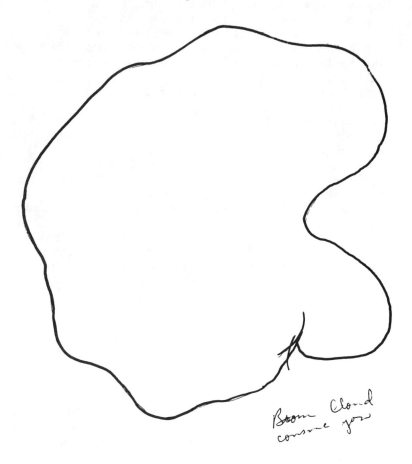

Boom Cloud consume you

Figure 6.8*b*

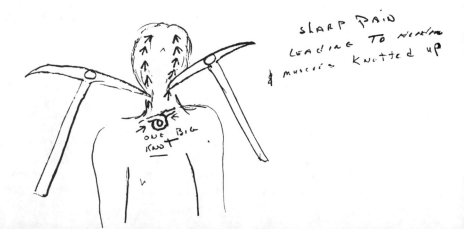

SHARP PAIN
LEADING TO HEADACHE
& MUSCLES KNOTTED UP

ONE BIG
KNOT

Figure 6.8c

Figure 6.8d

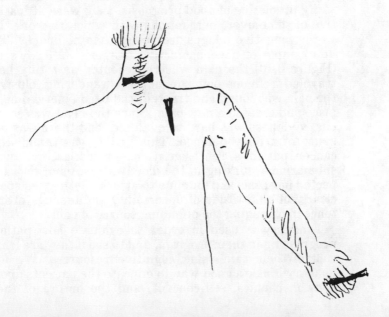

can be made to connect the intent of the pain symbol with other positive symbols like policemen and physicians.

Dynamics of pain intervention. The third evaluative dimension in the imagery is the patient's perception of the body's forces for combating the pain. If the pain symptom is a fire, does the body have the ability to put it out? If the pain is a thorn or knife, can it be dulled or broken? In chronic pain patients, the initial percepts are naturally void of bodily defense. However, as knowledge is gained and self-concepts change, positive symbols begin to emerge. This emergence is a very positive factor; the sooner it is evident, the more probable it is that pain management will be accomplished.

The case study of Jose is a fairly good example of a positive outcome reflected in imagery. Figure 6.9 shows Jose's drawing of his imagery while in a period of relaxation.

He saw his pain as a red ball of heat with radiating streams of irritation. The location of this ball was deep within his back. It was the size of a baseball, very hard and hot to the touch. After three days of relaxation and autogenic training, he began to see little flakes, colored metallic gold and silver, that cooled and softened the ball. He saw these flakes as being very powerful but quiet and deliberate. He also saw the control of these flakes as being under his direction during relaxation and eventually reaching the point of bringing about anesthesia of his entire body.

It should be pointed out that patients with the *most* negative results in treatment evidenced no imagery at all, nor could they relax to the point of focusing on any imagery. While images such as those about to be discussed were not necessarily predictive of good prognosis, they were at least indicative of some overt perceptions with which to work. In other words, negative images are better than no images. Tony's is an example of nonconstructive imagery. In Tony's drawing (Figure 6.10) the pain was represented as a tiny bead that traveled from one point to another: wandering, elusive. Once the pain was found and treated, the bead emerged at another place and created a new pain. Since the bead was so mysterious, vividness was hard to evaluate, and there was no emergence of a body defense. This image was reminiscent of a cancer patient's representations of his ascites tumors as submarines—lurking in the dark waters, emerging at unsuspected intervals and immune to attack. Both cases speak very clearly of an attitude of uncertainty and feelings of incompetence in managing the offending source of pain.

Imagery is used in order to evaluate how patients are progressing in their program, and to see if they are learning to control their pain using cognitive resources. We feel that imagery is also a good way to educate the patients about their body mechanics, self-concept, and the nature of their pain

Figure 6.9

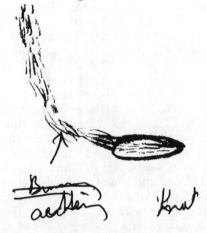

Figure 6.10

management skills. It is also a good medium for suggesting positive affirmations of security and support by having them focus on feelings and images evoked by such verbalizations as, "Every day I'm getting better and better," or "I see my body as becoming healthier," and "I am helping myself." A favorite affirmation of one pain patient is, "If it is to be, it's up to me." At first glance, this appears to be a rather liturgical approach, but such verbal concretion is both comforting and necessary to many people. It is also a format for thought stoppage of intervening negative cognitions and fantasies.

Imagery is the process of allowing patients to visualize their disease antibodies in a nonevaluative perspective. Without requiring judgments about goodness or badness, this process also allows them to communicate their feelings and dynamics without having to defend them. It is also a time of maximal receptivity to new information about their own responsibilities in health care and pain management.

Lifestyle Analysis. In this exercise each individual begins by describing his or her lifestyle. Inquiries from either the leader or the other members of the group are allowable. It is important to relate the lifestyles described to attitudes that will inhibit or facilitate rehabilitation efforts. Although there are many exceptions to the trends, the following developmental histories have been found to be useful ways to get at relevant attitudes.

1. *Birth order.* For the Adlerian therapist, these developmental histories should be no surprise. The relationship in a family hierarchy is the primal learning experience. Those individuals who were first born, especially females, often exhibit a great deal of guilt proneness regarding their lack of production. They often admit to a feeling of large responsibilities and frustration in fulfilling the demands of their families. The leader can point out how these guilt trips can intensify the perception of pain, especially when the anxiety is manifested muscularly. These patients usually do well in the program and are often the leaders of the group.

Last-born patients, especially the last girl of brothers or last boy of sisters, often have a perception of life in which they were passive recipients of care. They generally look to authority figures with different expectations than those people with more assertive lifestyles. Sometimes this dynamic may take the mode of identifying with those around them. For example, we had one patient—the youngest girl of a family of boys—who reported spending her early life as a tomboy. Her identity with those around her was evident in the clinic, because she began to dress like the staff and became "one of the gang." This particular style is usually positive with respect to attaining the goals within the program, but careful consideration should be made about placement. If placed back into an environment that promotes pain behavior, prognosis is poor. It appears that external stimulation is very difficult for these people to ignore, and it is easy for them to slip into the role of "the sick member."

Another variation of the last born is the last-born sister of a family of all girls, or brother of all boys. These individuals tend to report lifestyles of carefree, happy-go-lucky attitudes in which there is either an expectation that "everyone will take care of me" or else a cynical appreciation of rules. Regardless, this patient type tends to be manipulative of other patients and staff, argues a lot, and has more complaints than anyone else. An example is one patient who would have probably lived the rest of his life at the clinic, if allowed, and complained every minute he was there. Later we found that he had been in four prisons, was in the process of working his way through two marriages (at the same time), and had currently fallen in love with another patient. His pain (the roving kind) had a variety of routes throughout his body. Although discharged with manageable pain and vocationally placed, he has requested reentry to the program several times since.

Another birth-order consideration is the only-child syndrome, a kind of combination between the first born and last born. Only children tend to be similar to first borns in that they usually report a great deal of frustration in fulfilling their parents' expectations. They often report anxieties regarding their roles and social status. At the same time, they express that being raised in a world of adults stimulates a sensation of "always feeling like a child." The consequent behaviors are often related to the resolution of adult-child interactions: often rebellious in nature, sometimes overtly seductive. This type of patient usually improves impressively ahead of his or her peers, apparently seeking staff approval. It is as if the positive aspect of an achievement need is optimized, and some of our superstars are in this category.

Those individuals who come from large families are usually the most comfortable in hospital settings. They seem to fit in well with the group because they are accustomed to the interpersonal demands. They are not particularly outstanding in their progress through the program, but their congenial attitudes are very contagious. We find that they are the most cooperative and willing to participate in the activities we outline for them. On the other hand, we rarely find a leader among them in group activities.

2. *Cultural background.* People are often proud of their cultural backgrounds, and will usually readily discuss this aspect of their lives. Being relevant to the pain response, we have found it important to discuss this relationship early in the rehabilitation program.

Virtually all of the people that we have seen in the program so far have had similarities in their cultural developmental histories. They usually come from families that were either very poor or that evidenced turmoil and instability (divorce, parental neglect, abusive parents or siblings). The patients explain that this background allowed them to "learn about life" earlier. Often they express how physical activity could be extremely reinforcing to them. Some began manual labor at an early age (8-14); for many, sports activities became an outlet for energy and an important source of social contact. Regardless of the specific activity, they have related that this early experience of physical activity to them equaled productiveness, or peer acceptance, or pride.

As the individuals continue their life stories, it is obvious that these early learning experiences served them well in their jobs. They usually have excellent work histories, and their achievements are often beyond expectations. It is not unusual to see patients with 10th-grade educations who have obtained positions reserved for college graduates. Examples would run for pages. One man served as an engineer although he did not achieve a high school diploma. Many such patients had been promoted to supervisory jobs. One woman was vice president of a bank.

As group members describe themselves, it becomes apparent that the ambitious syndrome, or "Type A" personality, is common among them, and they affirm it with pride. The reaction to injury would be obvious, and we often use the analogy of the hard-working athlete who injures himself or herself. Given this singular view of self as a workhorse, all the patient's self-sentiment is contingent upon just one dimension of individuality.

The notion of productive behavior as positive is very consistent with goal attainment in a rehabilitation program. Yet the relentless application of this philosophy to every other aspect of life can be counterproductive. This stresses the individual to the point of building defensive mechanisms and manipulative behaviors against failure. Within three months, unless countered, the patient will be finding methods of avoiding work because of fear of failure. Another aspect is the usual response to pain: patients will often relate that their responses to the pain are like any other obstacle that they have encountered, except that this one (the pain) is beating them.

3. *Early memories and recollections.* Following Adlerian footsteps, patients are often asked about their earliest memories or recollections. Memories are differentiated semantically from recollections by defining recollections as a series of memories involving themselves and an incident, whereas memories may be only an isolated incident. We find

that this discussion helps stimulate insight into the inter-personal situation and the rehabilitation processes. It is important for the patients to consider their general attitudes about life and whatever obstacles they might present in the future.

After a recollection is presented, the task of the group is to discuss the "attitude" of life manifested and how it can help in rehabilitation. The simplest approach is to finish each recollection with the homily, ". . . and thus, is life." A good example was a young man whose pain appeared to be minimal. His employer felt that, with a little help, he could have great potential. He first recollected his early trials at riding a bicycle, with his father attempting to show him the technique. Every trial brought more and more frustration to his father and disappointment to the patient. Finally, the father left, and the boy, through his own independence and endurance, learned to ride his bicycle.

The relationship of his recollection to his program progress was illustrated in a variety of settings. His perception of being helped was representative of that early memory in the sense that he expected failure when it was associated with authority. His independence was a positive factor in his motivation to get well, but his interactions with the staff were characterized by a cynical attitude. When the explanation of the recollection was discussed by the group, he could admit to his attitudes and readily explored the positive and negative consequences.

4. *Names.* The first identifications we have in this world are our names, both family and personal. The identification of ourselves as a syllable or syllables has fascinating implications for self-concept and motivation.

Many names have cultural biases with positive or negative attribution. Johnny Cash's song, "A Boy Named Sue," is a good illustration of the lifelong programmed response to a name. Some people reject their names, rebelling at the connotations; others embrace their names, sometimes linking their self-esteem to the prestige of another person with the same name. Nicknames are especially interesting because of the information regarding the giver, the relationship between the two, and the implied message in the name. Names like Shortie, Fatso, Boy, Grease, Slick, Curlie, and Sonny are only a few that conjure a stereotype.

But it is not entirely the social stereotype of a name that is important to self-concept as it relates to rehabilitation. If the patient perceives his or her identification as evoking a loser image, then that person is reminded of potential failure every time someone calls his or her name. For example, Hank was a friendly man who was named after his father, Hank Sr. Hank Jr. had been successful in his job as a factory assembler, working his way to foreman before his injury. Hank Sr. had died an alcoholic and a failure in his son's eyes. Now, after experiencing a year of unproductive pain, he feared the same fate as his father. When this story was expressed to the group, everyone agreed that this patient needed a new name. After a thorough discussion, a new "identifier" was chosen— "Babe"—after his hero Babe Ruth and his lifestyle of swinging at anything. At a follow-up contact, his wife was addressing him as "Babe." Thus, the demise of Hank Jr. and the emergence of Babe signaled a change in outlook which was accompanied by insight and a new perspective on his problems.

Positive Attributions of Pain. Pain is usually seen as an enemy by both physician and patient. In a totally negative approach, our patients during one session took as their motto, "Kill the pain; it's my enemy." However, we have seen many patients utilize their pain in constructive ways. Our current philosophy accepts pain as a part of life, because it would be harmful to our outlook if we condemned *any* part of life as totally horrible or completely negative. Therefore, we set aside at least one session in which the patients are asked to think of ways in which pain has enriched their lives. Some of the most frequent replies are listed.

1) It (pain) helps me stop and look at myself.
2) It (pain) helped me realize what a wonderful family I have.
3) The pain and this program showed me the control I can have over my life.
4) The pain allowed me time to change my lifestyle and work habits.

Massage Techniques. We teach massage to the patients for two basic reasons: (1) because some patients need either the feedback of tension in their muscles in order to learn relaxation *or* require the external help massage affords in facilitating fuller relaxation; and (2) because the actual experience of being massaged becomes a training lesson in pain management through relaxation. With respect to the first reason, we find that many patients, whether pain patients or not, are unaware of their tension, especially in their legs and shoulders. Biofeedback can be utilized for this purpose, but it is quicker to have another person using the tactile sense (via massage) to relay the feedback. Additionally, training in the use of relaxation and massage for pain control is a technique directly transferable to the home setting. By using deep muscle massage as an adjunct to relaxation methods, we obtain a relatively quick and effective temporary relief of pain.

The principles, as explained to the participants, are based on a matrix which combines skeletal support with elements of behavioral response. Muscle structure is first described by using a picture of round muscle fiber (Figure 6.11). Muscles are combinations of tiny strands attached to bone and other muscles. Their function is to contract in order to move or support the skeletal frame. We also learn to restrict them in response to emotional feelings as if they were reacting to physical demands. For example, the shoulder muscles often tense when the person imagines a scene involving a great deal of responsibility. Many people tense their leg muscles when they are emotionally experiencing a need to achieve a goal or when experiencing a frustration in their schemes. Many such muscle sets are typically stressed as a result of emotional energy. From our experiences with patients presenting both physical and psychological distress, a very general topology can be outlined with caution, since there are many exceptions (Figure 6.12).

Normally, muscle is soft (even strong muscle) when not required to contract. This allows the opposite muscle—if required—to move the involved joints without resistance. When muscles are continuously tensed, blood is squeezed out, causing early fatigue and coolness. Sometimes muscles are partially tensed, causing tension to remain in a portion of the muscle with consequential contracture of that part. These muscular segments are referred to in the session as "knots," and are painful when massaged. We had a patient who had a knot in her back the size of an egg. As that region was deeply massaged, she reported that she had had that lump since she witnessed an automobile accident a year before. While she described her reactions, fears, and other anxieties, her muscle tension decreased. Certainly not all muscle knots are so specific to emotions, though many are—particularly those developed during specific postures, such as sitting at a typewriter, an activity during which many of the emotions related to the job may be "buried" or stored in the ache of pain.

The principle of massage is simply one of a milking motion directed toward the heart, with the intent of helping the blood and accompanying oxygen flow through the whole muscle and, particularly, the muscle knots. This motion needs to be deep and firm. Vegetable oils (such as coconut) are recommended for massage rather than mineral oils. The latter ultimately prove drying to the skin, whereas the vegetable oil is absorbed and softens as well as lubricates. The oil has a very specific purpose in addition to acting as a lubricant; it assists the person who is giving the massage in defining and feeling the knots with greater precision. A five-minute limit is

Figure 6.11

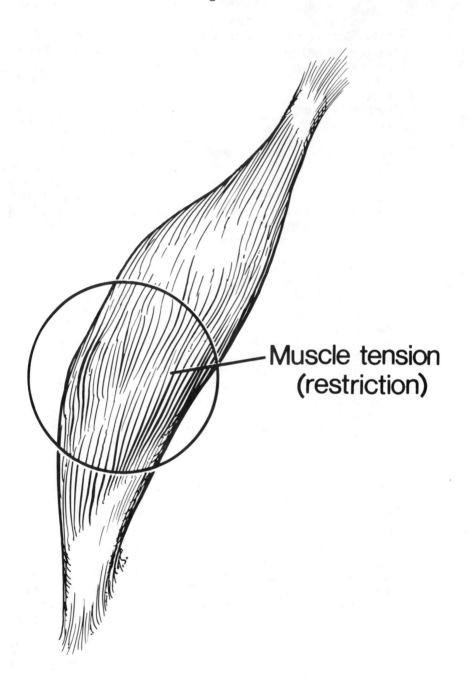

Muscle tension
(restriction)

Figure 6.12

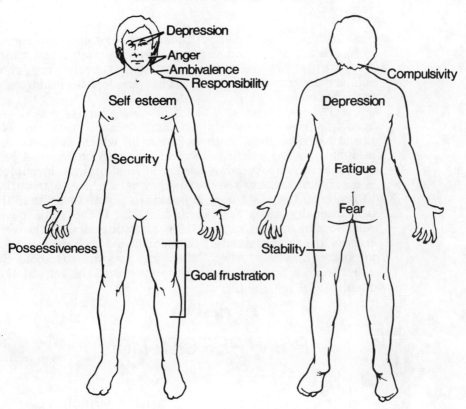

MUSCULAR STRESS REGIONS

recommended for any one set of muscles to prevent bruising the skin or outer layers of the muscle covering.

As patients experience the tension or pain held within a muscle, the typical physiological response is one related to fear and is the opposite of a state of relaxation. They usually hold their breath, tensing the entire body and withholding any communication. It should be pointed out that those responses only intensify the pain and extend the tension. Correct responses can be initiated at this time, as the discomfort is perceived. Breathing, even singing or growling, and relaxation of muscles allows the blood to flow and the knots to resolve themselves.

Pain Management Skills. Although all exercises presented here are intended to develop pain management, and range from attitude to physiological functioning, the following protocols are specific to this goal. These are ice, breathing, and verbal exercise.

1. *The ice exercise.* The ice pressor exercise was developed from research focusing on pain tolerance measures. The literature describes methodologies in which subjects are asked to submerge their hands and arms into ice water. A pain tolerance measure is defined as the amount of time the subject is capable of keeping the arms submerged. After attempting to replicate these studies, it became evident to us that the pain intensity had a curvilinear function. If the subject was relaxed and had no expectations of undue stress, the pain crested after approximately 60 seconds and then decreased in intensity. However, when the subject was anxious about the experience, it was not possible to experience the sensation of adaptation (Figure 6.13).

Figure 6.13

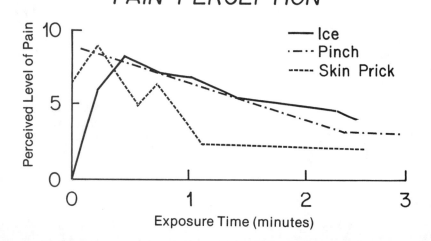

PAIN PERCEPTION

In the Spinal Pain Program, the cold pressor test has been adapted as a training task instead of a measure of pain tolerance. Each patient is first told about the phenomenon and the meaning of the outcome. Participating in the exercise necessitates the use of pain management skills on the part of the patient in order to allow the pain to crest and subside. Failure to perceive the decrease, and failure in management of the physiological pain response, implies a variety of motivational barriers: notably, anxiety, lack of trust, fear, and low aspiration.

2. *The breathing exercises.* Breathing exercises are designed to help the patients become more aware of their habitual breathing capacity. There are many extrapolations from these exercises to other situations; therefore, the practitioner should note some new possibilities with each exercise.

Patients are asked to lie down, close their eyes, and focus on their breathing. After a few moments, they are asked to breathe out all the air in their lungs with each breath. The therapist can apply physical pressure on the patient's body in order to aid maximum exhalation. This pressure also facilitates patient awareness of how rigidly the muscles involved in breathing may be held.

After this experience and a short recess, patients are asked to inhale in one breath and exhale in three breaths, repeating this exercise several times. After another short recess, patients are asked to inhale in three short breaths and exhale in one long breath. Many combinations and permutations are possible: inhaling in three breaths and exhaling in three breaths; inhaling in six breaths, exhaling in two breaths; etc.

Another exercise varies the inhalation, pause, and exhalation with respect to time units. Certain types of yoga practice recommmend a $1:4:2$, $1:1:1$, or $1:1:2$ ratio of timing. For example, the patient might be instructed to breathe in for one count, hold it for four counts, and breathe out for two counts.

Primary foci for subsequent discussion with the patient include:

1) How does deep breathing affect the rest of the body?
2) How does exhaling differ in difficulty from inhaling, or vice versa? (Sometimes one can use the analogy of extraversion-introversion.)
3) Although everyone breathes, there are different levels of skills.

Breathing may be the simplest, most basic bodymind bridge. Therefore, the exercises often serve to convince people who are not psychologically oriented of the powerful body control that can consciously be exercised. It is a nonoffensive exercise which requires little commitment to mentalistic notions and can be used to help the most concrete individual learn to center, relax, and focus inward.

3. *The verbal exercises.* Often, in order to affect deep-seated belief systems regarding health, an unusual impact is necessary. An old and valid way of accomplishing this goal is to utilize chanting as a common exercise. Religions and mystic sects, as well as governments, have long seen the value in repetitious verbal affirmation, whether of faith or allegiance. There is the obvious hope that, in addition to the altered state induced by chants, the meaning will also be adopted at an unconscious level.

Perhaps the methods of pain management greeted by patients and professionals as being the most outlandish are the exercises of singing, growling, and yelling. We have had many reactions, including having members of the hospital staff charge in to interrupt the session for fear someone was hurt. Yet these exercises seem to bring both physiological and psychological benefits. Physiologically, the activities facilitate better breathing, especially exhaling. As a result, there appears to be significant improvement in muscle tone and tension resolution. The psychological aspect of these exercises is related to the patients' need to express themselves more openly and, perhaps, in new ways. Many patients tell us that they had never yelled, growled, or even sung before in their lives. No patient has yet reported a lack of enthusiasm for the activities, and we treat instruction in a lighthearted, non-dogmatic fashion.

The exercises can be done with great flexibility, but we have found that two procedures appear to produce the most consistent results. We try to utilize opposing emotional responses in series. For example, anger is expressed for a while, followed by affection or pleasure. When the exercises are biased in one direction, patients often report a dissatisfaction with themselves, or "imbalance" of expression. Secondly, since most patients are inhibited in expressing themselves, the leader(s) should serve as models. A timid leader who is uncomfortable with the process is likely to engender only more discomfort in the participants. Some exercises we have found to be effective include:

1) Yelling "No"; "Yes"
2) Humming a favorite song
3) Growling like a bear
4) Whimpering like a hurt dog
5) Whispering or yelling "I love you"; "I hate you"
6) Expressing profanity

Self-Concept Training. Exercises for self-concept training are not unique and have been utilized in such areas as assertiveness training, interpersonal training, T-groups, etc. Working with self-concept in the Spinal Pain Program constitutes a significant challenge in many respects. The self-concept of the chronic back pain patient is typically restricted, focusing on negative traits. These individuals are often defensive about introspecting and are depressed. The task of the leader is *not* to conduct psychotherapy, however. Experience and the literature clearly support the conclusion that sessions organized around psychological problems tend to reduce self-esteem initially, at a time when patients are usually experiencing the greatest pain and the greatest need for support. The focus of the group must be designed to enlarge the possibilities of self-perception and to engage the patients in examining the resources available from within themselves as well as external to them. Our favorite exercises for accomplishing these purposes are: "first impressions," "funeral rites," and "secrets."

1. *First impressions.* This exercise is most often presented on the second or third day of the program. Each person is instructed to describe his or her first impression of every other patient in the group, giving an example of the trait or behavior which was the primary stimulus. We have never seen a patient give a negative first impression, and we build upon that probability. Usually, the patients are trying to be nice and pick out a positive quality in the others. These qualities are then reinforced and used as a focus around which to build supportive discussion.

Occasionally, another professional has criticized this procedure as nurturing unrealistic or superficial self-perceptions. Generally, we respond that our initial focus is on expansion of the self, not on restriction. The patients have a hard enough time faking positive responses, much less feeling them.

2. *Funeral rites.* This exercise is depressing to observers, but is often remembered by the patients as one of the more positive exercises in self-concept change. The exercise was designed to allow the patients to have a time for restructuring priorities, needs, memories, and goals.

Patients are instructed to lie down with eyes closed. After a period of relaxation, they are asked to imagine themselves at their own funerals. With that in mind, they are instructed to consider four questions (allow at least five minutes of time for each):

1) What would I like for people to say about my life?
2) What would be my message to my survivors?
3) If I were looking back over my entire life and focused on these weeks at the Pain Program, what would I say?
4) Now that I have a set of priorities, I will soon be opening my eyes and living again—a possibility few people ever have. How will I live my life differently? Where do I go from here?

The questions are obviously existential and serve as a springboard for discussion after the exercise. The patients have been very responsive and have used the experience for making important decisions. For example, it is not unusual to hear a person decide to change jobs, go back to school, or use resources to upgrade suitability for a less strenuous vocation. On a less drastic note, some patients make personal decisions to not work so hard and to settle for less. As one patient said, "I have learned that there is very little difference between $400 and $375, but that extra 25 bucks can tear you up for all the wear and tear."

Sometimes the decisions are not immediate. We had one patient who came into the clinic six weeks after discharge and said, "Last night it came to me. You know—about the funeral thing. I made a decision about my life and its priorities." Apparently, the exercise, for him, required an incubation period.

3. *Secrets.* Although the exercise of "secrets" is not used as a regular part of the program, we have found that it facilitates openness and helps to structure interpersonal communication. We sometimes find patients whose responses to their peers can be irritating; the "secrets" exercise is designed to promote communications training along with self-concept exploration.

Patients are instructed to write on uniform slip of paper a secret that they have not shared with anyone. They are also instructed not to write their names or to identify their stories in any way. After a pause, each folds his or her secret in a uniform way and puts it in a can or hat. The notes are shaken and mixed, letting each member draw one.

Each participant reads the selected note aloud, then relates the feelings as if he or she had the secret. For example, at one of our sessions the following secret and feelings were revealed:

> This note says, "I once had an affair, and I think of her a lot. I wonder if I can ever get over her." I think this person is having a lot of pain, both guilt and loneliness. I feel sorry for him.

This expression of empathy is reinforced and supported as a medium of communication. It establishes the ground rules for future group sessions: no moralistic advice nor negative opinions, just good support and high acceptance.

Biofeedback Techniques. Biofeedback centers have sprung up all over the country. Their success has been largely due not to the efficiency of the machines in doing something for the patient, but because they allow the patient to do something for himself or herself. The two modes of biofeedback we use for back pain patients are EMG and temperature. Muscle tension (EMG) is the primary measure for two major reasons: (1) the direct link of muscular tension itself to the continued pain, and (2) the fact that the cultural perspective of most of the pain patients is more amenable to a muscular interpretation. Explaining autonomic arousal, and the relationship between temperature and relaxation, only led to confusion in many instances.

We usually use the frontalis muscles in the forehead as a standard monitoring location. In addition, we have found specific muscle groups unique to each individual that should be considered as secondary feedback locations. For example, the calf and thigh muscles have been pain sites associated with emotional stress in several of our male patients, whereas muscles in the forearms are common emotional stress points in many females. These are generalizations, of course, and the opposite may just as often be true.

When temperature monitoring has been useful in treating patients, it appears to have been primarily helpful because of its inherent confidence-building qualities. Most people understand the concept of temperature and its measurement in the body, even if they do not understand how it relates to tension. When patients perceive the variance attributable to their own reactions, they are amazed at themselves. Especially if the machine is set in small increments, the interaction between patient and machine has a great impact upon the concept of self as a "master of the body." The patients are confronted with their own capabilities, and the implicit principles of the overall program are affirmed.

Besides being good for morale, the temperature feedback is useful for headaches. Occasionally, too, we have a patient who is allergic to the jelly necessary for muscle tension feedback. We then resort to temperature monitoring as the total biofeedback program.

Physical Exercises. The practitioner should be aware of the physical state of the patient, and of the need to deal with the muscular stress inherent in surgical and injury patients. This is important even when exercises are prescribed by orthopedists or physiatrists and conducted by physical therapists.

Most patients will have spasms and shortness of the lumbar muscles, due to the natural tendency for the body to splint itself. Sometimes this shortness will be primarily on one side, resulting in a scoliosis. If surgery has been performed, then scar tissue will be a problem. This scar tissue can be attached to a wide variety of structures: muscle to muscle, muscle to nerve, and muscle to connecting tissues such as tendons. Scar tissue is not so flexible as muscle, and, if the patient has been immobilized for a long time, that person will be very rigid as a result of the scar tissue restriction.

As long as the muscles or scar tissue are shortened, the patient will have pain when the back is bent. The pain, then, signals the need to lengthen the muscles and stretch the scar tissue. Like the athlete who injures a leg muscle, the rehabilitation process requires stretching exercises and will involve some discomfort. It takes three to six weeks for muscles to lengthen and accommodate a wider range of motion. However, scar tissue is another story; there is little flexibility, and the scar tissue will gradually break. This creates new, longer tissue.

As far as the back pain patient is concerned, rehabilitation requires physical exercise—though painful—in order to free the back of its rigidity. The patient will have to know that this transition, to hurt more, is a necessary evil which will have a major effect in successful rehabilitation. The positive aspect to this message is simply this: pain *can* go away, regardless of the origin, with or without surgery, with or without medication, and regardless of the amount of pain that is experienced presently, *if* the exercises described below are practiced regularly (Figure 6.14).

1. Pelvic tilts. One of the most conventional exercises to have the patient flatten and straighten the lumbar spinal area by tilting the pelvis backward. The easiest way to demonstrate the exercise is to have the person either stand with the back next to a wall, or to lie on the back. By tightening the abdominal and buttock muscles, the person bends the back so that it touches the wall or floor. The patient can use this exercise to teach the body better posture in both standing and walking situations, as well as to alleviate stress on the bone and nerve structures (Figure 6.14*a*).

2. Pull-ups. This exercise is perhaps the most misunderstood exercise. Done incorrectly, it will aggravate the pain and the stressed muscles. The mechanics of the pull-up exercise require the patients to lie flat on the floor with the knees bent. They raise *only* their heads and shoulders from the floor. Caution should be taken that overzealous patients do not try to bring their backs completely off the floor. That movement does not strengthen the stomach muscles, as is often thought, but actually tightens the thigh muscles and probably creates a more negative pelvic tilt than before (Figure 6.14*b*).

3. Knee chest. Similar to the pull-ups, patients are positioned with backs on the floor and knees bent. They are instructed to pull their knees to their chests, using *only* the stomach muscles and the arm muscles. In this exercise, the patients have a tendency to try to overuse the thigh muscles, which can complicate the outcome by strengthening the wrong

Figure 6.14

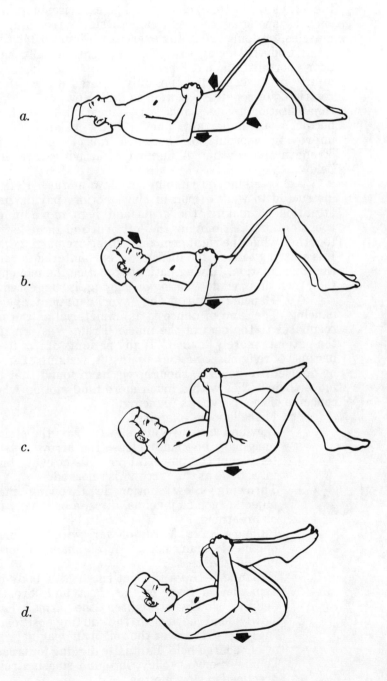

a.

b.

c.

d.

muscles. The exercise is designed to stretch the muscles in the lumbar areas as well as strengthen the stomach muscles. With the knees up in this position, other exercises can be added, such as swinging the legs side to side, stretching the hip muscles, or doing breathing exercises (Figure 6.14c,d).

4. Body-balancing exercises. Patients usually have very poor coordination, most probably due to the history of the injury or disease, but possibly related to a lifestyle of restricted or repetitive motion as well. However, if the goal of rehabilitation involves muscle re-education, "body balancing" becomes an important part. "Body balancing" involves improving coordination between muscle groups in both strength and rhythm. A number of activities are presented below.

a. Walking or running in slow motion. Patients are instructed to walk or run in slow motion, paying particular attention to making the arms and legs move in diagonal coordination, i.e., moving the left arm and right leg forward together while the right arm and left leg are moving back, etc. It is amazing to view the difficulties encountered in relearning this coordination. Having patients practice the movements on their own time, while walking or jogging, is suggested.

b. Dancing. One of the favorite patient exercises is dancing. The kind of dance is as immaterial as the patients' responses to the beat of the music. From Western to Disco, the patients merely "dance." If any patients object to dancing because of religious sanctions against it, walking exercises can be devised. In general, though, we have found that patients move their bodies with a much more fluid motion when they conceive of themselves as "dancing."

c. Miscellaneous exercises.

Bow and arrow—Very slowly draw the string of an imaginary bow and release the arrow. Sustain the tension of the powerful bow all the way, breathing in. Exhale as the "arrow" is released.

Throwing—Slow motion in throwing imaginary objects, such as javelins, discs, a ball, etc., focusing on breathing.

Pulling—Have a tug-of-war with an imaginary opponent: man, horse, or elephant, according to imaginative zest.

Expander—Have the patient hold a body-building expander in front of the chest and, breathing in deeply, slowly straighten the arms. Exhaling, slowly bend the arms to the starting position.

Digging—Turn over the soil in an imaginary garden, or dig a large hole. Fantasize digging for treasure.

Tennis—Serve, volley, lob, and smash strokes are practiced in slow motion.

Lifting—Weight-lifting or weight-training movements are basic to not only body coordination, but also to practical habits at work or home. With either real weights or imaginary ones, slow-motion actions can be re-enacted. Both muscle and breath control are emphasized.

Swimming—Swimming exercises are extremely beneficial for body coordination. If pool facilities are not available, some strokes can be practiced out of water. For example, the standing breast stroke is beautiful in motion and allows breathing exercises to be integrated with the arm movements.

General Rules of the Program. In the Pain Clinic there are basic rules which are explained to each patient and reinforced by the staff. We think that rules are needed in order to structure the environment for success. Otherwise, the tendency for patients to become depressed or manipulative is a distinct possibility.

Rule Number One: Some four letter words are not to be used. We explain to patients that we understand they are hurting and have been hurting for a long time. We try to express as much empathy as possible in order to communicate that we understand the extent of their problem and the disruption it has produced in their lives. Especially, we explain that we understand how the disease or injury has affected self-concept and mental attitude. However, after that transaction has taken place (usually the first day), they are told that, since we have heard all the details and acknowledge their validity, further expansion is not needed nor wanted. In fact, we explicitly state that any further magnification would be as boring to us as staff as it would be to any of the other patients. Moreover, it would possibly create some negative force. Far from being a nonhumanistic approach, this refusal to allow expanded detail has been most effective in allowing the therapy to proceed on a rapid course. We fully recognize that each patient is an individual with a unique expression of pain, and that some stories will have to be heard out. However, there are enough similarities with former patients to allow us to believe that we *do* understand enough to carry on without minute detailing of previous treatment, impact, and intricate nature of the existing pain. Therefore, four letter words, such as "pain" and "hurt" are to be eliminated from their vocabulary. If they experience some discomfort or stress, we tell them they can express it with positive words, such as "I am having fun," or "Joy! Joy!"

Rule Number Two: Pain medication is not good for a person. Most patients referred to the clinic have been on high dosages of muscle relaxants and pain killers. It has been our experience that, after two months, many of the medications have paradoxical effects; in a "rebound-like" phenomena, pain is actually increased following administration. There have been some patients who have had complete pain relief after only a short period of nonmedication. This observation is in line with the notion that the enkephalin system may be inhibited by pain killers.

Absolutely no injectables are used, because the injection itself appears to create patient passivity and dependence. If patients do appear to have withdrawal symptoms, or expect to have them, they are placed on the Pain Cocktail. The Pain Cocktail is merely an elixir which allows for gradual decrease in pain medication over a period of a week or so. The patients cannot tell how much actual pain medication they receive, and they usually are able to give it up in a few days. From our perspective, we would rather let their own bodies' natural enkephalins act on their pain. It is much more dignifying for the patient to rely on self, and certainly encourages fewer attempts at manipulation of the staff by patients' trying to receive medication.

Rule Number Three: Education is essential. A great deal of effort is expended in order to educate the patients. One reason for this effort is the fact that, if patients understand the mechanics of their bodies, they can participate and comply with the staff in their care much more easily. Secondly, the fear of treatment and staff is reduced significantly. The natural course for low back pain patients necessitates additional rehabilitation pain. If a patient does not know what is happening or what to expect, that person will probably get depressed, angry, and/or frightened.

We have found that patients want to know "how is it going to feel?" Factually, anatomical information is important, but what appear to be most critical are the sensory expectations for the treatment. The expectation of an initial increase in pain should be emphasized in any program.

Rule Number Four: Don't speculate—Ask us. Most of the time, patients will get the majority of their information from peers. This is a positive characteristic for mutual support and education. However, gossip can also nurture fear and anxiety. Questionable information should be discussed directly with the staff to prevent the circulation of harmful and erroneous rumors. The staff can encourage this only by providing straightforward, honest answers. Of course, patients who are absent should not be discussed, and any issue should be dealt with in an empathic and genuine manner.

Rule Number Five: Program for success. It goes without saying that the program is focused on success. On a day-to-day basis, this means that whatever happens, it can be reacted to as a positive element in a person's life. This general philosophy is illustrated by the following examples of events and their accompanying positive attitudes.

Event	Attitude
A patient has more pain	"You know that you are doing something. You need to do it more."
A patient needs corrective surgery	"Marvelous. When it's all over, you'll really be able to do something."
A patient wants to quit the program, stop work, and become bed dependent	"That's okay. That's your decision. You know the consequences. We at least know what your real goals are. If that is what you want, we can rejoice in your decision."

The last example may sound a bit cynical or like a less-than-sincere acceptance, but it does convey that, if a patient has thoughtfully chosen a negative outcome after being shown alternatives, we have no choice but to accept the decision. Of course, we cannot work with him or her any longer, but our only option is to make a positive reaction to whatever we can and go on.

Rule Number Six: We are what we eat. In essence, we tell the patients that what they eat will have an effect on their rehabilitation. We suggest that they keep a diary of some sort and correlate their feeling state to their eating habits. Though we recognize that there is a wide variance in patients' responses, we focus on emotional as well as physical meanings.

We explain that their bodies and minds *must* respond to differing foodstuffs, because they introduce different forms of energy into a system. We also stress that reactions to foods are highly individualistic responses and that, because bodies are not the same metabolically, there cannot be one correct way to eat. Certain bodies require more fat, others more protein, and still others minerals or vitamins far in excess of the minimum daily requirements. It is our opinion that the world of professional dietetics has been one of the last to recognize individual variations in nutritional needs, and that even food faddists are too quick to describe "the only true path." Our approach places responsibility directly on the patients' shoulders to eat as wisely as they know how and to observe carefully positive and negative responses. No machine or blood test can be as sensitive as one's own "energy" barometer. Much of the response to certain foods may well be emotionally based, in that a conditioned response has evolved which associates tastes with feelings. Whatever the case, whether metabolic differences or developmental history, paradoxical effects in response to identical foods are noted between patients. Coffee, for example, appears to trigger a hypoglycemia-rebound-type reaction in many people. On the other hand, we also have seen patients who perceive coffee as a source of comfort and pain relief. Sugar is commonly related to a syndrome of pain and depression, especially in a hypoglycemic state. However, for the very slow oxidizer of food, sugar apparently has little impact. Probably any food that can have a positive physical consequence can also have emotional benefits. For the pain patient, foods which are high in tryptophan have been shown to have a relationship to decreased pain.

Rule Number Seven: Lifestyle change. Whether or not the program accomplishes the goal of rehabilitation, it is our intention that the person's experience in the program will provide some alternative ways of thinking and living. Life may not become more productive, but, hopefully, a broader perspective will at least be gained. The basic philosophy is predicated on the belief that each person in the program deserves to learn something that they can use in a more adaptive lifestyle. People can change, and if a person has improved understanding, he or she will make better personal decisions.

Prolongation of a disease has wide-ranging implications, not only involving the patient's spirit and the management of monies, but also the relationships between the patient and the health-care professionals. As any disease process begins to alter a person's lifestyle, many other dimensions also shift. Moreover, as more protocols and/or surgeries are employed, medically induced disorders (iatrogenic) and complications geometrically increase, creating more pain and potentially addictive situations.

In addition to medical problems, the patient's response to treatment is likely to be lacking in enthusiasm, even if an implicit trust in the staff is maintained. Patient's lives, including their jobs, become permanently changed. A person may be relieved of his or her job because of physical requirements. The family role becomes one of dependency or isolation. The matrix of complications in chronicity frequently includes prescribed or nonprescribed drug abuse, as well as alcohol abuse. These substances are used initially to deaden physical pain and the pain of a deteriorating lifestyle. But, before long, they may also become problems. The physician begins to feel frustrated about the resistant symptoms and considers withdrawal from the patient, or referral; in short, the doctor/patient relationship is severely stressed.

As time creates distance from a life-oriented routine, the daily schedule becomes dependent upon disease or pain fluctuations. "Momma cannot get up in the morning before 9:00 a.m." or "Daddy cannot take care of the kids for longer than a hour or he starts having his pain." It is no wonder that we see the same phenomena that many pain researchers report, including Sternbach (1978), i.e., that psychological measures rise and fall according to the current status of pain.

The quest of pain management is not only to achieve effective management of disease, but also to win a race against the clock in the continuous erosion of a person's spirit. Whether or not it is an individual's "fault" that pain has become a chronic symptom is not a critical issue. The primary fact is just this: if a person is not inclined to do so anyway, chronicity of pain will compel some manner of compensation, emotionally and socially. Therefore, it is with some measure of missionary zeal that we attend to the earliest stages of rehabilitation, trying to minimize the tremendous costs of hesitation.

In summarizing the program, we can state that the treatment of back pain is evolving. Some patients respond to basic methods, such as biofeedback. Others require a more unique approach, or a combination of approaches. What is most important is the flexibility of the professional tools and the courage to utilize them.

CHAPTER VII

RHEUMATOID ARTHRITIS
A Psychological Perspective

Clinical
Description Arthritis is estimated to be a chief cause of physical disability in at least 50 million Americans, with approximately a half-million new cases reported each year. Due to severe, chronic pain, 17 million arthritics currently are receiving medical attention. The economic impact of arthritis is profound in terms of lost wages and the expense of chronic medical care, amounting to 13 billion dollars a year. Medical costs directly attributable to this disease amount to about four billion dollars per year and are growing rapidly. (Figures were obtained from *Arthritis: The Basic Facts*, a booklet published by the Arthritis Foundation.)

Several major types of arthritis may be diagnosed, with the incidence of each depending upon factors such as the age and sex of the afflicted individual. About 85% of arthritics are 45 years of age or older; of these, 60% have osteoarthritis. Rheumatoid arthritis (RA) affects the majority of arthritics who are 45 years or younger. An estimated five million Americans suffer from rheumatoid arthritis, including approximately 200,000 children, together with over two million adolescents and young adults. Significantly, rheumatoid arthritis afflicts approximately three times more women than men, and is considered to be the most crippling of all forms of arthritis.

Although the term "rheumatoid arthritis" was first used in the middle of the 19th century, a detailed description of the disease has only recently begun to emerge. Current clinical descriptions of RA characterize the disease as a generalized systemic illness (Williams, 1974). The systemic aspects of this disease are to be contrasted with the more commonly occurring osteoarthritis. According to Williams, "multiple extra articular areas of involvement, the constitutional symptoms, and the interesting generalized prodromata often antedate the illness by years or months." (p. 3)

Apparently, RA begins slowly, usually in one or two joints at a time. Many patients, however, recall a sudden dramatic onset. Shoulders, elbows, wrists, fingers, hips, knees, ankles, and feet are the most commonly involved areas. In some patients, various prodromal symptoms of fatigue, diffuse muscle stiffness, or paresthesias may occur. However, the ultimate severity of the disease cannot be predicted reliably by the presence or absence of prodromata, nor by the acuity of onset.

As the disease progresses, complaints of joint pain at rest and upon moving, swelling and stiffness of the involved joints after inactivity, and pronounced limitation of motion are typical. A symmetrical pattern of joint involvement is not unusual, although cases of nonsymmetrical involvement are also seen. Soft tissue swelling near involved joints is also common. Muscular atrophy may occur at an alarming rate, and subcutaneous nodules form in approximately one-fifth of all patients. Peripheral manifestations such as vasomotor instability, exemplified by cold hands or excessive peripheral sweating, are frequent symptoms. While the severity of symptoms may fluctuate over time, the most common complaints of the RA patients concern chronic pain, and the often dramatic reduction of mobility in the more advanced stages.

Underlying this symptomology there is also a predictable sequence of steps in the progression of the disease at the physiological level (Williams, 1974). Normally, a joint interior is lined with a synovial membrane which secretes a lubricating fluid. RA affects the synovial cells and causes them to multiply at an unnatural rate. This excess tissue creeps into the joint, creating a swelling which ultimately destroys the cartilage. Further erosion occurs as the ends of the bone become covered. At that point, the joint is rendered useless. In the most advanced stages, joint deterioration may cause the formation of scar tissue which, in turn, produces a joint that is knobby, deformed, and completely immobilized. The diagnosis of RA is deceptively simple, and is done on clinical grounds. The criteria for diagnosis have been outlined by the American Rheumatism Association and have been widely accepted (but not universally used). *Seven* of the *11* proposed symptoms must be observed by the physician in order to classify a patient as having classical rheumatoid arthritis. In abbreviated fashion, they are: (1) morning stiffness; (2) observed pain on motion or tenderness in at least one joint; (3) observed swelling (defined as soft tissue thickening or fluid, not bony overgrowth alone) in at least one joint; (4) observed swelling of at least one other joint within a three-month period from the first incident; (5) observed symmetrical joint swelling with simultaneous involvement of the same joint on both sides of the body (excluding the terminal joints of the fingers); (6) observed subcutaneous (under the skin) nodules on muscles that extend joints or are near a joint; (7) roentgenographic (a form of x-ray) changes typical of rheumatoid arthritis (which must include at least bony decalcification localized to, or most markedly adjacent to, the involved joints); (8) positive test for "Rheumatoid Factor" through standardized laboratory tests; (9) failure of mucus substances in joint lining fluid to settle into particles (fluid remains cloudy with mucus shreds suspended); (10) changes in the histology (composition and function) of the synovium with three or more of the following: (a) marked enlargement of the cells and a "shaggy" (villose) appearance of those cells, (b) overproduction of synovium surface cells, (c) marked infiltration of chronic inflammatory cells, (d) a buildup of numerous dead cells; (11) changes in the histology of nodules showing granulated tissue.

Efforts of the American Rheumatism Association have enhanced communication and standardized diagnosis among rheumatologists. However, such was not always the case. Criteria used in diagnosing the illness have been varied and often of a dysjunctive nature (Weiner, 1977). As a result, researchers may or may not have been studying RA, which accounts to some extent for inconsistencies in findings obtained from investigations of etiology and pathogenesis. Support for theories proposing an epidemiological, physiological, genetic, or psychological causal basis has also been inconsistent (King, 1955; Spergel, Erlich, & Glass, 1978; Weiner, 1977; Williams, 1974; Wolff, 1968). This situation may in some measure again be attributed to differences in diagnostic criteria.

No single treatment regimen is widely endorsed for RA, but chemotherapy is the most typical intervention. There are currently six types of medication in widespread use. Aspirin is used most frequently. Dosages are set at a "maintenance" level, i.e., the largest possible dosage that does not produce counterproductive side effects. Treatments based on nonsteroid anti-inflammatory agents, steroids, gold, penicilliamine, and cytotoxins follow aspirin in popularity. Reported success rates, in terms of stabilization or remission within the six medication paradigms, vary considerably.

Medical alternatives to drug regimens are also available (Silverman in Freedman, Kaplan, & Sadock, 1975). A comprehensive approach to intervention often requires a therapy team which, in addition to a physician, can involve a physical therapist, occupational therapist, social worker, psychiatric nurse, and a psychiatrist or psychologist. The physical therapy protocols are the most extensively developed of all the nonpharmacologic methods; and, while adequately controlled trials are lacking, there appears to be clinical validation of these interventions. Included are exercise, hot packs, paraffin treatments (particularly for hand involvement), cryotherapy (or cold therapy), and permutations and combinations of these.

The involvement of a psychologist in the treatment program may be extremely important, since chronic pain and the loss of mobility may create serious problems of psychological functioning, including depression, frustration, apathy, and a helpless outlook (Pelletier, 1977; Weiner, 1977). These psychological symptoms may act to undermine compliance with the treatment regimen, blocking any intervention strategy.

Further, psychological distress may antedate or exacerbate certain diseases, including RA (Solomon & Moos, 1964; Williams, 1974; Wolff, 1968). Therefore, treatment must involve a process of everchanging decisions and goals based on the patient's constantly shifting status of physical and psychosocial functioning (Katz, Vignos, & Moskowitz, 1968). The psychologist should theoretically assist the patient in minimizing maladaptive emotional reactions, provide adjunctive treatment which facilitates compliance with the medical regimen and hopefully aid the patient in the management of his or her pain. This is a tall order. Unfortunately, psychologists do not appear to have been offered much information about which techniques should be included in their treatment strategy in order to achieve these objectives.

Although areas of research in RA have varied, historically, psychological interest in the illness has been of a traditional psychodynamic nature. Relationships between rheumatoid arthritis and personality traits, defense mechanisms, and conflicts are among the most frequently investigated topics. Excellent critical reviews of psychological research methodology in this area have been offered by King (1955), Moss (1964), and Scotch and Geiger (1962). A most recent and complete review of the previous research and state of the art has been accomplished by Pierrko Kiviniemi (1978), in a monograph that contains 204 references. That particular article will certainly serve as an excellent source of information for all who are interested in the psychosocial dimensions of RA. Another recent review appears in Weiner's *Psychobiology and Human Disease* (1977). While Weiner's work contains up-to-date information on the immunological aspects of RA, it lacks any unique theoretical approach; nor does it offer any insights regarding intervention which might follow from a review of psychosocial factors.

Psychological Correlates of Rheumatoid Arthritis

Before reviewing the psychological literature on arthritis, it should be reemphasized that research conducted on arthritic patients is fraught with methodological flaws in design which hinder interpretation and contribute to the inconsistent findings often reported. Analysis of published results must be attempted cautiously, with an awareness that scientific rigor was not always maintained in many studies of RA. Indeed, we have no guarantee that the patients involved met the currently accepted diagnostic criteria for RA.

Typological Characteristics. As mentioned earlier, most psychological investigators historically have taken a typological or trait-oriented approach in researching RA. Many have concentrated, therefore, on delineating an "arthritic personality," or at least identifying configurations of traits, demographic variables, defense mechanisms, or conflicts which might be unique to that population. The intent has been to establish parameters that identify high-risk groups and that predict the likelihood of RA onset. As illustrated in Table 7.1, a second large segment of the literature includes reports on patient reaction to certain life events, including arthritis, as it affects the progression of the illness.

Among the earliest typological research studies was that by Halliday (1941, 1942). Believing he had identified a rheumatoid personality, Halliday described a small sample of female rheumatoids as consistently self-restricted, detached, emotionally calm, and markedly compulsive. Also, according to Halliday, most were independent and self-sufficient; strict parental discipline was common in childhood; and most lived a self-sacrificing, conscientious, quiet life. The patients reported few intensive friendships and often exhibited a domineering personality. Johnson, Shapiro, and Alexander (1947) reported findings which supported the compulsive aspect of Halliday's proposed configuration. Johnson et al. additionally cited a tendency among arthritic patients to report they had been vigorous and physically competitive as children. Supposedly, this activity represented an expression of suppressed rebellious resentment against parental dominance. (One also wonders, if true, what effect this early vigorous activity may have had in weakening joint structure enough to provide some interaction with a genetic predisposition toward the disease.)

Research interest in RA accelerated throughout the 1950s and early 1960s, with each investigator suggesting additional descriptive terms as well as speculations about childhood dynamics. For instance, Geist (1966, 1969) maintained that RA patients repressed hostility and thus were intrapunitive. These results coincided with and added to a multitude of earlier studies (Cobb, 1959; Cromier, et al., 1957; Ludwig, 1952, 1967; Mueller & Lefkovitz, 1956) characterizing rheumatoids as latently hostile, experiencing interpersonal difficulties, and as having unemotional mothers and authoritarian fathers. The descriptors eventually became so numerous that the notion of an arthritic personality suffered from a lack of specificity.

In the mid-1960s there was a proliferation of more adequately controlled studies. Several researchers attempted to delineate an arthritic personality profile using the relatively objective Minnesota Multiphasic Personality Inventory

(MMPI) rather than the less reliable projective personality tests of previous efforts (Bourestom & Howard, 1965; Moos & Soloman, 1964, 1965; Nalven & O'Brien, 1964. Although many descriptors were again generated, the most consistent finding was a neurotic pattern characterized by a high degree of bodily concern, depression, and somatization. However, these findings were significant only in contrast to a normal population. They were felt to be of little use in terms of differential diagnosis when comparisons were made to patients with other chronic diseases. As yet, a personality profile specific to RA does not seem to have been found, although there does appear to be a profile which is characteristic of individuals suffering from chronic disease in general. According to Moos and Soloman (1964) and others, this profile is characterized by intrapunitiveness, latent hostility, familial and interpersonal difficulty, shyness, rigidity, self-consciousness, an inability to express anger, masochism, and a perfectionistic standard of self-evaluation. Emotionally, moderate depression and a tendency to somatize are not uncommon.

Personality configurations of rheumatoids (although highly variable) overlap somewhat with this general chronic disease profile. Spergel, Ehrlich, and Glass (1978) go so far, however, as to call the arthritic personality a "psychodiagnostic myth." This seems a somewhat harsh condemnation of years of research and clinical observation, culminating in several hundred professional publications. The sweeping generalization is all the more unwarranted since these investigators used only two psychodiagnostics in examining the relationships of personality dynamics to rheumatoid affliction for a total of 46 patients. The tests in question—the MMPI and the Tennessee Self-Concept Scale—have not been found to be particularly powerful in studying reactions to physical disease. The answers, though, are clearly not all in.

Etiological Considerations. If nothing else, it is evident that attempts to find an arthritic personality focused much attention on the role of childhood conflicts. Alexander (1950) and Johnson (1947) both hypothesized that a specific childhood psychological conflict might predispose an individual to RA, provided that the person also possessed a certain predisposing physiological substrate. Based on clinical findings that were derived primarily from studies with women, Alexander and his associates (Alexander, 1950; Alexander, French, & Pollock, 1968; Alexander, Steward, & Duthie, 1968) further postulated that the core conflict in RA has its genesis in the restrictive parental attitudes experienced by the patient in childhood. The child presumably rebels but, due to an excessive dependency on the punitive parent (typically the mother), represses the rebellion for fear of rejection. For girls, "tomboyish" behavior supposedly provides an outlet for the repressed emotions of anger and hostility. According to Alexander, the rebellion later becomes transferred to men and involves rejection of the female role in favor of aggressiveness in sports, work, and environmental control. Any guilt which may be experienced is alleviated through serving others in some way. The disease purportedly has its onset when the patient can no longer discharge hostility by dominating others or relieve guilt by periodically serving other people.

Other investigators adhere to a nonspecific conflict etiology theory (Blom & Nichols, 1953; Cobb & Hall, 1965; Ludwig, 1952; Robinson, 1957; Schochet, Lisansky, Schubart, Fiocco, Kurland, & Pope, 1969). Although the advocates of the non-specific conflict theory accept hostility, resentment, over-control, and inhibited expression as centrally important, they do not tie these traits to definite childhood conflicts. This theory is more easily supported and also more difficult to empirically refute. To illustrate, Rimon (1969) conducted a study with female rheumatoid patients for whom no explicit environmental or physiological antecedents of the disease could be found. These subjects were significantly more inhibited in their expression of hostility and aggression than were patients who had a clearly identifiable precipitator of arthritis. They were also less aware of negative emotions. These data appear to support a relationship between repressed emotionality and the onset of the disorder in the absence of other salient antecedent conditions. Such findings are consistent with the fact that defense mechanisms most common to RA have consistently been found to be denial and avoidance (Cobb, 1959; Cobb & Hall, 1965; Ludwig, 1952; Schochet, et al., 1969). Reaction formation, isolation, intellectualization and undoing have also been frequently mentioned.

Despite the apparent significance of conflict in rheumatoid etiology, several researchers (Gregg, 1939; King, 1955; Nissen & Spencer, 1936; Pilkington, 1956; Rothermich & Phillips, 1963; Trevathan & Tatum, 1954) have reported a lower incidence of psychosis among RA patients than would be expected in the general population. Nissen and Spencer (1936), for instance, did not find one case of RA among 2,200 schizophrenic patients, nor did Gregg (1939), in 3,000 autopsied psychotics. Pilkington (1956) reports the highest incidence at only 0.8% of the psychotic population studies. These researchers generally expressed the opinion that conflict can be channeled either into somatic or psychological routes, and that these pathways appear to be mutually exclusive. Similar findings have also been reported concerning the selective immunity of the mentally disturbed population to other so-called psychosomatic diagnoses (Pedder, 1969) and to cancer (Achterberg, Collerain, & Craig, 1978).

The Role of Stress. Rather than describe the importance of personality dynamics in the etiology of RA, an extensive segment of the relevant literature has been devoted to the effect that general psychological factors may have on the status of the disease. Considerable data exist to support the conclusion that stress, emanating from numerous sources, can have an exacerbating effect on RA. This effect is independent of the specific origin of the stress; worry about financial matters, job absenteeism, anger, major surgery, divorce, death of a loved one, anxiety about prognosis or incapacitation, and intense competition have all been shown to be related to a worsened symptom pattern (Williams, 1968; Wyatt, 1969).

Pelletier (1977) and others (Cobb, 1959; Cromier, et al., 1957; Crown, Crown, & Fleming, 1974; Meyerwitz, 1971; Weiner, 1977) report that the illness may begin, or exacerbations may occur, in association with conscious worry, grief, depression, or with exposure to various life events perceived by the patient as stressful. A review of Table 7.1 from pages 264-265 leads to the conclusion that psychological stress may play some role in initiation or aggravation of symptomatology.

A review of two selected studies should help illustrate this association more clearly. Schochet, et al. (1969), in a study of 12 subjects, found a strong relationship between the occurrence of major life crises (e.g., separation from a loved one) and the temporary exacerbation of arthritic symptoms. Similarly, Rimon (1969) uncovered an unexpected amount of psychological distress in the life histories of 100 female patients diagnosed as having RA. The families of 25% of the patients had members with psychiatric disturbances, and 37% of the patients had come from homes where the parents had separated or divorced. Marital discord and/or sexual problems in the years immediately preceding the onset or serious exacerbation of the disorder were reported by 23%. Over half (55%) reported major life conflicts preceding onset, and, of these, 65% reported additional exacerbation related to a significant life crisis. Certainly, it would seem that the frequency with which stress precedes onset and exacerbation of RA far exceeds that which would be expected by chance.

The consistent reports of stress as an antecedent to flare-ups of RA are notable, given the usually contradictory evidence reported in the arthritis literature. Unfortunately, a hypothesis of arthritic pathogenesis connecting psychological and physiological functioning must await elucidation of the exact site at which the process begins. Clarification of the interaction also requires discovery of a pathogenetic agent. Currently, a variety of hypotheses exist which attempt to describe the physiological initiating agent. Major hypotheses include: infection by virus (Kilroy, et al., 1970; Phillips & Christian, 1970; Warren, Marmor, Liebes, & Hollins, 1969) or bacteria (Duthie, Brown, Knox, & Thomson, 1975; Sharp, 1971); immunopathology, i.e., rheumatoid factors (specifically antibodies directed against the body's own healthy blood cells) (Kellgren & Ball, 1959; Lawrence, Valkenburg, Fuxford, & Collard, 1971); and vascular lesions (Schumacher, 1975).

Without a full understanding of the nature of the interaction between psychological and physiological aspects of RA, effective treatment and prevention is unlikely. However, psychological stress appears to be an important piece of the elusive puzzle. Reduction of that stress is therefore regarded as a significant treatment adjunct.

No unequivocal evidence exists as to precisely how psychological stress impacts on the physiology of RA, but it is widely accepted that at least one mediator is probably increased muscle tension (Alexander, 1950; Gottschalk, Serota, & Shapiro, 1950). This seems plausible, as it is congruent with physiological models of the stress reaction (Cannon, 1934; Selye, 1950) and clinical observations that muscular tension often precedes sudden arthritic outbreaks. It is well documented that muscle tension can be produced by psychological stress (Moos & Engel, 1964; Morrison, Short, Ludwig, & Schwab, 1947; Rodnan, 1973; Selye, 1950). Demonstrations of the translation of stress into muscle tension have been achieved through the electromyographic monitoring of muscle activity while intermittently presenting stressful stimuli (Southworth, 1958). Based on these findings, it may be suggested that psychological conflicts, such as those espoused by the dynamic theorists as being central to the onset and/or exacerbation of illness, are simply nonspecific sources of stress which lead to muscle tension and a subsequent aggravation of inflamed joints. In other words, a stress—muscle tension—exacerbation cycle seems plausible.

Additional medical information has shed some light not only on a probable physiologic mechanism for stress exacerbation of RA, but also lends support to the use of stress intervention strategies for treating the condition. Horvath and Hollander in 1949 measured the intra-articular temperature of RA patients under a variety of conditions. It appeared that increases in joint temperature were related to: (1) superficial application of cold stimuli, (2) exercise, (3) smoking, (4) pain, and (5) states of fear or apprehension. This information was of only moderate interest 30 years ago when originally published, and the results have never been replicated. However, in view of our more enlightened immunological knowledge, these obscure findings gain significance.

RA is now considered to be characterized by an immunological system "gone haywire." It is frequently explained to patients as the body becoming allergic to itself or attacking itself. (An excellent discussion of this process for moderately

Table 7.1

THE RELATIONSHIP BETWEEN STRESS AND RHEUMATOID ARTHRITIS

Author/Date	Sample	Stressor	Outcome Measure	Results
Bourestom and Howard (1965)	94 Rheumatoids 74 multiple sclerosis patients 100 with spinal cord injuries	Various personal pathological patterns	Frequency of ego-dystonic pathology patterns among rheumatoids	Found the most common pathology for male rheumatoids was depression; for females, somatic concerns and inhibited emotional expression.
Cobb et al. (1969)	49 Rheumatoids	Patient/child conflicts in childhood	Frequency with which the rheumatoids described their mothers as arbitrary, severe, unreasonable and controlling	Found a significant trend for rheumatoids to describe mothers in this way.
DeWind and Payne (1976)	230 Bypass surgery patients	Bypass surgery	Type and frequency of complications occurring in two years following surgery	Nine percent of the men and 19 percent of the women reported onset of arthritis, greatly exceeding base rates for the general population.

Study	Sample	Variables	Outcome Measure	Findings
Heisel (1972)	34 Rheumatoids 68 Controls	Life change events as measured by questionnaire	Frequency on onset of rheumatoid arthritis	For year preceding onset, rheumatoids had life change scores averaging 166.98 versus 82.78 for controls ($p < .0005$).
Pipineli-Potamianoa (1976)	11 Rheumatoids	Overwhelming anxiety about aggressive impulses (various other dynamic conflicts as measured in two 1½-hour face association interviews.	Frequency of onset of rheumatoid arthritis	Psychoanalytic interpretation suggested that central to all rheumatoids were castration anxiety inducing factors.
Rimon (1969)	100 Rheumatoids 100 Matched Controls	Family mental illness, broken home background, personal mental illness, sexual problems, various major life crises	Frequency of onset and exacerbation of rheumatoid arthritis	Found significant relationship between identified stressors and rheumatoid arthritis in patients reporting acute initial onset. Those with insidious onset did not manifest such a relationship.
Schochet et al. (1969)	12 Rheumatoids	Life change events as measured by interview and questionnaire	Frequency of onset and exacerbation of rheumatoid arthritis	Onset and exacerbation were found to be significantly related to the occurrence of life crises, especially loss of loved ones.

well-educated patients and nonmedical professionals is provided in a paperback written by Darrell C. Crain entitled *The Arthritis Handbook*, 1976.) The body's normal protection system involves, among other things, the action of lymphocytes—a type of white blood cell. These defenders circulate and identify foreign substances, such as viruses or bacteria (called antigens). When these are identified, the lymphocytes manufacture antibodies which attack to immobilize the antigens. A second wave of white blood cells (the macrophages or "giant eaters") then act as scavengers, engulfing the antigens. The lysosomes—little sacs in the macrophage itself—contain enzymes which digest and dispose of the antigens.

With RA, the ability to correctly discriminate the intruders is lost; the living cells and cartilage of the joint are attacked instead, and the macrophage activity is accelerated. The net result is a hypermetabolic condition of greatly increased numbers of lysosomal enzymes which initiate and perpetuate more cartilage damage. One possible way to speed up this condition still more is by increasing the intra-articular temperature. On the other hand, cooling would be likely to reduce the activity (Smith & Polley, 1978). We have already mentioned the conditions which were found to increase intra-articular temperature, two of which can be of direct concern to the psychologist, i.e., pain and fear or apprehension. Presumably, then, negative emotional states are not only mediated by excessive muscle tension, but also via the autonomic system in some as yet unknown fashion that directly affects the level of enzyme activity.

Psychophysiological Aspects of Rheumatoid Arthritis

Certain well-known psychophysiological characteristics of RA preclude the usual psychotherapeutic approaches to treating chronic pain patients. On the other hand, behavioral intervention strategies which include specially adapted tactics can help to meet the treatment needs of the RA patient. Before these tactics or their role in a comprehensive treatment plan can be discussed, it is necessary to develop an understanding of the underlying psychophysiological aspects of the disease.

Alexithymia. An emotional "colourlessness," as Kiviniemi describes it, is frequently noted in RA patients which gives the impression of serenity, patience, and laissez-faire. Halliday (1942) concluded the patients were devoid of affect, without soul, with the result being an "impression of touching patience." The reasons given for the flat affect run the gamut, of course, from suggestions that it is the result of self-imposed restraint on the demonstration of feelings to what others suggest may instead be a true absence of feelings. We take yet a different approach and suggest that, in over 100 patient encounters, we saw repeatedly what Nemiah and his associates (Nemiah, Freyburger , & Sifneos, 1976; Nemiah & Sifneos, 1970) have termed "alexithymia"—a Greek word meaning "without words for feelings."

Nemiah et al. (1976) proposed that patients suffering from psychosomatic disorders have a structural defect (caused by an unknown genetic or developmental etiology) which has disrupted the neuronal connections between the limbic system and areas of the neocortex. This suggests that neural activity related to drive arousal is not processed through the higher cortical pathways but, rather, is short-circuited through the hypothalamic nuclei of the hindbrain and thereby accelerates or potentiates autonomic discharge. According to the model of the nervous system in Chapter III, this could involve a functional or structural lesion in either the right prefrontal lobe or in the frontolimbic pathways. As a result, of course, the somatic pathways would respond exclusively without evoking any activity in the cortical areas normally used to interpret and modulate sensory events. Thus, feelings would be transcribed directly into physical symptoms rather than words.

Steven (1973) and Nemiah et al. (1976) further suggest that the palaeostriatal dopamine tract is an area related to the alexithymic process. It, they believe, may act as a filter for limbic system discharges. Steven (1973) points to the typical accompaniment of schizophrenia by an uncontrolled flooding of sensations, emotions, and ideas which may well be the result of the *lack* of limbic filtering. Rheumatoid patients (and others with psychosomatic disorders) may have too complete a filter. The previously cited evidence for a negative correlation between RA and schizophrenia can be offered as support for this contention. All of this physiologizing might be considered mere speculation, yet it is one of the few instances in the psychosomatic literature where an objective, *testable* hypothesis has been offered.

Considering the physiology of RA, and in light of the alexithymic hypothesis, we submit the following mechanisms might be involved.

1) Stress, in the broad context of reactions to psychological and physical events and to the external environment, as well as to one's internal milieu, results in a *somatic* change. This change could be manifested in any of the autonomic responses accompanying fear, anger, love, or other feelings.

2) For some reason, neither the subjective right cerebral

hemisphere nor the verbal left cerebral hemisphere can process or label the information. What then occurs is a somatic emotional response, but a *defective* cognitive response.

3) The somatic response may well include muscle tension as an antecedent to symptoms. Muscle tension has been shown to increase joint pain and intra-articular temperature; hence, it may accelerate destructive activity in the joints themselves (Smith & Polley, 1978; Harvath & Hollander, 1949).

4) The diverted, unlabeled emotions may also be focused on hypothalamic activity, as suggested earlier. If so, the entire autonomic system could be affected. Similarly, the immune system—which is clearly under central nervous system control and *specifically* influenced by hypothalamic activity—would be involved. Rogers, Dubey, and Reich (1979), in an excellent critical review entitled "The Influence of the Psyche and the Brain on Immunity and Disease Susceptibility," have marshalled and summarized the evidence for central nervous system involvement, citing 94 references. These authors concluded that considerable evidence exists which indicates "that CNS change leads to immunologic change through the mechanism of *hypothalamic-pituitary-hormonal* stimulation." Further evidence can be cited for an afferent link, initiated by an immune mechanism, in which a message is sent to the hypothalamus whenever an immune reaction takes place (Besedovsky, Sorkin, Felix, & Haas, 1977). This may thus be a two-way process, with the hypothalamus responsive to immunologic changes as well as able to influence these changes. In an autoimmune disorder such as RA, perhaps the defect is not in the antibody-antigen reactions per se but, rather, in the signals from central nervous system areas (e.g., the hypothalamus) which trigger the reactions.

Discussions on denial of emotion appear throughout the literature on RA. We submit that the apparent denial is not denial in the usual psychoanalytic sense of having a mental block that serves as a defense mechanism. Instead, the denial relates to a very "real" problem of having, literally, no words for feelings; it reflects a patent failure to process the cognitions involved. One of the clearest examples of this phenomenon was a woman who was selected as part of an RA control group for a study to be described shortly. She was interviewed in the customary manner, but many of the questions led to great, uncontrollable outbursts of crying. The questions, which themselves were not particularly emotionally charged, included such innocuous items as "How many children are there in your family?" and "What makes you angry?" She was never able to give any reason for her profusion of tears. She did acknowledge that she frequently cried for no apparent reason, however.

Other women in our study would relate life experiences of misfortune with amazing calmness—la belle indifference. For instance, one woman seen at a charity hospital described an early life of high aspirations to a musical and scholarly career. She had even been offered a scholarship at the end of high school that would have allowed her to embark upon the pathway toward her goals. Her parents—particularly her father—believed that such achievement was unsuitable for girls and, instead, exhausted the family's resources in order to educate a son who was academically nonremarkable, to put it kindly. The woman had two children and four grandchildren of her own and was widowed when we met. She was living on modest social security payments in subsidized government housing. Self-education was a continuous process for her, and she enrolled in every free community education program in the city. She had studied Latin, math, and music in this fashion. Not once, even after repeated discussion, did any bitterness or tone of remorse creep into her voice as she related her parents' obviously oppressive behaviors and her own poor state which resulted from them. That was just the way things were. Certainly, this might represent a case of severely repressed hostility which was allowed to manifest itself only in the somatic realm. However, the concept of alexithymia posits a *lack* of cognitive processing of the emotions which might be experienced in such circumstances, not merely their repression as does the defense mechanism of denial in a psychiatric explanation.

The etiology of alexithymia is as speculative as the disorder itself. As with most diseases, the problem probably stems from an interaction between genetic tendency and environmental factors. Overt and covert behaviors which allow for the translation of stressful or emotionally charged events into somatic, rather than cognitive, pathways no doubt follow the most basic law of learning: reinforced behaviors continue while unreinforced behaviors cease. Patients with physical disorders that are precipitated or exacerbated by psychological distress, such as RA, may have learned at a very early age that the somatic channel was more likely to be reinforced. Whereas an occasional somatic response originally relieved the tension, however, sudden massive responding during a major life crisis could well overload the system. The likely focus of consequent physical attrition would depend on the particular response and individual predisposing characteristics.

We believe RA patients are, in large measure, alexithymic. That fact alone structures an approach to therapy. Whether it is true of most people with chronic disease or simply a function of culture, and whether or not there is some special relationship with arthritis itself, doesn't negate the need to recognize and deal with the issue in preparing a group or a therapeutic encounter.

In this regard, some interesting findings regarding emotions and change in disease that colors the development of a therapeutic encounter have been presented by Moldofsky and Chester (1970). These investigators report two types of RA patients: one group in which mood patterns appeared to either precede by one day or occur simultaneously with increased intra-articular pain, and another group, termed paradoxical, in which an asynchronous pattern was characteristic. The former lived up to expectations based on previous literature findings, in that negative emotional conditions produced pain or flare-up through the mechanism of muscle tension and possibly autonomic change. Paradoxically, the latter group did not show the predicted mood change. Instead, as their pain worsened, their reported mood-state improved. These were, incidentally, the "good" patients who suffered difficult medical regimens calmly and without complaint.

In follow-up studies of both groups, the paradoxical patients fared much worse physically. According to the authors, six of eight managed poorly, required lengthy hospitalizations, and had major medical difficulties. One died of a cerebral vascular accident, one experienced a temporary cardiac arrest, another underwent metacarpalphalangeal synovectomy and ureterolithotomy, and so on. Their familial and social relations were no less characterized by difficulty and distrust. "Most apparent was the rigidity of the mood-state of this group. They experienced great difficulty in altering their pessimistic outlook and seemingly purposeless existence." (p. 347)

In examining these data, we might assert that those individuals who *recognize* their feelings to the extent that they can label them reliably to coincide with disease change are, by definition, *less* alexithymic. Predictably, they also do better physically. For a therapist, a major goal would be to assist patients in the identification and subsequent labeling of feelings. A rationale for doing this is the fact that negative emotions tend to stress the physiological system, as well as to reflect its being stressed, and so appropriate emotional labeling allows for some prediction of change. The patient is thereby able to attribute a factor to physical change and is lifted out of the role of victim of disease to at least the role of predictor of disease change.

In this proposition, we are making the assumption that Moldofsky and Chester's paradoxical group were unable to *label* emotions, though they may have experienced the conditions that evoke an emotional response. The stress that precedes flare-up was present but was not cognitively mediated by the patient. There may be secondary gains associated with the *onset* of the flare-up based on the observation that as the physical condition worsened, mood improved. Perhaps, for them, the burden of uncertainty, of wondering when the next attack would occur, had been resolved.

The notion of the "burden of uncertainty," in fact, has formed the premise for a description of the psychological aspects of RA by Carolyn Weiner (1975). After interviewing 21 patients, she surmises that "all living requires tolerating a considerable amount of uncertainty—to state that is to state the obvious. But a study of the victims of rheumatoid arthritis provides an insight into the demands placed upon living when uncertainty is exaggerated beyond the usual level of toleration." (p. 97) If uncertainty is at issue, then gaining conscious mastery over it should prove broadly beneficial.

Pensee Operatoire. Far more speculative and less well documented, yet a trait that may be of greater importance than all the others associated with RA, is pensee operatoire. This phenomenon is often conceived as coexisting with alexithymia, and may certainly reflect merely an extension or more in-depth consideration of the same syndrome. Pensee operatoire captures the notion of an inability to fantasize. In the psychiatric sense, fantasy refers to that cognitive material which represents alternatives to what is defined by convention as external reality. Fantasies are personal thought forms which allow an individual to shift the patterns of sensory information, transcending—even projecting shape onto—the future. Form and substance are given to things not perceived in the usual way, i.e., through eyes and ears, and kinesthetic and proprioceptive senses, to mention the more familiar ones.

The inability to fantasize is felt to be a factor in psychosomatic disease, presumably using a mechanistic explanation similar to that presented earlier for alexithymia. Significantly, the portions of the brain which are assumed to be involved in the cognitive processing of emotional information are the same areas believed to be involved in the creation of images or fantasies. Especially implicated is the anterior aspect of the right frontal lobe. Of course, the redundancy and interdigitation of many cerebral functions caution us against locating functions with much assurance. Nevertheless, research findings presented in Chapter III allow us to speculate that a deficit in information *storage, processing,* or *retrieval*—for organic or functional reasons—would result in behaviors like those defined by the alexithymic and pensee operatoire terminology. In other words, deficits in the ability to fantasize and in verbalizing feelings would be expected.

The studies of psychological aspects, taken *in toto*, depict a profile of patients who find fantasy difficult; indeed, it does not seem to play much of a role in their inner lives. Repeated reports of rigidity in thinking, underproductivity of expression on projective tests, lack of richness in speech, restrictions in emotional response, and the inability to project a future (i.e., the burden of uncertainty) present a composite picture of a life devoid of daydreaming, of fantasy regarding the future.

We hesitate to assign etiologies in explaining this phenomenon. They could conceivably run the spectrum from an actual lesion in the central nervous system to a developmental learning explanation. The latter is the most parsimonious and does not require premorbid assignment of personality traits or deficiencies. For example, suppose a patient does in fact feel that life is so uncertain that—upon awakening—one never knows what the day will bring, much less what the year or the decade will produce. Hopes for improvement are dashed repeatedly, yet unexplainable long-term remission may be experienced. We assume that this ability to fantasize, like every other human trait, is subject to the laws of learning, i.e., behaviors that are reinforced continue and strengthen, while those that are not reinforced drop out of the repertoire. Using this kind of interpretation, we would conclude that rheumatoids, as a rule, have not been reinforced much for behaviors of fantasizing future outcomes.

As would be expected, those patients who do not fit into this sterotype appear to have a more positive disease outcome. That has been our observation throughout: the cancer patient who does not exhibit the passive, depressive, so-called cancer personality; the pain patient who psychologically differs from the pain-patient profile; these are the ones who are most likely to recover. This has been a grand source of confusion in psychosomatic thought, and perhaps the confusion has led to the inability to define consistently any disease/psyche profiles. The inclusion of data from patients who are likely to recover or stabilize must significantly bias the total profile.

In the arthritis literature, the previously cited work by Moldofsky is relevant. Patients who could predict the disease course by nature of their responses to psychological questions were found to do better physically. It is a fine line that discriminates between this kind of prediction and future reinforcement for fantasized outcomes. During the 1950s, when traditional psychosomatic studies were at a peak, another interesting observation was made. McLaughlin, Zabarenko, Diana, and Quinn (1953) studied the reactions of RA patients to a course of ACTH therapy. Certain psychological similarities were noted among those who responded well to treatment. Those patients who exhibited the best response were those *least* like the profile of the typical RA patient. They were significantly better at discussing their feelings (i.e., less alexithymic) and were better able to recall dreams. Their ability to process and report fantasy material, therefore, was notably better. By contrast, the researchers noted that "The patients who habitually could recall none of their dreams continued, while on ACTH, to repress the knowledge of their dreaming. These patients showed a strikingly poor response to the ACTH." (p. 197) These differences in dream recall, we believe, signify a cluster of characteristics which are predictive of disease response, regardless of treatment.

The inability to fantasize has a direct implication for psychological treatment, in that it is synonymous with the inability to image. The dysfunction appears to extend to disease imagery—the mental pictures of disease, treatment, and the body's recuperative ability. The ramifications for outcome of a cognitively oriented treatment that involves the development of somatic control, such as biofeedback or sundry relaxation strategies, are obvious. The implications are plain, too, for treatments such as Rational Behavior Therapy, Gestalt, Psychosynthesis, or, in fact, any type of psychotherapy that uses components of imagining in order to achieve attitudinal or behavioral change. Progress will be slow—perhaps negligible—and will depend on the extent to which the therapist is aware of, and willing to help develop, the patient's ability to image. Otherwise, both patient and therapist are sentenced to an exercise in frustration.

An Eclectic Approach to Treatment

It is our contention that any adjunctive medical treatment for RA patients will have to take into consideration the following factors:

1) An outpatient program is likely to be preferred by most patients, since they are typically not hospitalized except for surgery or, on rare occasions, rest therapy.

2) The program must be economical. Therefore, if support funding does not exist, only selected components of the total program might be offered. This economic consideration is necessary because, unlike low-back pain and other trauma patients, arthritics do not have hefty workmen's compensation payments; many are on Medicare and Medicaid (which, as of this writing, are not generous toward behavioral interventions); while others have no insurance at all and very limited financial resources. The massive amount currently estimated to be spent on medical costs for this disease— $4 billion per year in the United States alone—is not likely to be channeled the way of behavioral treatment. (In view of these facts, we are amazed at the $400 billion figure which Crain (1976) states is an estimate given by the Arthritis Foundation of what is being spent on "quackery" by arthritics each year.)

3) The program might best be developed in consort with other professionals and in conjunction with an already established treatment center designed for rehabilitation generally, or rheumatological disorders, specifically.

4) A knowledge of community resources—particularly free ones—and a good working relationship with the local arthritis association are essential and invaluable ingredients for any program. Indeed, they are useful also for the psychologist in private practice who may see an arthritic occasionally.

5) *Any adjunctive* treatment designed for arthritics should be adaptable to the patient's home environment, with the expectation that they may return to the practitioner for follow-up at well-spaced intervals. Many arthritics will manifest symptoms all of their lives and cannot be expected to participate in an intensive treatment program forever. The key here is *self-help;* and while many will return for medical assistance in finding more effective pain relief, they will largely be left to their own resources to find comfort and relief in other ways.

6) A chief objective, regardless of modalities of intervention, should be to assist the patient in becoming sensitive to the fine balance between the appropriate amount of activity and relaxation, and to help in managing the possible psychological and functional ramifications of this disease.

The components of the proposed program are discussed below, with emphasis on the behavioral dimensions.

Medical Evaluation. Ideally, this should be conducted on-site by a consulting physician, though we have had to rely on information from the patient's treating physician at times. The extent and thoroughness of evaluation depend upon the objectives of the behavioral program. If research is to be conducted, and statements are to be made about RA specifically, then a careful work-up would be advisable to determine existence and stage of disease. In another type of setting, it may be sufficient to simply understand something about the duration and extent of disease and the patient's functional capability in order to assist with behavioral interventions.

Variables which can be useful in assessing the degree of involvement and subsequent change in physical condition are: ring size, pain assessment, 50-foot timed walk, a count of painful or inflamed joints, duration of morning stiffness, time at onset of fatigue, and grip strength. Additionally, physicians will occasionally ask for an assessment of the patient's perceived extent of disability. The reader will no doubt have quickly surmised the potential unreliability of all these measures and may be somewhat disturbed. When one considers these factors are utilized to diagnose, it becomes apparent how differences of opinion regarding causes and cures can occur. Two more objective measures which can be obtained through routine lab tests are Erythrocyte Sedimentation Rate and RA Latex. The first gives an index of disease activity, and is considered reliable except that elevations may be related to infectious activity other than RA. Rheumatoid Arthritis Latex level is also useful in combination with symptoms, yet 15% of RA patients have negative latex readings so it can't be exclusively utilized to determine diagnosis.

Medical diagnosis, then, is deceptively simple. If it is crucial to include only RA patients, then the physician evaluation had best be considered integral to the program. However, if the consequences are minor when one includes someone with osteoarthritis (OA), or a mixture of OA and RA, then certainly there is some value in limiting the evaluation to only a few, pragmatic criteria. We were abruptly made aware of the problems in diagnosis when we screened approximately 150 women on a list of "known rheumatoids" provided by a local health service. Only approximately 30 of them could be considered classic or definite RA. Many had never been to a physician for their disease but simply *assumed* they had RA. Others had gone for treatment many years previously and thought they remembered being diagnosed as RA. It would be interesting to conduct a study on the extent of misconception, because this may be a serious issue for the patient. For example, they all seem to regard RA as the "crippling" kind of arthritis. To what extent might this be accompanied by an ever-present fear and a consequent vulnerability to the so-called home remedies and quack cures?

Regardless of the extent of medical evaluation, a careful monitoring of medication is of practical value even in behavioral programs. Our major concerns have been:

1) Types of medication, both for arthritis and coexisting conditions. Many patients are on steroids (which resemble mood elevators in their enhancement of well-being), and others have been given prescriptions for pain killers, tranquilizers, and sleeping pills;

2) Dosage and frequency of use if medications were taken PRN; and

3) Any change in medication during the course of treatment.

In discussing drug regimens with patients, we have received vital clues regarding behavior. For example, one 55-year-old woman we evaluated presented with Stage II (or moderate disease) involvement in only five joints, and with low disease activity as measured by Sedimentation Rate. Her behavior, however, was quite inappropriate for her condition; she essentially described herself as an invalid, used a cane, and took to her bed frequently. Her conversation was inappropriate, and, while she was clever and fairly creative in her speech, she was unable to focus on one topic for long. There was also something strangely familiar about her glassy, dilated eyes that was out of context for an arthritic. We soon found out that she was, apparently, unwittingly overmedicating herself with Percodan. Her mental confusion had been a source of bewilderment for her, too, and she was relieved to experience a cessation of ambiguity when the drug was gradually discontinued. Her condition, by any yardstick, did not warrant that kind of narcotic. Interestingly, she was demanding and critical of the therapists, and complained incessantly. One suspects that that kind of patient ultimately is overmedicated through an honest desire to ameliorate the distress.

A second example of the importance of drug information is illustrated in a composite picture of the many RA patients who are on Prednizone or other steroids. In the short run, these chemicals are like a miracle prescription. Pain and swelling subside; patients feel emotionally stable, even euphoric. However, long-term use is accompanied by untoward side effects, including a softening of bones, thinning and easy bruising of skin, and fluid retention. From a psychological standpoint, one of the devastating effects we see repeatedly when patients are taken off steroids (and almost all are sooner or later) is a depressive reaction. Many seem unaware that it is related to the medication withdrawal; and the inability to distinguish any other cause compounds the depression. We soon learned to inquire on each visit about any change in medications of this type since not only are psychological factors involved, but general physical distress may be present as well.

There is another practical reason for inquiring about amount or change of medication: the information can serve as a criterion variable for judging the success of intervention. Most patients are given sedatives and tranquilizers with the advice, "take as needed." Therefore, decreases in self-administration of both types of drug, while psychological condition or hours of sleep remain stable, can be indicative of patients beginning to use their own nonpharmacologic resources.

Functional Evaluation. The functional approach to RA evaluation resembles both medical and psychological evaluations in that all are based largely on *behavior* or subjective self-report. Nevertheless, some differences of focus do occur. In the functional evaluation, more attention is given to measuring the strength and range of motion of involved joints. In addition, the functional evaluation typically includes some type of assessment of activities routinely encountered in daily living. One of our instruments consists of a 3-point scale reflecting whether each activity can be accomplished all of the time (3), some of the time (2), or never (1). A total ratio score that gives a crude indication of functionality is found by adding together points from all items and dividing the sum by the total number of questions answered. Items tap areas of personal hygiene and grooming (Can you zip up a back zipper?), household chores (Can you pour from a pitcher?), as well as modes of transportation used, leisure activities pursued, etc. A total of 108 items were formulated (see Table 7.2).

Both the functional and medical evaluations (perhaps even more so than the psychological) are contingent upon the patient's *motivation* and the conditions under which they are required to respond. They walk faster, grip harder, and move with greater range when motivated to do so. This source of variance is unavoidable but should be recognized. Otherwise, the physical exams may be construed as totally objective. (It is a common misperception that they are objective and that the psychological evaluation is the subjective end of it all.)

We have found the total functional exam useful for pre- and post-treatment evaluation. Most measures showed some variation during a six-week study program that we conducted. A mid-treatment evaluation was discarded as too time-consuming for the patients to justify the small amount of information it yielded.

Psychological Evaluation. Our psychological evaluation was developed on the basis of literature findings of import in the understanding of RA and of specific research questions we were asking. It consists of three elements: (a) social history, (b) psychological tests, and (c) self-reports gathered at intervals to serve as criterion measures.

The evaluation was administered to 75 women diagnosed with Stage II or III rheumatoid arthritis. Many of these women were participants in a research project aimed at assessing the treatment effects of biofeedback and relaxation techniques relative to traditional physiotherapy techniques. Details of the study are presented later in this chapter.

The primary reason for doing such an evaluation, of course, is to locate characteristics which might be predictive of treatment progress. A secondary purpose of the psychological evaluation, though, is to provide a situation in which to establish a warm relationship with each of the patients, to relieve their anxieties about the program, and to learn something of their interpersonal styles. We mention it here, and will repeatedly refer to the fact that the rheumatoid patients we encountered did not tolerate much psychologizing. *They* made their distaste clear from the outset.

Table 7.2

DAILY ACTIVITY SCALE

NAME _____ Date _____

DOMINANT HAND _____

FUNCTIONAL EVALUATION FOR ARTHRITIS

SCORE ACTIVITIES ON SCALE OF 1 TO 3
  1 = Always can
  2 = Sometimes can
  3 = Never can
n/a = Not applicable

ACTIVITIES	SCORE	COMMENTS
PERSONAL HYGIENE		
1. Wash hands, face		
2. Bathe self		
3. Operate water faucets		
4. Get into and out of shower or tub		
5. Wring wash cloth		
6. Apply toothpaste to brush		
7. Brush teeth		
8. Get on and off toilet		
9. Shave or make up		
10. Shampoo hair		
11. Put up hair		
12. Comb or brush hair		
13. Clean and trim fingernails		
14. Trim toenails		
DRESSING		
1. Take clothes from closet		
2. Manage clothes independently		
3. Put on, remove button blouse		
gloves		
socks or hose		
slipover garment		
shoes or slippers		
slacks or shorts		
slip		
belt		
bra		
girdle		
sweater across shoulders		
4. Tie shoe laces		
6. Put on, remove glasses		
7. Wind watch		
8. Put object in pocket		
9. Remove object from pocket		
10. Manage zippers		
safety pins		
straight pins		
EATING		
1. Sit down and get up from dining table		
2. Pass food at table		
3. Pour from pitcher		
4. Use salt shaker		
5. Eat sandwich		
6. Pick up glass and drink		
7. Cut with knife		
8. Butter bread		
9. Eat with spoon or fork		
10. Eat soup with spoon		
HOUSEHOLD		
1. Walk carrying tray with dishes		
2. Pick up object from table		

Table 7.2 (Concluded)

	SCORE	COMMENTS
3. Wash, dry dishes (heavy pans)		
4. Empty trash		
5. Prepare foods for serving: a. peel, slice, mash		
b. use rolling pin		
c. use egg beater		
d. crack eggs		
e. open cans, bottles		
6. Cook food: a. lift pan to burner		
b. turn on stove		
c. stir food		
d. pour from pan into dish		
7. Put in, remove things from oven		
from refrigerator		
8. Set oven timer		
9. Pick up object from floor		
10. Dust, wax furniture		
11. Make bed		
12. Clean windows		
13. Sweep, mop floors		
14. Vacuum		
15. Laundry		
16. Hang up wash		
17. Iron: a. sprinkle clothes		
b. put up ironing board		
c. pick up iron		
18. Clean bathtub, commode		
19. Clean refrigerator		
20. Move furniture		
21. Remove, replace screw top from bottle		
22. Open prescription bottle		
23. Carry grocery bag		
24. Gardening: a. rake		
b. hoe		
c. dig		
d. pull weeds		
25. Home repair: a. hammer		
b. screwdriver		
c. paint		
d. pry open objects		

LOCOMOTION

	SCORE	COMMENTS
1. Ambulate unassisted		
2. Ambulate with crutches, cane		
3. Propel wheelchair		
4. Get in and out of bed		
chairs		
car		
5. Ride a bus		

COMMUNICATION

	SCORE	COMMENTS
1. Write name		
2. Write letter		
3. Position paper for writing		
4. Stamp letter		
5. Use eraser		
6. Sharpen pencil		
7. Handle money		
8. Dial phone		
9. Manage pay phone		
10. Hold book		
11. Handle newspaper		
12. Wrap, tie package		

APPARATUS

	SCORE	COMMENTS
1. Put on, remove hand splints or braces		
2. Put on, remove adaptive apparatus		

The social history is relatively brief and contains the usual demographic data. Additionally, we inquire about birth order, which we previously have come to trust as a rehabilitation indicator (See Chapter VI). We ask about early childhood activities to assess the extent of "tomboyism." We also obtain information on several questions regarding typical behavioral responses to frustration, hurt, or anger.

The types of diagnostics selected naturally depend upon one's purpose in testing the patients. For clinical purposes, a mood-state scale seems to be useful since moods may be predictive of, or at least correlated with, changes in physical condition. We have used the Profile of Mood States (POMS) and found it helpful. Other investigators (e.g., Moldofsky and Chester, 1970), using adjective check lists modified from Nowlis and Nowlis (1956-1957), have noted that moods heralded disease change in some patients.

An inquiry regarding stressful events also appears relevant since stress is a frequent precursor to disease onset or change. Discussion of these events or life changes also frequently serves as a stepping stone to awareness of the mind/body connection. We typically administer the Holmes and Rahe instrument (1967), although several other versions are available (Dohrenwend & Dohrenwend, 1974). Additionally, we ask patients to try to recall any stressful situations which might have transpired in the few months prior to the initial diagnosis. Besides giving us vital information, this procedure assists patients to conceptualize some relationship between their behavior and the disease. Strangely enough, most RA patients have already identified an event which they consider to be the triggering factor for their illness. These putative etiologies are highly variant, ranging from bee stings to pregnancy.

There may be some benefit in administering a test, such as the MMPI or 16 PF, which generates a character profile in order to facilitate an understanding of the person. Using the MMPI, Solomon and his associates have further demonstrated how the findings may be used to compare rheumatoid arthritic patients with nonarthritics and to discriminate those patients who do well from those who do poorly (see Solomon, Amkrant, & Kasper, 1974, for a review).

Finally, many investigators have used projective tests to assess RA patients. From their findings valuable formulations have been developed (Kiviniemi, 1978, reviews these). Both the Thematic Apperception Test and the Rorschach have been widely used in this regard, as well as lesser known instruments. Certainly, the clinician who is comfortable using these tests, and who feels information from them can be of use in determining the therapeutic strategy, will continue to administer them. Psychologists and others who are accustomed to using the projectives solely to seek out pathology, however, should be aware that they will probably find none. The same can be said of the more objective tests (e.g., MMPI); while variations within the normal range do give useful information and tend to discriminate among groups, psychopathology is rarely manifested.

We have found quantitative, self-report measures useful as criterion variables against which to judge improvement. They also help to assess current disease status. The format we use is illustrated in Figure 7.1.

Behavioral Intervention Strategies

Nemiah et al. (1976) advise that patients with psychosomatic disorders (and RA patients are included) probably benefit from mere supportive counseling provided outside a psychoanalytic framework. While not spelling out the nature of this counsel, one assumes that it ought to relate to the development of skills for coping with distress. Ross (1977) is more specific in his discussion of treatment approaches to the RA patient. Even though he does not overtly acknowledge the existence of an alexithymic syndrome per se, his advice is obviously geared toward a minimum of what we have called psychologizing and a maximum of attention to traditional medical, pharmacologic management of the emotional state. Among other things, it is advised that:

1) Personal conflict may precede or exacerbate the condition;
2) Patients do not generally confide emotional problems during the first interview (the implication being that *after* lab findings are made known and medication administered, the patient may then reveal frustrations and conflict);
3) Careful timing of referrals to a psychiatrist or psychologist is important and best awaits the patient's initiating a discussion of problem areas;
4) Hospitalization can be used effectively as a haven from stressful situations;
5) Medications need to be utilized cautiously, in that
   a) tricyclic antidepressants are most helpful if the drug is prescribed *after* the patient has verbalized feelings of discouragement. (It is noted that "At this point, the use of these drugs can facilitate the patient's verbal expression of aggression and aid him in constructive activity.")
   b) "If antidepressant medications or steroids are given soon, i.e., before the therapeutic alliance has developed, they may bolster a defense of denial and block

Figure 7.1

Interval   **Question**

Initial 3 Weeks Posttreatment Follow-up Follow-up

                              I. How many hours a day do you experience pain?

— — — — —   1. I do not have pain

— — — — —   2. 1 - 8 hours per day

— — — — —   3. 9 - 16 hours per day

— — — — —   4. 17 - 23 hours per day

— — — — —   5. Constantly

— — — — —   II. How many hours' sleep do you get each night?

— — — — —   III. How many times do you wake up?

                              IV. Check changes in work (including housework) activities since diagnosis.

— — — — —   1. do more

— — — — —   2. no change

— — — — —   3. considerable change

— — — — —   4. drastic change, I cannot do what I did before surgery

                              V. Changes in leisure activities.

— — — — —   1. Some activities I engaged in more (Specify) __

_____

— — — — —   2. No change. I participate in the same activities as before.

— — — — —   3. Some activities (but not all) I engage in less frequently.

— — — — —   4. I have had to curtail or decrease all leisure activities since surgery.

                              VI. Pain/discomfort scales (0 - 100)

— — — — —   1. pain severity (100 = worst pain imaginable, 0 = none)

— — — — —   2. physical activity (100% = totally disabled, 0 = no disability)

— — — — —   3. percent of time pain felt

— — — — —   4. effect on mood (100% = mood totally changed, 0 = no effect)

— — — — —   5. percent of body hurting

the patient from solving his personal problems."
(Regrettably, Ross does not expand upon this
notion, but presumably the resultant mood elevation
prevents an examination of issues. This presents a
rather ticklish situation for the therapist intent upon
uncovering latent conflict and assisting the patient
with insights. Many patients are given steroids for
their disease, not their mood, and rarely is consideration given to the subjective experience of well-
being that comes with the prescription. Likewise,
the depression that may occur after medication is
discontinued may not be discussed. For this reason,
the author advises that patients should not be
weaned from steroids at the time of discharge or
when time between office visits is expected to be
very long.

6) Supportive therapy plus medical management is probably the best approach for most patients, although some
   will benefit from insight therapy.

These suggestions certainly do not provide pragmatic information for the psychotherapist on *what* to do with an RA
patient. They do point out that the patient has a physical
problem which requires attention. Even after that is treated,
medication and rest are suggested for emotional or stress-
related disorders. This simple method is probably effective in
many instances. Medicine—not psychotherapy—is the
patient's relevant symbol of healing. Medicine gives patients
permission to heal and grants relief, even from depression,
anger, or thwarted conflict, and other assorted pains of the
soul. That does not particularly discriminate patients with
psychosomatic disorders from the population at large. What
does distinguish them is their somatizing of the conflict and
inability to benefit from insight into these matters for reasons
of alexithymia, repression, or whatever.

Group-Oriented Therapy. RA patients *do* vehemently express
discontent over problems encountered as a result of having
the disease, even though depression itself appears very concrete, fundamental, and attributed by them to the disorder itself. They seem to benefit from a mutual sharing of such problems, provided that pragmatic solutions are discussed. As
with many groups composed of people suffering from a specific
dysfunction, the discussion can rapidly degenerate into a general complaint session. While this may bolster the spirits of a
few ("After all, there *is* someone worse off than me."), most
participants leave feeling worse than when they came. To prevent this development, the leaders should be well informed
about arthritis and its complications, as well as group processes. The possibility is ever present that some spunky

person will say, "Sonny, don't tell *me* about arthritis unless
you've had it." If the group experience is made rewarding
enough, though, initial objections are soon forgotten. Unfortunately, almost nothing has been written about initiating and
managing groups designed expressly for RA patients. One
suspects the reputed failure of such groups to endure beyond a
few sessions may have something to do with this omission
from the literature. Schwartz, Marcus, and Condon (1978),
though, have reported on an apparently successful group
therapy approach for the psychosocial treatment of RA. Their
group lasted eight months; 14 patients participated in the
sessions, but only six attended regularly. The three physician
leaders were specialists in the areas of rheumatology, psychiatry, and physical medicine (physiatry). Discussion was
steered away from medical issues, which were handled only
during a designated period at the end of each session. The
goals, which appeared largely to encourage communication
among patients, their families, and physicians, were judged as
having been met on the basis of several qualitative observations.

1) The physician/patient relationship improved as a result
   of having more *time* available together.
2) Compliance and clinic attendance improved, possibly
   fostered by the group interactions.
3) Families and patients became more understanding of
   one another's situation and feelings.
4) Patients learned to share problems and solutions relating to activities of daily living.
5) Physicians, too, apparently gained insight into their
   patients' behaviors.

The group itself was not structured "along traditional psychoanalytic lines," but rather was more directive. The psychological content of the meetings was reportedly centered upon
such issues as alterations in physical appearance, whether to
undergo surgery, dependency/independency fears, and the
related feelings of responsibility/guilt that emerge as the
physical condition deteriorates. The authors mention that "as
the group developed a sense of cohesiveness and trust," and
presumably not until then, the patients began to explore the
relationship between their feelings and the disease itself. The
authors also comment that, as the time approached to disband
the group, separation anxiety and fears of worsening disease
were voiced. Sure enough, some of the fears were self-
fulfilling, inasmuch as three patients of this small group
suffered flare-ups after termination.

Skirting about the issues of feelings, touching upon them
only lightly, and then when the subject is initiated by the
patients themselves, showing empathy for the many changes
that come with chronic disease, offering education and a place

to socialize seem to be the key ingredients in group process for RA patients. This is pretty tame fare for many psychologists who have the expectation that the group will somehow work miracles or provide a vehicle for that elusive breakthrough to understanding psychological dynamics. It is also pretty mundane, compared with the dramatic group experiences some of us have been fortunate enough to encounter with patients who reexamine their lives in order to save their lives.

Stress Management Techniques. The previously cited information on the relationship between stress, muscle tension, and the exacerbation of pain (and perhaps even disease) points clearly toward intervention mechanisms which can be readily adapted to RA. Specifically, techniques which aid and train relaxation appear relevant. The rheumatoid may have had a long history of muscular and joint distress in view of the repeated reports of tomboyism. We, too, in interviewing patients, elicited frequent reports of excessive physical activity when young. Often it took the form of gymnastics or dancing instead of tree climbing, but was nevertheless present. Again, as with the condition of alexithymism, it matters little as far as therapeutic design whether excessive muscle tension is specific to RA, or whether it reflects age and cultural concerns. It was, and is, a factor to be contended with by both therapists and patients.

The women whom we have studied seem to be extraordinarily in need of physical activity to justify their existence. Many remembered having worked physically hard all of their lives and were proud of it. Few seemed comfortable with the periodic inactivity imposed upon them by the disease. Approximately one-third of those interviewed stated they had always "worked out" their anger by throwing themselves into some physical task or sport. This method of relieving tension was no longer available to them because it now resulted in greater pain. Therefore, other means of dissipating muscular tension could be learned with profit.

The assessment and treatment of subjective stress is a potentially important component of planned intervention for any physical disorder. For RA patients, regardless of differential stresses in their lifestyles, pain is a common denominator and a major source of salient stress, with possibly auto-exacerbating effects. An effective treatment program for arthritis should therefore minimize subjective distress, whether of an internal (pain) or external origin. Several different intervention components will be described which are designed to achieve that goal.

An individual's response to stress is said to be as variable as the situations which produce it (Wolff, 1968). Yet, regardless of the manner of expression, all stress reactions are characterized by physiological arousal (Selye, 1950; Williams &

Gentry, 1977; Wolff, 1968). Increased attention, muscle strength and tonus, respiration, and heart rate are all typically observed in states of arousal. Obviously, short-term physiological arousal would seem to provide an organism with an adaptive advantage, in that there is a mobilization of defensive biological responses, such as "fight or flight" (Selye, 1950). However, extreme and/or long-term arousal actually may be counterproductive.

One of the psychologist's most effective means for combating inappropriate and maladaptive physical stress is by training deep muscle relaxation as a response that is incompatible with arousal (Suinn, 1977; Suinn & Richardson, 1971). Although indirect approaches (jogging, listening to music, reading, and consuming alcohol) yield a degree of relaxation, clinical application of direct relaxation techniques allow greater control. These alternatives include massage, relaxation, imagery, meditational instruction, and biofeedback. Of these, biofeedback and relaxation are the most readily applicable and testable, although only two applications have appeared in the literature (Wickramasekera, 1976; Denver, Laveault, Girard, Lacourciere, Latulippe, Grove, Preve, & Doiron, 1979). Findings on a number of criteria were positive in both studies, but the samples were small.

Biofeedback. Although the two above-mentioned studies are the only published reports specifically concerned with its use in RA treatment, biofeedback has been used widely in the treatment of the chronic pain which accompanies a variety of other disorders. Biofeedback has been employed for this purpose because of its versatility. Most physical therapy techniques such as heat, traction, and massage do not teach the patient relaxation skills which could be used outside of the clinical setting. On the other hand, biofeedback training teaches the patient a method of breaking the pain-tension-pain cycle which can generalize to situations outside of the clinic. By providing information about a physiological system that covaries with tension, such as electrical activity in muscles or skin temperature, the patient is trained to recognize and modify deviant states which might exacerbate pain.

In general, the use of biofeedback in the treatment of physiological disorders has distinct advantages relative to the more traditional medical approaches. It offers a viable alternative to long-term chemotherapy which often produces undesirable side-effects. The active participation of the patient in treatment is probably another important advantage. RA ents with "type A," high-achiever personalities, or who aps exhibit a history of physical activeness, possibly rience an exacerbation of symptomatology when ated in treatment to the unaccustomed role of passivity. y, biofeedback therapy probably elicits from the patients an increased sense of responsibility and motivation, and feelings of frustration and helplessness are minimized. For these reasons, biofeedback training was included as a major component of the treatment program proposed for rheumatoid arthritis.

Verbal relaxation. A treatment strategy often coupled with biofeedback training is that of verbally induced relaxation (Goldfried & Davidson, 1976; Rimm & Masters, 1975; Williams & Gentry, 1977). Broadly conceived, such techniques as progressive muscular relaxation (Jacobson, 1948), autogenic training with imagery (Luthe, 1969), and meditation to elicit the "relaxation response" (Benson, 1975) are all verbally induced relaxation procedures. It has been demonstrated repeatedly that voluntary muscular relaxation markedly reduces subjective stress and anxiety (Bernstein & Borkovec, 1973; Goldfried & Trier, 1974; Jacobson, 1948; Lang, Melaned, & Hart, 1970; Paul, 1969b). It should also be noted that the vocal instructions for relaxation can be tape recorded for use in home practice as well as in clinical training sessions. (Lang et al., 1970; Achterberg & Lawlis, 1978). The simplicity of the treatment procedure is enhanced by an impressive pool of favorable research findings. Verbal relaxation, like biofeedback, has been used at least as an adjunctive treatment of numerous physical disorders. A brief summary of representative studies demonstrating the efficacy of verbal relaxation training is provided in Table 7.3.

Research Support for Behavioral Intervention Strategies. A combination of the biofeedback and relaxation or meditation appears to be most effective for many physical disorders as compared to biofeedback alone (Green & Green, 1977; Patel, 1973; Gaardner & Montgomery, 1977). Although recognizing that the design was "messy" from a research standpoint, since the contribution of biofeedback and relaxation separately to the end results could not be known, we chose to utilize a combined approach in our work. Actually, our intention was to design a strategy which took into consideration previous research findings, and which was most likely to guarantee success in terms of pain and stress reduction (Achterberg, McGraw, & Lawlis, 1980).

In this study, two groups of female patients were taught a relaxation technique (via a tape recording which focused on the relaxation of all major muscle groups) and then trained in either (a) *temperature elevation,* or (b) *temperature decrease.* Some of the women (15) were diagnosed by a rheumatologist; hence, they constituted a homogeneous disease group of Stage II and III patients—classic or definite RA. Another 12 women were self-referred, and diagnoses were verified with the family physician. (In line with previous discussion regarding the

Table 7.3

DATA ON THE EFFICACY OF VERBAL RELAXATION TRAINING*

Author/Data	Target Behavior	Treatment Method[s]	Results
Alexander, Miklich, & Hershkoff (1971)	Expiratory Flow in Asthmatic Children	Systematic verbal relaxation training as compared to quiet rest.	Patients receiving verbal relaxation training achieved a significant mean increase in expiratory flow versus a nonsignificant decrease for patients receiving rest only. (All patients in relaxation group were able to achieve the relaxed state.)
Bassett, Blanchard, & Estes (1977)	Anxiety as measured by questionnaire	Verbal relaxation training with high, medium, or low expectancy set versus soothing music with same three expectancy sets.	All subjects receiving verbal relaxation training achieved significant reductions in anxiety independent of expectancy set.
Craighead (1973)	Snake fear	SD, SD without relaxation, verbal relaxation with childhood scenes and verbal relaxation.	All subjects receiving relaxation training mastered the response, and all groups significantly reduced their fear of snakes. Treatments were equivalent.
Freeling & Shemberg (1970)	Test anxiety	SD, SD without relaxation, and verbal relaxation.	Subjects in SD and verbal relaxation groups all mastered the relaxation response. SD and verbal relaxation groups were equal, and both exceeded SD without relaxation.
Gershman & Clouser (1974)	Insomnia	SD and verbal relaxation	All subjects mastered the relaxation response and treatments were equally effective.

McGlynn (1971)	Mouse fear	SD and verbal relaxation with imagery (pleasant scenes)	All subjects mastered the relaxation response and made significant progress in overcoming mouse fear. The two treatments did not differ.
Mitchell & White (1977)	Predormital insomnia	Progressive verbal, mental, and muscle relaxation and cognitive control procedures.	All subjects in relaxation phases mastered the response and reduced presleep tension. Intensive cognitions were controlled by cognitive intervention.
Ratliff & Stein (1968)	Scratching associated with neurodermatis	Aversion therapy and verbal relaxation.	The subjects mastered the relaxation response. Aversion therapy controlled scratching in session, and the relaxation response was employed as a competing response when an urge to scratch occurred between sessions.
Tasto & Chesney (1974)	Dysmenorrhea	Verbal relaxation training with imagery of reduced menstrual pain.	All patients mastered the relaxation response and reported success in obtaining relevant images. Results were positive.
Taylor (1972)	Frequent urination	Verbal relaxation training and SD.	A case study in which the patient mastered the relaxation response, allowing progression through the hierarchy and ultimate control of the target behavior.
Zeisset (1968)	Interview anxiety	Verbal relaxation training versus SD.	All subjects were able to master the relaxation response, and reductions in anxiety were significant in comparison to no-treatment controls. Verbal relaxation and SD groups did not differ.

*Inasmuch as verbal relaxation is an integral facet of systematic desensitization (SD), studies investigating the effects of SD on various disorders are considered appropriate and are included in this table.

number of arthritic subtypes that are frequently diagnosed RA, we first considered these women separately. However, no significant differences between the two patient types were noted in response to treatment, so they were combined for the experimental analysis.)

Temperature biofeedback was selected for investigation in view of the repeated reports on the effectiveness of this modality for stress-related syndromes, and because it provides information about physiological change along a dimension of sympathetic nervous system arousal (Gaardner & Montgomery, 1977). Additionally, the vasodilation which produces the increased skin temperature is a primary effect of both heat and cold applications, and of aspirin, the most common treatment for RA (Hollander & McCarty, 1972). Also, the muscle atrophy noted in RA may be attributed to the significant reduction of muscle blood flow as a result of the vasculitis of small blood vessels (Oka, Rekonen, & Elomaa, 1971). Taking all of this information into consideration, it is clear that a rationale exists for training RA patients to attain some control over their vascular system.

Considering other available medical information about the disease, application of heat may be beneficial because it results in subsequent *decreases* in articular temperature (Horvath & Hollander, 1949). As pointed out earlier, these same investigators have demonstrated empirically, by inserting thermisters into the articular cavity of the knees of rheumatoid arthritic patients, that *increases* in joint temperature are related to: (1) superficial cold application (although a rebound warming effect did occur), (2) smoking, (3) pain, and (4) fear and apprehension. The disease itself is characterized by hypermetabolic lysosomal enzyme activity which accelerates cartilage destruction. Heat, of course, would speed up this process, while cooling, such as has been demonstrated during rest, may reduce destructive activity (Smith & Polley, 1978). A few investigators report the benefits of cryotherapy (or cold packs) as having exceeded those of the usual heat treatments for RA in clinical trials (Pegg, Littler, & Littler, 1969).

In summarizing the issue, it appeared to us that reduction of intra-articular temperature was obviously desirable, that relaxation would allow that to occur, but that the issue regarding the direction of temperature biofeedback training required investigation. Also, since many of the physiological effects of traditional physiotherapy would be duplicated by temperature biofeedback and relaxation, a direct comparison between these techniques would be valuable. Criteria included psychological tests, functional/physical evaluations, and questionnaire items related to pain, sleep, and other activities. These comprised the evaluations conducted at pre-, mid-, and posttreatment.

Results revealed positive changes following treatment which were primarily related to pain, tension, and sleep patterns for both groups, but no differential effects were noted between the group trained in temperature elevation and the one trained in reduction. This was attributed to the fact that both groups maintained temperatures above baseline during biofeedback training. Next, a group of 15 patients receiving biofeedback and relaxation was compared with eight patients who received traditional physiotherapy. The results of the second study consistently favored the biofeedback/relaxation over the physiotherapy group on the significant physical/functional indices. The psychological measures tended to remain constant throughout both studies with only minor exceptions, thus lending support to the conclusion that the effectiveness of treatment was fairly specific to physical functioning rather than to a psychological enhancement of well-being.

Both the biofeedback/relaxation and the physiotherapy groups significantly improved in walking time and in activities of daily living (Table 7.2). The significant interactions were particularly interesting, in that *all* favored the biofeedback/relaxation group: (a) for joint count, the physiotherapy group began with approximately the same number of involved joints and deteriorated, while the biofeedback/relaxation group improved; (b) for a self-report measure of physical activities, the physiotherapy group reported less involvement in physical activity, while the biofeedback/relaxation group reported being more active; and (c) on a pre- and post-measure of pain severity, the physiotherapy group began the study reporting more pain than the other group and got worse, while the biofeedback/relaxation group reported less pain at the termination of the study than at the beginning.

A general positive trend in both groups was reflected in a blood measure of disease or infectious activity—Erythrocyte Sedimentation Rate (ESR). This test is not used as an indicator of RA activity in and of itself, but rather adds to the information of the clinical picture in combination with other indices. Blood analyses were available pre- and post-treatment on nine biofeedback/relaxation participants and three physiotherapy participants. All nine of the biofeedback/relaxation participants experienced either stable rates or improvement, and two of the three physiotherapy patients showed improvement.

The combined studies described above represent an initial attempt at delineating the efficacy of biofeedback and relaxation treatment techniques for the rheumatoid arthritic patient. In the first study, it was established that biofeedback and relaxation were related to an improvement in condition, but that the specific type of biofeedback (e.g., training for temperature elevation or reduction) did not differentially affect the outcome. The second study compared biofeedback and relaxation training with traditional physiotherapy modalities. In other words, it compared an unknown treatment to a known one—a common tactic in medical or pharmaceutical research. Here, too, it was determined that biofeedback and relaxation together were equal or superior to physiotherapy in terms of the outcome measures.

With RA, finding a suitable control group presents a particular problem. First of all, one needs to determine what to control *for* (and nowhere is that made clear). Secondly, if attentional or motivational factors are agreed to be at issue, then difficulties arise. Unlike hypertensives or diabetics, or even cardiac patients, there is no medical reason to frequently examine RA patients. For many of them, pain and stiffness are debilitating; the incentive to present for either repeated examinations, or to participate in a control group that did not offer some somatic relief, would have to be creative indeed.

The failure of psychological indicators to change in either study is interesting in that an overall enhancement of well-being might have been expected due to the so-called placebo effect. The noteworthy changes in the physical/functional realm concerned those measures primarily involving sleep and pain. Sleep, particularly, is an important criterion variable. It is indicative of several factors—including pain and discomfort, tension and anxiety. Many patients described to us their gratitude at being able to sleep through the night with minimal awakening. Normally, pain and soreness present a need to change position for comfort, seriously disrupting sleep patterns. Most of the patients used relaxation instructions from the study in order to return to sleep. Another change was the increased level in their activities of daily living. From a clinical perspective, it appeared they had more energy and were motivated to extend themselves to attempt activities they had protected themselves from previously.

The biofeedback technicians and researchers who participated in this project agreed that this population appeared to have more difficulty than usual in integrating the instructions pertinent to biofeedback training. During training, several appeared to us to simply lie there, waiting for the machine to "do something." The magnitude of temperature change was also less than we had anticipated, based on our clinical experience and on literature findings. Further, cognitive representations (or images) of the disease and treatment process, as well as conceptualizations of internal change required to achieve the relaxation and biofeedback responses, were difficult to elicit from them verbally. Whether due to differences inherent in the physiology of RA, to longstanding chronic pain, or to psychosocial issues, learning biofeedback and relaxation presented special problems for this group. Some conceptual gap may have to be bridged before physiological control can be accepted as a possibility by RA patients.

Another observation was a general decline in attitude at midterm. We attributed this to the fact that RA patients tend to approach each new treatment with some optimism. When neither relief nor cure occurred immediately, depression may have set in, along with an attitude of hopelessness and of having gotten trapped in yet another futile attempt toward health. Normally, at midterm evaluation, we had an opportunity to address these feelings in conjunction with several of the interview questions; subsequently, attitude seemed to improve in most cases.

A further observation that may account for the effectiveness of biofeedback training is the previously noted fact that RA patients frequently cannot identify any relationship between their behavior and the course of their malady. As a consequence, they may express feelings of being totally victimized and helpless. The recognition that there *can* be conscious control over physiological processes, no matter how slight, may serve to alleviate this attitude of helplessness. In addition, when patients are trained to be more sensitive to body signals and cues, it is quite possible that the events that provoke disease exacerbation can be better identified, that inappropriate or excessive physical activity and muscle tension can be immediately recognized and countered, and that psychological stress which results in undue tension on muscles and strain on joints can be avoided or rechanneled.

Imagery
and RA We began to have a sense of the patients who would respond successfully to biofeedback during our first interviews with them. In our study, those patients who could describe images of their disease, treatment, and recuperative process with some vividness were the same ones who were able to learn to control their physiology via temperature biofeedback. Also, they were the same individuals who experienced the most noteworthy and positive change in disease status. Our work therefore replicated the findings of McLaughlin et al., in some respects.

What began as an effort to apply IMAGE-CA tactics to another disease was undermined by a combination of the patients' impoverished creative constructs and several naive interviewers. We did learn a great deal from our efforts, however, in lieu of the quantitative answers for which we had hoped. The patients were requested to draw pictures of their images of the diseased joints following a tape-recorded relaxation and education procedure. A structured interview was then conducted to expand upon the drawings and to provide detail. During the course of the biofeedback sessions, repeated images were suggested of both the musculature and blood flow changes. The patients were also encouraged to envision the joints themselves. Rarely did this procedure enhance the richness of the protocols, though. Most unusual, too, was a resistance to drawing anything but the external features of the joints. We had not encountered this phenomenon with such consistency in any other patient group. Arthritis, certainly, is a difficult disease to conceive in creative constructs, yet we were not particularly successful in eliciting even anatomical pictures. This was especially surprising in view of the well-illustrated literature produced by the Arthritis Foundation to which all patients had been exposed at one time or another.

The illustrations in Figures 7.2 through 7.6 were very typical for the group. Figure 7.2 was produced by a 24-year-old woman who experienced most of her pain in her ankles. She was high-school educated, very attractive, and worked full time. Her disease was fairly stable and controlled by gold shots. She spoke in a quiet, soft voice (as soft as the lines that she drew) and never exhibited any emotional change or inflection. Figure 7.3 was produced by a young woman of 32 who had a Master's degree in accounting. She was well over 6 feet tall and weighed close to 300 pounds. She was far more psychologically oriented than most, and had "straightened some things out" in psychotherapy. The picture of her involved vertebrae was less than 1-inch square. The lightness and hesitation of the lines belie the fact that she did not have any hand involvement. Figures 7.4 and 7.5 were also produced by women with no hand involvement. The drawings are typical, again, in their diminutive size, lack of detail, and light lines.

Figure 7.6, at first glance, appears to be more of the same story. Yet, it came from one of the most unusual patients we saw. The woman had experienced a dramatic remission of her disease three months prior to the interview. She had been diagnosed as a classic stage II rheumatoid with significant elbow, hand, and shoulder involvement. She attended a healing service at a charismatic church in Dallas, and during the service was overcome with a feeling of intense fever. The fever remained for two days; when it remissed, she had regained strength and range of motion in her affected joints. Fortunately, she was undergoing physical therapy at the time, and we were able to obtain verification of her story. We entered her as the first patient in our biofeedback study. We did not use her data in the results but, rather, used her as our teacher. She holds the local record for increasing fingertip

Figure 7.2

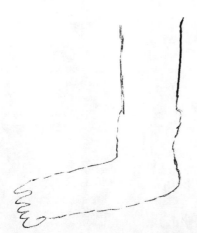

WBC

Figure 7.3

vertebra near waistline

Figure 7.4

wrist

Figure 7.5

Figure 7.6

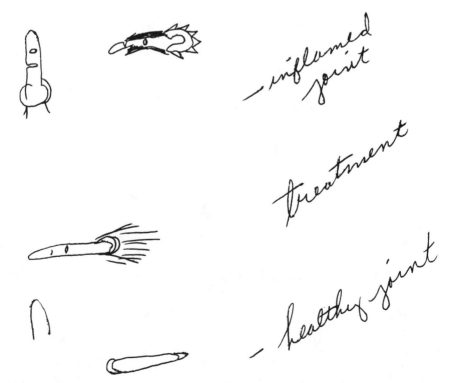

temperature (97.5), among other things! The only problem remaining when we saw her was a "loose" finger joint, a result of long-term inflammation and cartilage destruction. Her pictures of this joint are neither significant in detail nor particularly symbolic, yet the lines are sure and the drawings are the same size as those made by other women whose affected joints actually were many, many times larger (e.g., ankle or vertebrae).

In summary, the arthritic patients expressed disease and treatment constructs that were characterized overtly by weakness of lines, lack of detail, and a general tendency to describe only the external manifestation of the disease. Further, during the six weeks of treatment, which implicitly contained imagery suggestions, the drawings and constructs remained constant in their barrenness. We observed slightly more symbolism in the responsive patients; for example, the sensory aspects might be described as bee stings, the treatment as warm oil bathing the joints. However, these were rare cases and of negligible richness compared with drawings by cancer patients, diabetics, or even blue-collar, low-back-pain patients described in earlier chapters. We have struggled with and vacillated in our interpretation of these phenomena. We are struck by the homogeneity and consistency, realizing that it "must mean something," but are reluctant to over-interpret the significance of the findings at this time. At the least, it can be said that the drawings depict an uncertainty of body or "self"-concept that is not warranted by the amount of exposure to information about body function. The frequent refusal to draw or adequately describe internal events and the restriction of drawings to *percepts* (i.e., that which one can actually see on the outside of the body), indicates a functional deficit of the creative process. Perhaps this represents a second-order indication of the armoring of thought defense mechanism which many told us they employ—the "I just try not to think about it" approach to disease.

As always, though, a small number of patients took us by the hand and led us through the woods, showing us glimpses here and there of the creative bridges that allowed physiological events to be transcribed. From those glimpses, we have developed a series of concepts for RA patient education. Kathy Matulaitus, a nurse, provided the artwork. The pictures and a brief description of each are illustrated in Figures 7.7 through 7.14.

Figure 7.7

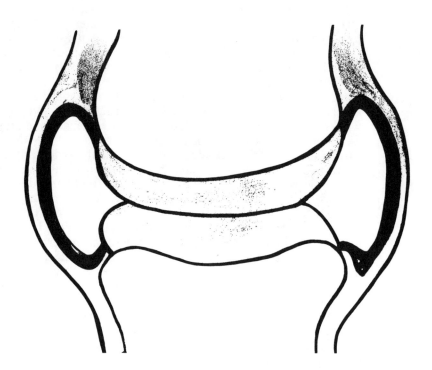

This figure represents the joints. Included are bones, cartilage, synovial lining, and intra-articular space. Rheumatoid arthritis is a disease of joints which may affect as many as 5 million Americans. Symptoms include morning stiffness, pain or tenderness in at least one joint, joint swelling, nodules under the skin, X-ray changes, a positive test for the rheumatoid factor in the blood, cloudy fluid in the joint lining, and changes in the composition of the synovia. The patient may exhibit some or all of these symptoms (but at least seven must be observed in order to classify one as rheumatoid arthritic).

Figure 7.8

Rheumatoid arthritis is called an autoimmune disease. Its causes are unknown, but we know a great deal about how it affects the immunological system. First, it is necessary to relate something about the immune response itself. The body's normal protection system contains, among other things, lymphocytes, which are a type of blood cell. They are shown here in the intra-articular space as small soldiers. Their purpose is to circulate and identify foreign substances such as viruses or bacteria (antigens). When these are identified, the lymphocytes manufacture antibodies (ammunition) which attack to immobilize the antigens. The furry creatures represent the successfully immobilized antigens in this drawing.

Figure 7.9

A second wave of blood cells is also involved in the body's defense system. They are called macrophages (literally, "giant eaters") and act as scavengers, engulfing the immobilized antigens. They are shown here as gourmets, obviously enjoying their meal. The macrophages contain lysosomes, which are little sacs in the macrophage itself. Lysosomes contain enzymes which digest the antigens and allow for their disposal. In the normal body, this is a very efficient system which allows us to live in a sea of germs and still maintain our health.

Figure 7.10

In the case of rheumatoid arthritis, something appears to go awry, and the body acts as if it has become allergic to itself. No one knows what starts this process; it is assumed that both heredity and environment play a role. Stress is also thought to be a factor in triggering it. For simplicity, one can think of rheumatoid arthritis as the lymphocytes' having lost the ability to correctly identify intruders into the system. The living cells of the synovial lining are attacked, and more and more macrophages are called to the scene as the debris increases. Their excessive activity results in increased amounts of enzymes' being vomited into the system. These enzymes, in and of themselves, are destructive to cartilage. The gourmets of the body have become gourmands.

Figure 7.11

One of the ways in which the inflammatory processes can be halted is simply to slow down the migration of the lymphocytes to the area of the joints. It is believed that the lymphocytes are escorted or carried to the areas where they must do their job by substances called prostaglandins. It would seem that, if the prostaglandins could be decreased or slowed down, then fewer white blood cells would migrate to the areas where the inflammation occurs. The prostaglandins are shown here as jeeps transporting the soldiers.

Figure 7.12

Many of the medications given for rheumatoid arthritis are believed to be effective because they slow down or decrease the prostaglandins. Here, the medications are shown shooting the tires out of the transport vehicles.

Figure 7.13

Therapy for the rheumatoid arthritic involves reeducating the body's defenders. This can be done in a number of ways, including pharmacologic treatment, rest, exercise, nutritional information, and biofeedback or other relaxation techniques. Typically, a combination of these elements are recommended to the patient. According to some authorities, the keystone of good medical management is a medication which subdues the inflammatory process, and then patients themselves learn to achieve a delicate balance between exercise and rest.

Figure 7.14

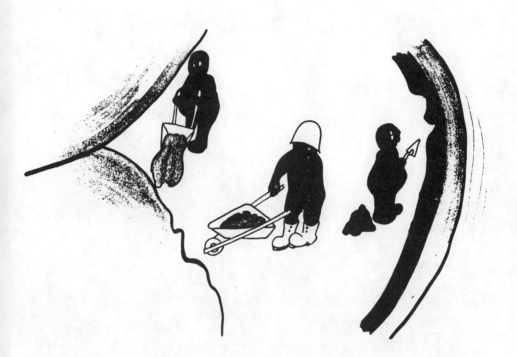

Finally, if inflammation can be controlled and damage has not been extensive, some repair can take place. In fact, a sizable percentage of the rheumatoid arthritics (some authorities estimate as many as $\frac{1}{3}$) have only one attack and go into permanent lifetime remission. Approximately another third continue to have active diseases, but the disease is kept in check by good medical management and by adaptation of lifestyle that allows the body to operate as well as possible. Finally, in the other third of the population with the disease and for whom the condition is more problematic, it is advised by rheumatologists and the American Arthritis Foundation that the crippling of the past is no longer an inevitability. So, while known cures for rheumatoid arthritis do not exist, there is a general optimism about the management of the disease. This can be conveyed to relieve the patient's burden of uncertainty.

CHAPTER VIII

ALCOHOLISM
Disease of a Lifestyle

Alcoholism is one of contemporary America's most serious social and medical problems. Although present estimates of the number of alcoholics range from four to six million, it is quite possible that these figures are conservative. It is not known whether alcoholism is increasing or decreasing, but it is apparent that alcohol consumption itself is increasing as indicated by continued expansion of the liquor industry.

One of the problems in obtaining statistical information about alcoholism is lack of a good definition of the problem. Literally hundreds of definitions have evolved from divergent research approaches. However, the definition offered by the American Medical Association (1967) seems to have elicited considerable support:

> Alcoholism is an illness characterized by preoccupation with alcohol and loss of control over its consumption, such as to lead to intoxication if drinking is begun; by chronicity; by profusion; and by tendency toward relapse. It is typically associated with physical disability and impaired emotional, occupational, and/or social adjustment as a direct consequence of persistent and excessive use. (p. 3)

Alcoholism is thus a moral problem, a mental disturbance, a social concern, and an emotional maladaptation; but most of all, it usually becomes an issue of medical concern. Generations ago, alcoholism was considered to be an act of the devil, a dire sin of the soul. Legally, imprisonment is still the most typical "rehabilitation" effort. In more recent times, alcoholism has been considered a disease entity much like diabetes. In this context, alcoholism is then classified as a disease characterized by alterations in body chemistry as well as behavior.

The basis for the analogy with diabetes has some validity in the sense that there is sociological and physiological evidence that some people are more or less sensitive to alcohol than others. For example, the American Indian apparently lacks tolerance to alcohol; whereas Jewish and some Oriental groups exhibit remarkably low incidences of alcoholism. The individual differences are due to genetic structure, socioeconomic status, and cultural influences, with no single factor completely explaining the occurrence.

The diagnosis of an alcoholic is also variable. Whether or not one could be labeled an alcoholic is dependent upon who makes the diagnosis. Alcoholics Anonymous (AA) defines an alcoholic as one whose life is seriously affected by drinking. Others might include the number of drinks taken daily or the circumstances, such as whether consumption is motivated by stress reduction or social relationships. Our preferred definition for alcoholism follows: A person is considered an "alcoholic" if that person abuses alcohol as an alternative and maladaptive behavior for dealing with stress, whether or not there is drug dependency or even habitual use of alcohol. The description posits a potential for such behavior, however. Implied in this definition are a number of specific treatment modalities.

The term "abuse" is a medical term and is a highly important one. A person abuses a substance or activity when it is destructive to the person. One can abuse food, running, working, and even water intake. Alcohol—even to the point of drunkenness—can serve a constructive purpose. In a few cases we are sure it has served as a pain drug and as a tranquilizer. With this in mind, we are always careful not to take alcohol away without first making a better choice available to the patient. Alcohol and many other drugs are usually employed as informal methods of stress management, a socially learned behavior. At some time its use may have been appropriate, but later became inappropriate. Therefore, the first step toward a rehabilitation plan is the *willful* decision to learn new responses to stress.

Personality Alcoholics have been tested in a multitude of ways, and the results are consistently inconsistent. It is our overall conclusion that alcoholics can be either greater or less than average on any one particular measure. A flood of dissertations have used numerous batteries (but primarily the MMPI) in deriving a formidable number of hypotheses, generally classifying alcoholism as a personality disorder. Some authors have sought to distinguish a major personality characteristic of "abusive drinkers." Thus, alcoholics have been described as egocentric, narcissistic (Hart, 1930; Machover & Puzzo, 1959; Tiebout, 1945); materialistic (Lentz, 1943); passive (Halpern, 1946; Klebanoff, 1947; Machover & Puzzo, 1959); and generally maladjusted (Billig & Sullivan, 1943; Halpern, 1946; Lentz, 1943; Seliger & Rosenberg, 1941). They have been further described as ambivalent (Machover & Puzzo, 1959), self-critical, and pessimistic (Lentz, 1943; Williams, 1965). Klebanoff (1947) and Wittman (1939*a*, *b*, *c*) found alcoholics insecure, while Fisher and Fisher (1955) considered them rigid in ego-involving situations. Several authors have described alcoholics as having low frustration tolerance, numerous conflicts, and an inability to endure anxiety (Billig & Sullivan, 1943; Buhler & Lefever, 1949; Carver, 1931; Felix, 1944; Fox, 1958, 1961). The increased hostility and resentment of alcoholics have frequently been stressed (Button, 1956a; Fox, 1958; Jellinek, 1952; Klebanoff, 1947; Norbury, 1942), as have feelings of depression (Fox, 1958) and guilt (Button, 1956a; Machover & Puzzo, 1959; Tiebout, 1945; Wittman, 1939a, b, c).

Although alcoholics seem to have a low conception of themselves (Fox, 1958), they are also described as having grandiose fantasies and feelings of superiority (Hart, 1930; Tiebout, 1945, 1953, 1954; Machover & Puzzo, 1959). Furthermore, the alcoholic has demonstrated needs for elation and excitement (Meerlo, 1952), needs for self-identity (Hershenson, 1965), and needs to remove inferiority feelings (Ansbacher & Ansbacher, 1946; Klebanoff, 1947). Other investigators stress the alcoholic's need to escape from reality. It appears these individuals are incapable of facing the demands of reality and thus become dependent on the illusionary escape of intoxication (Bird, 1949, Buhler & Lefever, 1949; Carver, 1931; Hart, 1930; Seliger, 1939; Seliger & Rosenberg, 1941; Strecker & Chambers, 1937). Alcoholics are also characterized as having feelings of isolation (Fox, 1958; Singer, Blane, & Rasschau, 1964), having poor social adjustment (Machover & Puzzo, 1959), and exhibiting tendencies toward withdrawal and regression (Billig & Sullivan, 1943).

Fox (1958) and Halpern (1946) hold the opinion that alcoholics take risks and act out impulses. In other studies (McCord & McCord, 1959), the preadolescent characteristics of later problem drinkers were said to be impulsiveness and exaggeration of the masculine role. Machover and Puzzo (1959) listed denial as the most commonly used defense mechanism of the alcoholic. Vogel (1953) agreed that denial was a major defense, but also added projection and rationalization as important escape devices. However, Coppersmith (1964) found the alcoholic to have a very limited defensive system.

The dimension of introversion/extroversion has been investigated by several authors, and the results have produced conflicting positions. Strecker and Chambers (1937) found 90% of their subjects predominantly introverted, while other authors found extroverted personalities more prevalent among alcoholics (Hart, 1930; Hoch, 1940; Miles, 1937; Wenger, 1944). Davidoff and Whitaker (1940) found equal numbers of introverts and extroverts among their subjects. However, since the subjects were alcoholics with psychoses, the results apply only to a particular group of alcoholics. Norbury (1942) found 75.2% extroverts and 20.9% introverts in the case histories of 105 alcoholics. He postulated that the extroverted alcoholic is attempting to achieve social acceptance, which results in the seeming sociability, talkativeness, and gaiety of many alcoholics.

Psychoanalytic authors tend to agree that the alcoholic is attempting to satisfy unconscious, infantile needs, and that alcohol provides the means for weakening self-criticism, inhibitions, and repressions. They feel that the alcoholic is fixated at the oral level of psychosexual development. The "oral personality" is characterized by passive-dependent needs, intolerance of any kind of psychic tension, and inability to endure pain, frustration, or postponement of need satisfaction. Alcohol provides an escape from painful realities and facilitates regression to early forms of gratification (Glover, 1927; Knight, 1937a, b; Richman, 1925; Sillman, 1949; Simmel, 1930; Wall, 1936, 1945).

Studies of intellectual capacity indicate no deviations of alcoholics from normals in either direction (Button, 1956b; Halpern, 1946; Moore & Gray, 1941; Murphy, 1953). Halpern (1946) states that there are no structural differences in intelligence among alcoholics as compared with the general population, but their emotional difficulties seem to prevent full use of their intellectual abilities. Kaldegg (1956) pointed out uneven intellectual performances, including frequent discrepancies between verbal IQ and performance IQ. Fitzhugh and Reitan (1960) found alcoholics did not differ significantly from normals in general intelligence, although the alcoholics did more poorly on abstraction and adaptive tasks.

The studies that have received the greatest popular support are those that hypothesized the "alcoholic personality" to be synonymous with psychopathology and psychiatric diagnosis. In 1964, McAndrews and Geertsma tested 300 psychiatric patients with three widely used scales derived from the MMPI by Hampton (1951), Holmes (1953), and Hoyt and Sedlacek (1958). It was found that none of the scales significantly differentiated alcoholics from a normal population. The authors concluded that the scales measured general maladjustment rather than alcoholism. In a smaller study, Quaranta (1949) also found no significant differences between two populations of 30 alcoholics and 30 normal controls.

McAndrews and Geertsma (1964) reviewed the literature and concluded that the *Pd* scale yielded more information than other MMPI scales. To determine the reasons, they tested 200 male hospitalized alcoholics and 200 male nonalcoholics from a private clinic, using the MMPI. A factor analysis of the *Pd* scale resulted in the isolation of five distinct factors: (*a*) desurgency, (*b*) acceptance by others, (*c*) discontent with family situation, (*d*) social deviance, and (*e*) remorseful intrapunitiveness. The alcoholics scored significantly higher on the factors of social deviance and remorseful intrapunitiveness, but when the most discriminating items were removed from these factors, the significance disappeared. The content of the discriminating items concerned excessive alcohol use, arrest history, and morality/integrity of lifestyle.

Manson (1948) obtained mixed results when comparing 123 alcoholics and 123 normal subjects on the *Pd* scale. The alcoholic group was comprised of both active drinkers and AA members. He found no differences between the two alcoholic groups; but when compared to the normal population, the alcoholic groups scored significantly higher on the *Pd* scale. The author suggested that the MMPI could not differentiate between subgroups of alcoholics, but that the test could distinguish alcoholics from nonalcoholics.

A persistent MMPI finding is the existence of a marked psychopathic trend among alcoholics. *Pd* elevations suggest to several researchers the potential for alcohol dependency (Hampton, 1951; Harris & Ives, 1947; Hewitt, 1943; Manson, 1948; Mathias, 1955; Modlin, 1947; Rubin, 1948; Quaranta, 1949). Evidence indicates that, in addition to psychopathy, alcoholics show conflict and concern over their behavior. Thus, the alcoholic may act out impulses with apparent disregard for personal welfare and that of others, but does not escape without a guilty conscience.

Developmental Aspects

It seems fair to say that the potential alcoholic does not represent a singular syndrome or distinct personality type. However, we have found striking similarities among alcoholics in some aspects of developmental or learning backgrounds. In hundreds of interviews there are basic elements that turn up again and again.

The potential alcoholic remembers an early childhood filled with turmoil, either in terms of parental rejection, neglect, or overindulgence. This is not to say that the perception is necessarily accurate, but rather that the person usually recalls events from his or her own frame of reference. Rejection is typically expressed as a mother or father overtly declaring the child unworthy of care, sometimes in direct comparison to a sibling. Perceived neglect is most often associated with absence of parental supervision. For example, many potential alcoholics tell of being left alone at night as a child. Overindulgence is reflected in the dominance of a child through a smothering relationship, sometimes resulting in an abnormal "favorite child" expectation that generates tremendous guilt feelings toward siblings. Frequently, a potential alcoholic confesses the secret feeling that the opposite sex parent could have overwhelmed him or her with sexual advances. They would live day to day in fear that the advance would begin and there would be no defense or escape.

These perceptions lead to a parentification of the child. Parentification is the process by which someone is emotionally placed in the parental role. The potential alcoholics, as children, were placed in the role of meeting the needs of their parents through such actions as physically taking care of them (preparing meals and taking care of the other children), offering emotional support (calming, forgiving, counseling), and, in some cases, actually dominating them. In all these cases, the child was given an early responsibility to help the parents by assuming some parental role.

The resultant learning that often takes place in parentification relationships is threefold. The child develops a tremendous guilt reaction regarding events of the world. The parent blames the child because of the parentification; however, the child has none of the usual defenses against such irrational attacks. The child also develops an unresolved hostility that is inexpressible due to the situation. Finally, finding reality unresponsive to his or her needs, the child turns inward for support. Thus, the ingredients are present for the classical passive-aggressive reaction to authority, especially to confrontation. This is *not* to say that all potential alcoholics are passive-aggressive; however, it should be pointed out that the alcoholic typically has learned behaviors similar to those that characterize passive-aggressives.

Games
Alcoholics Play
Although an overused term, the "games" that the potential alcoholics utilize are important to recognize. Games are manipulative strategies that individuals use in order to facilitate their belief system and establish or maintain their power base. It is as if the person wants everyone to play by his or her rules, thereby maintaining the illusion that the person's perception of reality is in fact true. All interactions are forced to end in the same predictable manner, usually failure. The following scenarios are a few of the most common.

A. *I'm Sorry, I'm Sorry, I'm Sorry, etc.* In the game, "I'm sorry, I'm sorry, etc." (abbreviated IS, IS), it is the strategy of the alcoholic to ruminate about his or her shortcomings for as long as it takes to convince whoever is listening that pity and forgiveness are deserved. Of course, the game *is* a game because the alcoholic is manipulating the listener in order to foster the conviction that he or she is willing to change lifestyles. Being disarmed with such a defenseless approach, the helper often jumps at the opportunity to aid in the rehabilitation.

This game (IS, IS) is played out a hundred times a day, especially between husband and wife. It is one of the most insidious to combat because of the sincere desire on the part of all concerned to see positive behavioral change.

The therapist should quickly extinguish the behavior. Usually agreement and/or rule establishment can diffuse the situation. We use such phrases as, "You are right. You are at the bottom of the barrel. You have convinced us. Now, we do not want to hear any more about it." This sounds simple and harsh, but directiveness is critical.

B. Got You Last. The strategy of "got you last" is a revenge game in which the patient uses the drinking behavior as a means to communicate to whomever is encouraging rehabilitation that he or she cannot be defeated by giving up the habit. Drinking is the weapon with which the battle is fought. While the patients may feel they are winning over the therapist, they are losing their lives.

This game needs to be confronted with an Adlerian-type approach—natural consequences. The idea is to develop an agreement with the patient so the consequences of drinking reflect *solely* upon his or her own survival and not upon the needs of the therapist, spouse, parent, or other concerned individual. We usually have the patient take out a temporary life insurance policy of sufficient amount to support the family in case he or she should die while intoxicated. This action effectively negates the possibility of manipulating fear of absence and the conflict over survival needs. Then the patient's spouse is given instructions to have the patient committed or jailed during the next episode, thus letting someone else deal with the hassle of the drinking behavior.

Because of the social implications, spouses are extremely reluctant to refer to a law agency. The point hopefully to be made, though, is that the whole family can participate in stopping the behavior by making the patient take the responsibility for the natural consequences of drinking.

C. Help Me Make It Through the Night. Although this game has manipulative characteristics, it should be pointed out that it is also a sincere plea. It is like yelling "Help!" at a swimming pool—sometimes it is a matter of life and dealth, sometimes it can be a game of manipulation. The life guard has to make that discrimination, and the costs are great.

The game is based on the need of one person to become the center of attention for another person or other people, and the need of the other person(s) to rescue or save the first one. The rules are basic—the alcoholic uses drinking as a lever to get the helper to help him or her. Some likely phrases are, "If you would just hold my hand this night. . . ," and "It would mean so much if you could just be here."

All of these actions and reactions *can* be appropriate to the situation. Rehabilitation is a lonely process and interpersonal support can be critical. This is a major component of AA. Nevertheless, when the plea becomes chronic, and when the help does not affect the drinking behavior, the interaction is likely to be a game. We have a rule of thumb: if the behavior occurs six times under a given set of environmental conditions, it will happen a seventh.

This game is usually countered with two steps. First, the helper must be willing to stop the rescuing and let the natural consequences occur. This can be fairly traumatic for the helper, especially if there is a need to nurse the drinker. Second, the alcoholic is made to work for the attention. We have had people jog a certain number of miles per hour, pay money, and give trading stamps for the attention time. It is surprising how many people get better when they have to pay for it.

D. Jack and the Beanstalk. This game is only a game in the sense that so many people risk their lives on the wisdom of the drinker, and he or she trades it off for as little as three beans. In this case, the drinker does not take the active role of manipulating other people, but other people are trying to manipulate him or her into a positive lifestyle. The drama is usually observed when money and other advantages are offered time and time again in the hope that the drinker will eventually "see the light." Yet all the while he or she does not seem to care. We have seen people contribute new cars, homes, jobs, and money to the cause only to see them get wrecked, lost, or otherwise destroyed in sundry ways.

The point is that the alcoholic may not care, or—more important—may not have the judgment for appropriate management. All the gifts and handouts in the world will not prevent anyone from "screwing up" their lives. Usually the people behind the scenes are the ones who need to be controlled and counseled. Perhaps they may have to accept the fact that although Jack may be lovable, good looking, and have boundless potential, he is also ineffective in handling responsibility. He may need a little education and experience in the college of hard knocks.

In order to minimize the confusion between personality types and interaction games, it should be pointed out that personality is a stable entity and maintains a specific function related to chronic needs within the self-structure. Interpersonal games are usually situational and functions of communication styles. One personality type can utilize a wide variety of games, including two or more at the same time. For example, the alcoholic can play "I'm Sorry" with a spouse, "Got You Last" with a boss, and "Help Me Through the Night" with a lover.

Group Intervention Techniques

One major topology of alcoholism utilizes an analogy of social development to indicate that persons classified into any given category have characteristic defenses that they use in their management of anxiety: moving against people (aggressive neurotic), moving toward people (sociopath), and moving away from people (inhibited neurotic). For example, the alcoholic classified as aggressive neurotic is usually the one who, when anxious or guilt-ridden, will resort to aggressive behavior. It is as if the person feels bad about the day and so takes it out on everyone else. The alcoholic diagnosed as inhibited neurotic is more of an intropunitive reactor, hiding his or her feelings from the world. The sociopathic alcoholic has learned to become self-indulgent and attempts to release tension by acting irresponsibly. All these interpersonal modes are a result of the guilt and learned helplessness growing out of the earliest childhood experiences. (Lawlis & Rubin, 1971; Costello, Lawlis, Monder, & Celistino, 1978).

The three personality types require differential treatment plans; accordingly, the differential model divides the personality categories into respective needs. The aggressive neurotic, who already fosters an assertive social approach, is taught more appropriate and effective means of communicating his or her anxiety. The inhibited neurotic, who has already learned an introspective social demeanor, is taught a more assertive and expressive means of social anxiety management. The sociopath, who already possesses the skill of shrugging off tension-producing agents, is placed on a contingency program by which he or she is helped to endure stress in order to gain positive conclusions.

The general formats as described above can be included as part of a variety of therapies. The therapist is, of course, encouraged to utilize other appropriate resources and skills that may be available. However, we have found the following specific techniques especially helpful and present them here for those times when all else fails.

A. The Inhibited Neurotic. Probably the most frequently published techniques for alcoholism intervention have been aimed at the inhibited neurotic type. Essentially, the goal is to stimulate new behaviors with which to respond to stress. The following interventions are representative.

1. Growling, singing, and yelling at others. As a part of an assertiveness training, we often have the participants express their frustrations toward others without any words. We give instructions like, "For the next three days, growl at a friend. You do not have to explain yourself or give reasons for your behavior. Just "growl" (sing, yell, snarl, etc.).

The exercise gives the person an opportunity to experience a new outlet, to find out that people will not be destroyed by their expression, and to give themselves a better perspective on their frustration.

2. Surveying. We find that many of these individuals have a very narrow view of what people are like. A direct method of exploring feelings and thoughts of others is to interview them. We require the person to formulate a short and concise questionnaire for this purpose. A necessary part of the program is to supervise the questions so they are meaningful. We have found that, for the most part, the inhibited neurotic alcoholic types have a most difficult time deciding on questions.

The next critical issue is whom to ask. They always want to use their friends, but we have reservations about this because they usually know how their friends think. We like for them to survey a variety of people: college students, bank presidents, athletes, coaches, preachers, salesmen, etc.

This exercise has proved an extremely insightful one for the participants. They begin to experience the wide variety of responses and to appreciate the quality of responses associated with successful people. As one group member expressed it, "I guess I am still like a kid. It amazed me when I heard how the people who hire and fire people stereotype others on the basis of dress. I can fight it or change, I guess." We explained that the information gained can be used for meeting their own needs. This particular person began to dress for success and learned to adapt very well.

3. Social activities. Even though special activities are uncomfortable for the inhibited neurotic, we think it is doubly painful to continue a self-indulgent withdrawal. We program them into social activities centered around the development of social skills. In most communities there are wide selections such as square dancing, ballroom dancing (even disco), bridge clubs, jogging clubs, and Jaycees. AA has excellent resources and activities in social contexts, as do the YMCA, YWCA, church groups, etc.

B. The Aggressive Neurotic. Perhaps the most misunderstood, and the least successful, alcoholic type is the aggressive neurotic. The goal of intervention is to develop a more inward-directed and self-controlled person. The following representative techniques have often been successful in meeting this goal.

1. Fire therapy. As opposed to the typical therapeutic goal of fostering expression, the aggressive neurotic needs exercises to help him or her center and turn inward. One of the most successful and unique therapies is one we call fire therapy. Basically, it involves a focusing on fire when confronting problems instead of acting out. Fire has a calming influence much like that experienced while watching a campfire or fireplace. It invariably elicits a response.

The person is allowed to burn birthday candles one by one. We have also used popsicle sticks, toothpicks, and small pieces of firewood, but the candles appear to be the most manageable and practical. They are probably the safest and smell the best as well. Problems are discussed, memories are explored, and plans are laid during the burning ritual.

Some of the participants find images within the tallow, others project their feelings into the fire. No consequence of the experience other than a "peaceful feeling" has so far been reported. Most people do not verbally associate the fire with the process of release, but we have not found it necessary for them to attain such a conscious awareness. If they appear able to reduce tension by this means, we encourage a daily practice.

2. Biofeedback. In order to facilitate a self-regulation of tension, we have frequently used biofeedback techniques with this group. Using temperature monitoring of the hand as a medium, the patient is asked to relax and to note the subsequent temperature change. Interestingly, the usual response is one of amazement at the variation in temperature. Then a sense of pride emerges as it is realized that some control over body functions can be organized. We have even had one person make professional contacts to show the world how he could move his temperature up and down in a 10-degree range.

Having developed confidence in physiological control, and also implanted the concept of self-responsibility for emotional control, the biofeedback procedures are practiced in tension-producing situations instead of drinking behaviors. This transfer of learning is a long leap for many people, and success has not been very high (probably 30-50 percent). It is as if the biofeedback training is interesting and supportive, but too abstract to relate to everyday experience. The equipment is "at the doctor's office." There is also the natural inclination of this particular type of personality to be competitive. "Beating"the machine is seen as just one more challenge. Without generalization to internal resources and some introspection, the potential alcoholic may simply pass through all the procedures without any appreciation for their meaning.

3. Relaxation strategies. The biofeedback program and relaxation programs are similar in concept. Biofeedback utilizes physiological feedback to organize the person's thought processes. Relaxation programs tend to be much more didactic, like a step-by-step instructional package.

We often have outpatients listen to individualized cassette tapes a minimum of three times daily, especially during periods of high tension. The results have been rewarding for the compliant ones. Whether in one session or in a serial program, specific instructions need to take into account these characteristics. The first phase is a muscle relaxation sequence, often incorporating breathing exercises to facilitate relaxation. It is important to reassure the individual with simple statements such as, "Very good, very good," or "You are doing very well." Another method of support involves giving a cue of success, such as instructing the person to become aware of a warming, tingling, or pulse within the body as confirmation that he or she is doing it "right." It cannot be overemphasized that the alcoholic has a self-concept of defeat; even a simple exercise is feared as another trial.

The second phase is a series of statements about cleansing of the body. It is pointed out that as a person relaxes and breathes, muscles and organs are cleansed and poisons are freed in order to be filtered out more efficiently. It is useful to emphasize that the individual has the power not only to rid the body of the toxic effects of alcoholism, but also of the perceived sin of indulgence.

The third phase is to educate the person about relaxation as a method of stress management that is amenable to every-day use. In fact, by their participation, the individuals have actually resolved some of their stresses. Some suggested cues for new awareness that are helpful in providing confirmation include noting a lightness in the chest and easier breathing, a freer mind with less pain, and a feeling of energy running throughout the body with less obstruction.

4. Running, jogging, exercise. Physical exercise is a good approach to many health problems. The increased blood flow and respiration help clear out emotional stress as well as build up physical reserves. It is also an expression of motivation. If a person is not willing to walk at least three miles a day, then we consider that individual's needs to be focused in some direction other than rehabilitation.

For the aggressive neurotics, it is essential that an independent program be developed in which they are exercising by themselves. Because of their need to compete, they will often try to outrun or outdistance any fellow exercisers. The general rule is to exercise (jog, swim, walk fast) for 20 minutes' duration, regardless of how far or how fast. An individual gains the maximum benefit in that amount of time, so the clock is the criterion against which they compete.

Most of the patients respond well to the exercise routine. It gives them an athletic image, and to most of them it makes sense. The aggressive alcoholic is typically hypomanic anyway, and drinking has served as either a tranquilizer or boredom fighter. As a prescribed routine, exercise meets both of these needs.

Exercise alone has also helped many individuals to have an autopsychotherapy session. They report experiences, after they get into shape, in which they reach a trance-like state while exercising. After a few minutes at this level, an amazingly calming perception occurs. This behavior is antagonistic to destructive drinking and thus allows for the possibility of more adaptive stress management.

C. The Sociopathic Personality. The general aim of intervention is to reconstruct the individual's mode of interacting with the environment in order to help achieve the most appropriate and constructive response. This goal includes a primary concern for making sure the individual develops a responsible attitude. The following are techniques which have been used successfully and which illustrate the principles involved.

1. Contracts. A contract between therapist and patient is not a new concept, but the technique should be exaggerated for the sociopathic alcoholic. It is essential to clarify individually each point of agreement so the participants acknowledge their respective responsibilities and the consequences of default.

It is also a good idea to include as part of the contract behaviors that are not particularly a matter of social conformity. For example, we usually write down something like, "Eat at least one banana split per month." This sort of demand gives participants permission to try something different while allowing them to experience lifestyle changes in an unthreatened manner. It also helps to make treatment a somewhat more enjoyable experience.

The protocol in Figure 8.1 is an example of a behavioral contract. It should be pointed out that, for many of the behaviors, the negative consequence is a discontinuance of therapy. Other behaviors do not have obvious consequences attached to them, such as #3—"go to movies." The reason for this openendedness is to allow freedom of exploration in determining what consequences can occur.

2. A better crook. Others generally have very little control over the sociopath's behavior. Sometimes it is more effective to make the individual better at what he or she wants to do. If the alcoholic wants to manipulate others, why not give that person better skills at doing precisely that?

Figure 8.1

CONTRACT

between Barbara M.   and   G. Frank Lawlis

	Consequences of
Behaviors	**Completion (+) or Failure (−)**

1. Run 3 miles a week

    (+) Become healthier
    (−) Become depressed;
        discontinue therapy

2. Get up in the morning early enough to eat breakfast and get to work on time

    (+) Better job performance
    (−) Poor job performance;
        discontinue therapy

3. Go to movie twice a week

    (+) No consequences ?
    (−)

4. Learn to drive

    (+) Better mobility
    (−) Continued lack of mobility

5. Attend 5 social functions this week

    (+) Feel more support and contact
    (−) Continue to withdraw; discontinue therapy

_____
Date

_____
Signature of 1st party

_____
Signature of 2nd party

We have instituted a didactic and experiential program in interpersonal skills for several groups of sociopathic alcoholics, focusing on empathy, warmth, and genuineness. We worked from the notion that if they had a natural, non-aversive way of handling others, it would prove adaptive.

The participants were excellent students, attaining empathy scores (judged by independent raters) equivalent to those achieved by the psychologists and counselors at the end of the training sessions. As a final examination, we required them to go out into the community and change somebody's mind. One individual talked a traffic officer out of a ticket. Another ran for political office. (She did not win, but the effort was productive.)

One might be concerned with the moral position in which we put ourselves. No doubt we made some manipulative people better manipulators. But we did not have one single case return for treatment, and—as far as we know—no one ended up in jail. Furthermore, some individuals reported that for the first time they felt good about themselves and about their skills; they even became active members of AA in order to help others. Perhaps we only tapped the potential that had been utilized solely for destructive purposes and turned it around for constructive goals.

Basic Principles of Alcoholic Behavioral Management

In this chapter we have presented a summary of the research on personality and alcoholism and ways that the various needs predicated by the personality types can be met in treatment. Other investigators, though, have focused on the antecedent and consequent events associated with drinking as a basis for both functional analysis of the behavior and treatment prescription. Sobell and Sobell (1973, 1977), for example, have developed a technology called "Problem Solving Skills Training" that is based on functional analysis of drinking and involves a broad-spectrum approach to treatment. The stages of the training are: (1) Problem identification (when and where does drinking occur?); (2) Delineation of behavioral options (what other behaviors are possible in problem situations?); (3) Evaluation of each behavioral option for its possible outcome (what are total, short-, and long-term consequences?); and, finally, (4) Employing the behavioral options evaluated to have the best total consequences. Sobell and Sobell (1977) also describe specific treatment procedures such as relaxation training, assertion training, contingency management and behavioral contracting that are similar to methods previously outlined in this chapter. In addition, they describe two methods that, although frequently utilized, have enjoyed only limited success. One method, aversion conditioning, involves pairing an aversive event (shock, or a nausea inducing chemical) with drinking behavior in a Pavlovian (classical) conditioning paradigm. The other method, avoidance conditioning, involves delivery of a mild shock for "inappropriate" drinking and is based on the notion that appropriate drinking behavior (rather than abstinence) can be trained.

The Sobells wisely caution that, though behavioral approaches to alcoholism have been developed and tested in research settings, whether generalization to clinical settings will be effective or not is still unknown. In general, the intent and content of the behavioral treatments proposed by the Sobells and others are not divergent from what we have presented. They have, however, stayed closer to a behavioristic method and terminology that lends itself to systematic observation and reporting.

There are a number of clinical considerations involved in the practical application of these behavioral principles to the alcoholic which are worthy of review. First of all, the role of the professional is often determined by the treatment setting, as well as by one's professional identity and philosophical bent. In medical settings, alcoholism may well be regarded as a physical disease, something that requires prescription and treatment by a medical doctor. In volunteer groups such as AA, alcoholism is viewed as a condition which can only be understood and ameliorated by another alcoholic. In other agencies, both state and church sponsored, alcoholism may be regarded as either a moral matter or as one that requires concrete social welfare services; the appropriate personnel would include social workers or pastoral counselors. In psychologically-oriented settings, alcoholism is usually considered a problem of behavior and of relationships. Here, behavioral scientists from several backgrounds may designate treatment. Quarreling among professionals has continued over the years about not only *how* to treat alcoholism, but also about *who* should treat alcoholics. No resolution is in sight, but it is certain that any one person can have only a very limited impact on the alcoholic. It would take a TV Dr. Welby, who has only one patient to see each week, to manage all the resources for one alcoholic. It is therefore essential to establish a team, or at least a network of resources for total management.

Although we have not concerned ourselves here specifically with the need for emotional growth, it is implicit. The communication of understanding and acceptance is a therapeutic ingredient critical to the beginning of trust, especially with respect to the alcoholic's perception of competence on the part of the therapist. This is not to say that all interactions must take place under the guise of psychotherapy. In fact, quite the opposite is true. Although psychotherapy is defined as a therapeutic environment, it is often threatening to those individuals who are not psychologically oriented. Nevertheless, the therapeutic role of the professional must pervade all interactions with the participant.

Relationship variables are critical for understanding the expectations of all parties. Four basic dynamics are recognized which have been found to contribute to positive relationship building: parental-respect, problem-solving, identification, and sexual-affection. Parental-respect is a relationship in which one person perceives another as having strength and wisdom, and therefore depends upon that person for support. Problem-solving relationships are based upon a mutual trust and equal distribution of responsibility. These types are objective and are based on a mutual need to accomplish some task, e.g., a task-oriented relationship. Identification relationships are based on perceived similarities between individuals. These similarities can have several aspects, including dress, friends, hobbies, or other interests. The sexual-affection relationship has its positive element in the physical and nurturing needs of its participants.

The therapeutic relationship encompasses elements of all relationship dimensions; however, the growth curves are quite different from one another. As can be seen in Figure 8.2,

Figure 8.2

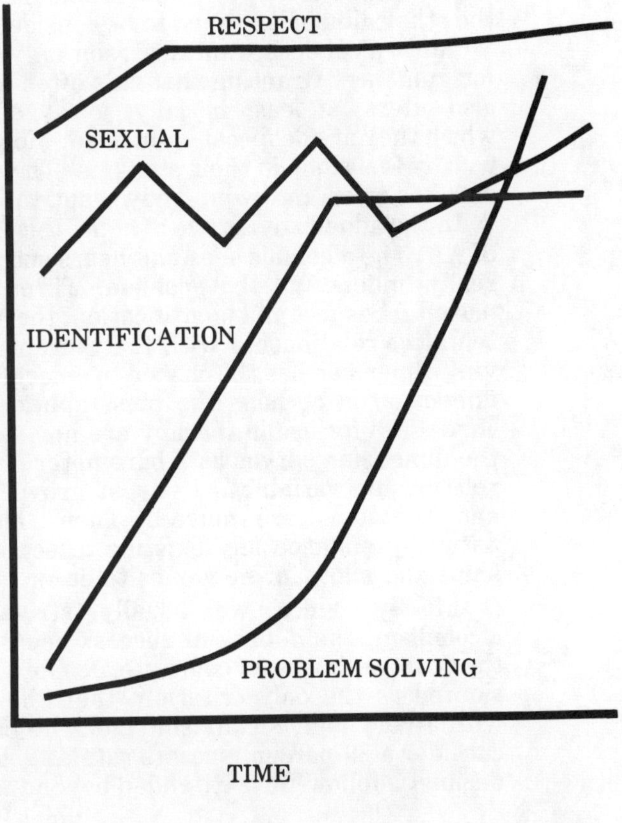

RESPECT

SEXUAL

IDENTIFICATION

PROBLEM SOLVING

TIME

the parental-respect dimension is based on expectancies. As the other person can accommodate to that image, the respect continues to grow (Lawlis, 1973). Identification begins at point zero; as the individuals perceive more similarities, the relationship grows. Since sexual-affection is so affected by personal needs, this relationship tends to be unstable over time. The problem-solving dimension, the primary element in psychotherapy, begins in the negative range. This is due largely to the need to work and to have a problem on which to work. Nobody likes to have to work on a problem, of course, much less have to deal with another personality. As time passes and a history of trust accumulates, though, a problem-solving relationship increases in intensity.

Alcoholics who come into a therapeutic situation do not generally want a problem-solving relationship. Even sincere patients have uneasy feelings about accepting self-responsibility. It is no wonder that many alcoholics discontinue professional contact when they hear statements like, "I am here to help *you* help yourself." Their histories of failures would not allow them to justify an expectation of success. Consequently, the other dimensions need to be considered.

Most alcoholics want a person on whom they can depend for guidance. Granting that this often fosters dependency, it also offers, at least initially, a ray of hope—something of which they are desperately in need. Moreover, most alcoholics usually feel alone in their struggle. They want to see someone who has tried and won. They want to identify with success. With the added advantage of hope, this is a major contribution of AA. The alcoholic sees and hears successful people who can really understand the problem. Through the dimensions of parental-respect and identification, the alcoholic can develop a tentative relationship with the therapist until a problem-solving dimension has the chance to emerge. The sexual-affection dimension is perhaps the most subtle, yet complex, of all. Guidelines for use in therapy are non-existent. Nevertheless, the dimension serves as a barometer of change for all of the relationship variables. As trust grows, identification occurs and problems are solved. Then, feelings of self-worth naturally enhance any existing affection or sexual relationships and allow for new ones to occur.

Finally, since we usually strive for success with alcoholism, the *degree* of success needs to be considered. If the strict definition of complete alcohol abstinence is to be considered as the only criterion, then the practitioner is faced with a very high recidivism rate. The best programs usually consider a 30-percent success rate as good, even with a sharp decline as follow-up is extended beyond 30 days.

A more liberal measure of success would focus upon the quality of life itself. If the person improves his or her lifestyle as a result of intervention, then some success can be claimed. At least a modicum of success could help others determine a consistent form of therapy. A brief list of quality-of-life items that we use to ascertain the degree of improvement, as well as the most critical issues in a person's drinking behavior, is presented in Figure 8.3.

Alcoholism is a medical, psychological, and social concern. It is complex to the point of being too cumbersome for any one discipline to address. Yet, because it is a disease of a lifestyle, it may prove to be one of the more fruitful areas for behavioral interventions.

Figure 8.3

PROBLEM AREA CHECKLIST	Non Significant	Significant	Very Significant
1. Trouble in meeting minimal requirements of job (time promptness, loss of time, etc.)	( )	( )	( )
2. Trouble in interpersonal relationships with spouse	( )	( )	( )
3. Trouble in interpersonal relationships with friends	( )	( )	( )
4. Trouble in making decisions	( )	( )	( )
5. Trouble with memory	( )	( )	( )
6. Trouble in sleeping at night	( )	( )	( )
7. Trouble in sexual relationships	( )	( )	( )
8. Trouble in imagining what he/she wants in life	( )	( )	( )
9. Trouble in feeling guilty	( )	( )	( )
10. Trouble in getting the things he/she wants	( )	( )	( )

CHAPTER IX

CLINICAL RESEARCH

The material in previous chapters of this book represents a wide variety of research efforts. However, one particularly rich and unique approach deserves attention as we expand the common grounds of understanding shared by psychology and medicine. This branch of methodology, called "clinical research," utilizes the insights of practitioners and patients themselves. It takes courage and energy to derive a belief from a research methodology, to defend it, and to generalize the conclusions to theory, especially if all components have been derived from a single case. The mission, though, of operationalizing the wonderful patient stories and those close, intimate encounters that appeared to be associated with recovery has been all-involving, demanding our best efforts and wisdom.

Historically, the biological sciences began to emerge from natural observation and then moved on to apply scientific methodology with its implicit requirement of constant control. The model which became the prototype for all physical sciences characteristically utilized a laboratory setting and emphasized rigorous control of all variables except the experimental or dependent variable. Eager to gain the prestige of a scientific discipline in the modern technological era, psychological and medical researchers quickly embraced this methodology and the implicit requirement of constant control. The infinity defined by the classification "all other variables" (as in "all other variables were held constant"—a frequent research statement) proved impossible to specify, let alone control, in psychology as well as in medicine. Actually, "all other variables" have never been held constant even in physics (as we now know from the work of quantum physicists), the area in which the scientific method has been honed to its purest form. Nevertheless, the magnitude of error introduced by the inconstancy of "other variables" in the physical sciences was trivial, especially with regard to statistical design (Eber, 1975).

Faced with this dilemma, the social sciences (especially psychology) began to develop more sophisticated approaches to methodology. Utilizing computer technology and a normative model, a psychometric perspective was established. Measurement was essentially modeled upon a bell-shaped curve. Such procedures require large numbers of experimental subjects in order to meet the assumptions implicit in the statistical derivations.

Where does this historical chronology leave the clinical researcher, the person who does not enjoy the luxury of matching each of many patients with others who have some designated identical properties, and who cannot submit the matched groups to different procedures? Further, the clinician is unlikely to have the expectation that 100-200 patients of a specific disease or syndrome will grace his or her treatment facility within a reasonable predetermined time frame. What happens to the practitioner who sees people instead of numbers, and yet is in the best position to note the greatest variation between all patients and to spot unusual aspects of response? All too often the critics in research design lay such a heavy emphasis on control and randomization that the clinician is hesitant to participate in any type of research activity.

We have spent some time and effort encouraging and developing methods in clinical research because of a strong feeling that significant gains in knowledge are largely due to the hints and hunches, the intuitions and dreams of clinicians *and* patients. Large research projects are economically and logically feasible *only* for evaluating what we think we already know. Clinical research, on the other hand, provides a vehicle whereby new ideas may be more readily explored.

In addition to the satisfaction that can accrue from a study, there are other benefits of clinical research. On a purely economic level, it becomes important to know the beneficial impact of any single component of a treatment program. For example, in one particular practice it was the usual procedure to have a psychiatric staffing once a week on all patients. The staffing was composed of the physician, a psychologist, a social worker, and a technician (psychometrist). The mission of the group meeting was to determine appropriate treatment and direction of therapy. After the approach was subjected to evaluation, it was found the staffing had very little substance of value for patient treatment, since it did not change either diagnosis or intervention. The sessions did appear to meet staff needs, however, in that they served as a vehicle for gaining assistance on personal problems encountered in the setting. A better solution proved to be a briefer weekly meeting in which special cases could be brought forth, as well as programmatic discussion. Expending large amounts of professional time in areas which are not enhanced by the effort is economically unsound. Yet, until the impotency of the procedure is demonstrated using reliable figures, such practices are likely to continue out of habit and misplaced faith.

Clinical research also provides a method of identifying needs specified by the patient population. Perhaps the patients' symptoms are more efficiently treated through group experience, biofeedback, or hypnosis, factors which should be empirically decided. Not only is research important to the conduct of the clinical program, but also it is critical to the application of innovative and unprecedented modes of therapy. As new approaches are discovered, the responsibility of the clinician is to share them with other professionals and to determine their efficacies. This must be so, or advances are prohibited.

Research

Designs We return to the same dilemma: How can a practitioner serve any research needs if he or she cannot meet the rigid guidelines of acceptable designs? We feel that clinical research deserves special consideration and should be accorded greater latitude by the purists of either academic or bureaucratic ivory-tower backgrounds who think a study is not a study unless it is defined by Winer or Kirk (two authors of well-known statistical texts).

Grand projects test the assumptions of group averages. Clinical research tests the subtle variances between people. Classical experimentation in a historical psychological framework emphasizes a theoretical base for methodology, whereas clinical experimentation is more related to theory-building activity. As one patient resembles another—or differs—a tentative hypothesis is born, and is maintained or destroyed as the third and fourth patients are followed. Another discrimination which can be made between the classical and the clinical models of research is that of the conclusiveness for acceptance or rejection of a formalized statement of opinion. In classical designs, hypotheses are made which are not accepted or rejected until after the project is completed. In clinical research, the results are immediately utilized for feedback. In fact, that is one of the reasons for the difficulties in generalization. If a pain patient begins to show improvement as a result of electrical stimulation, for example, the clinician is apt to continue to explore that modality intensively rather than set up a controlled study in which patients are randomly divided into treatment-versus-no-treatment groups. The distinguishing features of the two research orientations are summarized in Table 9.1.

What are the methodologies available to the clinical researcher? Basically, the question involves the general research strategies in psychological and medical research and the specific clinical applications. The general strategies to be discussed are condensation, group or treatment differences, and relationship.

Condensation. The term "condensation" means that the researcher is attempting to condense results into a much smaller

Table 9.1

**DIFFERENCES BETWEEN CLASSICAL AND CLINICAL
RESEARCH DESIGN**

Classical	Clinical
1. Group averages are basis of conclusion	1. Individual variances are basis of conclusion
2. Theory explains methodology	2. Theory building explains methodology
3. Conclusions support or reject an opinion or statement	3. Conclusions are utilized for continuous feedback

body without sacrificing information. This is accomplished by omitting or combining redundant information and even omitting nonusable material. For instance, patients may be asked both their ages and dates of birth. If the function of these questions is solely to determine how old the patient is, the two answers are redundant and one can be eliminated. Another form of condensation is to summarize several responses into one global response. The most obvious example of this is in test construction. The 566-item test called the Minnesota Multiphasic Personality Inventory (MMPI) is summarized in 10 clinical scales and 3 validity scales. In medical examinations, too, quite frequently a number of observations are summarized into one single comment. For example, general appearance or function may be noted as "good," "fair," or "grossly intact" rather than itemizing each observation that led to the conclusion.

Factor analysis is the most often used systematic technique designed for condensation. The basic rationale for this technique is to clump every measure with every other similar measure in a given array into units called factors. The factors are statistically independent, meaning that each clump will tend to be more related to one concept than to others, with little or no overlap among clumps. If all responses were highly related and redundant, they would all flock to the first factor. In this instance, all responses would be summarized into one statement. For example, if the items were: (1) fear of snakes, (2) fear of worms, (3) fear of lizards, then a general factor might be summarized as "fear of long-bodied, slippery animals."

The strategies for purifying and identifying the clusters are mathematical, but the general picture is one of the clinician, over time, gathering responses of patients and condensing the data into global units. It is necessary for the clinician to develop a uniform response code that allows each person to respond to every item, and that enables the evaluator/examiner to interpret each item with a minimum of confusion. After administrations to a number of people (50-100 is typical), an analysis can be computed to determine the clusters or dimensions into which the information may be condensed.

Another condensation technique that is important to the field of clinical research is people-clustering. Clinicians have always noted some typologies. By observation, Freud classified neurosis into dynamic types (hysteric, obsessive, etc.), and Jung classified his patients into other modes (intuitive, sensory, etc.). In medicine, too, people are classified into diseases which represent clinical judgments determined on the basis of presence or absence of symptoms, rather than upon any single, absolute diagnostic factor. Rheumatoid arthritis is an example of a disease determined by multiple judgments. Further, individuals who are diagnosed in this manner are then clustered into *stages*, on the basis of the number of the extent of diagnostic criteria observed. A subjective (rather than mathematical) kind of clustering was used to determine all these typologies. Perhaps the number of variables to be considered exceeds the differentiating capacity of any one human, but the concept of factor analysis can be easily applied through the use of computer resources.

To illustrate the power of this technology, in one application we found there was more than one clump of personality types within the large diagnostic category designated "alcoholic" (Lawlis & Rubin, 1971; Costello & Lawlis, 1978). The implications of this finding for differential treatment were discussed in Chapter VIII. The original data for this work were collected from existing files, not generated specifically for this purpose. Thus, even with a technique as seemingly complicated as factor analysis, the collection efforts are well within the clinician's reach.

Group and Treatment Differences. Hopefully, most investigators have finally learned that in human medical research there is rarely (if ever) such a thing as an appropriate control group (i.e., one which received no treatment at all). It is generally considered unethical to withhold treatment, even where the treatment has been shown to have minimal value, such as in certain chemotherapy protocols. Further, the primary design used throughout the medical research world asks the question: Does the group A treated with X differ from the group B treated with Y? Unfortunately, assuring that groups A and B are alike in all respects except for treatment (so an unqualified statement can be made regarding the differences in response that are attributable to treatment) is impossible.

The tendency to match groups on the basis of age, sex, and diagnosis (the traditional "big three") disregards other important variables that are likely to contribute to response variance, such as socioeconomic status, motivation, and geographical distribution. Cancer patients who are indigent, for example, have a poorer prognosis for recovery from the disease than do more affluent patients suffering from the identical type of cancer (Berg, 1977). Yet this variable (socioeconomic status) has never been controlled in cancer experimentation, so the findings of many studies must be called into question. The point is that even the most acceptable designs overlook vital factors; and should one choose such a design with the intention that these factors *not* be overlooked (i.e., control for all error), then one could plan on conducting a single experiment for decades. If one has enough time and enough subjects, the error or the uncontrolled variation will eventually cancel out through randomization.

The most popular design is the pre/postmeasurement type in which the subjects are randomly assigned to either a treatment or a comparison group. This design requires a surprisingly small number of subjects (at least 20) and is fairly easy to conduct. Nevertheless, the assumptions regarding the nature the data are difficult to meet under practical conditions: (1) randomization of subjects to each group; (2) matched subjects with regard to a wide variety of measures, such as socioeconomic status, age, diagnosis; (3) homogeneity of variance; (4) double-blind effects.

What the clinician lacks is the a priori, or predetermined, expectation of the factors that are important. Again, we are suggesting a more exploratory posthoc design. Instead of blindly preselecting variables, it would be a good idea to merely code any differences between treatment or categorical designations noted in the records. In this way, data could be compared at a later time, perhaps as a curiosity only, or perhaps as a more structured endeavor to present informally to colleagues. For example, the following classifications would be invaluable for the most sophisticated of designs: sex type, chief complaint, race, previous disease history, preliminary impressions, and outcome. If even only these few pieces of information were coded for each patient, certainly some important findings would emerge.

The key word is "coded." Our experience in several projects where we were called in after the effort was well underway—or even over—and asked to do an evaluation, led us to the conclusion that open-ended clinical notes were worthless. Unless a consistent format was used, regardless of how much information was contained in the case reports, the observations simply could not be compared. Coding means to limit or classify the general statement into discrete categories, thereby making one record comparable to another. For example, some options are only one way or the other: sex type is easily coded as male (0), female (1). A mood status could be more extensive, such as depressed (-1), normal (0), or manic (1). A severity of emotional response scale can be implemented which has the advantage of being quantified along a low-to-high continuum, such as very excited and agitated (5), mildly excited and agitated (4), appropriate (3), mildly sullen or moody (2), or depressed (1). Another coding strategy is to have yes-no response choices, such as to problems: sexual (y/n), schoolwork (y/n), family (y/n), etc. In this latter illustration, the coder does not have to be confined to only one response. The patient may have more than one problem, or all problems. Regardless of the coding strategy used, the clinician will have to design the code according to obvious needs and constraints of the situation, sometimes missing important information. With this possibility in mind, it is always a good idea to evaluate the code sheet itself for appropriate usage.

The basic objective of coding is to facilitate retrieval of the available data to resolve some question of differences, utilizing one of many statistical procedures. Standard statistical tests exist that approach the problem in terms of the probability that differences as large as those observed could have occurred by chance. The more popular and simpler ones, the t-test and F-test, treat one variable at a time, basing the determination of significance on a ratio of differences obtained to error (difference variance to error variance).

The term "significantly different" has both statistical and clinical implications. For the clinical researcher, it may be more appropriate to specify what is to be considered "significant" before analyzing the data. For example, an average difference of only .5 in standard I.Q. scores between patients who do or do not respond positively to biofeedback may be *statistically* significant. *Practically*, however, such slight differences between groups may be meaningless. In medical research, too, different protocols may yield statistically significant differences in longevity, in blood pressure, or in some blood chemistry analysis. Yet, the actual differences may be so trivial that any clinical change or benefit to the patients from the favored protocol is non-existent. Significant differences do not specify a criterion for discriminating among individual patients, nor do they help when the span of separation is so minuscule.

Another approach is to begin with a clinical criterion, not a research one, and determine the frequency with which people deviate in a practical sense from that criterion. In our previous example, consider the researcher who is questioning the relationship of biofeedback response to intelligence, and who begins with the notion that an I.Q. score in the range of 100 ± 10 is the criterion which defines an average response potential to the treatment. The researcher also decides that an I.Q. score lower than 85 (allowing 86-90 for an uncertainty of measurement) constitutes a difference of significant proportions for determining response potential to biofeedback treatment techniques. A 2 X 2 table like that of Table 9.2 would demonstrate graphically any differences in treatment response between patients in these two intelligence groups. A chi-square statistic could also be computed to determine the degree of confidence with which conclusions might be drawn about the frequency distribution. Accordingly, the hypothetical data presented in Table 9.2 for our example could not be considered sufficient to establish a relationship between intelligence level and treatment response, at least for the differences specified. Of course, the analyses could be extended by subdividing or re-establishing the criterion of separation (I.Q. below 80, below 70, etc.). The results, whether or not they showed significant differences, would be directly related to clinical practice and yet would not create elaborate confusion regarding the statistics utilized.

Table 9.2

TREATMENT RESPONSE AS A FUNCTION OF INTELLIGENCE

	I.Q.	
	110 — 90	85
High Response to Biofeedback	50	40
Low Response to Biofeedback	40	50

Another interesting statistical procedure is that of discriminant function analysis, which calculates group differences from a combination of variables instead of one at a time. It accomplishes the combination of variables by determining linear equations and solving for the best "fit" in optimizing group differences. Consequently, if the researcher wants to see which combination of variables best separates groups, this procedure can be of great value.

Returning to the more pragmatic problem of determining what impact a treatment has upon an individual, it is often recommended that the individual be his or her own control.

After all, the best determination of change is in relationship to the person's own past, not someone else's response. As implied, the person's past behaviors are monitored before the intervention actually begins. Then any differences in behaviors can be attributed to the treatment. If appropriate, the treatment can be suspended to see if previous behaviors return. By pinpointing the onset of the intervention and change of behavior, a strong argument can be made for impact. An example of behavioral reactions to food illustrates this approach. A woman had been suffering from headache pain for several years; frequency of pain-hours was recorded. After a trial-and-error period it was found that absence of cane sugar reduced her pain-hours. The resultant graph displayed in Figure 9.1 shows clearly the effect of sugar ingestion on her metabolism.

Lawlis (1976) has shown that other variables can serve as controls, or baselines, in order to understand change more completely. In his study, he used one set of recurring measures as indices of change; other variables were used as controls to determine if a researcher could exactly specify the changes that would take place. Similarly, in our example with the woman and headache pain, one could make it a stronger study by utilizing some variables like levels of anxiety, frustration, and anger to obtain additional baseline measures. If these latter variables remained relatively stable and the pain variables still fluctuated as predicted, then the researcher could reasonably contend that the nutritional elements were not influencing mood states, but were influencing pain alone. A relatively clean relationship would thereby have been demonstrated.

Relationship. Covariation is another approach to understanding relationships between events and observations. If one watches natural events long enough, certain relationships begin to reaffirm themselves day after day. Temperature relates to direct sunlight, speed of a car relates to how quickly it can come to a stop, certain behaviors relate to approval responses from others, and so on. Relationships between observations and outcomes are discussed widely, and journal editors are usually eager to publish any additional consistencies of practical value. How do psychological variables predict surgery outcome, rehabilitation of prisoners, marriage/divorces, or response to favorite football team's fortunes? Any insight into the future demands attention.

As a surprising number of researchers do not know, there are a variety of basic correlation coefficients that describe relationships in a manner so they can be compared. All are

Figure 9.1

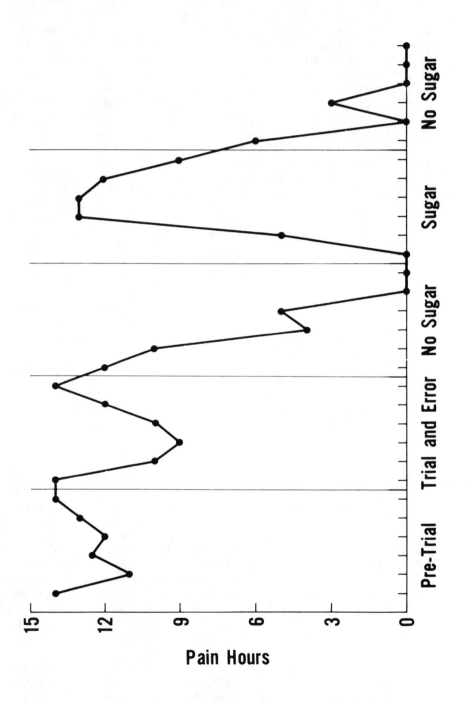

based on a square root of the ratio of covariation (the measured relationships between variables) to the total possible relationship (the relationships of the variables with themselves). Hence, the correlation coefficient of .5 would describe $(.5)^2$ or 25 percent predictability between two events or observations. The product-moment (PM) coefficient is the most popular technique and is a measure of the *linear* relationship between two distributions. Therefore, if we calculated a .50 PM correlation between a football team's total weight and its win/loss record, we could predict with 25 percent accuracy how well they would do in their future games. Another possible application would be to relate ego strength, or existence of pending lawsuit, to pain reduction.

What if we found two or three observations that related to football team performance, such as coach's intelligence, team spirit, and overall team speed? Insofar as they were not redundant with one another, each could be added for a better prediction. The combining of relationships to explain one outcome is called multiple correlation or multiple regression analysis. The strategy for utilization by the practitioner is similar to previous discussions regarding posthoc analysis; as long as consistency of coding is maintained throughout record keeping, there is always the potential for computing a multiple regression. Incidentally, it is not necessary to preselect the arrangement of the combination. Some computer programs will combine the prediction variables for the maximum relationship, allowing the researcher to obtain the most profitable prediction equation.

In the way of an example, since we are always interested in prediction of pain reduction, we used the scales of the MMPI as a means of understanding the final disposition of a pain measure (0-100% of tolerable pain) for one treatment program. As expected, Scales 1, 3, and 8 (*Hy, Hs,* and *Sc*) together accounted for 20 percent of the observed variations in response outcome among patients. In other words, the three scales in combination predicted change in pain status as a result of the treatment with 20 percent accuracy. We are now comparing other prediction equations, but at least we do have confirmation that psychological variables are related to the outcome. More important for the theme of this chapter, the analysis resulted from a curiosity about data that already existed in the files.

Strategy of
Analysis In the vast majority of psychological research designs, the validity of the research hypothesis is determined by what is called the .05 level of significance. Statistically, this

means that the observed differences or correlations are so great that the chances of obtaining such a result accidentally are only 5 times in 100 trials; therefore, the result cannot be dismissed as pure coincidence. The .05 level of significance itself, however, is only an arbitrary criterion, intended to serve as a decision guide in hypothesis testing; it represents just one theoretical issue within statistics, per se. Traditional hypothesis testing is an approach to logic formulated to divide all decisions into a dichotomous arrangement: to be or not to be, or to believe or not to believe. When the .05 level is not achieved, the research hypothesis is automatically rejected from further consideration and the alternative (null) hypothesis that no difference or relationship actually exists must be retained. Thus, the .05 level of significance is merely preselected by convention as the cutoff point for deciding in favor of the research hypothesis, but its choice may have nothing to do with the realities of a given situation.

In clinical research, this system of logic can be accepted if one also has the luxury of knowing what to expect. We recommend instead using the significance level as a confidence index, depicting a general internal range of support for the strength of relationships. The researcher also has the latitude to suspend these logic principles for others. We recommend, therefore, an approach that is oriented more to data-analysis rather than to hypothesis-testing. We utilize the same statistical procedures as described above, but instead of testing a formal research hypothesis against a preselected criterion of probability, we determine our significant findings on other bases, principally by means of the following rules:

1. Is the finding meaningful and explainable with respect to existing theory and understanding?

2. Are the levels of association (correlation, differences, or condensation) great enough to make an impact on practice, either affirming previous actions or defining new ones?

3. Does the finding simplify life? It is our belief that research should magnify the consistency of nature, and any discovery of significance should remedy previous frustrations. For example, if condensation demonstrates that one is treating a heterogeneous population, one once thought to be homogeneous, then that discrimination might explain differential results of treatment. If results show only slight correlation to diagnostic predictions, then the energy needed to justify an explanation can be minimized.

Regarding the issue of significant findings, the researcher must decide what is impressive enough to report. The answer is completely related to the art of the field and the cost of accepting the conclusions. For example, a .25 statistical significance may be very meaningful if it is an exploratory finding improving the survival of heart attack victims, but a

.001 probability may have a minor impact if related to vice-presidential election polls.

The researcher must understand the desirability of communication to other consumers of information in the field. Consequently, the author of relevant findings must achieve two goals: a most complete and rigorous understanding of his or her own results and a clear communication of the relevant parts to the professional community. Although these aspects may be complementary, the issues sometimes become cloudy.

During this chapter we have recommended the use of record-keeping files in order to "data snoop," but the obvious question is what to keep and record and what to throw away. That is the biggest question of all, yet it is impossible to answer and is often met with a shrug and a smile. Nevertheless, it is interesting to note what current journal articles have to say about important variables. We found a list of relatively important items—at least important to the consumers of mental health delivery systems—by Weinstein (1975, pp. 398-399).

1. Admission information. Identifying the person—Where is he from? What is he like? Social and economic resources? Who sent him? What previous services has he received? Where? And how long? Problems presented? Seriousness of the problems? Tentative program assignment?

2. During services. Plans for dealing with problems? Program involved? Staff providing services? Progress? Changes in plans? Why?

3. Conclusion of services. Services rendered? Further care indicated? Referred? Where? Party responsible for payment? How much? Condition of presenting complaints? Present complaints?

4. Follow-up. Work/school performance? Family? Others? Recurrent symptomatology? How long since services? Services elsewhere?

Research is aimed primarily at building knowledge and understanding. The clinician, on the other hand, is also oriented toward good patient management. Nonetheless, while research and human services may be viewed as distinct endeavors, each is essential for a rational and effective treatment program. To be meaningful, the researcher must deduce some certainty with which a professional can provide useful services. This may mean some results could only pertain to a single situation, such as the personality of a staff member, or political considerations. This goal is entirely appropriate if the clinician is aided by nothing more than personal insight and gratification. To the extent that results can be generalized to another setting, the net effect of the effort is doubled. In this regard, it becomes critically important to communicate with each other about our results and to become responsive to our own attainments.

BIBLIOGRAPHY

Achterberg, J., Collerain, I., & Craig, P. A possible relationship between cancer, mental retardation, and mental disorders. *Journal of Social Science and Medicine*, May, 1978, *12*, 135-139.

Achterberg, J., & Lawlis, G. F. Psychological factors and blood chemistries as disease outcome predictors for cancer patients. *Multivariate Experimental Clinical Research*, 1977, *3*(3), 107-122.

Achterberg, J., & Lawlis, G. F. *PERCEPT programs in relaxation and imagery*. Dallas: Medisette, 1978.

Achterberg, J., & Lawlis, G. F. *Imagery of cancer: A diagnostic tool for the process of disease*. Champaign, Ill.: Institute for Personality and Ability Testing, 1978.

Achterberg, J., & Lawlis, G. F. A canonical analysis of blood chemistry variables related to psychological measures of cancer patients. *Multivariate Experimental Clinical Research*, 1979, *4*(1 & 2), 1-10.

Achterberg, J., Lawlis, G. F., Carlton, A., & Smith, P. *The ostomate: Variables in physical and psychosocial rehabilitation*. Paper presented at the American Congress of Physical Medicine and Rehabilitation, New Orleans, 1978.

Achterberg, J., Matthews, S., & Simonton, C. *Stress, psychological factors and cancer: An annotated and edited bibliography*. Ft. Worth: New Medicine Press, 1976. (Available through Cancer Counseling & Research Center, Ft. Worth.)

Achterberg, J., McGraw, P., & Lawlis, G. F. Rheumatoid arthritis: A study of relocation and temperature biofeedback training as an adjunctive therapy. Accepted for publication, *Biofeedback & Self-Regulation*.

Agrippa, H. *Three books of occult philosophy or magic*. Chicago: Hahn & Whitehead, 1898.

Alexander, A. B., Miklich, D. R., & Hershkoff, H. The immediate effects of systematic relaxation training on peak expiratory flow rates in asthmatic children. *Psychosomatic Medicine*, 1971, *34*(5), 388-391.

Alexander, F. *Psychosomatic medicine*. New York: Norton, 1950.

Alexander, F., French, T. M., & Pollock, G. H. *Psychosomatic specificity: Experimental study and results*. Chicago: University of Chicago Press, 1968.

Alexander, W. R. M., Steward, S. M., & Duthie, J. J. R. Etiological factors in rheumatoid arthritis. In J. J. R. Duthie & W. R. M. Alexander (Eds) *Rheumatic disease*. Edinburgh: Edinburgh University Press, 1968 (Pfizer Medical Monographs No. 3).

Alvarez, W. C. *Nervous disease and pain*. New York: Harper & Brothers, 1954.

American Medical Association. Is alcoholism really an illness? In R. J. Shearer (Ed.), *Manual of alcoholism*. Health, Education & Welfare, 9801-967-25M, MH#3, 1967.

Andersson, S. A. Hansson, G., Holmgren, E., & Renberg, O. Evaluation of the pain suppressive effect of different frequencies of peripheral electrical stimulation in chronic pain conditions. *Acta Orthopedic Scandinavia,* 1976, *47,* 149-157.

Ansbacher, H., & Ansbacher, L. *The individual psychology of Alfred Adler.* New York: Basic Books, 1946.

Auden, W. H. "Miss Gee" from E. Mendelson (Ed.), *Collected Poems.* New York: Random House, 1940.

Bacon, C. L., Renneker, R., & Cutler, M. A psychosomatic survey of cancer of the breast. *Psychosomatic Medicine,* 1952, *14,* 543.

Bahnson, C. B., & Bahnson, M. B. Denial and repression of primitive impulses and of disturbing emotions in patients with malignant neoplasms. In D. M. Kissen & L. LeShan (Eds), *Psychosomatic aspects of neoplastic disease.* Philadelphia: Lippincott, 1964, 42. (a)

Bahnson, C. B., & Bahnson, M. B. Cancer as an alternative to psychosis. In D. M. Kissen, & L. LeShan (Eds), *Psychosomatic aspects of neoplastic disease.* Philadelphia: Lippincott, 1964, 184. (b)

Bahnson, C. B., & Kissen, D. M. (Eds), Psychophysiological aspects of cancer. *Annals of New York Academy of Sciences,* 1966, *125*(3), 773-1055.

Baker, L., Barcai, A., Kaye, R., & Hague, N. Beta adrenegric blockade and juvenile diabetes: Acute studies and long term therapeutic trial. *Journal of Pediatrics,* 1969, *75,* 19-29.

Barber, T. X. The effects of hypnosis on pain: A critical review of experimental and clinical findings. *Psychosomatic Medicine,* 1963, *23,* 303-333.

Barchas, J., Akil, H., Elliott, G., Holman, R., & Watson, S. Behavioral neurochemistry, neuroregulators and behavioral states. *Science,* 1978, *200,* 965-973.

Bassett, J. E., Blanchard, E. B., & Estes, L. D. Effects of instructional-expectancy sets on relaxation training with prisoners. *Journal of Community Psychology,* 1977, *5*(2), 166-170.

Bell, C. C. Endurance, strength and coordination exercises without cardiovascular or respiratory stress. *Journal of the National Medical Association,* 1979, *71*(3), 265-270.

Benson, J. *The relaxation response.* New York: William Morrow, 1975.

Berg, J. W., Ross, R., & Latourette, H. B. Economic status and survival of cancer patients. *Cancer,* 1977, *39,* 467-477.

Bernstein, D. A., & Borkovec, T. D. *Progressive relaxation training: A manual for the helping profession.* Champaign, Ill.: Research Press, 1973.

Besedovsky, H., Sorkin, E., Felix, D., & Haas, H. Hypothalamic changes during the immune response. *European Journal of Immunology,* 1977, *7,* 323-325.

Billig, O. E., & Sullivan, D. J. Personality structure and prognosis of alcohol addiction. *Quarterly Journal of Studies on Alcohol,* 1943, *3,* 554-573.

Binder, G. A. *Great moments in medicine.* Detroit: Parke-Davis, 1966.

Bird, B. One aspect of causation in alcoholism. *Quarterly Journal of Studies on Alcohol,* 1949, *9,* 532-543.

Blake, B. G. A follow-up of alcoholics treated by behavior therapy. *Behavior Research and Therapy,* 1967, *5,* 89-94.

Blom, G. E., & Nichols, G. Emotional factors in children with rheumatoid arthritis. *American Journal of Orthopsychiatry,* 1953, *24,* 101-104.

Blumberg, E. M., West, P. M., & Ellis, F. W. A possible relationship between psychological factors and human cancer. *Psychosomatic Medicine,* 1954, *16*(4), 276-286.

Bogen, J. E. The other side of the brain: An oppositional mind. *Bulletin of the Los Angeles Neurological Society,* 1969, *34,* 135-162.

Booth, G. Cancer and humanism. In D. M. Kissen & L. LeShan (Eds), *Psychosomatic aspects of neoplastic disease.* Philadelphia: Lippincott, 1964, 159.

Bourestom, N. C., & Howard, M. T. Personality characteristics of three disability groups. *Archives of Physical Medicine,* 1965, *36,* 626-629.

Bradley, L., Prokop, C., Margolis, R., & Gentry, D. Multivariate analysis of the MMPI profiles of low back pain patients. *Journal of Behavioral Medicine,* 1978, *1,* 253-271.

Broca, P. Remarques sur le siege de la faculte du lanajage articule: Suivies d'une observation d'aphemil (perte de la parole). *Bulletin de la Societe Anatomique de Paris,* 1861 (2nd series), *6,* 330-357.

Brown, B. Biofeedback: An exercise in "self-control." *Saturday Review,* February 22, 1975, 22-26.

Buchbaum, M., & Fedio, P. Visual information and evoked responses from the left and right hemispheres. *EEG and Clinical Neurophysiology,* 1969, *26,* 266-271.

Bugental, J. F. T. Discussion of E. M. Blumberg's article, Results of psychological testing of cancer patients. In J. A. Gengerelli & F. J. Kirkner (Eds), *The psychological variables in human cancer.* Berkeley: University of California Press, 1954, 95.

Buhler, C., & Lefever, D. W. A Rorschach study of the psychological characteristics of alcoholics. *Quarterly Journal of Studies on Alcohol,* 1949, *8,* 197.

Bunnell, B. N. Amygdaloid lesions and social dominance in the hooded rat. *Psychonomic Science,* 1966, *6,* 93-94.

Burtle, V., Whitlock, D., & Franks, V. Modification of low self-esteem in women alcoholics: A behavioral treatment approach. *Psychotherapy: Therapy, Research and Practice,* 1974, *11,* 36-40.

Button, A. D. A study of alcoholics with the MMPI. *Quarterly Journal of Studies on Alcohol,* 1956, *17,* 263-281. (a)

Button, A. D. The genesis and development of alcoholism. *Quarterly Journal of Studies on Alcohol,* 1956, *17,* 671-675. (b)

Callan, J. P. Holistic health or holistic hoax? *Journal of the American Medical Association*, March 16, 1979, *11*, 241.

Campbell, J., & Taub, A. Anesthesia from Percutaneous Electrical Stimulation: A peripheral mechanism. *Archives in Neurology*, 1973, *28*, 347-350.

Cannon, W. B. *Bodily changes in pain, hunger, fear and rage* (2nd ed.). New York: Appleton-Century, 1934.

Canter, F. M. Personality factors related to participation in treatment of hospitalized male alcoholics. *Journal of Clinical Psychology*, 1966, *22*, 114-116.

Carver, A. E. The psychology of the alcoholic. *British Journal of Medical Psychology*, 1931, *11*, 117-124.

Cattell, R. B. *Handbook supplement for form C of the 16 PF*. Champaign, Ill.: Institute for Personality and Ability Testing, 1962.

Chaves, J., & Barber, T. X. Cognitive strategies, experimenter modeling, and expectation in the alternation of pain. *Journal of Abnormal Psychology*, 1974, *83*, 356-363.

Cobb, B. A socio-psychological study of the cancer patient. Unpublished doctoral dissertation. University of Texas, Austin, 1952.

Cobb, S. Contained hostility in rheumatoid arthritis. *Arthritis Rheumatism*, 1959, *2*, 419-423.

Cobb, S., & Hall, W. A. A newly identified cluster of diseases—rheumatoid arthritis, peptic ulcer, and tuberculosis. *Journal of the American Medical Association*, 1965, *193*, 1077-1079.

Cobb, S., Schull, W. J., Harburg, E., & Kasl, S. The intrafamilial transmission of rheumatoid arthritis: Summary of findings. *Journal of Chronic Disease*, 1969, *22*, 193-195.

Coppen, A. J., & Metcalfe, M. Cancer and extraversion. In D. M. Kissen & L. LeShan (Eds), *Psychosomatic aspects of neoplastic disease*. Philadelphia: Lippincott, 1964.

Coppersmith, S. Adaptive reactions of alcoholics and non-alcoholics. *Quarterly Journal of Studies on Alcohol*, 1964, *25*, 262-277.

Costello, R., Lawlis, F., Monder, S. K., Celistino, J. F. Empirical derivation of a partial personality typology of alcoholics. *Journal of Studies on Alcohol*, 1978, *39*, 125-126.

Craig, K., & Best, H. Perceived contol over pain: Individual differences and situational determinants. *Pain*, 1977, *3*, 127-135.

Craig, K., Best, H., & Ward, L. Social modeling influences on psychophysical judgment of electrical stimulation. *Journal of Abnormal Psychology*, 1975, *84*, 364-365.

Craighead, W. E. The role of muscular relaxation in systematic desensitization. In R. Rubin (Ed.), *Advances in behavior therapy* (Vol. 5). New York: Academic Press, 1973.

Crain, D. C. *The arthritis handbook*. New York: Arco, 1976.

Critchley, M. *The parietal lobes*. London: Edward Arnold, 1953.

Cromes, G. F. Implementation of interdisciplinary cancer rehabilitation. *Rehabilitation Counseling Bulletin*, 1978, *21*(3), 230-237.

Cromier, B. M., Wittkower, E. D., Marcotte, Y., & Forget, F. Psychological aspects of rheumatoid arthritis. *Canadian Medical Association Journal*, 1957, *77*, 533-545.

Crown, S., Crown, J. M., & Fleming, A. Aspects of the psychology of rheumatoid disease. *Rheumatological Rehabilitation*, 1974, *13*(4), 167-168.

Davidoff, E., & Whitaker, C. A. Prepsychotic personality in alcoholic psychoses. *Psychiatric Quarterly*, 1940, *14*, 103-120.

Delgado, J. M., Roberts, W. W., & Miller, N. E. Learning motivated by electrical stimulation of the brain. *American Journal of Physiology*, 1954, *179*, 587.

Dement, W., & Wolpert, A. The relation of eye movements, body mobility, and external stimuli to dream content. *Journal of Experimental Psychology*, 1958, *55*, 543-553.

Denver, D. R., Laveault, D., Girard, F., Lacourciere, Y., Latulippe, L., Grove, R. N., Preve, M., & Doiron, N. *Behavioral medicine: Bio-behavioral effects of short-term thermal biofeedback and relaxation in rheumatoid arthritic patients*. Paper presented at the 10th Annual Meeting of the Biofeedback Society of America, San Diego, 1979.

Derogatis, L. R., Abeloff, M. D., & Melisaratos, N. Psychological coping mechanism and survival time in metastatic breast cancer. *Journal of the American Medical Association*, 1979, *242*(14), 1504-1507.

DeWind, L. T., & Payne, J. H. Intestinal bypass surgery for morbid obesity, long term results. *Journal of the American Medical Association*, 1976, *236*(20), 2298-2301.

Dick-Read, G. *Childbirth without fear*. New York: Harper & Row, 1953.

Dohrenwend, B. S., & Dohrenwend, B. P. (Eds). *Stressful life events: Their nature and effects*. New York: Wiley & Sons, 1974.

Dumas, R., & Morgan, A. EEG asymmetry as a function of occupation task, and task difficulty. *Neuropsychologia*, 1975, *13*, 219-288.

Dunbar, F. *Emotions and bodily changes* (2nd ed.). New York: Columbia University Press, 1935.

Duthie, J. J., Brown, P. E., Knox, J. D. E., & Thomson, M. Course and prognosis in rheumatoid arthritis. *Annals of rheumatoid disease*, 1975, *16*, 411-417.

Dychtwald, K. *Bodymind*. New York: Pantheon, 1977.

Eber, H. W. Multivariate methodologies for evaluation research. In I. E. L. Struening & M. Guttentag (Eds), *Handbook of evaluation research*. Beverly Hills: SAGE, 1975.

Eddy, M. B. *Science and Health*. Boston: First Church of Christ, Scientist, 1934.

Ellis, F. W., & Blumberg, E. M. Comparative case summaries with psychological profiles in rapidly and slowly progressive neoplastic diseases. In J. A. Gengerelli & F. J. Kirkner (Eds), *The psychological variables in human cancer.* Berkeley: University of California Press, 1954, 72.

Evans, E. *A psychological study of cancer.* New York: Dodd, Mead & Co., 1926.

Evans, R. B., Stern, E., & Marmorston, J. Psychological-hormonal relationships in men with cancer. *Psychological Reports,* 1965, *17,* 715.

Ferguson, M. Karl Pribram's changing reality. *Re-Vision,* 1978, *1*(3/4), 8-13.

Felix, R. H. An appraisal of the personality types of the addict. *American Journal of Psychiatry,* 1944, *100,* 462-467.

Fenna, D., Mix, L., Schaefer, O., & Gilbert, J. A. L. Ethanol metabolism in various racial groups. *Canadian Medical Association Journal,* 1971, *105,* 472-475.

Fisher, S., & Fisher, R. Application of rigidity principles to the measurement of personality disturbance. *Journal of Personality,* 1955, *24,* 86-93.

Fitzhugh, L. C., & Reitan, R. M. Adaptive abilities and intellectual functioning in hospitalized alcoholics. *Quarterly Journal of Studies on Alcohol,* 1960, *21,* 414-423.

Foque, E. Le Probleme du cancer dans ses aspects psychiques. *Gaz. Hop. Paris,* 1931, *104,* 827.

Fowler, J. E., Budzynski, T. H., & VandenBergh, R. L. Effects of an EMG biofeedback relaxation program on the control of diabetes: A case study. *Biofeedack and Self-Regulation,* 1976, *1*(1), 105-112.

Fox, B. Premorbid psychological factors related to incidence of cancer: Background for prospective grant applicants. *Document issued by National Cancer Institute in conjunction with Request for Proposals,* 1976.

Fox, J. An overview of alcoholism research. *Public Health Reports,* 1961, *76,* 223-231.

Fox, R. A multidisciplinary approach to the problem of alcoholism. *International Journal of Psychiatry,* 1958, *5,* 34-44.

Frank, J. D. *Persuasion and Healing.* Baltimore and London: Johns Hopkins University Press, 1973.

Freedman, A., Kaplan, H., & Sadock, B. (Eds). *Comprehensive textbook of psychiatry* (Vol. 2). Baltimore: Williams & Wilkins, 1975.

Freeling, N. W., & Shemberg, K. M. The alleviation of test anxiety by systematic desensitization. *Behavior Therapy and Research,* 1970, *8,* 293-296.

Freud, S. *The complete psychological works of Sigmund Freud.* (J. Strachey, Ed. and trans.). Hogarth Press and Institute of Psychoanalysis, 1953, Vol. 7.

Gaardner, K., & Montgomery, P. *Clinical biofeedback: A procedural manual.* Baltimore: Williams & Wilkins, 1977.

Galin, D. Implication for psychiatry of left and right cerebral specialization. *Archives of General Psychiatry*, 1974, *31*, 572-583.

Galin, D., & Ornstein, R. Individual differences in cognitive style—I. Reflective eye movements. *Neuropsychologia*, 1974, *12*, 367-376.

Galin, D., & Ornstein, R. Lateral specialization of cognitive modes: An EEG study. *Psychophysiology*, 1976, *9*, 412-418.

Gazzaniga, M. S. *The bisected brain.* New York: Appleton-Century-Crofts, 1970.

Gazzaniga, M. S., & LeDoux, J. E. *The integrated mind.* New York: Plenum Press, 1978.

Geist, H. *The psychological aspects of rheumatoid arthritis.* Springfield, Ill.: Charles C Thomas, 1966.

Geist, H. Can rheumatoid factors and anger equal arthritis? *Medical World News*, 1969, *10*, 23.

Gentry, W. D., & Bernal, G. A. A. Chronic pain. In R. B. Williams, Jr., & W. D. Gentry (Eds), *Behavioral approaches to medical treatment.* Baltimore: Ballinger, 1977.

Gengerelli, J. A., & Kirkner, F. J. *The psychological variables in human cancer.* Berkeley: The University of California Press, 1954.

Gershman, L. M., & Clouser, R. A. Treating insomnia with relaxation and desensitization in a group setting by an automated approach. *Journal of Behavior Therapy and Experimental Psychiatry*, 1974, *5*, 31-36.

Gibbs, H., & Achterberg, J. The spouse as facilitator for esophageal speech: A research perspective. *Journal of Surgical Oncology*, 1979, *11*, 89-90.

Gibbs, H. W., & Achterberg-Lawlis, J. Spiritual values and death anxiety: Implications for counseling with terminal cancer patients. *Journal of Counseling Psychology*, 1978, *25*(6), 563-569.

Gifford, S. D. *A comparison of drug treatment for insomnia and the effect of causal attribution.* Unpublished doctoral dissertation, North Texas State University, 1979.

Glover, E. The etiology of alcoholism. *Royal Society of Medicine*, 1927, *21*, 13.

Goldfried, M. R., & Davidson, G. C. *Clinical behavior therapy.* New York: Holt, Rinehart, & Winston, 1976.

Goldfried, M., & Trier, C. S. Effectiveness of relaxation as an active coping skill. *Journal of Abnormal Psychology*, 1974, *83*, 348-355.

Goldstein, S., & Linden, J. Multivariate classification of alcoholics by means of the MMPI. *Journal of Abnormal Psychology*, 1969, *74*, 661-669.

Goleman, D. Holographic memory. *Psychology Today*, February, 1979, 71-84.

Gorman, W. *Body image and image of the brain.* St. Louis: Warren H. Green, 1969.

Gorrell, R. Perspectives in pain control. *Today's Clinician*, February, 1978, 52-55.

Gottschalk, L. A., Serota, H. M., & Shapiro, L. B. Psychologic conflict and neuro-muscular tension. I. Preliminary report and a method, as applied to rheumatoid arthritis. *Psychosomatic Medicine*, 1950, *12*, 315-319.

Graffenried, B., Adler, R., Abt, K., Nuesch, E., & Spiegel, R. The influence of anxiety and pain sensitivity on experimental pain in man. *Pain*, 1978, *4*, 253-263.

Grant, I., Kyle, G. G., Teichman, A., & Mendels, J. Recent life events and diabetes in adults. *Psychosomatic Medicine*, 1974, *36*, 121-128.

Gregg, D. The paucity of arthritis among psychotic patients. *American Journal of Psychiatry*, 1939, *95*, 853-854.

Green, A., & Green, E. *Beyond biofeedback*. New York: Delta/Dell, 1977.

Greene, W. A. Psychological factors in reticuloendothelial disease. *Psychosomatic Medicine*, 1954, *16*, 220.

Greene, W. A. The psychosocial setting of the development of leukemia and lymphoma. *Annals of the New York Academy of Science*, 1966, *125*, 794-801.

Greene, W. A., Young, L., & Swisher, S. M. Psychological factors and reticuloendothelial disease. II. Observations on a group of women with lymphomas and leukemias. *Psychosomatic Medicine*, 1956, *18*, 284.

Grinder, J., & Bandler, R. *The structure of magic, II*. Palo Alto: Science and Behavior Books, 1976.

Gross, C. G., & Weiskrantz, L. Some changes in behavior produced by lateral frontal lesions in the macaque. In J. M. Warren, & K. Akert (Eds), *The frontal granular cortex and behavior*. New York: McGraw-Hill, 1964, 74-101.

Gross, W. F., & Carpenter, L. L. Alcoholic personality: Reality or fiction? *Psychological Reports*, 1971, *28*, 375-378.

Guyton, A. *Textbook of medical physiology*. Philadelphia: W. B. Saunders, 1971.

Hague, W. H., Donovan, D. M., & O'Leary, M. R. Personality characteristics related to treatment decisions among inpatient alcoholics. *Journal of Clinical Psychology*, 1976, *32*, 476-479.

Halliday, J. L. The concept of psychosomatic rheumatism. *Annals of Internal Medicine*, 1941, *15*, 666-673.

Halliday, J. L. Psychological aspects of rheumatoid arthritis. *Proceedings of the Research Society in Medicine*, 1942, *35*, 71-76.

Halpern, F. Studies of compulsive drinkers: Psychological test results. *Quarterly Journal of Studies on Alcohol*, 1946, *6*, 468-479.

Hamilton, M. *Incubation or cure of disease in pagan temples and Christian churches*. London: 1906.

Hampton, P. J. A psychometric study of drinkers. *Journal of Consulting Psychology,* 1951, *15*, 501-504.

Hardy, J. D., Wolff, H. G., & Goodell, H. *Pain sensations and reactions.* New York: Hafner, 1967.

Harris, R. E., & Ives, V. M. A study of the personality of alcoholics. *American Psychologist,* 1947, *2*, 405.

Hart, H. H. Personality factors in alcoholism. *Archives of Neurology and Psychiatry,* 1930, *24*, 116.

Hartman, F. *Paracelsus: Life and prophecies.* Blauvelt, N.Y.: Rudolf Steiner, 1973.

Head, H. *Studies in Neurology.* Oxford: Oxford University Press, 1920.

Healey, L. A. The management of rheumatoid arthritis. *Resident and Staff Physician,* August, 1978, 50-56.

Hebb, D. O. On imagery. *Psychological Review,* 1968, *75*, 466-477.

Heidt, P. Patients tell their stories. Paper presented at the Second Annual Conference on Imaging and Fantasy Process, Chicago, November, 1978.

Heisel, J. S. Life changes as etiological factors in juvenile rheumatoid arthritis. *Journal of Psychosomatic Research,* 1972, *16*, 411-417.

Hershenson, D. B. Stress-induced use of alcohol by problem drinkers as a function of their sense of identity. *Quarterly Journal of Studies on Alcohol,* 1965, *26*, 213-222.

Hewitt, C. C. A personality study of alcohol addiction. *Quarterly Journal of Studies on Alcohol,* 1943, *4*, 368-386.

Hinkle, L. E., Evans, F. M., & Wolf, S. Studies in diabetes mellitus IV. *Psychosomatic Medicine,* 1951, *13*, 184-202.

Hinkle, L. E., & Wolf, S. The effects of stressful life situations on the concentration of blood glucose in diabetic and non-diabetic humans. *Diabetes,* 1952, *48*, 383-392. (a)

Hinkle, L. E., & Wolf, S. The importance of life stress in the course and management of diabetes mellitus. *Journal of the American Medical Association,* 1952, *148*, 513-520. (b)

Hoch, P. H. Personality factors in alcoholic psychoses. *Psychiatric Quarterly,* 1940, *14*, 338.

Holden, C. Cancer and the mind: How are they connected? *Science,* 1978, *200*, 1363-1369.

Hollander, J. L., & McCarty, D. J., Jr. *Arthritis and allied conditions.* Philadelphia: Lea & Febiger, 1972.

Holmes, T. H., & Masuda, M. Life change and illness susceptibility. Presented as a part of a "Symposium on separation and depression: Clinical and research aspects," Chicago, December 26-30, 1970.

Holmes, T. H., & Rahe, R. H. The Social Readjustment Rating Scale. *Journal of Psychosomatic Research*, 1967, *11*, 213-218.

Holmes, W. O. The development of an empirical MMPI scale for alcoholism. Unpublished manuscript, 1953.

Hoover, J. Complex questions, complex answers. *Diabetes Forecast*, 1978, *2*, 28-29.

Horney, K. *Our inner conflicts: A constructive theory of neurosis.* New York: Norton, 1945.

Horvath, S. M., & Hollander, J. L. Intra-articular temperature as a measure of joint reaction. *Journal of Clinical Investigation*, 1949, *28*, 469-473.

Hoyt, D. P., & Sedlacek, G. M. Differentiating alcoholics from normals and abnormals in the MMPI. *Journal of Clinical Psychology*, 1958, *14*, 69-73.

Hughes, J. (Ed.). *Centrally acting peptides.* New York: Macmillan, 1978.

Inman, O. B. Development of two different types of cancer in a patient undergoing psychoanalytic treatment. In D. M. Kissen & L. LeShan (Eds), *Psychosomatic aspects of neoplastic disease.* Philadelphia: Lippincott, 1964.

Isaacson, R. L. *The limbic system.* New York & London: Plenum, 1974.

Izak, F. C., & Medalie, J. H. Comprehensive follow-up of carcinoma patients. *Journal of Chronic Disease*, 1971, *24*, 179-191.

Jackson, H. *Selected writings of John Hughlings Jackson.* J. Taylor (Ed.). New York: Basic Books, 1958.

Jacobs, J. S. L. Cancer: Host resistance and host acquiescence. In J. A. Gengerelli & F. J. Kirkner (Eds), *The psychological variable in human cancer.* Berkeley: University of California Press, 1954, 128.

Jacobsen, C. F. Studies of cerebral function in primates: I. The functions of the frontal association areas in monkeys. *Comparative Psychology, Monographs*, 1936, *13*, 3-60.

Jacobson, E. *You must relax* (3rd ed.). New York: McGraw-Hill, 1948.

Jellinek, E. M. Phases of alcohol addiction. *Quarterly Journal of Studies on Alcohol*, 1952, *13*, 673.

Jellinek, E. M. *The disease concept of alcoholism.* New Haven: Hill House, 1960.

John, E. R., & Killiam, K. F. Electrophysiological correlates of avoidance conditioning in the cat. *Journal of Pharmacology and Experimental Therapeutics*, 1959, *125*, 252-274.

Johnson, A., Shapiro, L., & Alexander, F. Preliminary report on a psychosomatic study of rheumatoid arthritis. *Psychosomatic Medicine*, 1947, *9*, 295-302.

Johnson, J. E. Effects of accurate expectations about sensations on the sensory and distress components of pain. *Journal of Personality & Social Psychology*, 1973, *27*, 261-275.

Johnson, J. E., Rice, V. H., Fuller, S. S., & Endress, M. P. Sensory information instruction in a coping strategy, and recovery from surgery. *Research in Nursing and Health*, 1978,*1*(1), 4-17.

Kaldegg, A. Psychological observations in a group of alcoholic patients with an analysis of Rorschach, Wechsler-Bellevue and Bender-Gestalt test results. *Quarterly Journal of Studies on Alcohol*, 1956, *17*, 608-628.

Katz, S., Vignos, P. J., & Moskowitz, R. W. Comprehensive outpatient care in rheumatoid arthritis. *Journal of the American Medical Association*, 1968, *206*, 1249-1253.

Kazdin, A. E., & Wilcoxin, L. A. Systematic desensitization and non-specific treatment effects: A methodological evaluation. *Psychological Bulletin*, 1975, *83*, 5.

Kellgren, J. H., & Ball, J. Clinical significance of the rheumatoid serum factor. *British Medical Journal*, 1958, *1*, 523-531.

Kilroy, A. W., Schaffner, W., Fleet, W. F., Jr., Lefkowitz, L. B., Jr., Karzon, D. T., & Fenichell, G. M. Two syndromes following rubella immunization. *Journal of the American Medical Association*, 1970, *214*, 2287-2291.

King, S. H. Psychosocial factors associated with rheumatoid arthritis. *Journal of Chronic Disease*, 1955, *2*(3), 287-302.

Kissen, D. M. The significance of personality in lung cancer in men. *Annals of New York Academy of Science*, 1966, *125*, 820-826.

Kissen, D. M. Psychosocial factors, personality and lung cancer in men aged 55-64. *British Journal of Medical Psychology*, 1967, *40*, 29-43.

Kissen, D. M., & Eysenck, H. J. Personality in male lung cancer patients. *Journal of Psychosomatic Research*, 1962, *6*, 123.

Kissin, B., Platz, A., & Su, W. H. Selective factors in treatment choice and outcome in alcoholics. In N. K. Mello & J. H. Mendelson (Eds), *Recent advances in studies of alcoholism*. Washington, D. C.: U. S. Government Printing Office, 1972.

Kiviniemi, P. Emotions and personality in rheumatoid arthritis. *Scandinavian Journal of Rheumatology*, 1978, Supplemental Monograph No. 18, *6*.

Klebanoff, S. G. Personality factors in symptomatic chronic alcoholism as indicated by the Thematic Apperception Test. *Journal of Consulting Psychology*, 1947, *11*, 111-119.

Klopfer, B. Psychological variables in human cancer. *Journal of Projective Techniques*, 1957, *21*, 331-340.

Knight, R. P. The dynamics and treatment of chronic alcohol addiction. *Bulletin of Menninger Clinic*, 1937, *1*, 233, (a)

Knight, R. P. The psychodynamics of chronic alcoholism. *Journal of Nervous Mental Disease*, 1937, *86*, 538-548. (b)

Knorring, L., Almay, B., Johansson, F., Terenius, L. Pain perception and endorphin levels in cerebrospinal fluid. *Pain,* 1978, *5,* 359-365.

Koenig, R., Levin, S. M., & Brennan, M. J. The emotional status of cancer patients as measured by a personality test. *Journal of Chronic Disability,* 1967, *20,* 923.

Korneva, F., & Khai, L. Effect of destruction of hypothalamic areas on immunogenesis. *Fiziol. Sechenov,* 1963, *49,* 42.

Krug, S. (Ed.). *Psychological assessment in medicine.* Champaign, Ill.: Institute for Personality and Ability Testing, 1978.

Kuhn, T. *The structure of scientific revolutions.* Chicago & London: University of Chicago Press, 1962.

Lachman, S. *Psychosomatic disorder: A behavioristic interpretation.* New York: Wiley & Sons, 1972.

Lambert, P. L., Harrell, E. H., & Achterberg, J. The effect of hypothalamic stimulation on the phagocytic activity of the reticuloendothelial system. Paper presented at the Annual Meeting of the Southwestern Psychological Association, San Antonio, 1979.

Lang, P. J., Melamed, B. G., & Hart, J. A psychophysiological analysis of fear modification using an automated desensitization procedure. *Journal of Abnormal Psychology,* 1970, *76,* 220-234.

LaPatra, J. *Healing: The coming revolution in holistic medicine.* McGraw-Hill, 1978.

Lashley, K. In search of the engram. *Symposium for the Society of Experimental Biology,* 1950, *4,* 425-482.

Lawlis, F. *The measure of interpersonal dimensions.* Wichita, Ks: Test Systems, Inc., 1973.

Lawlis, F. Multivariate methodology for N = 1. *Multivariate Experimental Clinical Research,* 1976, *2,* 101-106.

Lawlis, F., Mooney, V., Selby, D., & McCoy, E. A motivational scoring system for spinal pain. Submitted for publication to *Spine.*

Lawlis, G. F., & Rubin, S. E. 16-PF study of personality patterns in alcoholics. *Quarterly Journal of Studies on Alcohol,* 1971, *32,* 318-327.

Lawrence, J. S., Valkenburg, H. A., Fuxford, A. F., & Collard, P. J. Rheumatoid factor in the United Kingdom: II. Associations with certain infections. *Clinical Experimental Immunology,* 1971, *9,* 519-528.

Leavitt, F., Garron, D., Whisler, W., Sheinkop, M. Affection and sensory dimensions of back pain. *Pain,* 1978, *4,* 278-281.

Lentz, T. F. Personality correlates of alcoholic beverage consumption. *Character and Personality,* 1943, *12,* 54-70.

LeShan, L. Psychological states as factors in the development of malignant disease: A critical review. *Journal of the National Cancer Institute*, 1959, *22*, 1-18.

LeShan, L. An emotional life history pattern associated with neoplastic disease. *Annals of the New York Academy of Science*, 1966, *125*, 780-793.

LeShan, L., & Worthington, R. E. Some recurrent life-history patterns observed in patients with malignant disease. *Journal of Nervous & Mental Disease*, 1956, *124*, 460.

Levenson, H. Distinctions within the concept of internal-external control: Development of a new scale. *Proceedings of the American Psychological Association*, 1972, 259-268.

Levine, L., Gordon, N., & Fields, H. Hormones and behavior. *The Lancet*, 1978, *11*, 654.

Levy, J., Trevarthen, C., & Sperry, R. W. Perception of bilateral chimeric figures following hemispheric deconnection. *Brain*, 1972, *95*, 61-78.

Lisonsky, E. Clinical research in alcoholism and the use of psychological tests: A re-evaluation. In R. Fox (Ed.), *Alcoholism: Behavioral research and therapeutic approaches*. New York: Springer, 1967, 3-15.

Loeser, J. D. Relief of pain by transcutaneous stimulation. *Journal of Neurosurgery*, 1975, *42*, 308-314.

Long, D. External electrical stimulation as a treatment of chronic pain. *Minnesota Medicine*, 1974, *57*, 195-198.

Lorr, M., McNair, D. M., & Weinstein, G. H. Early effects of librium used with psychotherapy. *Journal of Psychiatric Research*, 1962, *1*, 257-270.

Ludwig, A. O. Psychogenic factors in rheumatoid arthritis. *Bulletin of Rheumatoid Disease*, 1952, *2*, 33-37.

Ludwig, A. O. Rheumatoid arthritis. In A. M. Freedman, & J. J. Kaplan (Eds), *Comprehensive textbook of psychiatry*. Baltimore: Williams & Wilkins, 1967.

Luria, A. *The mind of a mnemonist*. New York: Basic Books, 1968.

Luthe, W. *Autogenic therapy*. New York: Grune & Stratton, 1969, Vol. 1-7.

MacDonald, M. J. Equal incidence of adult onset diabetes among ancestors of juvenile diabetics and non-diabetics. *Diabetologia*, 1974, *10*, 767-773.

Machover, S., & Puzzo, F. Clinical and objective studies of personality variables in alcoholism: Clinical investigation of the "alcoholic personality." *Quarterly Journal of Studies on Alcohol*, 1959, *20*, 258.

Management of chronic pain: Medicine's new growth industry. *Medical World News*, 1976, 49.

Manson, M. P. A psychometric differentiation of alcoholics from non-alcoholics. *Quarterly Journal of Studies on Alcohol*, 1948, *9*, 175-206.

Manson, M. P. A psychometric analysis of psychopathic characteristics of alcoholics. *Journal of Consulting Psychology*, 1949, *13*, 111-118.

Mark, V. H., & Ervin, F. R. *Violence and the brain.* New York, Evanston, & London: Harper & Row, 1970.

Martarano, R. Mood and social perception in four alcoholics: Effects of drinking and assertive training. *Quarterly Journal of Studies on Alcohol*, 1974, *35*, 445-457.

Marty, P., & de M'Uzan, M. La pensee operatoire. *Rev. Franc. Psychoanalysis*, 1963, *27*, Supplement, 1345.

Mathias, R. E. An experimental investigation of the personality structure of chronic alcoholic, alcoholic anonymous, neurotic, and normal groups. Unpublished doctoral dissertation, University of Buffalo, 1955.

McAndrews, C., & Geertsma, P. A critique of alcoholism scales derived from the MMPI. *Quarterly Journal of Studies on Alcohol*, 1964, *25*, 68-76.

McClelland, D. C., Dorris, W. N., Kerline, R., & Wanner, E. *The drinking man.* New York: The Free Press, 1972.

McCord, W., & McCord, J. Some current theories of alcoholism: A longitudinal evaluation. *Quarterly Journal of Studies on Alcohol*, 1959, *20*, 727-749.

McCreary, C., Turner, J., & Dawson, E. Differences between functional versus organic low back pain patients. *Pain*, 1977, *4*, 73-78.

McGill, J. Pain profiles related to outcome. Unpublished doctoral dissertation, North Texas State University, 1979.

McGlynn, F. D. Experimental desensitization following three types of instructions. *Behavior Research & Therapy*, 1971, *9*, 367-369.

McKelvy, P. L. Clinical report on the use of specific TENS units. *Physical Therapy*, 1978, *12*, 1474-1477.

McLaughlin, J. T., Zabarenko, R. N., Diana, P. B., & Quinn, G. Emotional reactions of rheumatoid arthritis to ACTH. *Psychosomatic Medicine*, 1953, *15*(3), 187-199.

McMahon, C. E. The role of imagination in the disease process: Pre-Cartesian history. *Psychological Medicine*, 1976, *6*, 179-184.

McQuade, W., & Aikman, A. *Stress.* New York: Dutton, 1974.

Meerlo, J. A. M. Artificial ecstasy: A study of the psychosomatic aspects of drug addiction. *Journal of Nervous & Mental Disease*, 1952, *115*, 246-266.

Melzack, R. *The puzzle of pain.* New York: Basic Books, 1973.

Melzack, R., & Wall, P. D. Pain mechanism: A new theory. *Science*, 1965, *150*, 971-979.

Melzack, R., Weisy, A., & Sprague, L. Strategies for controlling pain: Contributions of auditory stimulation and suggestions. *Experimental Neurology*, 1963, *8*, 239-247.

Meyer, A., & Beck, E. *Prefrontal leucotomy and related operations: Anatomic aspects of success or failure.* Springfield, Ill.: Charles C Thomas, 1954.

Meyer, A., Bollmeier, J., & Alexander, F. Correlation between emotions and carbohydrate metabolism in two cases of diabetes mellitus. *Psychosomatic Medicine*, 1945, *7*, 335.

Meyerwitz, S. The continuing investigation of psychosocial variables in rheumatoid arthritis. *Modern Trends in Rheumatology*, 1971, *2*, 92-105.

Miles, W. R. Psychological factors in alcoholism. *Mental Hygiene*, 1937, *21*, 529-548.

Miller, R. F., & Jones, H. W. The possibility of precipitating the leukemia state by emotional factors. *Blood*, 1948, *8*, 880.

Milner, B. Interhemispheric differences in the localization of psychological processes in man. *British Medical Bulletin*, 1971, *27*, 272-277.

Minuchin, S., Rosman, B., & Baker, L. *Psychosomatic families.* Cambridge, Mass.: Harvard University Press, 1978.

Mitchell, K. R., & White, R. G. Self-management of severe predormital insomnia. *Journal of Behavior Therapy & Experimental Psychiatry*, 1977, *8*(1), 57-63.

Modlin, H. C. A study of the MMPI in clinical practice with notes on the Cornell Index. *American Journal of Psychiatry*, 1947, *103*, 758-769.

Moldofsky, H., & Chester, W. J. Pain and mood patterns in patients with rheumatoid arthritis: A prospective study. *Psychosomatic Medicine*, 1970, *32*, 309-318.

Moore, M., & Gray, M. Alcoholism at the Boston City Hospital. *Quarterly Journal of Studies on Alcohol*, 1941, *2*, 18-34.

Moos, R. H. Personality factors associated with rheumatoid arthritis: A review. *Journal of Chronic Disease*, 1964, *17*, 41-59.

Moos, R. H., & Engel, B. T. Pychophysiological reactions in hypertensive and arthritic patients. *Journal of Psychosomatic Research*, 1964, *8*, 17-21.

Moos, R. H., & Solomon, G. F. Psychologic comparisons between women with rheumatoid arthritis and their non-arthritic sisters. *Psychosomatic Medicine*, 1965, *25*, 153.

Morrison, L., Short, C., Ludwig, A. O., & Schwab, R. The neuromuscular system in rheumatoid arthritis. Electromyographic and histologic observations. *American Journal of Medical Science*, 1947, *214*, 33-37.

Mueller, A. D., & Lefkovitz, A. M. Personality structure and dynamics of patients with rheumatoid arthritis. *Journal of Clinical Psychology*, 1956, *12*, 143-148.

Muldoon, J. F. The diabetic's guide to the health care system. *Visual Impairment and Blindness*, November, 1978, 348-353.

Murphy, M. M. Values stressed by two social class levels at meetings of Alcoholics Anonymous. *Quarterly Journal of Studies on Alcohol*, 1953, *14*, 576-585.

Muslin, H. L., Gyarfas, K., & Pieper, W. J. Separation experience and cancer of the breast. *Annals of the New York Academy of Science*, 1966, *125*(3), 802.

Nalven, F. B., & O'Brien, J. F. On the use of the MMPI with rheumatoid arthritic patients. *Arthritis Rheumatism*, 1964, *7*, 18-29.

Nauta, W. J. H. Some efferent connections of the prefrontal cortex in the monkey. In J. M. Warren, & K. Akert (Eds), *The frontal granular cortex and behavior*. New York: McGraw-Hill, 1964, 397-409.

Neisser, V. The processes of vision. *Scientific American*, 1968, *219*(3), 204-214.

Neisser, V. The process of vision. In A. Richardson (Ed.), *Perception: Mechanism and models*. San Francisco: W. H. Freeman, 1972.

Nelson, C. G., & Pyke, D. A. Viruses and the etiology of diabetes: A study of identical twins. *British Medical Journal*, 1975, *4*, 249-251.

Nemeth, G., & Mezei, A. Personality traits of cancer patients compared with benign tumor patients on the basis of the Rorschach test. In D. M. Kissen, & L. LeShan (Eds), *Psychosomatic aspects of neoplastic disease*. Philadelphia: Lippincott, 1964, 12.

Nemiah, J. C., Freyberger, H., & Sifneos, P. E. Alexithymia: A view of the psychosomatic process. In O. W. Hill (Ed.), *Modern trends in psychosomatic medicine* (Vol. 3). London: Butterworths, 1976, 430-439.

Nemiah, J. C., & Sifneos, P. E. Affect and fantasy in patients with psychosomatic disorders. In O. W. Hill (Ed.), *Modern trends in psychosomatic medicine* (Vol. 2). London: Butterworths, 1970.

Nerviano, V. J., & Gross, W. F. A multivariate delineation of two alcoholic profile types on the 16 PF. *Journal of Clinical Psychology*, 1973, *29*, 371-374.

Netzer, M. The body image of women under study for cancer. Unpublished doctoral dissertation, Yeshiva University, 1965.

Newfeld, R. The effects of experimental altered cognitive appraisal on pain tolerance. *Psychonomic Science*, 1970, *20*, 106-107.

Nissen, H. A., & Spencer, K. A. The psychogenic problem (endocrine and metabolic) in chronic arthritis. *New England Medical Journal*, 1936, *214*, 576-579.

Norbury, F. G. Some mental mechanisms in alcoholism. *Journal of the American Medical Association*, 1942, *118*, 25-28.

Nowlis, V., & Nowlis, H. H. The description and analysis of mood. *Annals of the New York Academy of Science*, 1956-195, *65*, 345-355.

Oka, M., Rekonen, A., & Elomaa, I. Muscle blood flow in rheumatoid arthritis. *Acta Rheumatology Scandinavia*, 1971, *7*, 203-208.

Olds, J., & Milner, P. Positive reinforcement produced by electrical stimulation of septal area and other regions of rat brain. *Journal of Comparative & Physiological Psychology*, 1954, *47*, 419-427.

Olds, M. E., & Olds, J. Approach - avoidance analysis of rat diencephalon. *Journal of Comparative Neurology*, 1963, *120*, 259-295.

Ornstein, R. E., & Galin, D. Physiological studies of consciousness. In P. Lee, R. Ornstein, D. Galin, A. Deikman, & C. Tart (Eds), *Symposium on consciousness*. New York: Viking, 1976.

Osler, W. *The evolution of modern medicine*. New Haven: Yale University Press, 1921.

Paget, I. *Surgical pathology* (2nd ed.). London: Longmons, 1870.

Paivio, A. *Imagery and verbal processes*. New York: Holt, Rinehart &Winston, 1971.

Paloucek, F. P., & Graham, J. B. The influence of psychosocial factors on the prognosis in cancer of the cervix. *Annals of the New York Academy of Science*, 1966, *125*(3), 814.

Papez, J. W. A proposed mechanism of emotion. *Archives of Neurology & Psychiatry*, 1937, *38*, 725-744.

Patel, C. H. Yoga and biofeedback in the management of hypertension. *The Lancet*, November 10, 1973, 1053-1055.

Paul, G. L. Outcome of systematic desensitization. II. Controlled investigations of individual treatment technique variations, and current status. In C. M. Franks (Ed.), *Behavior therapy: Appraisal and status*. New York: McGraw-Hill, 1969.

Pedder, J. Psychosomatic disorder and psychosis. *Journal of Psychosomatic Research*, 1969, *13*, 339-347.

Pegg, S. M., Littler, T. R., & Littler, E. N. A trial of exercise and ice therapy in chronic arthritis. *Physiotherapy*, 1969, *55*, 51-86.

Pelletier, K. R. *Mind as healer, mind as slayer*. New York: Dell, 1977.

Pelletier, K. R. *Toward a science of consciousness*. New York: Dell, 1978.

Penfield, W., & Rasmussen, T. *The cerebral cortex of man*. New York: Macmillan, 1950.

Perls, F., Hefferline, R., & Goodman, P. *Gestalt therapy*. New York: Dell, 1951.

Phillips, P. E., & Christian, C. L. Myxovirus antibody increases in human connective tissue disease. *Science*, 1970, *168*, 982-984.

Pilkington, T. L. The coincidence of rheumatoid arthritis and schizophrenia. *Journal of Nervous & Mental Disease*, 1956, *124*, 604-607.

Pilowsky, I., Chapman, C., & Bonica, J. Pain, depression and illness behavior in a pain clinic population. *Pain*, 1977, *4*, 183-192.

Pipineli-Potomianoa, A. Stress and anxiety in psychosomatic diseases: Research on cases of rheumatoid arthritis. *Transnational Mental Health Research Newsletter*, 1976, *18*(3-6), 13-14.

Quaranta, J. V. Alcoholism: A study of emotional maturity and homosexuality as related factors in compulsive drinking. *Quarterly Journal of Studies on Alcohol*, 1949, *10*, 354.

Ransford, A. O., Cairns, D., & Mooney, V. The pain drawing as an aid to the psychologic evaluation of patients with low-back pain. *Spine*, June, 1976, *1*, 127-135.

Ratliff, R. G., & Stein, N. H. Treatment of neurodermatitis by behavior therapy: A case study. *Behavior Research & Therapy*, 1968, *6*, 397-399.

Ray, C., & Maurer, D. A review of neural stimulation system components useful in pain alleviation. *Medical Progress through Technology*, 1974, *2*, 121-126.

Reznikoff, M. Psychological factors in breast cancer. *Psychosomatic Medicine*, 1955, *17*, 96.

Rickman, J. Alcoholism and psychoanalysis. *British Journal of Inebriation*, 1925, *23*, 66.

Riley, V. Mouse mammary tumors: Alteration of incidence as apparent function of stress. *Science*, 1975, *189*, 465-467.

Rimm, D. C., & Masters, J. C. *Behavior therapy: Techniques and empirical findings.* New York: Academic Press, 1974.

Rimon, R. A psychosomatic approach to rheumatoid arthritis. *Acta Rheumatology Scandinavia*, 1969, *13*, 1-11.

Robinson, C. E. Emotional factors and rheumatoid arthritis. *Canadian Medical Association Journal*, 1957, *77*, 344-357.

Rodnan, G. P. Primer on the rheumatic diseases. *Journal of the American Medical Association*, 1973, *224*, 663-669.

Rogers, M. P., Dubey, D., & Reich, P. The influence of the psyche and the brain on immunity and disease susceptibility: A critical review. *Psychosomatic Medicine*, 1979, *41*, 2.

Ross, W. D. Musculoskeletal disorders. In E. D. Wittkower, & H. Warnes (Eds), *Psychosomatic medicine: Its clinical application.* New York: Harper & Row, 1977.

Rosvold, H. E., & Szwarchart, M. K. Neural structures involved in delay-response performance. In J. M. Warren, & K. Akert (Eds), *The frontal granular cortex and behavior.* New York: McGraw-Hill, 1964, 1-15.

Rothermich, M. O., & Phillips, V. K. Rheumatoid arthritis in criminal and mentally ill populations. *Arthritis Rheumatism*, 1963, *6*, 81-86.

Rubin, H. The MMPI as a diagnostic aid in a veterans' hospital. *Journal of Consulting Psychology*, 1948, *12*, 251-254.

Rubin, S., & Lawlis, F. A model for differential treatment for alcoholics. *Rehabilitation Research & Practice Review*, 1970, *1*, 53-58.

Safer, M. A., & Leventhal, H. Ear differences in evaluating emotional tones of voice and verbal content. *Journal of Experimental Psychology: Human Perception & Performance*, 1977, *3*, 75-82.

Samuels, M., & Bennett, H. *The well body book.* New York: Random House/Bookworks, 1973.

Samuels, M., & Samuels, N. *Seeing with the mind's eye, the history, techniques and uses of visualization.* New York: Random House, 1975.

Scheflen, A. E. Malignant tumors in the institutionalized psychotic population. *Archives of Neurological Psychiatry*, 1951, *64*, 145-155.

Schilder, P. *The image and appearance of the human body.* London: Kegan Paul, 1935, 11.

Schmale, A. H., & Iker, H. Hopelessness as a predictor of cervical cancer. *Journal of Social Science and Medicine*, 1971, *5*, 95-100.

Schochet, B., Lisansky, E., Schubart, A., Fiocco, V., Kurland, S., & Pope, D. M. A medical psychiatric study of patients with rheumatoid arthritis. *Psychosomatics*, 1969, *10*, 3-8.

Schumacher, H. R., Jr. Synovial membrane and fluid morphologic alterations in early rheumatoid arthritis: Microvascular injury and virus-like particles. *Annals of New York Academy of Science*, 1975, *256*, 39-43.

Schutz, W. C. *The FIRO-B Scales: Manual.* Palo Alto, Calif.: Consulting Psychologists Press, 1967.

Schwartz, G. E., Davidson, R. J., & Maer, F. Right hemisphere specialization for emotion: Interactions with cognition. *Science*, 1975, *190*, 286-290.

Schwartz, L. H., Marcus, R., & Condon, R. Multidisciplinary group therapy for rheumatoid arthritis. *Psychosomatics*, 1978, *19*(5), 289-293.

Scotch, N. A., & Geiger, H. J. The epidemiology of rheumatoid arthritis: A review with special attention to social factors. *Journal of Chronic Disease*, 1962, *15*, 1037-1042.

Seliger, R. V. Working with the alcoholic. *Medical Records; New York*, 1939, *149*, 147-150.

Seliger, R. V., & Rosenberg, S. J. Personality of the alcoholic. *Medical Records; New York*, 1941, *154*, 418-421.

Selye, H. *The stress of life.* New York: McGraw-Hill, 1956.

Serber, M. Teaching the non-verbal components of assertive training. *Journal of Behavior Therapy & Experimental Psychiatry*, 1972, *3*, 179-183.

Service, E. R. *A profile of primitive culture.* New York: Harper & Brothers, 1958.

Shafii, M. Psychotherapeutic treatment for rheumatoid arthritis. *Archives of General Psychiatry*, 1973, *29*, 14-17.

Shapiro, A. K. The placebo effect in the history of medical treatment: Implication for psychiatry. *American Journal of Psychiatry*, 1959, *116*, 298-304.

Sharp, J. T. Mycoplasmas and arthritis. *Arthritis Rheumatism*, 1971, *13*, 263-266.

Sillman, L. R. Chronic alcoholism. *Journal of Nervous Mental Disorders*, 1949, *107*, 127.

Silverman, A. J. Rheumatoid arthritis. In A. Freedman, H. Kaplan, & B. Sadock (Eds), *Comprehensive textbook of psychiatry* (Vol. 2). Baltimore: Williams & Wilkins, 1975.

Simmel, E. Morbid habits and cravings. *Psychoanalytic Review*, 1930, *17*, 481.

Simonton, C., Simonton, S., & Creighton, J. *Getting well again.* Los Angeles: J. P. Tarcher, 1978.

Sims, D. Please don't tell me what to do unless you tell me why: A diabetic speaks out. *The Diabetes Educator*, 1977-1978, *3*, *4*, Winter.

Singer, E., Blane, H., & Rasschau, R. Alcoholism and social isolation. *Journal of Abnormal & Social Psychology*, 1964, *69*, 681-689.

Sjolund, B., Terenius, L., & Eriksson, M. Increased cerebrospinal fluid levels of endorphins after electroacupuncture. *Acta Physiology Scandinavia*, 1977, *100*, 382-384.

Skinner, H. A., Jackson, D., & Hoffmann, H. Alcoholic personality types: Identification and correlates. *Journal of Abnormal Psychology*, 1974, *83*, 658-666.

Slawson, P. F., Flynn, W. R., & Kollar, E J. Psychological factors associated with the onset of diabetes mellitus. *Journal of the American Medical Association*, 1963, *185*, 166-170.

Smith, R. D., & Polley, H. F. Rest therapy for rheumatoid arthritis. *Mayo Clinic Proceedings*, 1978, *53*, 141-145.

Snow, H. *Cancer and the cancer process.* London: 1893.

Snyder, S. Our body's own narcotics. *Scientific American*, 1977, *18*, 129-139.

Sobell, L. C., & Sobell, M. B. Alcohol problems. In R. B. Williams, Jr., & W. D. Gentry (Eds), *Behavioral approaches to medical treatment.* Cambridge: Ballinger, 1977.

Sobell, M. B., & Sobell, L. C. Individualized behavior therapy for alcoholics. *Behavior Therapy*, 1973, *4*, 49-72.

Solomon, G. F., Amkraut, A. A., & Kasper, P. Immunity, emotions and stress. *Annals of Clinical Research*, 1974, *6*, 313-322.

Solomon, G. F., & Moos, R. H. Emotions, immunity and disease: A speculative theoretical integration. *Archives of General Psychiatry*, 1964, *11*(6), 657-674.

Sontag, S. *Illness as metaphor*. New York: Farrar, Straus & Giroux, 1977.

Southworth, J. Muscular tension as a response to psychological stress in rheumatoid arthritis and peptic ulcer. *Genetic Psychological Monographs*, 1959, *57*, 337-351.

Spergel, P., Erlich, G. E., & Glass, D. The rheumatoid arthritic personality: A psychodiagnostic myth. *Psychosomatics*, 1978, *19*(2), 78-86.

Stein, S. P., & Charles, E. Emotional factors and juvenile diabetes: A study of early life experiences of adolescent diabetes. *Journal of the American Medical Association*, 1975, *128*, 238.

Sternbach, R. A. *Pain patients: Traits and treatment*. New York: Academic Press, 1974.

Sternbach, R. A. Treatment of the chronic pain patient. *Psychosomatics*, September, 1978, 11-15.

Steven, J. An anatomy of schizophrenia. *Archives of General Psychiatry*, 1973, *29*, 177.

Stoddart, A. M. *Life of Paracelsus*. London: 1911.

Strecker, E. A., & Chambers, F. T., Jr. *Alcohol—one man's meat*. New York: Macmillan, 1937.

Suinn, R. M. Type A behavior patterns. In R. B. Williams, Jr., & W. D. Gentry (Eds), *Behavioral approaches to medical treatment*. Baltimore: Ballinger, 1977.

Suinn, R. M., & Richardson, F. Anxiety management training: A nonspecific anxiety control. *Behavior Therapy*, 1971, *4*, 498-503.

Swearingen, R. L. A humanistic approach to the management of fractures. *Today's Clinician*, February, 1978, 21-25.

Sweney, A. *Leadership: Management of power and obligation*. Wichita, Ks.: Test Systems, Inc., 1979.

Swerdlow, M. (Ed.). *Relief of intractable pain*. New York: Excerpta Medica, 1974.

Tarlau, M., & Smalheiser, I. Personality patterns in patients with malignant tumors of the breast and cervix: An exploratory study. *Psychosomatic Medicine*, 1951, *13*, 117.

Tasto, D. L., & Chesney, M. Muscle relaxation treatment for primary dysmenorrhea. *Behavior Therapy*, 1974, *5*, 668-672.

Taub, E. Self-regulation of human tissue temperature. In G. E. Schwartz, & J. Beatly (Eds), *Biofeedback: Theory and research*. New York: Academic Press, 1977, 265-300.

Taub, E., & Emurian, C. S. Feedback aided self-regulation of skin temperature with a single feedback locus. I. Acquisition reversal training. In J. Kamiya, T. X. Barber, N. E. Miller, D. Shapiro, J. Stoyval (Eds), *Biofeedback and self-control*. Chicago: Aldine, 1977.

Taylor, D. W. Treatment of excessive frequency of urination by desensitization. *Journal of Behavior Therapy & Experimental Psychiatry*, 1972, *3*, 311-313.

Thomas, C. B. Precursors of premature disease and death. *Annals of Internal Medicine*, 1976, *85*, 653-658.

Thomas, C. B., & Duszynski, K. R. Closeness to parents and the family constellation in a prospective study of five disease states: Suicide, mental illness, hypertension and coronary heart disease. *Johns Hopkins Medical Journal*, 1974, *134*, 251-270.

Thomas, C. B., & Greenstreet, R. L. Psychobiological characteristics in youth as predictors of five disease states: Suicide, mental illness, hypertension, and coronary heart disease. *Johns Hopkins Medical Journal*, 1973, *132*, 16-43.

Tiebout, H. M. The syndrome of alcohol addiction. *Quarterly Journal of Studies on Alcohol*, 1945, *5*, 535.

Tiebout, H. M. Surrender versus compliance in therapy with special reference to alcoholism. *Quarterly Journal of Studies on Alcohol*, 1953, *14*, 58-68.

Tiebout, H. M. The ego factors in surrender in alcoholism. *Quarterly Journal of Studies on Alcohol*, 1954, *15*, 610-612.

Trevathan, R. D., & Tatum, J. C. Rarity of concurrence of psychosis and rheumatoid arthritis in individual patients. *Journal of Nervous & Mental Disease*, 1954, *120*, 85-88.

Tucker, D. M., Roth, R. S., Arneson, B. A., & Buckingham, T. M. Right hemisphere activation during stress. *Neuropsychologia*, 1977, *15*, 697-700.

VandenBergh, R. L., Sussman, K. E., & Titus, C. Effects of hypnotically induced acute emotional stress in carbohydrate and lipid metabolism in patients with diabetes mellitus. *Psychosomatic Medicine*, 1966, *28*, 383-389.

VandenBergh, R. L., Sussman, K. E., & Vaughn, G. D. Effects of combined physical-anticipatory stress on carbohydrate lipid metabolism in patients with diabetes mellitus. *Psychosomatic Medicine*, 1967, *8*, 16-20.

Vogel, S. An interpretation of medical and psychiatric approaches in the treatment of alcoholism. *Quarterly Journal of Studies on Alcohol*, 1953, *14*, 620-631.

Vogel-Spratt, M. Alcoholism a learned behavior: Some hypotheses and research. In R. Fox (Ed.), *Alcoholism: Behavioral research and therapeutic approaches*. New York: Springer: 1967, 46-54.

Volgyesi, F. A. "School for patients" hypnosis-therapy and psychoprophylaxis. *British Journal of Medical Hypnosis*, 1954, *5*, 8-17.

Wall, J. H. A study of alcoholism in men. *American Journal of Psychiatry*, 1936, *92*, 1389-1401.

Wall, J. H. Psychotherapy of alcohol addiction in a private mental hospital. *Quarterly Journal of Studies on Alcohol*, 1945, *5*, 547.

Wallace, R. K., Benson, H., & Wilson, A. F. A wakeful hypometabolic physiologic state. *American Journal of Physiology*, 1971, *221*, 795-799.

Wallston, B. S., Wallston, K. A., Kaplan, G. C., & Maides, S. A. Development and validation of the health locus of control scale. *Journal of Consulting & Clinical Psychology*, 1976, *44*(4), 580-585.

Walshe, W. A. *The nature and treatment of cancer.* London: Taylor & Walton, 1846.

Warren, S. L., Marmor, L., Liebes, D. M., & Hollins, R. L. An active agent from human rheumatoid arthritis which is transmissible in mice. *Archives of Internal Medicine*, 1969, *124*, 629-633.

Weiner, C. L. The burden of rheumatoid arthritis: Tolerating the uncertainty. *Social Science & Medicine*, 1975, *9*, 97-104.

Weiner, H. M. *Psychobiology and human disease.* New York: Elseiuer, 1977.

Weiner, M. Psychological aspects of diabetes treatment. *The Diabetes Educator*, 1977, *3*, 6-9.

Weinstein, A. S. Evaluation through medical records and related information systems. In E. L. Struening, & M. Guttenberg (Eds), *Handbook of evaluation research* (Vol. 1). Beverly Hills: SAGE, 1975.

Weller, C. The effects of hypnotically induced emotions on continuous uninterrupted blood glucose measurements. *Psychosomatics*, 1961, *2*, 375-383.

Wenger, P. History of a drinking habit in 400 inmates in a penal institution; with special consideration of personality and prognosis. *New York Journal of Medicine*, 1944, *44*, 1898-1904.

Wheeler, J. I., Jr., & Caldwell, B. M. Psychological evaluation of women with cancer of the breast and of the cervix. *Psychosomatic Medicine*, 1955, *17*(4), 256-268.

White, K. D. Salivation: The significance of imagery in its voluntary control. *Psychophysiology*, 1978, *15*(3), 196-203.

White, M. A. The social significance of mental disease. *Archives of Neurological Psychiatry*, 1929, *22*, 873.

Wickramasekera, I. The management of rheumatoid arthritic pain: Preliminary observations. In I. Wickramasekera, X. T. Truong, M. Bush, & C. Orr (Eds), *Biofeedback behavior, therapy, and hypnosis: Potentiating the verbal control of behavior for clinicians*, 1976, 47-55.

Williams, A. F. Self-concepts of college problem drinkers: A comparison with alcoholics. *Quarterly Journal of Studies on Alcohol*, 1965, *25*, 586-594.

Williams, R. C. *Rheumatoid arthritis as a systemic disease.* Philadelphia: Saunders, 1974.

Wilson, D. H., Reeves, A. G., Gazzaniga, M. S., & Culver, C. Cerebral commissurotomy for the control of intractable seizures. *Neurology*, 1977, *27*, 708-715.

Wittman, P. A controlled study of the developmental and personality characteristics of chronic alcoholics. *Elgin Papers*, 1939, *3*, 77. (a)

Wittman, P. A differential analysis of chronic alcoholics and controls. *Elgin Papers*, 1939, *3*, 85. (b)

Wittman, P. Diagnosis and analysis of temperament for a group of alcoholics compared with controls. *Elgin Papers*, 1939, *3*, 94. (c)

Wolf, S. Effects of suggestion and conditioning on the action of chemical agents in human subjects. The pharmacology of placebos. *Journal of Clinical Investigation*, 1950, *29*, 100-109.

Wolff, B. B. Rheumatoid arthritis - assessment. In J. R. Nichols, & W. H. Bradley (Eds), *Proceedings of a symposium on the motivation of the physically disabled*. London: National Fund for Research in Crippling Diseases, 1968.

Wolpe, J. *Psychotherapy by reciprocal inhibition*. Stanford, Calif.: Stanford University Press, 1958.

Wolpin, M., & Kirsch, I. Visual imagery, various muscle states and desensitization procedures. *Perceptual & Motor Skills*, 1974, *39*, 1143-1149.

Wyatt, H. J. Psychologic factors in arthritis. In S. Light (Ed.), *Arthritis and physical medicine*. Baltimore: Waverly, 1969, 176-190.

Zeisset, R. M. Desensitization and relaxation in the modification of psychiatric patients' interview behavior. *Journal of Abnormal Psychology*, 1968, *73*, 18-24.

Zimmermann, M. *Neurophysiology of nociception pain abstracts* (Vol. 1). Second World Congress on Pain, International Association for the Study of Pain, 1978, 173-174.

AUTHOR INDEX

SUBJECT INDEX